M000290416

Internal Credit Risk Models

Internal Credit Risk Models

CAPITAL ALLOCATION AND PERFORMANCE MEASUREMENT

Michael K. Ong
ABN Amro Bank

Published by Risk Books, a division of the Risk Waters Group.

Haymarket House
28–29 Haymarket
London SW1Y 4RX
Tel: +44 (0)20 7484 9700
Fax: +44 (0)20 7484 9758
E-mail: books@risk.co.uk
Sites: www.riskbooks.com, www.riskpublications.com

ISBN 1 899332 03 0 Reprinted by Risk Books, 2000

British Library Cataloguing in Publication Data
A catalogue record for this book is available from the British Library

Risk Books Commissioning Editor: Conrad Gardner
Copy edited by Romilly Hambling, Special Edition
Typeset by Corinne Orde, Special Edition

Printed and bound in Great Britain by Bookcraft (Bath) Ltd, Somerset.
Covers printed by Bookcraft.

All chapters are published here for the first time with the exception of the following, slightly revised, articles from *Risk* magazine: the appendix of the epilogue: "History Repeating", *Risk* (January, 1998); "RAROC Remodelled", *Risk* (September, 1992); "Many Happy Returns", *Risk* (June, 1998); "Reconcilable Differences", *Risk* (October, 1998); "Refining Ratings", *Risk* (August, 1998); "A Credit Risk Toolbox", *Risk* (December, 1998).

About the Author

Michael K. Ong is a senior vice president and head of enterprise risk for ABN Amro Bank. He is responsible for the management information and decision support function for the executive committee on enterprise-wide market, operational, credit and liquidity risk, as well as RAROC and ROE models. Before joining ABN Amro, Michael was head of the corporate research unit at First Chicago NBD Corporation, where he was chair of the global risk management research council and head of the market risk analysis unit. Prior to First Chicago NBD, he was responsible for quantitative research at Chicago Research and Trading Group (now Nations Banc-CRT) and has served as an assistant professor of mathematics at Bowdoin College. Michael is also an adjunct professor at the Stuart School of Business of the Illinois Institute of Technology. He received a BS degree in physics, *cum laude*, from the University of the Philippines and degrees of MA in physics and MS and PhD in applied mathematics from the State University of New York at Stony Brook. Michael is a member of the editorial boards of the *Journal of Financial Regulation and Compliance* and the *Journal of Risk.*

Acknowledgements

I owe a debt of gratitude to many people for this book. Behind every good book is an excellent team, and I am very fortunate to have two excellent teams of people on both sides of the Atlantic. First, I extend my infinite appreciation to Conrad Gardner, Senior Commissioning Editor of Risk Books, for recognising the value of this book even from its initial glimmering. It was his enthusiasm and belief in the importance of the subject matter, and his confidence in my writing ability, that gave me the chance to proceed. In my futile search for thoughtful proverbs for the dedication page, Conrad Gardner brilliantly offered some – "Whoever understands the first truth, should understand the ultimate truth …" Thank you Conrad for seeing the first and the ultimate truth, as I hope readers of this book will likewise do.

I am also deeply honoured to be the first single author ever published by Risk Books. My profound gratitude goes to Shân Millie, publisher of Risk Books, for her willingness and enthusiasm to stake Risk's reputation in publishing my work and allowing me the platform to be candid and unrestrained in voicing out my thoughts in writing. Without the assistance of very able editors in crafting the proper phrasing and wording, the voice of reason – no matter how profound the thoughts of the author – would remain unheard. To this end, I am indebted to Ben Mullane, Desk Editor, who carefully and skilfully crafted and shaped the core truths of the book into all that it is. Many thanks also to Romilly Hambling and Corinne Orde, who diligently assisted Conrad Gardner in the technical editing and typesetting of the book.

On this side of the Atlantic, my colleagues who performed the real work in the trenches deserve much praise. First and foremost, this book could not have been written without the assistance of my colleague, Dr Yang Song, who worked painstakingly through the mathematics and single-handedly implemented the internal credit risk model framework. Many of the technical appendices, though not credited to anyone in particular, are clearly reflective of her work. She performed the calculations for almost all of the numerical examples in the book, and truly she deserves to be considered a co-author of this book. Heartfelt thanks are due to my colleague, Dr Stevan Maglic, who performed all the Monte Carlo simulation exercises and thought of clever ways to simulate the loss distributions of very large portfolios. He was also responsible for preparing two important appendices. I extend my gratitude to my colleague, Dr Weixiong Li, for extending our preliminary internal model into one that has the capability of performing mark-to-market valuation, credit migration, multi-year analysis and macroeconomic risk analysis. Notwithstanding being the most junior of our team, Thanh Tran was outstanding in his graphic illustration work and carefully performed due diligence tests on the numerical calculations of our internal model. To him I extend my sincere thanks.

How useful this book is remains to be seen. I was given a rare opportunity to speak my mind and to present sensible solutions to a very delicate dilemma in our industry, and I took it. Curiously, my intent in writing this book is not that people will simply read it like a text, but more to open up a dialogue on a fundamentally difficult and political topic that goes to the heart of the financial industry and the function of its regulatory supervisors.

Finally, much gratitude is owed to all the unsung heroes on the Street who have advocated reform since our initial debate on market risk capital adequacy many, many years ago.

Michael K. Ong Chicago, April 1999

In memory of my father,
to my mother,
and to George

Contents

Lightning flashes,
Sparks shower,
In one blink of your eyes,
You have missed seeing.

*

It is too clear and so it is hard to see,
A dunce once searched for fire with a lighted lantern,
Had he known what fire was,
He could have cooked his rice much sooner.

*

Whoever understands the first truth,
Should understand the ultimate truth,
The last and first,
Are they not the same?

Hyakujo Ekai (720–814)

Introduction

The Case for Internal Credit Risk Models

It is no big secret that the 1988 Basle Capital Accord underlying the risk-based capital adequacy requirement imposed on banks* has serious flaws even though its original intent was noble – "to strengthen the soundness and stability of the international banking system" and to promote a fair and a "high degree of consistency in its application to banks in different countries with a view to diminishing an existing source of competitive inequality among international banks" (Basle Committee on Banking Supervision, 1988).

It is also no longer a secret that the anomalies in the Capital Accord have been universally exploited by big banking institutions through clever innovations in the capital markets with the use of such vehicles as asset securitisation programmes, credit derivatives and other recent technological and financial innovations. In effect, banks have been able to lower their risk-based capital requirements significantly without actually reducing the material credit risk embedded in their banking portfolios.

While the 1996 Amendment to the 1988 Capital Accord requiring capital adequacy for market risk is an attempt to correct some of these anomalies by allowing banks to use their own internal models (under the broad heading "value-at-risk" (VAR)) for their trading books, it is at best an inadequate solution that addresses the dichotomy between the banking book and the trading book of an institution – the former subject to the Accord; the latter subject to

*Throughout the book "banks" is used as a generic term referring to bank holding companies, insurance companies and other financial institutions that are subject to capital adequacy standards.

market risk standards. For the most part, the basic core of the 1988 Capital Accord regarding credit risk remains unchanged.

Furthermore, under this amendment and the capital arbitrage opportunities the Accord imprudently provides, a bank, through the use of internal VAR models, can in principle reduce its minimum risk-based capital requirement from 8% to much smaller percentages by judiciously shifting the risks of these assets from its banking book to its trading book, whenever accounting rules allow it.

The irony of it all is that the Accord, which originally provided an international credit risk capital standard for G10 countries, was subsequently more widely adopted as the *global* benchmark for regulatory credit risk capital adequacy standards for the world's largest banks. Within the European Union, the Accord was first adopted for banks through two directives, the Solvency Ratio and the Own Funds directives, and was later also applied to investment banks. Within the United States the Prompt Corrective Action and other provisions of the FDIC Improvement Act of 1991 explicitly linked regulatory policies to the Basle framework on required capital ratios. The continued usage of a flawed framework with such global implications is definitely unconscionable and, therefore, irresponsible.

A further irony is that the regulators themselves are perplexed:

> With the formal RBC (risk-based capital) ratios rendered less useful, judgmental assessments of capital adequacy through the examination process necessarily have assumed heightened importance. Yet, this process, too, has become problematic as regulatory capital arbitrage has made credit risk positions less transparent. While examination assessments of capital adequacy normally attempt to adjust reported capital ratios for shortfalls in loan loss reserves relative to *expected* future charge-offs, examiners' tools are limited in their ability to deal effectively with *credit risk* – measured as the *uncertainty* of future credit losses around their expected levels. (Federal Reserve System Task Force on Internal Credit Risk Models, 1998)

Indeed, banks themselves, having recognised the inadequacy of these risk-based capital rules and the quandary within regulatory circles, have begun in earnest – for some time now since the industry's acceptance of trading VAR models for market risk – to develop their own internal credit risk models for quantifying the credit risk in their banking books. Analogous to the trading book VAR models, internal credit risk models are rapidly being developed to support internal capital allocation schemes and economic capital adequacy in lieu of regulatory capital. These laudable initiatives not only provide the banks with a more sophisticated and appropriate mechanism for managing portfolio credit risk, but an internal credit risk model can also serve as a basis for estimating the risk-adjusted profitability of the various lines of business, which, in turn, can be used to evaluate performance and compensation.

More importantly, the combined effort invested in internal credit risk modelling and economic capital allocation schemes has, slowly but surely, been incorporated into the risk management processes of these banks, directly affecting day-to-day portfolio credit risk management, the risk-adjusted pricing and hedging of transactions, portfolio concentration and diversification effects, collateral management and other strategic decision-making processes. All of these are important ingredients of prudent risk management across the enterprise and, consequently, of the prudential assessment of bank capital adequacy – the basic tenet of the Capital Accord.

OBJECTIVES OF THE BOOK

So, what really is an internal credit risk model? What is it supposed to do? And what components must it have? This book seeks to answer these questions (readers are referred to the last part of chapter 2 for a preview of its contents). Given the inadequacy of the 1988 Capital Accord and the developmental efforts of major banking institutions, it is only a matter of time before internal models for credit risk are the main risk management tool of the banking book. In the meantime, it is important for both the industry and the regulatory supervisors to agree swiftly on a common framework for measuring and managing credit risk, thereby accelerating the near-term use of internal models and promoting greater transparency in the market.

It is not too early to start a dialogue along the lines of a possible near-term use of internal credit risk models. In fact, there is no better place to begin the experiment than within the banks themselves. The regulators concurred with this thought by announcing recently that:

> Given the ongoing progress in credit risk modeling techniques, it is conceivable that further improvements could redress many, if not most, of the concerns raised by the Task Force. However, in the interim, as traditional techniques for assessing capital adequacy are rapidly becoming outmoded, improved supervisory methods are needed if capital-based prudential policies are to remain viable even over the shorter term. Because the most accurate information regarding risks in likely to reside within a bank's own internal risk measurement and management systems, supervisors should utilize this information to the extent possible. (Federal Reserve System Task Force on Internal Credit Risk Models, 1998)

This book is written in response to that call to action. Through simple explanations and accessible mathematics, the intention is to make the fundamental building blocks of the modelling effort, albeit quantitative, more transparent and accessible to a wider audience. Given the paucity of usable and coherent data on credit risk, the parameterisation of the internal model is, however, best left to the institution and the regulators to argue about in the years to come.

1

On Basle, Regulation and Market Responses – Past and Present

In recent years regulators have increasingly sharpened their focus on the capital adequacy of banking organisations. The period from the late 1980s to the early 1990s saw important changes that contributed to growing regulatory and market pressures on banks to increase capital ratios. The global adoption of the 1988 risk-based capital standards loudly trumpeted a greater regulatory interest in both the on- and off-balance sheet activities of major international banks. In the US, the 1991 Federal Deposit and Insurance Corporation Improvement Act (FDICIA) enforced punitive actions (the so-called "prompt corrective action") against banks with inadequate regulatory capital ratios. There is ample evidence to indicate that regulators have had a significant influence on the capital ratios of a large proportion of banks in the period since the 1980s.

The major banking institutions have responded creatively to these regulatory challenges. Because capital ratios as dictated by capital adequacy regulations have become a primary measure of a bank's financial condition, it is important to understand how banks respond to binding capital regulation. It has, after all, become an exercise in "game theory". Consequently, because the reactions from banks take various forms, regulators must consider what response they wish to elicit when formulating new regulations so that the game is played in a prudent and transparent manner.

We therefore need to ask many interrelated questions, such as, What is capital? Why do banks need to hold capital to conduct their business? What is the role of capital in banking? How much capital should banks be required to hold? How do banks respond to different types of capital regulation?

ORIGINS OF THE REGULATORY CAPITAL FRAMEWORK

Following a consultative process among the Group of Ten (or G10)[1] countries during the previous year, in July 1988 the Basle Committee on Banking and Supervisory Services circulated a final version of the document entitled the "International Convergence of Capital Measurement and Capital Standards". The Committee meets every quarter year under the auspices of the Bank for International Settlements (BIS)[2] in Basle, Switzerland – hence the appellation "Basle Committee".[3]

The document was a statement by the Committee, agreed by all its members, which set out details of the agreed framework for measuring capital adequacy and the minimum standard that the supervisory authorities represented on the Committee intend to implement in their respective countries. The capital framework was subsequently endorsed by the Group of Ten central bank governors. Although the agreements set forth in the capital accord are not legally binding, member countries of the G10 are morally bound to implement the framework in their respective supervisory functions and to turn it into national law by December 1992. As it stands today, the Basle Capital Accord of 1988 ubiquitously remains the definitive global benchmark for solvency requirements among the world's largest banks.

Prior to the full implementation of the Basle Accord in 1992, capital regulations consisted primarily of minimum capital standards uniformly applied to banks, regardless of their risk profiles and ignoring off-balance sheet activities. The 1988 agreement marked the first time that international minimum capital guidelines were linked to banks' capital requirements, albeit only to the credit exposures in their portfolios.

The capital adequacy framework currently in vogue – commonly known as the "1988 Basle Capital Accord" or, simply, the "Capital Accord" or the "Basle Accord" – has two fundamental objectives, namely:

❑ First, the framework sought "to strengthen the soundness and stability of the international banking system" by creating common minimum capital adequacy requirements for internationally active banks that are commensurate with the amount of credit risk each bank takes in its portfolio.

- ❑ Second, by reducing global systemic risk achievable through the first objective, the Capital Accord additionally sought to create a level playing field among international banks by establishing that "the framework should be fair and have a high degree of consistency in its application to banks in different countries with a view to diminishing an existing source of competitive inequality among international banks."

Indeed, the 1988 Basle Capital Accord marked a major step forward in introducing risk differentiation into the regulatory framework – the so-called "risk-based" capital standards. This will be elaborated in greater detail later on in the chapter. For the moment, one can briefly say that the capital framework was designed to provide a simple and crude distinction between the main types of credit risk. Specifically, the capital framework requires banks to hold capital equal to some percentage of all the "risk-weighted" assets in their portfolios. The assignment of risk weights is based on the perceived credit quality of an individual obligor, measured on an instrument-by-instrument basis. Consequently, at the core of the Capital Accord is the differentiation of credit risks into four broad categories:

- ❑ Government exposures with OECD (Organization for Economic Cooperation and Development) countries receive no credit risk capital charge.
- ❑ OECD banks and non-OECD governments receive a 1.6% capital charge.
- ❑ A 4% capital charge is levied on mortgages.
- ❑ Other banks, all corporates, and other remaining exposures require an 8% capital charge.

The framework was originally directed mainly at the assessment of capital in relation to credit risk – specifically, the risk of counterparty failure – but other risks (eg, market risk, liquidity risk, etc), although recognised by the Committee, were intentionally not addressed. More recently, the 1996 amendment[4] to the Capital Accord extended the initial requirement to include risk-based capital adequacy for market risk and specific risk in the trading books of the banks (Basle, 1996).

Clearly, even since the inception of the new credit risk capital regime, as nobly articulated by the two objectives and its differentiation of risk types, the 1988 Basle Capital Accord has sought to cover both credit risk and systemic risk in the banking industry as its most urgent vocation.

What was the cause of this urgency? What prompted the promulgation of the 1988 Basle Capital Accord? Many think, incorrectly, that the 1988 Accord was the genesis of risk-based regulatory capital requirement. It was not. In fact, capital requirements existed prior to 1988.

At this juncture in the exposition it should be reiterated that even though the most important issue at hand – the management of credit risk and its attendant modelling effort – was conveniently lumped under the guise of regulatory capital requirement, it would not be beneficial for all parties involved (regulators and practitioners alike) to misconstrue the primary intent here of addressing credit risk modelling. Capital requirement, with its attendant allocation issue, should be treated as a simple corollary of the more important effort of managing and containing credit risk.

The next few sections continue with a historical perspective of the events that led to the establishment of the Accord.

SOME HISTORICAL PERSPECTIVES

Declining capital ratios

As reported by Berger, Herring and Szegö (1995), the history of capital requirements in the United States reveals a remarkable, century-long decline from the levels that prevailed before the introduction of the federal "safety net". The term "safety net" refers to all governmental actions – regulations and enforcement of capital requirements – designed to enhance and protect the safety and soundness of the banking system in the United States. The safety net may include deposit insurance, unconditional payment guarantees, access to discount windows and other government actions enacted to regulate the banking system in general.

> In 1840, equity funded over 50% of banks' assets, after which the ratio (equity to assets) fell fairly steadily for about 100 years until it settled in the 6% to 8% range from the mid-1940s to the 1980s. Prior to the start of the National Banking era of 1863, capital ratios were already declining significantly. As the efficiency of the U.S. financial system improved from geographic diversification, development of regional and national money markets, and introduction of clearing-

> houses and other mutual guarantee associations, the probability of bank failures declined. (Berger, Herring and Szegö, 1995)

Similar developments occurred elsewhere, particularly in Europe. Empirical data support the hypothesis that, with stabilising factors established in the market, increasingly less capital is needed to protect against financial distress.

The National Banking Act of 1863 required national banks to deposit $10 in US government bonds with the Comptroller of the Currency for each $9 of national bank notes issued, effectively collateralising the notes issued so that the safety of the bank notes did not depend on the solvency of the bank. In principle, a national bank could effectively have a 10% capital-to-asset ratio by simply raising $9 in deposits for each dollar of equity and buying government bonds. Ironically, the implicit ceiling of 10% of regulatory capital ratio was less than a quarter of the average capital ratio of the time. Empirical data show an accelerated decline of capital ratios after 1863.

The creation of the Federal Reserve System in 1914 also contributed to the reduced risk of bank failures by permitting banks to obtain liquidity by discounting assets at the Federal Reserve rather than by selling distressed bank assets to meet liquidity needs and thereby incurring losses. Data provided by Berger, Herring and Szegö (1995) suggest that the creation of the Federal Reserve led to, at most, a small reduction in capital ratios.

The creation of the Federal Deposit Insurance Corporation (FDIC) in 1933 provided unconditional government guarantees for most bank creditors. The FDIC brought about regulations that restricted the interest rate banks could pay on deposits. The safety net of the insurance provided a guarantee of repayment to depositors even if the bank failed. These two actions, in essence, provided an additional subsidy to banking that made uninsured bank debt safer, reducing capital requirements further. By the early 1940s capital ratios had dropped to the 6% to 8% range, where they remain today.

The Great Depression

The Great Depression in the US lasted from late 1929 to 1939. During this time the prices of stocks fell 40%. Nine thousand banks became insolvent and nine million savings accounts were wiped out. 8,600 businesses failed and wages fell by an average of 60%.

The unemployment rate jumped from 9% to 25%, and there were about 15 million jobless people.

The Great Depression had many causes, but a major source of destabilisation of the American economy was the huge discrepancies in international wealth distribution. While America prospered in the post-World War I 1920s, European nations were struggling to rebuild themselves. During the First World War the US government extended to its European allies approximately $7 billion worth of loans, and then another $3.3 billion by 1920. Through the Dawes Plan of 1924 the US started lending to Germany. US foreign lending continued to climb to $900 million in 1924 and to $1.25 billion by 1928. Of these funds, more than 90% was used by the European allies to purchase US goods. However, the nations (Britain, Italy, France, Belgium, Russia, Yugoslavia, Estonia, Poland and others) to which the US had extended credit were in no position to pay off their debts quickly. Their gold reserves had flowed into the US during and immediately after the war in great quantity, and rapid repayment in gold would cause the ruin of their own currencies. This was, indeed, a period of American hegemony. Historian John D. Hicks (1960) describes the Allied attitude to repayment of the US loans:

> In their view the war was fought for a common objective, and the victory was as essential for the safety of the United States as for their own. The United States had entered the struggle late, and had poured forth no such contribution in lives and losses as the Allies had made. It had paid in dollars, not in death and destruction, and now it wanted its dollars back.

There were several causes of this imbalance of wealth between the US and its European counterparts. Most obvious is the fact that the First World War had devastated much of Europe, requiring considerable time and money to rebuild. An equally important cause of the disparity in wealth distribution was the tariff policies of the United States, which were enacted as a protectionist mechanism to safeguard domestic businesses. Protectionism reached an all-time high in the 1920s and early 1930s. Starting with the Fordney McCumber Act of 1922 and ending with the Hawley–Smoot Tariff of 1930, the United States increased many tariffs by 100% or more. These tariffs effectively limited the quantity of goods the Europeans were able to sell in the United States.

In the 1920s the United States was trying "to be the world's banker, food producer, and manufacturer, but to buy as little as possible from the world in return" (McElvaine, 1981). By maintaining high trade barriers to protect its own industries, the United States effectively hindered the ability of European countries to repay interest on its loans. The ensuing weakness of the international economy certainly contributed to the Great Depression. By 1929, 10% of the US gross national product went into exports. When foreign countries were no longer able to buy US goods, exports fell immediately by 30%, representing $1.5 billion of foreign sales lost between 1929 and 1933. This amount was one-eighth of all US sales lost in the early years of the depression.

Era of regulation and protection

It is interesting to observe that during this period, beginning with 1920, there were 31,000 commercial banks in the US with total assets of $53 billion. By 1930 there were 24,273 banks with $140 billion in assets. By 1940 there was a decline of 40% to 15,000 banks, with total assets of $179 billion. In 1950, less than 50% of the number of banks in 1920 remained, with 14,676 banks and assets of $230 billion – a fourfold increase of the 1920 asset levels (Williams, 1995).

The harsh realities of the Great Depression in the US and the hyperinflation in Europe during the 1930s contributed to a highly regulated and protected banking system throughout the world. Banking activities, understandably, were highly constrained by their national regulators, and in return banks were protected from competition, takeover and turf-incursion.

In contrast, when the economy expanded after the Second World War there were only 44 bank failures between 1945 and 1954. Competition between various types of financial institutions was largely circumscribed by law and regulations.

The Bretton Woods agreement

The Bretton Woods System,[5] or international monetary system, was established in 1944. Under this system the International Monetary Fund (IMF) charter stipulated that the price of the US dollar be fixed in terms of gold (initially at $35 per ounce) and that all other currencies be pegged to the US dollar. The system was, essentially, the last vestige of the gold standard. The monetary agreement held up for over a quarter century until its initial collapse in 1971 and ultimate demise in 1973.

Basically, the international monetary system consisted of a policy of fixed exchange rates, the elimination of exchange restrictions, currency convertibility and the development of a multilateral system of international payments. Exchange rates were based on a par value system that required member countries to constrain fluctuations in their exchange rates to within a margin of plus or minus 1% around a par value expressed in terms of US dollars, which in turn were directly convertible into gold at a fixed rate. Unless a country developed a "fundamental disequilibrium" in its balance of payments (usually interpreted as a "large and persistent" deficit or surplus) and obtained prior approval from the IMF to change the pegged value of its currency, the member country would have to maintain the exchange rate through the purchase or sale of US dollars.

There are many theories regarding the ultimate demise of the Bretton Woods system in 1973. One very important contributing factor was the progressive dismantling of direct controls and relaxation of controls on international capital flows. As member countries continued to focus on their domestic priorities (eg, inflation and unemployment) and with disagreement over the shared burden of adjustment to domestic policies between the surplus and the deficit countries, the objective of Bretton Woods was slowly defeated.

Linking currencies to gold did not completely restrain governments from manipulating the value of their currencies. In order to finance expenditure by printing money, governments could suspend the gold standard in time of war. Furthermore, countries periodically redefined the value of their currencies in terms of gold. Instead of allowing gold or foreign reserves to leave their coffers, they would choose to devalue their currencies. If a country appeared to be about to devalue its currency, massive speculative attacks would ensue during which investors quickly divested themselves of that currency. Eventually, the country would lose large amounts of gold or foreign currencies in its reserves.

The period from 1960 to 1971 witnessed waves of speculation against a number of different currencies. Between 1966 and 1967 Britain lost nearly 28 million ounces of its gold reserves when investors lost confidence in the pound. On a single day (November 17, 1967) it lost reserves equivalent to more than $1 billion. The destabilising effects of these speculative currency attacks and the persistent US balance of payments deficits were seen as the ultimate reasons for the final collapse of the Bretton Woods system in 1973.

The United States was reluctant to devalue the dollar despite its persistent deficit. In the meantime, surplus countries chose to add dollars to their reserves rather than revalue, thereby ballooning the amount of US dollars held abroad to meet the need for a reserve currency. In retrospect, some countries blamed the US for not being a pillar of responsibility for them to lean on but, instead, forcing them to finance the continuing deficits. Ultimately, confidence in the US dollar as a reserve currency waned. Following the 1971 decision by the United States to suspend the convertibility of dollars into gold, the ministers and central bank governors of the Group of Ten ratified the Smithsonian Agreement, which resulted in a 10% devaluation of the dollar and a realignment of exchange rates, including wider margins of fluctuation in lieu of par values. This interim adjusted par value system was abandoned in 1973 when European Community countries introduced a joint system of floating their currencies against the dollar.

Once the United States and the rest of the world broke away from the gold standard, inflation rates rose almost universally and, in some cases, spun rapidly out of control.

HISTORICAL RATIONALE FOR THE CAPITAL ACCORD

Efforts to save the Bretton Woods fixed but adjustable exchange rate system in the early 1970s were complicated by global economic uncertainties brought about by successive hikes in world oil prices and soaring gold prices. The Arab oil embargo exacerbated the inflation that had originally been brought on by the Vietnam War in the 1960s.

The sudden increase in uncertainty in the wake of the collapse of the Bretton Woods system in 1973 led to worldwide inflation far into the 1980s. The breakdown of the controlled exchange rate system brought about increasing volatility and widely fluctuating foreign exchange and interest rates. In the US there was double-digit inflation – as measured by the Consumer Price Index, the inflation rate rose from 4.9% in 1976 to 13.3% in 1979, levelling at

12.5% in 1980. Furthermore, short-term interest rates rose from around 11% in late 1979 to 17% by April 1980 and ultimately to around 20% by early 1981 – the like of which had never before been seen in US economic history. By the late 1970s the Federal Reserve had lost its credibility as an inflation fighter and defender of the purchasing power of the dollar. The only solution was deregulation of the banking industry. The gradual relaxation of exchange control regulations forced many central banks to influence the movement of money supply to local banks, effectively putting a tight reign on interest rates. The Federal Reserve finally used a series of very sharp tightenings and succeeded in bringing inflation in the US down to around 4% in 1982.

Additionally, after the collapse of Bretton Woods, floating currencies came into vogue. The major currencies – the dollar, the yen and the major European currencies, as well as a number of others – floated against each other. In principle, floating allows countries the leverage to pursue independent macroeconomic and fiscal policies more suited to their domestic needs; but floating also resulted in periodically disorderly markets, causing wide fluctuations in both real and nominal exchange rates, thereby reducing the potential macroeconomic benefits of international trade and investment.

In response to the suddenly volatile environment of exchange rates a huge global trading market quickly developed. Eurocurrency instruments sprung up rapidly. There was a swift development of the capital markets as an alternative source of funding. The highly regulated banking industry (especially the commercial side of the industry) was shocked in the 1970s not only by a turbulent interest rate environment but also by new, fierce competitors from the non-banking world. Although the deregulation that followed freed banks from the more restrictive mandates, banks in general had to raise their combative spirits to ward off competition from outside their immediate industry. With increased sensitivity to interest rate fluctuations, borrowers and investors alike began to scour the global markets for the smallest financial advantage. This set the stage for what was to come in a decade of banking crises during the 1980s.

The enterprising spirit in search of better return ratios did not, in fact, emerge out of the blue. In the mid-1960s, when the economy expanded rapidly and inflation was low, each segment of the financial services industry was able to maintain good profit margins. Because of this there was little need for turf-intrusion and hostile competition. As rates rose, however, deposits began to move out of the rate-restricted banking institutions into higher-yielding alternatives – a phenomenon known as "financial disintermediation". Consequently, new forms of liabilities (eg, jumbo CDs, NOW and money market accounts), as well as assets of increasingly lower quality, began to appear in banks' balance sheets. The Federal Funds market, which had been absent since the 1920s, was revived and the eurodollar market expanded rapidly outside of US regulatory constraints. The sudden abundance of funds provided opportunities for yield-seeking investors and resulted in creative and aggressive banking in search of higher credit volumes. On the cusp of the Bretton Woods collapse, banking in general had been transformed from conservative asset management into aggressive liability management. By the end of the 1960s the managements of some major banks were claiming that a bank could borrow its liquidity from the markets and that, effectively, it did not need any capital (Williams, 1995).

> The old careful concern about asset quality, with deposits taken as a given, changed into the new aggressive liability management dictating the acquisition of financial assets at higher rates to cover liability costs. This is a traditional fault of the banking industry, forgetting that interest rates are not just a function of market conditions but also of risk. To replace higher quality customers, who were now borrowing more cheaply in the commercial and Eurodollar markets, many banks were reaching out for credits of lesser quality with higher risks to realize higher returns. (Manuels, 1997)

In retrospect, the consequences of deregulation were predictable.

1980s and afterwards: a period of bank failures[6]

From 1965 to 1981 there were 135 bank failures in the United States, averaging about eight per year. Table 1.1 shows that there was an increasingly distressed period in the banking industry, reaching a peak during the late 1980s.

The number of bank failures during this period was unprecedented since the Great Depression. The period of successive bank failures in the mid-1980s has come to be known in the US as the "S&L crisis" – the savings and loan crisis. In response to concerns

Table 1.1 A period of bank failures

Period	Bank failures	Bank failures per year
1945–54	44	4.4
1955–64	Unknown	Unknown
1965–81	135	8
1982–84	170	57
1985–90	1,065	177
1991–92	249	124

Source: Williams (1995).

over the S&L bailouts and the potential for a similar bailout of banks, the US Congress swiftly passed the FDIC Improvement Act (or "FDICIA") of 1991. This was intended as a stopgap measure to reduce taxpayers' and the government's exposure to problematic financial institutions. Among the provisions is the so-called "prompt corrective action", which imposes increasingly strict limits on a bank as its capital ratio declines. The act provided for a five-tier classification of capital ratios, the lowest tier having a capital-to-assets ratio of less than 2%. Regulatory supervisors are strongly encouraged to close down any bank that falls into the lower tier if it is unable to raise its capital ratio within 90 days of falling below the minimum 2%. Table A.1.1 in Appendix A summarises the "prompt corrective action" provision of the FDICIA of 1991.

In 1980, a total of 14,163 banks in the US held $2.9 trillion in assets. By the end of 1990 there were 12,300 banks with a total of $3.4 trillion in assets. As we head into the year 2000, there is increasing competitive pressure to consolidate the number of banks in the financial services industry. It is still too early to judge the outcome at this time.

Discounting the external macroeconomic elements that contributed to the tangible causes of the crisis, there were other intangible causes. C. C. Hope, director of the FDIC in 1989, offered this explanation:

> ... the OCC [Office of the Comptroller of the Currency] completed a review of the causes of national bank failures between 1979 and 1987. The study found that in 89% of the failures, deficiencies in management were a contributing factor. In 81% of the failures, loan policies were ignored or banks had no loan policies at all.

Other contributing factors suggested were deficient system controls, overaggressive lending, economic conditions and dishonesty.

In the United Kingdom the so-called "secondary banking crisis" broke out in December 1973, requiring a rescue operation ("Lifeboat") mounted by the Bank of England with the help of London and Scottish clearing banks. The secondary banks concerned were largely deposit-taking finance houses, which had grown in number and size during the late 1960s and early 1970s. In the early 1970s these institutions, drawing funds largely from the money markets and also from depositors, lent heavily for property development. Tightening monetary policy in 1973 created acute liquidity problems for these houses as money market funds were withdrawn, resulting in insolvency and collapse. At the peak of the crisis in 1975 more than 20 firms received support from the Lifeboat operation.

Elsewhere around the globe, during the same period between the collapse of the Bretton Woods agreement and the mid-1980s, a banking industry which was primarily protected and restricted and not accustomed to fierce competition suddenly found itself relieved of constraints, regulations and governmental protection. Predictably, the results were catastrophic. The ominous confluence of several unfortunate factors – deregulation, the relative calmness of the 1960s, the opening of new markets and the intense competition for higher profit margins – let loose a massive offshore expansion of credit extensions and aggressive lending among many banks in the G10 countries, particularly Japan. As the saying goes, the rest is history.

From 1977 onwards,

> [a] huge borrowers' market in international banking funds emerged, which enabled non-oil developing countries to substantially increase their foreign exchange reserves through bank borrowing. A very important element in the rapid emergence of this borrower's market was the extent to which the U.S. deficit was adding to the world's net liquidity. During 1976–78 the sum of the cumulative deficits on the current account and on the net direct investment of the U.S. balance of payments came to nearly $50 billion. In addition, part of the liquidity that fuelled this borrowers' market was endogenous to the market, in that it came from the re-depositing in the Euro-market of dollar reserve accruals that themselves resulted from the lending operations of Euro-banks. (BIS, Reserves and International Liquidity, June 1988)

From 1979 on, after the second oil shock and the beginning of efforts made by many industrialised countries to reduce inflation – which in turn produced greater volatility in interest rate levels – the international liquidity situation of many countries deteriorated progressively.

During most of this period international bank lending continued to grow strongly (except to eastern European countries after 1980) until well into 1982, despite the fact that external indebtedness, particularly in the many non-oil developing countries, was clearly growing at an unsustainable rate. Beginning with the Mexican crisis of August 1982, and leading into the more general, catastrophic Latin American debt crisis that preoccupied much of the 1980s, voluntary new bank lending to Latin America as a whole came to a virtual halt. The consequent deterioration of bank capital ratios alarmed the regulators, with potential failures of large banks in the industrialised nations looming on the horizon.

This was the exciting backdrop against which the Basle Capital Accord was formulated in December 1987 and finalised in July 1988.

1988 onwards: the era of the Basle Capital Accord

As articulated at the beginning of the chapter, the primary objective of the Basle Capital Accord was to strengthen the soundness and stability of the international banking system by creating minimum *risk-based* capital adequacy requirements for internationally active banks that are commensurate with the amount of credit risk each bank takes in its portfolio, thereby reducing global systemic risk without unduly compromising the competitive differences between countries. The translation of these objectives is simple: to prevent bank failures without undermining the international competitiveness of the banking industry.

The 1988 Accord was by no means a first attempt in requiring risk-based capital standards. The US bank regulators have been refining their capital regulation rules since the early 1970s, but there were no rules that specified minimum capital ratios. In the early 1980s, as the regulators became more disenchanted with, primarily, the larger banking organisations and their declining capital ratios, specified minimum numerical capital-to-asset ratios became a requirement for almost all banks. The remaining banks

Table 1.2 Overview of major changes in capital regulation in the US, 1981 to 1992

1981	The Federal Deposit and Insurance Corporation (FDIC) sets out numerical guidelines for all the banks it regulates.
1981	The Office of the Comptroller of the Currency (OCC) and Federal Reserve divide banks into three categories: community, regional and multinational (the 17 largest banking organisations). Numerical guidelines are set for the community and regional banks. No standards are set for the multinational banks, but they are encouraged to raise their capital ratios.
1983	The OCC and Federal Reserve impose the regional bank numerical guidelines on multinational banks.
1985	The FDIC, OCC and Federal Reserve establish a common set of capital guidelines that apply to all banking organisations.
1990	Interim risk-based capital guidelines take effect for all banking organisations. The risk-based guidelines are supplemented by leverage guidelines.
1991	The FDIC Improvement Act, which establishes five categories, is passed. Regulators are given a menu of mandatory and optional enforcement actions which they may undertake as a bank's capital ratios decline. Regulators ultimately define the categories in terms of both risk-based and leverage ratios.
1992	Final risk-based capital guidelines based on the 1988 Basle Accord take effect for all banking organisations. The risk-based guidelines are still supplemented by leverage guidelines.

Source: Wall and Peterson (1996).

were brought under the same numerical standards in 1983. After the adoption of the guidelines in 1981, the banking industry in the US increased its capital ratios in the years that followed.

Table 1.2 presents an overview of the major changes in capital regulation in the United States during the period from 1981 to 1992. The 1988 Basle Accord took effect in 1992.

In the United States, the combined effect of the Basle Accord and the Federal Deposit and Insurance Corporation Improvement Act is to make capital ratios one of the primary regulatory measures in gauging the financial condition of banks. Appendix A summarises the "prompt corrective action" provisions of the FDIC Improvement Act of 1991 and the required capital ratios.

CREDIT RISK, REGULATORY CAPITAL AND THE BASLE ACCORD

What is the rationale for requiring banks to hold regulatory capital?

Given the tainted history of the global banking industry and the well-known fiascos that have arisen from lapses and failures of credit risk management, the fundamental objective underlying capital regulation has always been very simple: to reduce the number of bank failures. Sufficient capital must, therefore, be maintained to provide a cushion to absorb losses that would otherwise cause a bank to fail. A corollary to this fundamental objective is: to reduce the losses to depositors and the deposit insurer when a bank fails.

Of the myriad risks that confront the large international banks, which were the specific focus of the Basle Accord and capital regulations, credit risk is still fundamentally the most important and most pressingly urgent issue. In the light of past and current banking crises that are directly attributable to the mismanagement and mis-measurement of credit risk, the current intense debate on capital adequacy has forced the convergence of two words: risk and capital. It also brought severe criticism and intense scrutiny of the 1988 Basle Accord, even though the Accord (and its ancillary requirements) has reversed the decades-long decline in bank capital cushions.

In a speech (February 27, 1998) addressing capital adequacy regulation and the road ahead, Tom de Swaan,[7] an executive director of the Netherlands Bank and a standing member of the Basle Committee, made the following statement:

> Capital requirements foster the safety and soundness of banks by limiting leverage and by providing a buffer against unexpected losses. Sufficient capital also decreases the likelihood of a bank becoming insolvent and limits – via loss absorption and greater public confidence – the adverse effects of bank failures. And by providing an incentive to exercise discipline in risk-taking, capital can mitigate moral hazard and thus protect depositors and deposit insurance. Admittedly, high capital adequacy ratios do not guarantee a bank's soundness, particularly if the risks being taken are high or the bank is being mismanaged. Therefore, supervisors consider a bank's capital adequacy in the context of a host of factors. But the bottom line is that capital is an important indicator of a bank's condition, also for financial markets, and minimum capital requirements are one of the essential supervisory instruments ... Therefore, it

> should be absolutely clear that, when it assesses the treatment of credit risk, the Basle Committee has no intention whatsoever of reducing overall capital adequacy requirements, maybe even the contrary. Higher capital requirements could prove necessary, for example, for bank loans to higher risk countries. In fact, this has been publicly recognised by bank representatives in view of the recent Asian crisis. More generally, we should be aware of the potential instability that can result from increased competition among banks in the United States and European countries in the longer run. And we should not be misled by the favourable financial results that banks are presently showing, but keep in mind that bad banking times can – and will – at some point return. In those circumstances, credit risk will turn out to be inflexible, difficult to manage and undoubtedly the primary source of banks' losses. Absorption of such losses will require the availability of capital. A reduction of capital standards would definitely not be the right signal from supervisors to the industry, nor would it be expedient. (*BIS Review*, 1998)

As we approach the conclusion of the tenth anniversary of the 1998 Basle Accord, I ask: are the criticisms of the Accord – from the banking industry and bank regulators alike – really levelled against the amount of the required capital ratios or at its ineffectiveness[8] in measuring credit risk? Or is it really the widespread realisation that the weaknesses of the Accord are being exploited and played with, thereby rendering it ineffective and negating its noble objectives? The answer is obvious!

EVOLUTIONARY NATURE OF CAPITAL REGULATION

It should be noted that "the agreed framework was designed to establish *minimum* levels of capital adequacy for internationally active banks. National authorities will be free to adopt arrangements that set higher levels" (Basle Committee on Banking Supervision, 1988). The interpretative reading of this quotation implies that the Capital Accord provides for a *de minimis* level of capital required of international banks engaged in credit risk-taking activities. But, as it turns out, the minimum level has become irrelevant. The admirable, but highly inadequate, risk differentiation provided for in the Accord has inadvertently encouraged banking activities and innovations in the capital markets (eg, asset securitisation and credit derivatives, etc) to shroud the material credit risk embedded in banking portfolios and has, in fact, created a disparity in the level playing field competitiveness of international banks, allowing – contrary to its stated prime objective – the principle of regulatory capital arbitrage.

The crux of the criticisms, and therefore of the perceived problem, is that the Basle framework has not kept up with the rapidity of financial evolution. In his speech (February 26, 1998) on the role of capital in optimal banking supervision and regulation, Alan Greenspan, the Chairman of the US Federal Reserve System, remarked (*BIS Review*, 1998):

> To begin, financial innovation is nothing new, and the rapidity of financial evolution is itself a relative concept – what is 'rapid' must be judged in the context of the degree of development of the economic and banking structure. Prior to World War II, banks in this country did not make commercial real estate mortgages or auto loans. Prior to the 1960s, securitization, as an alternative to the traditional 'buy and hold' strategy of commercial banks, did not exist. Now, banks have expanded their securitization activities well beyond the mortgage programs of the 1970s and 1980s, to include almost all asset types, including corporate loans. And most recently, credit derivatives have been added to the growing list of financial products. Many of these products, which would have been perceived as too risky for banks in earlier periods, are now judged to be safe owing to today's more sophisticated risk measurement and containment systems. Both banking and regulation are continuously evolving disciplines, with the latter, of course, continuously adjusting to the former.

On the evolutionary nature of capital regulations, he added:

> It is argued that the heightened complexity of these large banks' risk-taking activities, along with the expanding scope of regulatory capital arbitrage, may cause capital ratios as calculated under the existing rules to become increasingly misleading ... While no one is in favor of regulatory complexity, we should be aware that capital regulation will necessarily evolve over time as the banking and financial sectors themselves evolve. Thus, it should not be surprising that we constantly need to assess possible new approaches to old problems, even as new problems become apparent. Nor should the continual search for new regulatory procedures be construed as suggesting that existing policies were ill-suited to the times for which they were developed or will be ill-suited for those banking systems at an earlier stage of development. (Greenspan, 1998)

MARKET RESPONSE: CLAMOUR FOR INTERNAL CREDIT RISK MODELS

Given the rapid evolutionary nature of the financial world, the response from the market has been swift and coherent. The response was based on three fundamental criticisms of the 1988 Basle Accord as applied to the activities of the largest and most complex international banking institutions.

- First, because the capital ratio requirements have not been prescribed along with standards for the probability of insolvency, they are, for the most part, arbitrary.
- Second, except for the requirement set by the 1996 amendment of the Accord to incorporate capital adequacy due to market risk, no operating capital is required for other forms of risk.
- Third, other than the recognition of portfolio aggregation for market risk using the internal models approach, current capital standards do not provide for hedging, diversification or advances in risk management techniques – especially portfolio credit risk management.

Following on this theme, Greenspan, in his speech, put two very significant questions that merit discussion:

- How should the "soundness" of a bank be defined and measured?
- What minimum level of soundness should be set by regulators?

Even before these questions were raised, the banking industry had responded unilaterally by investing heavily in the research and development of internal risk measurement and management processes. Beginning with the 1996 amendment (and its full implementation in 1998) to incorporate market risk in the trading books, banks have been allowed to develop and use their own internal value-at-risk models for risk management purposes and, more importantly, for market risk capital adequacy purposes. In recent years, the impetus among international banks to include internal credit risk models for credit risk management and capital adequacy quickly raised concerns about the stringent but outmoded provisions of the 1988 Capital Accord.

Against the backdrop of the criticisms highlighted earlier, the industry has begun to lobby for the adoption of internal credit risk models as either an alternative or a supplement to the Accord. For internal purposes, large banking institutions have attempted to quantify their market, credit and operating risks through the use of loss probability distributions for the various risk positions. The resulting economic capital, as distinct from regulatory capital, is then allocated internally to the different lines of business within the bank in accordance with the probability of insolvency perceived by the institution.

The implication of all these developments is that the proof of "soundness" of the banking concerns rests with the banks themselves. Greenspan seemed to agree with this point: "These internal capital allocation models have much to teach the supervisor, and are critical to understanding the possible misallocative effects of inappropriate capital rule." A further caution was provided:

> Given these difficulties with the one-size-fits-all nature of our current capital regulations, it is understandable that calls have arisen for reform of the Basle standard. It is, however, premature to try to predict exactly how the next generation of prudential standards will evolve … . Proponents of an internal-models-based approach to capital regulations may be on the right track, but at this moment of regulatory development it would seem that a full fledged, bank-wide, internal-models approach could require a very substantial amount of time and effort to develop. [Researchers have expressed] their concerns over the reliability of the current generation of credit risk models. They go on to suggest, however, that these models may, over time, provide a basis for setting future regulatory capital requirements. Even in the shorter term, they argue, elements of internal credit risk models may prove useful within the supervisory process. (*BIS Review*, 1998)

The most prudent solution, it seems, is to continue on a track of collaborative efforts between regulators and banks. After all, the Basle Accord was never intended to be a static framework that would be resistant to market changes and advances. As we shall see in the chapters to come, given the intrinsic difficulty associated with credit risk modelling, no single entity has exclusive access to the ultimate truth. The only truth about credit risk modelling is that it, too, needs to be evolutionary in nature or it will cease to be useful.

Appendix B gives a concise summary of the regulatory capital rules (the 1988 Basle Accord and the 1996 amendment) so that the reader can become acquainted with the actual capital rules that have caused much consternation among the banks.

GAME THEORY: REGULATORY CAPITAL ARBITRAGE

The late 1980s and early 1990s witnessed several important changes that may have contributed to both regulatory and market pressures on banks to maintain high capital ratios. The implementation of the 1988 risk-based Capital Accord certainly triggered more intense scrutiny of financial institutions' off-balance sheet activities. The penalties provided in FDICIA 1991 and the FDIC's resolution of failed thrifts have also had a significant influence on the increased level of banks' capital ratios. In light of the market response of increasing capital ratios, the question really is: to what extent are these increases merely cosmetic in nature and what are the different strategies that banks have employed to provide real, tangible increases in their capital cushions?

Wall and Peterson (1996) summarised these cosmetic responses by the banks as follows.

- ❑ First, banks increase their capital but at the same time increase their risk. Whether the increase in risk will more than offset the rise in capital and increase their probability of failure is unclear. Empirical evidence indicates that increases in capital are partially offset by greater risk-taking. However, none of the empirical studies indicate that higher regulatory capital requirements actually increase the likelihood of bank failure.
- ❑ Second, banks raise their regulatory capital levels in ways that do not increase the market value of their capital. Accounting tricks to achieve this include accelerated recognition of gains (but not losses) by deferring the recognition of losses on loans and recognising gains from trading with securities. However, empirical evidence suggests that window-dressing activities such as these are sometimes transparent to the market and will, accordingly, reduce the equity price of the bank. In principle, regulators can require mark-to-market accounting treatment to eliminate the opportunities for window-dressing.

Aside from cosmetic responses to capital regulation, we saw in the previous section that the more philosophical market response to the Basle Accord has been the rapid development and deployment of credit risk models for internal use. But the most important – and decidedly straightforward "in your face" – response is that of *regulatory capital arbitrage* through the use of market innovations.

"If there are weaknesses, exploit them to the utmost" appears to be the blunt maxim followed by the banking industry nowadays. A purely proactive response from the market, regulatory capital arbitrage can be construed as a form of "game" theory, and this forced the regulators to take notice quickly and accelerate the current debate on credit risk modelling and capital adequacy.

"Regulatory capital arbitrage", as Greenspan emphasised in his speech of February 26, 1998,

> is not necessarily undesirable. In many cases, regulatory capital arbitrage acts as a safety-valve for attenuating the adverse effects of those regulatory capital requirements that are well in excess of the levels warranted by a specific activity's underlying economic risk. Absent such arbitrage, a regulatory capital requirement that is inappropriately high for the economic risk of a particular activity, could cause a bank to exit that relatively low-risk business, by preventing the bank from earning an acceptable rate of return on its capital. That is, arbitrage may appropriately lower the effective capital requirements against some safe activities that banks would otherwise be forced to drop by the effects of regulation. (*BIS Review*, 1998)

Banks can effectively increase their regulatory capital ratios and their true capital cushions by reducing the size of their loan portfolios. This can be accomplished either by an outright sale of loans to other financial intermediaries or by restricting the amount of new loans. Both, however, have unsatisfactory results. The negative consequences can range from potential damage to client–bank relationships because of loans sales to the danger of a perceived "credit crunch" because of restrictions on new loans. It has been widely argued that the so-called credit crunch of the early 1990s which resulted from a large reduction in new loan volumes was an unintended consequence of both FDICIA and risk-based capital standards imposed on banks. Therefore – in what was another unintended consequence of regulatory capital requirements – the more viable alternative was regulatory capital arbitrage.

What is the nature of this regulatory capital arbitrage and how is it done? Faced with binding regulatory capital requirements, major banking institutions can accomplish such arbitrage in several ways. Two major approaches are based on the securitisation of assets and the use of credit derivatives. These are described in the following sections.

SECURITISATION OF ASSETS

Broadly, asset securitisation refers to the process whereby loans, receivables and other illiquid assets with similar characteristics in the balance sheet are packaged into interest-bearing securities that offer attractive investment opportunities. Sometimes the securitised assets are collateralised to enhance the yields of the resulting securities.

Securitisation transforms traditionally non-traded bank assets into marketable securities. In addition to collateralisation as a form of credit enhancement, it may also involve off-balance sheet guarantees such as standby letters of credit or loan commitments that back up the issuance of commercial papers. From the perspective of credit originators (eg, banks), the asset-backed market enables them to transfer some of the risks of ownership to parties who are more willing or able to manage them in exchange for a variety of financial benefits.

From a balance sheet perspective, the big secret about asset securitisation is that illiquid assets – such as whole loans, for example, that might otherwise have to be classified as "hold-to-maturity" – can now be repackaged, securitised, collateralised, yield-enhanced and then jettisoned (at least partially) from the balance sheet into the capital markets. This is pretty much an arbitrage between regulatory and economic capital in its purest form. Of course, the regulators hover keenly over this "window-dressing" activity like vultures and, predictably, will soon issue new regulations to plug some of the loopholes. But who is to blame?

The increasing use of asset securitisation is a clever response by many financial institutions to risk-based capital adequacy guidelines mandated by the various regulatory bodies. The risk-based capital adequacy guidelines required of financial institutions generally place a higher risk weight on loans than on securities. Therefore, to lower its regulatory capital a financial institution can either buy securitised assets rather than whole loans or instigate an asset securitisation programme. Either way, this immediately reclassifies the illiquid assets into a lower risk weight category, resulting in a lower regulatory capital requirement.

Asset securitisation originally began in the 1970s with the structured financing of mortgage pools. In the US, the creation of the national agencies – for example, the Government National Mortgage

Association (GNMA), the Federal National Mortgage Association (FNMA) and the Federal Home Loan Mortgage Corporation (FHLMC) – facilitated the flow of funds into the primary market of mortgage origination through the purchase of a variety of whole mortgages from the originators and their securitisation as mortgage-backed securities (MBS). With an implicit guarantee backed by the full faith and credit of the US Federal government, the involvement of these national agencies in the capital markets facilitated the creation of derivatives products such as collateralised mortgage obligations (CMO) and MBS strips.

After the success of the mortgage-backed securitisation vehicle, impediments (such as the lack of federal guarantees) to the development of similar vehicles in the non-mortgage markets have largely been solved through a host of technological advances in off-balance sheet credit enhancements. Examples of these are subordination features, pool insurance, standby letters of credit, collateralisation and other private guarantees. The first non-mortgage asset-backed security, a computer-lease-backed transaction, was issued by the Sperry Corporation in March 1985, followed by the securitisation of automobile loans during the same year. In 1986 the first significant bank credit card sale involving a private placement was issued. The first few spectacular successes in the securitisation of loan pools convinced banks of the benefits of receiving sales treatment for accounting and regulatory purposes, both of which provide substantial easing of balance-sheet and regulatory capital constraints, in addition to the steady receipt of servicing fees while retaining origination rights.

In general, the securitisation of loans improves return on capital by transforming an on-balance sheet lending business into an off-balance sheet fee income stream that places fewer constraints on regulatory capital. Of course, this was possible only because of the risk-differentiated capital treatment provided for in the 1988 Basle Capital Accord and its risk-based progeny. Depending on the types of structures provided, the securitisation process can also lower funding costs for the bank, improve both asset/liability and credit risk management and may provide additional capital relief for reinvestment purposes.

Increasingly over the past four years, securitisation programmes have been actively pursued by major international banks with the primary goal of seeking capital relief. The crux of this regulatory capital arbitrage lies in risk-based capital guidelines that often place a significantly higher risk weight on loans than on securities. This means that a bank can frequently lower its regulatory capital requirements by buying securitised assets rather than whole loans or by securitising whole loans instead of accumulating them in its balance sheet.

For instance, based on the guidelines of the Basle Accord, a bank that originates uninsured single-family residential mortgage loans is levied a risk-weight capital charge of 50%, whereas an agency-sponsored (say, FNMA or FHLMC) mortgage pass-through requires only a 20% risk weight. It therefore behoves the bank to securitise its mortgage obligations in conformity with agency provisions. In addition, by securitising and selling the loans while retaining servicing rights, a bank effectively converts its capital-intensive assets into a less intensive one of servicing and origination fees without the need to increase its capital base, thereby increasing its return on capital.

CONCERNS RAISED BY SECURITISATION

Despite the universal appeal of securitisation programmes to banks, the explosive growth of securitisation activities in recent years has raised some very important and nagging questions for regulators and practitioners alike.

Before the 1996 amendment to the Basle Accord to incorporate market risk for off-balance sheet activities, most securitisation programmes of the 1980s and early 1990s offered off-balance sheet guarantees that were not subject to regulatory capital. Depending on the ensuing structures and tranches of the resulting securities, the material credit risk did not need to be fully jettisoned from the balance sheet. In fact, "capital standards in the 1980s led to allocative inefficiency by favoring the use of off-balance sheet guarantees even when it may have been more efficient to provide traditional bank loans. Moreover, off-balance sheet guarantees allowed banks with binding regulatory capital requirements to increase portfolio credit risk" (Berger, Herring and Szegö, 1995).

The biggest dilemma engendered by asset securitisation programmes is best summarised by the Office of the Comptroller of the Currency's *Handbook for Asset Securitization* (November, 1997).

A bank that sells assets in a securitisation transaction confronts three major manifestations of credit risk.

- *Residual exposure to default* In many securitisation programmes the material credit risk of the pool is normally relegated to the residual tranche of the structure. Whether or not the entire residual tranche sits in the bank's balance sheet depends on the structures embedded in the security. Even though the security has effectively lowered capital requirements, the material credit risk might not have been completely expunged from the balance sheet. Therefore, securitising banks must assess how much residual default risk remains with them after a sale. In most structures credit risk is allocated so that the originator bears the loss from default up to a certain point. As pool performance deteriorates and charge-offs increase, excess spread declines. Once excess spread is exhausted, the risk of default is shifted to the credit enhancers up to some additional multiple of projected losses. Since losses of the magnitude required to trigger credit enhancements are rare, the originators effectively absorb a substantial portion of realised losses in the securitised pool. Because risk-based capital rules are ineffective in assessing credit risk in this context, it has always been argued that an internally developed credit risk model that takes into account unexpected losses should be applied.
- *Credit quality of the remaining on-balance sheet portfolio* The greatest fear regulators have about securitisation is that banks might "cherry-pick" their portfolios for securitisation. Since higher-quality assets provide steadier and more predictable cashflow streams, these assets require less credit enhancement and produce higher excess spread income. As a consequence, banks may be tempted to securitise the better-quality assets in their portfolios while retaining the worse ones in their balance sheets, thereby increasing their loan loss reserves significantly. The converse is also possible: banks might cherry-pick only the weakened assets in their portfolios through securitised structures, leaving the market and the investors with "lemons" and rendering the securitisation process a proverbial "sale of lemons".
- *Possibility that banks will have to provide moral recourse* Originators of asset-backed securities may be compelled to protect their reputation in the marketplace by providing support for poorly

performing loan pools. The systemic risk associated with such an unexpected rescue has accounting, legal and regulatory costs that might cause disruptions to the market.

There are still other credit quality issues. Even though a bank may not be the originator of the loan pools used in securitisation, by becoming a provider of credit enhancement for assets originated by a third party the non-originating bank could find itself unavoidably entangled in a credit or liquidity crisis.

ROLE OF CREDIT DERIVATIVES

Credit derivatives are, by definition, a specific class of financial instruments whose value is derived from an underlying market instrument driven primarily by the credit risk of either private or government entities. The underlying instruments of credit derivatives are generally in the form of corporate debt and securities issued by sovereign entities.

Traditional financial derivatives, as we have known them, facilitate the separate trading of the individual attributes of the asset in isolation from the asset itself. They do not allow the separate trading of the risk margin and the risk of default embedded in the asset. Credit derivatives, by their very construction, facilitate the separate trading and risk management of these credit-related risk attributes.

As pointed out by Das (1998), the principal feature of these credit derivative instruments is that they separate and isolate credit risk, thereby facilitating the trading of credit risk with the purpose of: replicating credit risk; transferring credit risk; and hedging credit risk.

These new mechanisms for taking on or off-loading credit risk with predefined risk and reward parameters add value to a portfolio without the acquisition of the credit-risky asset itself. On the flip side, the provider of the credit derivative (normally the originator of the risky asset) can easily jettison the unwanted credit risk from its portfolio.

The principal credit derivative products widely available in the market comprise three main categories, namely:

- total return swaps (also known as loan swaps);
- credit spread products; and
- credit default products.

Total return swaps are off-balance sheet items that synthetically embed the returns of credit-risky assets into traditional swap structures. The key characteristic is that, being an off-balance sheet transaction, a total return swap obviates the need to arrange a loan or purchase a bond. Credit spread products are generally forwards or options on the margins of credit-sensitive assets, while credit default products take the form of put options on credit-risky assets that guarantee payoffs contingent on the occurrence of specific default events.

Credit derivatives are beginning to play a very important role within the overall credit risk management functionality of leading banks. Banks and financial institutions, in particular, are now using such derivatives to manage the credit risk in their balance sheets and to streamline their regulatory capital usage. Among the areas witnessing rapid growth in today's changing credit market landscape are:

- primary – loan syndication;
- secondary – institutions making markets specifically for yield pick-up; and
- tertiary – credit portfolio and balance sheet management in banks.

Credit derivatives are widely used today as part of the overall loan syndication strategy. In preparation for a turn in the credit cycle, syndication agents are using them to entice an ever increasing number of hedge funds into an already crowded loan market.

The preferred vehicle is usually a total return swap whereby the investor (generally a hedge fund) puts up collateral and borrows (up to several times the amount of the collateral) from the lender at a substantial premium. In return, the investor receives the cash-flows linked to the total return of an underlying asset (normally a loan or a high-yield bond). Since the investor is leveraged, its return is substantially high. In addition, the investor also receives the yield on the collateral pledged, which is usually a risk-free instrument such as treasuries. The lender, on the other hand, receives the substantial premium on the investment-grade loan to the investor while, at the same time, reducing its exposure to the underlying asset.

Through the total return swap vehicle the arranger bypasses the upfront fees normally required of ordinary loans in the primary market and receives a relatively wide margin on a high-grade loan to the hedge fund. Both sides appear to have benefited from the transaction.

Credit risk concentration and the credit paradox

Why do banks continue to find it beneficial to use credit derivatives in their balance sheet management function even though doing so often results in a loss?

The simple answer lies in what is collectively known as the "credit paradox". A credit portfolio that is not well diversified will generally be characterised by an excess in the two measures of portfolio risk – expected loss and unexpected loss – relative to a more diversified portfolio of similar size and other characteristics. The reasons for this are that credit losses in the portfolio are highly correlated and that the risk of default between individual obligors is not sufficiently mitigated by portfolio effects.

It is generally not "cheaper" to accept more credit risk since the bank needs to charge an increasingly larger credit spread as its exposure to a specific obligor rises. This phenomenon is very unlike going for volume in market risk. The larger spread is required to compensate the institution for the increase in the expected and unexpected losses in line with greater exposure to the obligor. However, in hopes of retaining the goodwill of such a borrower, banks rarely charge more. On the contrary, relationship managers normally argue for higher levels of exposure as a means of maintaining a cosy relationship with their primary clients. A problematic paradox hereby exists, resulting in significant concentration risk for the bank.

Several important factors contribute to concentration risk in the balance sheets of banks. First, most banks and financial institutions, by virtue of their expertise or lack of it, tend to specialise in specific industries or regions. This causes their credit portfolios to be highly concentrated on clusters of clients that tend to have similar default characteristics and whose businesses tend to be highly correlated with the economic cycles they are in. Second, as a consequence of current credit trends in the market (eg, the direct issuance of securities to investors and capital-raising in the capital markets), larger corporations have succeeded in bypassing bank financing, leaving a concentration of less creditworthy borrowers who do not have easy access to the capital markets for financing. Thus, some banks are beginning to accumulate a disproportionately large concentration of lower-quality borrowers in their credit portfolio. Finally, in order to preserve a cosy client relationship in the hope of generating more non-credit-related business down the road, many institutions have struggled with the dilemma of increasing their commitment to individual borrowers beyond what is considered profitable for the organisation. Consequently, faced with the inability to off-load the larger credit exposures directly, many institutions incur substantial concentration risk with specific borrowers.

Given these factors that collectively contribute to the credit paradox phenomenon – and, of course, the inevitable increase in regulatory capital requirements – banks are turning swiftly to the credit derivatives market for solutions in addition to instigating asset securitisation programmes. In spite of the early indications that they have not been able to use the credit derivatives vehicle to alleviate their concentration risk too profitably, the resulting capital relief has, nevertheless, allowed banks to employ these capital savings to generate earnings elsewhere. The capital relief and the new business opportunities provided by this form of regulatory capital arbitrage have, it seems for now, adequately compensated them for the loss in using credit derivatives.

Together with the asset securitisation vehicle, credit derivatives potentially allow a substantial amount of credit risk and its associated concentration effects to be lifted from the balance sheet. The amount of credit relief and capital reduction depends heavily on the tranches embedded in the asset securitisation and the kinds of credit derivatives that are structured.

Short of regulatory intervention, banks currently have at their disposal a considerable arsenal of innovative products that allow them to align their capital structure with the businesses they engage in while at the same time shifting the credit content of their balance sheets to more favourable positions.

Credit derivatives and regulatory capital

Unlike the asset securitisation vehicle, credit derivatives are the first mechanism through which credit instruments can be executed with reasonable liquidity and without the risk of a short squeeze.

Credit derivatives, except when embedded in structured notes, are off-balance sheet instruments. As such, they offer considerable flexibility in terms of leverage. Amazingly, the degree of leverage is defined and controlled by the user. And, interestingly, as we shall see in the example that follows, the degree of leverage also dictates the level of regulatory capital arbitrage that is feasible.

Because of the absence of a credit repo market, the return on capital offered by bank loans has been unattractive to institutions that do not enjoy access to unsecured financing. However, by taking exposure to bank loans using say, a total return swap (eg, receiving the net proceeds of the loan after financing), a hedge fund can both synthetically finance the position more cheaply and avoid the administrative costs of direct ownership of the asset. The bank, on the other side, stands to benefit from a reduction in regulatory capital usage and thereby achieve a better return on capital. The degree of leverage that can be achieved using this total return swap example will depend on the amount of up-front collateralisation and the underlying structure of the swap. The user controls this leverage.

The following example, which is a modification of an illustration given by Wong and Song (1997), demonstrates the effect of return on regulatory capital when a simple credit derivative swap is used.

Example 1.1 – Using credit derivatives to manage regulatory capital and returns

Consider two banks, each funding a $10 million BBB-rated corporate loan. The current Libor rate is 5.625%. The regulatory capital requirement for loans is 8% of the appropriate risk weighting. The risk weighting is 100% if the counterparty is a corporate and 20% if the counterparty is another OECD bank. (Refer to Appendix B for a detailed discussion of risk-weighted assets and how the regulatory rules are to be applied.)

Figure 1.1 shows each bank going its separate way, financing the corporate loan at Libor plus 0.375%. Each bank must put up $800,000 of its own equity. Bank A (higher quality) and Bank B (lower quality) fund at Libor – 0.20% and Libor + 0.25%, respectively. The returns on regulatory capital are 12.6% and 7.4%, respectively.

Figure 1.1 Returns on capital for banks not using credit derivatives

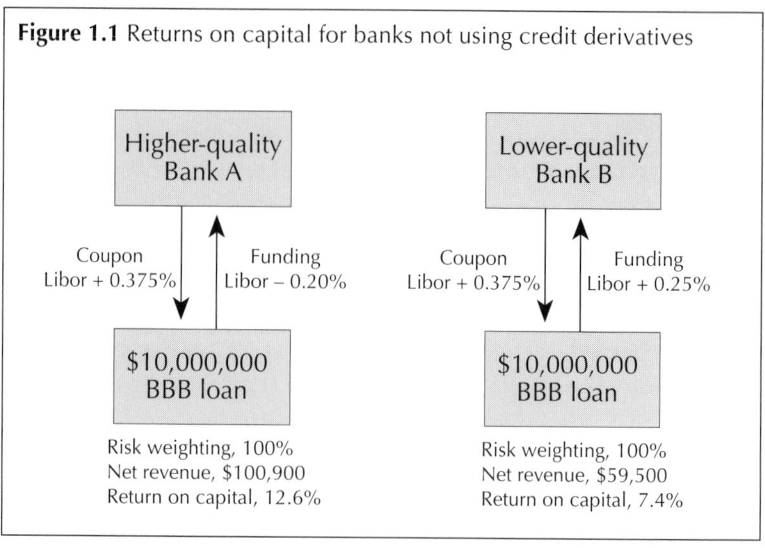

Figure 1.2 shows the two banks using a credit swap to end up in a "win–win" situation. The better-rated Bank A funds the $10 million loan and swaps the credit risk out to the lower-rated Bank B via a default put. Bank A is now exposed to the default risk of the lower-rated Bank B instead of the corporate. The new risk weighting for Bank A is 20% and the required regulatory capital is now reduced to $160,000. As a result, Bank A's return on regulatory capital increases to 17.9% although its net revenue falls. In addition, Bank A, having effectively "hedged" this credit exposure, can now free up credit lines and continue to lend to a valued customer even though it would exceed the original credit limits.

Bank B also wins. For receiving the put premium of $37,500 per annum, the lower-rated Bank B takes on the $10 million default risk of the corporate and has to put up $800,000 as equity capital. Investing the $37,500 in treasury bills (assuming a rate of 5.29%), Bank B increases its revenue to $79,800 and improves its return on capital to 10.0%.

The credit swap, of course, sits off balance sheet and is subject to daily mark to market, and it should therefore be passed to the trading portfolio for risk management.

Figure 1.2 Returns on capital for banks using credit derivatives

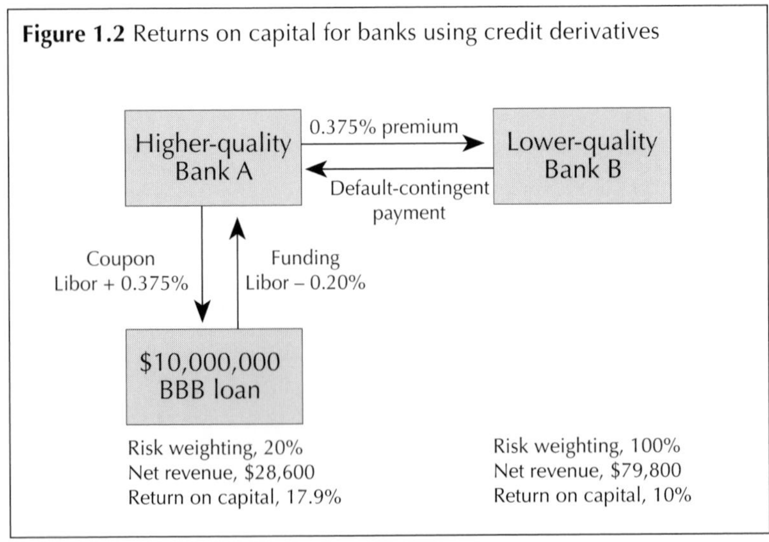

APPENDIX A – SUMMARY OF FEDERAL DEPOSIT INSURANCE CORPORATION IMPROVEMENT ACT 1991

In the 1980s, systemic problems at US depository institutions prompted a major overhaul of banking legislation unprecedented since the Great Depression. At the core of the new legislation was the Federal Deposit Insurance Corporation Improvement Act (FDICIA) of 1991, which emphasised early intervention and early closing of failing banks by regulators.

The "prompt and corrective action" provisions contained in the Act aimed to limit the number and cost of bank failures by intervening earlier in problem banks and by encouraging banks to become better capitalised. Table A.1.1 (overleaf) provides a brief summary of these provisions.

Table A.1.1 Summary of prompt corrective action provision of the Federal Deposit Insurance Corporation Improvement Act of 1991

	Mandatory provisions	Discretionary provisions	Capital ratios (%) Risk-based Total	Risk-based Tier 1	Leverage Tier 1
Zone 1 Well capitalised			>10	>6	>5
Zone 2 Adequately capitalised	1. No brokered deposits, except with FDCI approval		>8	>4	>4
Zone 3 Undercapitalised	1. Suspend dividends and management fees 2. Require capital restoration plan 3. Restrict asset growth 4. Restrict deposit interest rates* 5. Pay of officers restricted	1. Order recapitalisation 2. Restrict inter-affiliate transactions 3. Restrict deposit interest rates 4. Restrict certain other activities 5. Any other action that would carry out prompt corrective action better	<8	<4	<4
Zone 4 Significantly undercapitalised	1. Same as for Zone 3 2. Order recapitalisation* 3. Restrict inter-affiliate transactions* 4. Restrict deposit interest rates* 5. Pay of officers restricted	1. Any Zone 3 discretionary action 2. Conservatorship or receivership if fails to submit or implement plan or recapitalise pursuant to order 3. Any other Zone 5 provision, if such action is necessary to carry out prompt corrective action	<6	<3	<3
Zone 5 Critically undercapitalised	1. Same as for Zone 4 2. Receiver/conservator within 90 days* 3. Receiver if still in Zone 5 four quarters after becoming critically undercapitalised 4. Suspend payments on subordinated debt* 5. Restrict certain other activities				<2

*Not required if the primary supervisor determines that action would not serve the purpose of prompt corrective action or if certain other conditions are met.
Source: Board of Governors of the Federal Reserve System.

APPENDIX B – REGULATORY CAPITAL RULES

The regulatory capital rules have two major components: the 1988 Basle Capital Accord itself; and the 1996 Amendment to incorporate market risk.

The 1988 Basle Capital Accord

The 1988 Accord defined a common measure of solvency, called the Cooke ratio, which covers only the credit risk of the bank. Capital, in the regulatory context, is defined on a two-tiered basis:

- *Tier 1 capital* (or "core" capital). This includes stock issues (shareholders' equity) and disclosed reserves. Disclosed reserves can be in the form of loan loss reserves set aside to cushion future losses or for smoothing out income volatility.
- *Tier 2 capital* (or "supplementary" capital). This includes perpetual securities, unrealised gains on investment securities, hybrid capital instruments (eg, mandatory convertibles), long-term subordinated debt with maturity greater than five years and hidden reserves, such as excess allowance for losses on loans and leases.

A 1995 proposal[9] also provided for a third tier of capital consisting of short-term unsecured subordinated debt which can only be used for meeting market risk capital requirements.

There are limits and restrictions, such as that the total of tier 2 capital is limited to a maximum of 100% of the total of tier 1 capital; subordinated term debt is limited to a maximum of 50% of tier 1 capital; and others.

The Accord further requires tier 1 and tier 2 capital to be at least 8% of the so-called total "risk-weighted assets" (RWA) of the bank. These are simply the assets of the bank weighted in accordance with their relative credit riskiness. Table B.1.1 sets out the four risk-weight categories for on-balance sheet assets.

The Basle rules are simple. Capital adequacy for on-balance sheet exposures, as measured by the two-tiered capital regime, will result in a risk-weighted ratio in which the bank's total capital requirement is related to the different categories of on-balance sheet exposures, weighted according to the four relative riskiness categories displayed in Table B.1.1. The aggregate dollar amount in each risk category is then multiplied by the risk weight assigned to

Table B.1.1 Risk weights of on-balance sheet assets

Risk weight (%)	Asset category
0	Cash and gold held in the bank Obligations on OECD governments and US treasuries
20	Claims on OECD banks Securities issued by US government agencies Claims on municipalities
50	Residential mortgages
100	All other claims such as corporate bonds, less-developed countries' debt, claims on non-OECD banks, equity, real estate, plant and equipment, mortgage strips and residuals

that category. The resulting weighted values from each of the risk categories are then added together. This sum is the bank's total risk-weighted assets, which forms the denominator of the Cooke ratio. Finally, the required capital for the bank must be equal to at least 8% of the total risk-weighted assets in the bank's portfolio.

Some simple examples are in order.

Examples B.1.1 – On-balance sheet exposures

B.1.1a An unsecured loan of \$100 to a non-bank requires a risk weight of 100%. The risk-weighted asset is therefore

$$RWA = \$100 \times 100\% = \$100$$

A minimum 8% capital requirement results in

$$8\% \times RWA = 8\% \times \$100 = \$8.00$$

B.1.1b A residential mortgage loan of \$100 requires a risk weight of 50%, so

$$RWA = \$100 \times 50\% = \$50$$

The minimum 8% capital ratio results in

$$8\% \times RWA = 8\% \times \$50 = \$4.00$$

Table B.1.2 Risk weights of off-balance sheet assets

Risk weight (%)	Type of counterparty
0	OECD governments
20	OECD banks and public sector entities
50	Corporates and other counterparties

Table B.1.3 Credit conversion factors for OBSI (non-trading assets)

CCF (%)	Types of off-balance sheet exposure
0	Undrawn commitments with an original maturity of one year or less
20	Documentary credits relating to shipment of goods
50	Transaction-related contingencies – eg, performance bonds, bid bonds and warranties. Undrawn portion of commitments with original maturity greater than one year
100	General guarantees, standby letters of credit, banker's acceptance, sale and repurchase agreements, forward purchase of assets

Off-balance sheet items

In addition to on-balance sheet activities, the Basle framework also takes into account the credit risk of off-balance sheet items (OBSI) by applying so-called "credit conversion factors" (CCF) to the different types of off-balance sheet assets. Table B.1.2 displays the risk weights for off-balance sheet assets categorised by counterparty type.

It is important to note that the Basle rules distinguish between *trading-* and *non-trading*-related assets in OBSI. Later on, in Table B.1.4, we shall account for trading products differently.

OBSI (non-trading assets)

Table B.1.3 shows the CCF for *non-trading*-related off-balance sheet item exposures. The calculation of capital adequacy for these is a two-step process:

❑ *Step 1* The "credit-equivalent amount" of an OBSI is determined by multiplying the notional amount by a credit conversion factor (CCF).

- *Step 2* The credit-equivalent amount is then treated as an on-balance sheet item and risk-weighted according to its risk category classification. The resulting risk-weighted asset is finally multiplied by the minimum capital ratio requirement.

The capital calculation for the non-trading products in the OBSI is demonstrated with the following example.

Examples B.1.2 – Off-balance sheet exposures (non-trading assets)
An unsecured facility of $100 is granted to a non-bank with an original term of greater than one year. Calculate the required capital for the case when the facility is (1) not utilised and (2) 80% utilised.

B.1.2a Since the commitment is not utilised and is greater than one year, the credit-equivalent amount (CEA) is

$$CEA = \$100 \times CCF = \$100 \times 50\% = \$50$$

A minimum 8% capital requirement results in

$$8\% \times CEA = 8\% \times \$50 = \$4.00$$

B.1.2b Because 80% of the $100 commitment is utilised, $80 is considered to be an unsecured loan. The counterparty is a non-bank, which carries a risk weight of 100%. Thus, the risk-weighted asset for this portion is

$$\$80 \times 100\% = \$80$$

The remaining undrawn amount of $20 is treated as part (1) with a CCF of 50%, so the credit-equivalent amount is

$$CEA = \$20 \times 50\% = \$10$$

The total RWA for both portions is $80 + $10 = $90.

A minimum 8% capital ratio requires a capital of

$$8\% \times \$90 = \$7.20$$

OBSI (trading assets)

For trading-related products that are off-balance sheet items the calculations are different. Trading products in the context of the Basle Accord refer to those OBSI classified as derivatives: interest rates, foreign exchange, equity derivatives and commodities.

The Accord recognises that the credit risk exposure of over-the-counter financial products (more specifically, long-dated ones) fluctuates with market volatility. Consequently, there are two contributions to the total credit exposure of these bank assets:

- *Current exposure* (CE), which is estimated as the current marked-to-market value; and
- *Potential exposure* (PE), which is an estimate of the potential future increase in credit exposure over the remaining life of the derivative contract.

The sum of the two items is the credit-equivalent amount of the derivative contract. In practice, since the marked-to-market value is normally obtainable only from some in-house or external valuation models, it should more appropriately be referred to as the "marked-to-model" value.

The wisdom behind the CEA concept, as we saw earlier for the non-trading-related off-balance sheet items, is that trading products in OBSI can likewise be placed on the same level of comparison with other assets in the balance sheet. Hence, trading assets in OBSI also need to be converted first to their credit-equivalent amounts. The resulting CEA are then treated in the same manner as balance sheet assets by using the risk-weighting factors given in Tables B.1.1 and B.1.2.

From the bank's perspective, only the positive marked-to-market value of the derivative contract matters since a negative marked-to-market value implies that the bank owes money to the counterparty and is, therefore, not exposed to default risk of the counterparty. Thus, the replacement cost of a derivative contract with negative marked-to-market value is zero. For this reason, the potential exposure (PE) is also known as the "liquidation value" or "current replacement value". The PE is also normally known as an "add-on" to the current exposure.

Table B.1.4 displays the CCF for *trading*-related off-balance sheet item exposures.

Table B.1.4 Credit conversion factors for OBSI (trading assets)

Remaining maturity	Interest rates	FX and gold	Equity derivatives	Precious metals	Commodity contracts
Less than 1 year	0.0%	1.0%	6.0%	7.0%	10.0%
1–5 years	0.5%	5.0%	8.0%	7.0%	12.0%
More than 5 years	1.5%	7.5%	10.0%	8.0%	15.0%

Exceptions to the credit conversion process include: all foreign exchange trades with original maturities of less than 14 days; all exchange-traded products that require margin variations; and all written option contracts that are not financial guarantees.

For risk-based capital purposes, even if a derivative contract has a negative marked-to-market value (so that its CE equals zero), the PE add-on is not zero. The PE of a derivative contract is determined by multiplying the notional principal amount of the contract by the appropriate credit conversion factors in Table B.1.4. The credit conversion factors are also known as "add-on factors". The following example demonstrates some calculations.

Examples B.1.3 – Off-balance sheet exposures (trading assets)
B.1.3a An interest rate swap of notional amount $100 with an OECD bank, with remaining maturity of less than one year, has a current exposure (CE) – say, a marked-to-market value from some model – of

$$CE = \$10$$

From Table B.1.4, the remaining maturity of less than one year requires a CCF of 0%, so the potential exposure (PE) is

$$PE = \text{Notional} \times CCF = \$100 \times 0\% = 0$$

Thus, the credit-equivalent amount (CEA) is

$$CEA = CE + PE = \$10$$

We can now treat this credit-converted amount like a balance sheet item. An OECD bank requires a risk weight of 20%, so the risk-weighted asset (RWA) is

$$RWA = CEA \times 20\% = \$10 \times 20\% = \$2.00$$

The minimum 8% capital requirement for the bank is

$$RWA \times 8\% = \$2.00 \times 8\% = \$0.16$$

B.1.3b A foreign exchange forward contract with a corporate, of notional amount $100 and with 20 months remaining maturity, has

$$CE = \$3$$

say, from some model, and

$$PE = \$100 \times 5\% = \$5$$

The credit-equivalent amount is

$$CEA = CE + PE = \$8$$

The minimum capital requirement is

$$\$8 \times 50\% \times 8\% = \$0.32$$

Netting agreements

In April 1995 the Basle Accord was amended so that banks can effectively reduce their credit-equivalent exposures when bilateral netting agreements are in place. For banks using the "current exposure" method outlined above, credit exposure on bilaterally netted forward transactions is calculated as the sum of the net marked-to-market replacement cost, if positive, plus an add-on based on the notional amount of principal. But this time the add-on, representing potential exposure, is multiplied by a reduction factor given by a formula which reflects the fact that the potential change in value of a netted portfolio is less than one where no netting is allowed.

The *reduction factor* is given by

$$0.4 + (0.6 \times NGR)$$

where NGR is the ratio of the replacement value after netting to the replacement value before netting or

$$NGR = (\text{Net replacement cost})/(\text{Gross replacement cost})$$

Observe that in the absence of netting agreements, the netted and un-netted replacement values are identical, so that $NGR = 1$ and the formula becomes 1.0, implying no reduction in potential exposure. In the case where the replacement values net out to zero (so that $NGR = 0$), observe that the 1995 rule still imposes a minimum 40% of the total add-on amounts from the potential exposure.

In summary, in the presence of bilateral netting agreements, the potential exposure is calculated as

$$PE\text{ (with netting)} = \text{Notional} \times CCF \times [0.4 + 0.6 \times NGR]$$

or, more concisely,

$$PE\text{ (with netting)} = PE\text{ (without netting)} \times [0.4 + 0.6 \times NGR]$$

Example B.1.4 – Capital requirement with netting agreements
Suppose there are three different derivative contracts with the following characteristics. What is the effect of netting on the capital requirement?

	CCF	Notional	CE (MTM)
Contract 1	0.5%	$100	$20
Contract 2	1.5%	$50	–$5
Contract 3	8.0%	$100	–$10

The potential exposure based on the original 1988 rule without netting is

$$PE(\text{no netting}) = \sum_{i=1}^{3} \text{Notional}_i \cdot CCF_i = \$9.25$$

To determine the potential exposure using the 1995 rule for netting, we need to calculate other quantities first. The net replacement cost (NRC) is the sum of current exposures, viz:

$$NRC = \sum_{i=1}^{3} CE_i = \$5.00$$

The gross replacement cost (GRC) is the sum of only the *positive* marked-to-market or current exposures:

$$GRC = \sum_{i=1}^{3} \max(CE_i, 0) = \$20.00$$

The net-to-gross ratio (NGR) is, therefore, given by

$$NGR = \frac{NRC}{GRC} = 0.25$$

so that the reduction factor is

$$0.4 + (0.6 \cdot NGR) = 0.55$$

This means that, in the presence of netting agreements, the potential exposure using the 1995 amendment is

$$PE\,(\text{with netting}) = \sum_{i=1}^{3} \text{Notional}_i \cdot CCF_i = \$5.09$$

which is a significant 55% reduction on the 1988-based potential exposure.

The capital requirement is simply the risk-weighted sum of the potential exposure (either on the 1988 or the 1995 basis) and the current exposure of \$20 multiplied by the minimum ratio of 8%. As before, the risk weight is dependent on the risk category of the counterparty. For practical purposes it is important to note that the 1995 rules allow the calculation of NGR at a counterparty-to-counterparty or at a sub-portfolio aggregate level.

The 1996 Amendment to incorporate market risk

Beginning with the early 1990s, the traditional banking industry – which previously had tended to place more emphasis on credit-related businesses – moved rapidly into other areas such as investment banking and trading activities in the capital markets. The result was a dramatic increase in exposure to market risk. In 1996, in accordance with the Bank for International Settlement's desire to engage more actively in the evolutionary nature of capital adequacy regulations and to be in better alignment with industry developments, the 1988 Basle Capital Accord was amended to include capital adequacy for the market risk-taking activities of banks.

The "1996 Amendment",[10] as it is now called, came into force in January 1998 and requires banks to satisfy risk-based capital guidelines covering market risk in addition to those specified in the original Accord on credit risk. Many articles and books have already been written on the subject, so here we shall only highlight the important points of the Amendment, which are often overlooked.

Since market risk was defined in the Amendment as the "risk of losses in on- and off-balance sheet positions arising from movements in market prices", the capital guidelines identified four broad categories of products that generate market risk – namely, interest rate risk, foreign exchange risk, equities risk and commodities risk.

Earlier in this appendix we saw that the initial 1988 Capital Accord applied risk-based capital adequacy rules for credit risk to both the banking and trading books, covering both on- and off-balance sheet activities. Although the 1996 Amendment applies to only the market risk of on-balance sheet assets, off-balance sheet derivatives assets (eg, interest rate options, swaps, etc) are subject to *both* market risk and credit risk capital charges. The reason for the dual emphasis on both types of risk is that the 1996 Amendment considers market risk as comprising two fundamental risk items: general market risk and specific risk.

"General market risk" refers to changes in market value due to broad market movements. "Specific risk" refers to changes in the value of an individual security due to factors related to the individual issuer of the security (eg, credit quality and liquidity) that are outside of broad market movements. The specific risk capital charge is primarily intended as an add-on charge to debt securities.

In addition to these two risk items comprising market risk delineated along the four categories of product risk, the Amendment explicitly recognises the treatment of non-linear options risk in banks' portfolios.

There was a major twist in the 1996 Amendment for incorporating market risk capital adequacy. The Basle Committee and the major regulatory supervisory bodies around the world collectively recognised the significant internal development of risk management and risk measurement systems within large banks. In view of this, the regulatory supervisors have decided that the most sophisticated banks, which already have an independent risk management division in place and implement sound risk management practices, should be allowed to choose between their own internally developed "value-at-risk" (now universally known as VAR) models and the BIS "standard model". Consequently, these two approaches have become known in the financial industry as the "internal models approach" and the "standardised approach", respectively.

Internally developed VAR models for assessing market risk capital adequacy have essentially the same purpose as that advocated in this book for the evaluation of credit risk capital adequacy.

Internal value-at-risk models for market risk

Although criticism, both fair and unfair, continues to be levied against the VAR approach, I am of the opinion that, overall, the wisdom of allowing the rapid development of internal VAR models – initially in the large banks and currently among second-tier banking institutions, mutual funds, insurance companies, other general financial institutions and, finally, non-financial corporations engaged in derivatives activities – has indeed proved itself by advancing the frontiers of and the awareness required for prudential risk management. Never before has there been a more coherent awareness of the financial risks that confront us in the industry. Even though, as recently as 1998, there continue to be well-publicised financial losses, the fact remains that the debate surrounding the acceptance of internal VAR models during the mid-1990s has contributed significantly to a heightened awareness of the importance of risk, capital and portfolio management. And this cannot be a bad thing for the banking industry as a whole.

Following the decision by the regulatory supervisors to allow banks to use internal market risk models, two separate so-called *qualitative standards* and *quantitative requirements* are imposed on a bank before it is allowed to use its own internal VAR model. The qualitative standards relate to sound risk management practices and the systems infrastructure already in place within the bank. The quantitative requirements concern certain standardisations of inputs and methodology in the implementation of the internal model.

The main quantitative requirements are:

- The internal VAR number shall be derived on the basis of a uniform set of quantitative inputs, eg:
  - a 10-trading day horizon that can capture the movements of rates and prices during the period of analysis;
  - a 99% confidence level based on the assumption of a one-tailed normal distribution; and
  - an observation period based on at least one year of historical data and updated at least once every quarter period to estimate volatilities and correlations.
- Banks will be allowed to use correlations among the four major risk categories (interest rate, foreign exchange, equities and commodities) provided that the historical data used for the calculations are updated at least once every quarter period. If empirical information on correlations is not available, banks are required to aggregate the different risk categories in an arithmetic simple sum manner without the benefit of offsetting risk reductions.
- The calculated daily value-at-risk number shall be grossed up by the 10-day horizon using the "square root of time" rule, viz:

$$VAR = \sqrt{10} \cdot VAR_{\text{daily}}$$

- The regulatory capital required for market risk corresponds to the maximum of the previous day's VAR or a "multiplier", M, times the average VAR over the past 60 days:

$$\text{Market risk capital}_t = \max\left[VAR_t, \frac{M}{60} \sum_{i=1}^{60} VAR_{t-i} \right]$$

The multiplier, M, is either three or four, depending on the overall assessment of the local supervisor. A multiplier greater than three is intended as a punitive measure, the value applied being based on the number of exceptions in the required quarterly back-testing results *vis-à-vis* the actual calculated daily VAR number.

- For options portfolios, the internal VAR model must in addition be able to capture not only "linear" risk (eg, delta risk) but also "non-linear" risks (eg, gamma and vega risks).

To address the concerns raised regarding the robustness of internal VAR models, the regulators strongly encouraged stress-testing of model assumptions to test the validity of the 99% confidence level for capital adequacy. However, no explicit guidelines on stress-testing were circulated for discussion.

New calculation of capital ratios

The new capital guidelines set out in the 1996 Amendment have themselves undergone modification. At the discretion of their national banking supervisors, banks may now employ a third tier of capital, "Tier 3", which consists mainly of short-term subordinated debt subject to certain conditions and which can be used solely to meet the daily market risk capital requirement. Tier 3 capital is expressed by the formula given above for "market risk capital" using the internal VAR model.

Banks shall be required first to allocate tier 1 and tier 2 capital to meet credit risk capital adequacy according to the 1988 Capital Accord. The sum of the two must represent 8% of the risk-weighted assets, adjusted for positions that are no longer subject to the 1988 rules – for example, traded debt securities and equities on the balance sheet which are already subject to specific risk charges according to the 1996 Amendment. To ensure consistency in the calculation of capital for both credit and market risks, the market risk capital charge formula given above needs to be multiplied by 12.5 (ie, the reciprocal of the minimum capital ratio of 8%); the resulting figure is then added to the sum of risk-weighted assets compiled for credit risk purposes only.

By regulatory intent, tier 1 capital should constitute the major portion of a bank's capital requirement. Additional provisions are that:

- ❑ Tier 1 capital should represent at least 50% of a bank's total eligible capital (ie, the sum of tiers 2 and 3 should not exceed the total of tier 1).
- ❑ Long-term subordinated debt is limited to a maximum of 50% of tier 2 capital.
- ❑ Tier 3 capital is limited to 250% of a bank's tier 1 capital that is required to support market risks (ie, a minimum of about 28.5% of market risk must be met by tier 1 capital).

In summary, a bank's eligible capital is the sum of (1) tier 1 capital, (2) tier 2 capital under the limits imposed by the 1988 Accord, and (3) some of its tier 3 capital subject to the provisions of the 1996 Amendment.

1 The Basle Committee on Banking Supervision comprises representatives of the central banks and supervisory authorities of the Group of Ten countries (Belgium, Canada, France, Germany, Italy, Japan, Netherlands, Sweden, the United Kingdom and the United States) as well as Switzerland and Luxembourg. Thus, 12 countries are represented on the committee.

2 The Bank for International Settlements, located in Basle, Switzerland, was founded in 1930 and is an important forum for banking supervisors and central banks of the major industrialised nations to discuss and coordinate risk policies.

3 The Basle Committee, originally known as the Cooke Committee after its chairman, is in fact not a part of the BIS organisation.

4 Basle Committee on Banking Supervision, Bank for International Settlements, January 1996, *Amendment to the Capital Accord to Incorporate Market Risks.*

5 The International Monetary Fund was established in December 1945 following ratification of the Articles of Agreement of the Fund, which were formulated at the United Nations Monetary and Financial Conference held at Bretton Woods, New Hampshire, in 1944. In addition to the IMF, the World Bank was subsequently created as part of the Bretton Woods Institutions.

6 Parts of this section were derived from an unpublished manuscript by E. J. Manuels (Erasmus University, Rotterdam), 1997.

7 Tom de Swaan is currently a member of the managing board at ABN AMRO.

8 A major criticism of the Accord concerns its provisions for a minimum capital ratio requirement that is not based on a maximum probability of insolvency.

9 Basle Committee on Banking Supervision, Bank for International Settlements, *Proposal to Issue a Supplement to the Basle Capital Accord to Cover Market Risks,* April 1995.

10 Basle Committee on Banking Supervision, Bank for International Settlements, January 1996, *Amendment to the Capital Accord to Incorporate Market Risks.*

2

Overview of Approach

As we saw in the previous chapter, many of the criticisms levelled against the regulatory capital standards are well founded. More specifically, the failure of the current capital regime to capture the intrinsic credit risk in either the banking or the trading books of the world's major international banks has led to a unanimous clamour for the acceptance of internally developed credit risk models. The response from the industry has been swift and deliberate.

In particular, the weaknesses of the current capital regime, as pointed out by the industry group the International Swaps and Derivatives Association (ISDA, March 1998), can be grouped as follows.*

Limited differentiation of credit risk The 1988 Basle Capital Accord, as we saw in chapter 1, provides for only four, broad "capital buckets" – namely, 0%, 1.6%, 4% and 8% capital charges, corresponding to the four broad risk weightings of 0%, 20%, 50% and 100% based on an 8% minimum capital ratio requirement. The hope is that an internal credit risk model that took into account the bank's own internal risk rating system would result in a more granular differentiation of credit risk classes and so be more in tune with the bank's own assessment of intrinsic risk in the banking portfolio.

Static measures of default risk A fundamental assumption of the current credit risk capital regime is that a minimum 8% capital ratio is sufficient to protect banks from insolvency. The crux of the matter is that default risk is dynamically driven over time in response

*The positions taken by the ISDA are understandably slanted towards the trading books of banks. It is not my intent in this book, however, to address fully issues related to the trading book even though the issues arising from the banking and trading books are fundamentally similar.

to overall economic circumstances. Therefore, measures of default risk which do not take into account the probability of insolvency are, for the most part, arbitrary in nature. An internal models approach could overcome this dilemma of arbitrariness by incorporating probabilities of default associated with the granular risk classes. In so doing, it would also provide some statistical confidence measure for the solvency requirement and for the economic capital required to act as a buffer against insolvency.

No recognition of term structure of credit risk Current capital charges for the banking book are set at the same level regardless of the maturity of a credit exposure – contrary to the industry risk management practice of distinguishing risk exposures arising from different maturities. The application of credit migration risk techniques in an internal modelling approach, coupled with recognition of the forward credit curve, would improve on the regulatory rules.

Simplified calculation of potential future counterparty risk Although the capital rules for off-balance sheet activities have been amended several times by the Basle Committee to allow the recognition of close-out netting agreements, the potential exposure capital charges associated with a counterparty continue to be subsumed under the broad categories of credit rules for the banking book. The current capital regime effectively ignores the different levels of risk associated with different currencies or national indexes. Though the main focus of this book is the banking book, it is worth noting that a simple extension of the internal models approach to off-balance sheet counterparty activities can easily incorporate portfolio considerations and thereby perform the proper netting of risks. In addition, by incorporating term structure effects, the issue of potential future exposure is also resolved.

Constraints on an integrated view of credit risk As correctly pointed out by the ISDA, the current capital regime (setting aside for the meantime the recognition of portfolio effects) improperly views the world of credit risk under three broad categories: banking book credit risk; trading book-specific risk (including default and event risk); and counterparty credit risk. This arbitrary distinction imposes constraints on a more comprehensive view of internal risk management mechanisms by banks. With suitable extensions to an internal modelling approach the distinction would eventually disappear, to be replaced by a more integrated view of credit risk.

Lack of recognition of portfolio diversification effects For the most part, current capital rules call for the simple sum of individual risk exposures, ignoring the beneficial effects of portfolio risk management. This is contrary to the fundamental wisdom of risk reduction through diversification. As we shall see in later chapters, the sum of the individual risk exposures is much greater than the totality of risk intrinsic to the portfolio as a whole. An internal credit model that properly incorporates portfolio effects allows the bank a much more effective risk management and capital allocation scheme within the organisation.

Two additional issues pointed out by the ISDA, which are related more specifically to the trading book, are the limited recognition of the use of collateral and of offsets in the presence of hedging activities. Taking into account additional twists and interpretations, the views and criticisms presented above are pretty much a current consensus among industry practitioners and regulators.

The regulatory rules were sharply criticised for their overly simplistic interpretation of the world of credit risk. It many senses, however, the criticisms are unfair since the regulatory rules were promulgated to meet very pressing practical needs – for example, uniformity of interpretation and ease of implementation. It is very easy to get carried away by the mumbo-jumbo of quantitative risk modelling techniques. It is also very easy to derive risk measures that are difficult to implement owing to lack of data or otherwise. Therefore, whatever building blocks one chooses for implementation in an internal modelling project, one must be very cognisant of these very same issues or risk having one's efforts subjected to a similar round of sharp criticism.

Hence, a big and fundamental question remains: "In view of the weaknesses of the current capital regime and its oversimplistic treatment of credit risk, what important components or mechanism must be incorporated into a sound, but ultimately practical, internal credit risk model?" The next section attempts to outline the pieces of the solution from a practical perspective.

ESSENTIAL COMPONENTS OF THE INTERNAL CREDIT RISK MODEL

The issues considered above mean that the fundamental goal of the internal credit risk models approach must be to address these criticisms by providing alternative, but improved, solutions. Proposed solutions that focus only on the capital adequacy portion of the criticism, although necessary, are decidedly myopic and are, therefore, incomplete and insufficient. Alternative solutions must, in addition, consider how to devise new quantitative measures and introduce them into the credit risk management process.

From first principles, it is necessary to ask: "What are the consequences of the anomalies in the current regulatory capital standards?" In the previous chapter I discussed some of the unintended consequences of the current capital regime – the most egregious of which is the "game theory" of regulatory capital arbitrage through securitisation programs and the use of credit derivatives. From a more down-to-earth perspective of prudent risk management and capital allocation, the Federal Reserve System Task Force on Internal Credit Risk Models (1998) identified two key consequences:

- ❑ The regulatory measures of capital may not represent a bank's true capacity to absorb unexpected losses.
- ❑ The denominator of the risk-based capital ratios (ie, the total risk-weighted assets) may not be an accurate measure of total risk.

What kinds of risk measures, therefore, need to be introduced to achieve a more accurate assessment of credit risk? In contrast to the one-size-fits-all risk-based capital standards, what level of granularity is necessary to capture the risk in the portfolio with greater specificity? Analogous to the VAR model that is used on trading book data to estimate capital adequacy for market activities, what mechanism must exist within the internal credit risk model to give it a similar capability to estimate the economic capital needed (with defined confidence levels) to support a bank's credit activities?

As a corollary to the questions above, we need to ask further how, given these economically driven measures of credit risk, they can, in turn, be used in measuring the risk-adjusted performance of various business activities in a consistent portfolio context?

Based on both the risk and the return measures of individual credit exposures *vis-à-vis* the bank's overall portfolio, what criteria should be established so that credit services offered by the bank are priced in a manner that is consistent with the risk and return profile of the bank? And, finally, given the answers to all these questions, what criteria should be set to establish portfolio exposure, concentration limits and hurdle rates in line with the bank's objective of enhancing shareholder value?

OUTLINE OF MODEL COMPONENTS

In the chapters that follow we will go through a lengthy and detailed discussion of the credit risk modelling process. At this point, it is very important to preview what is to come and ponder for a moment how each model component is related to the others as we tackle the ultimate issues of *economic capital allocation* and *performance measurement*.

What is considered a "sound" internal credit risk model? The description should be accorded to a system only when it meets the practical needs of the end-users (eg, banks) and wins the approval of the regulatory supervisors. Briefly stated, it should be able to accomplish two important objectives:

- ❑ An internal credit risk model must be able to accurately assess and quantify the intrinsic credit risk embedded in the bank's portfolio. In so doing, it should introduce both quantitative and qualitative measures that facilitate prudential portfolio risk management.
- ❑ Ultimately, an internal credit risk model must provide a mechanism that can be used to determine the economic capital requirement of a bank, and the resulting capital allocation framework must be robust enough to be used for risk-adjusted pricing and other strategic purposes.

The diagram in Figure 2.1 is a simplified attempt to establish graphically the linkages between the essential components of a "sound" internal credit risk model. Clearly, the initial inputs to the model are crucial. For the most part, these are highly dependent on the existing systems infrastructure and data warehousing within the bank. The ability to extract customer-related information and current market rates on demand is vital. As an initial benchmark

Figure 2.1 Essential components of a sound internal credit risk model

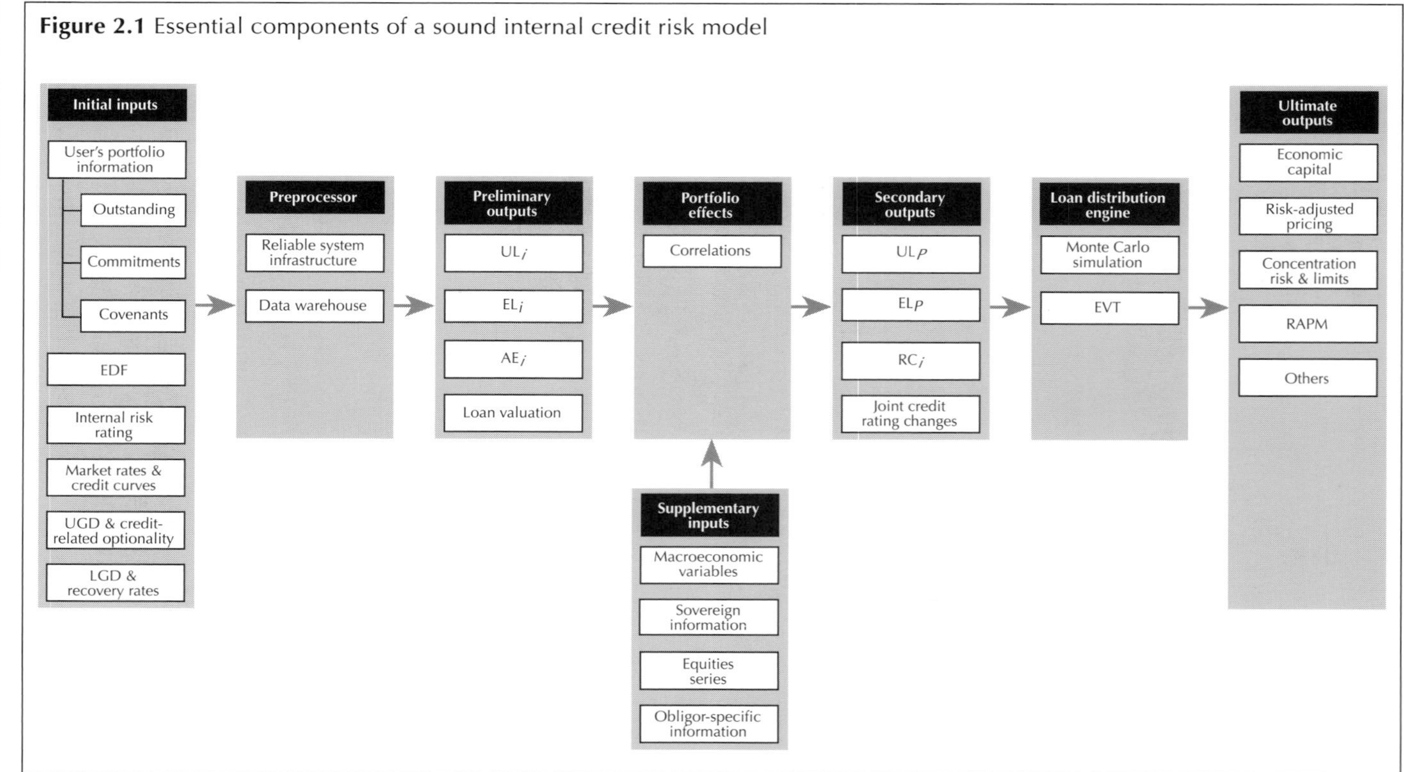

for assessing the creditworthiness of an obligor, the bank's own internal risk rating system must be sufficiently robust and granular to distinguish the different levels of credit quality. Other input required is obligor-specific information, such as default probabilities, recovery rates, outstandings, commitments and covenants.

The next component of the model is the ability to calculate individual risk measures – for example, expected loss, unexpected loss, adjusted exposure and the marked-to-market valuation of the underlying loan. Subsequently, given supplementary information such as macroeconomic variables, default correlation, sovereign-related quantities and other obligor-specific information, aggregate risk measures can be calculated on a portfolio basis.

In order to attach a statistical confidence level to the capital required as a buffer against insolvency, the bank needs to use tools like Monte Carlo simulation and extreme value theory to arrive at a desired loss distribution for the portfolio. This leads to the ultimate outputs of the internal model, such as risk-adjusted performance measurement, risk-adjusted pricing and economic capital requirement.

PREVIEW OF THE FOLLOWING CHAPTERS

To provide a short preview of the rest of the book, highlights of the modelling process are presented and some of the components outlined in Figure 2.1 are introduced. All these items will, of course, be covered in succession later.

Risky debt models

I begin with an outline of the state of current research in credit risk models for the valuation of risky debt. Although credit risk models were originally intended for the valuation of credit derivatives, the mathematical foundation for the analysis of credit risk, as a general daily process, and the assessment of the appropriate return measures for a credit portfolio are exactly the same as those used for valuation purposes. To achieve consistency with the way the market – through the opinions of the public rating agencies – views default, it is important to choose a risky debt model that allows some flexibility to incorporate publicly available information. The *instantaneous risk of default* models are one such class of flexible models.

Expected loss

To answer the loaded questions, "How much credit exposure does a bank have in the event of default or credit migrations, and how much of that exposure is the bank likely to lose?", one needs to be able to quantify several things. The first is the *expected loss*. The expected loss that the bank is likely to incur is the difference between the promised (or contracted) amount and what the obligor will eventually be able to pay if it defaults. This requires an assessment of several factors:

Expected default frequency (EDF) The probability that the obligor will default before the maturity of the contracted obligation to pay.

Loss given default (LGD) The fraction of the exposure amount that will be lost in the event of default or, more appropriately, the fraction of the debt the bank is likely to recover from the obligor once it has defaulted. The LGD is simply one less this *recovery rate*.

Adjusted exposure (AE) In the presence of covenants, the adjusted exposure is that portion of the totality of all exposures that the bank would not be able to recover in the event of default. This requires a detailed knowledge of *outstandings* and *commitments* and of the covenants which are embedded in the contractual obligation. In particular, it also requires an estimate of the *usage given default* provided for in the covenant. The usage given default is the additional draw-down of the unused part of the commitment that the borrower is likely to draw in the event of default.

The expected loss, as will be demonstrated, is the product of the three items above. The *expected loss* is, therefore, the amount the bank can expect to lose, on average, over the period of time in which it extends credits. It is also the amount that should not cause any surprise to the bank if lost as it is the credit exposure for which the bank should normally (and prudently) have set aside specific loan-loss reserves in the normal course of doing business.

Unexpected loss

Regardless of how prudent a bank is in managing its day-to-day business activities, there are market conditions that can cause uncertainty in the amount of loss in portfolio value. This uncertainty, or more appropriately the volatility of loss, is the so-called *unexpected loss*. Unexpected losses are triggered by the occurrence of default and unexpected credit migrations. Mathematically, such loss is the standard deviation of the change in asset value at the end of the horizon. This implies that unexpected loss is the estimated volatility of potential loss in portfolio value around the expected loss. If it is to be able to continue its daily business activities, it is imperative that a bank set aside sufficient capital to sustain this fluctuation in portfolio value. While it might appear to be a surprise, unexpected loss is, in fact, an inevitable, and unpleasant, consequence of holding a credit portfolio.

Risk contribution

In a portfolio context, the *risk contribution* of a risky asset to an unexpected loss in portfolio value, or *portfolio unexpected loss,* is defined as the incremental risk that the exposure of a single asset contributes to the total risk of the portfolio. Due to correlation effects, the sum of all the individual unexpected losses is not the same as the unexpected loss in portfolio value. The introduction of risk contribution as a risk measure, therefore, allows us to measure incremental risk to the portfolio.

Correlation of default

In a portfolio context, there is a very close relationship between the three general effects: *default correlation, concentration risk* and *diversification*. This link is a direct consequence of the relationship between the portfolio unexpected loss and the risk contribution of the individual assets to the portfolio's overall risk characteristics. The quantity that ties the risk contribution of a risky asset to the portfolio is default correlation. An aggregate of risk contributions from several risky assets dictates the effects of concentrated risk exposure in the portfolio. And, finally, the level of concentration risk determines the degree of diversification in the portfolio.

Economic capital

As market conditions deteriorate beyond a certain point, defaults of catastrophic magnitude are bound to occur more frequently. This corresponds to an *extreme loss* situation. The question now becomes:

"What level of capital is necessary for the bank to remain solvent in the event of such catastrophic or extreme losses?" The answer to this lies in *economic capital*. Briefly, economic capital is the number of standard deviations away from the expected loss that is necessary to cushion the bank from becoming insolvent in the event of extreme losses in the bank's portfolio due to default risk. The necessary cushion is the amount of capital the bank needs to set aside in anticipation of such disastrous market conditions.

Loss distribution

To address the issue of economic capital, one is inevitably led to the question: "How bad could the extreme loss be?" There is, however, no easy answer. Extreme events are associated with non-normal phenomena and are, therefore, quite difficult to quantify. In addition, the analysis of extreme events also requires that the associated *loss distribution* be known *a priori* with some level of certainty. This, of course, is circuitous. However, borrowing some tools and concepts from actuarial science, we shall eventually develop the ideas of *extreme value theory* through which the tail of an empirically observed loss distribution, however incomplete, can be fitted to some analytical "extreme distributions", thereby facilitating an inroad to the analysis of tail or extreme events.

Extreme value theory (EVT)

There exists a very large class of extreme value distributions under the heading "generalised Pareto distribution", which will be shown in later sections to be quite suitable (under certain assumptions) for analysing tail events associated with default risk.

In addition, we will demonstrate the usefulness of combining *Monte Carlo simulation* with EVT in the reconstruction of tail probabilities from the simulated loss distribution. In so doing, the steps leading to a robust simulation of loss distribution will be outlined in detail.

Risk-adjusted performance measurement (RAPM)

Once all the necessary pieces concerning credit risk are properly quantified, including the difficult issue of determining economic capital, it becomes important to develop tools for assessing the performance of the bank's credit portfolio. The performance measurement must also be extended to individual transactions on a "risk-adjusted" basis. The profitability of the different lines of the bank's business that are subject to intrinsic credit risk can only be appropriately and fairly analysed on a *risk-comparable* basis if the returns are measured in conjunction with the risks that are undertaken by those lines of business. The process whereby returns from dissimilar businesses are measured on a level playing field is called *risk adjustment*. The calculation of measures using a risk adjustment process is called *risk-adjusted performance measurement*. One such measure is commonly known in the market as *risk-adjusted return on capital*, or RAROC.

Implementation and interpretation of RAPM

Once the theoretical constructs delineated above are well understood, the next phase of the challenge involves implementing such a risk-adjusted performance measurement framework across the enterprise. In addition to the difficult systems challenges, the sometimes *political* interpretation of the results needs to be handled delicately. Regardless of how correct and mathematically precise the risk and return measures are, the rest of the battle needs to be waged among the users from across the enterprise. For what is the sense of building such a sophisticated risk management and measurement system if the users cannot be persuaded to use it properly?

The credit paradox and risk-adjusted pricing

Finally, banks may be the most efficient generators of loans because of their superior access to corporations, but, since credit risk increases exponentially with concentration, they are not always the best holders of these loans. The *credit paradox* is a phenomenon associated with the dramatic rise in the loan spreads required as exposure to the same obligor increases. The phenomenon forces many banks to take on larger amounts of credit exposure in search of larger spreads, thereby exposing themselves to an even larger probability of suffering from default.

How much, therefore, should a bank charge for taking on incremental credit risk from a specific obligor in exchange for some desired risk-adjusted return? In other words, what is the required spread the bank needs to charge given a particular level of risk-adjusted return? The answer can be found in the discussion on *risk-adjusted pricing*.

It is readily seen from the points outlined above that it takes an inordinate amount of effort to quantify credit risk before the very important issues of performance, return and risk-adjusted pricing can be addressed. In many regards it might seem that the risk-adjusted performance measurement stage is a trivial follow-on from the formidable task of credit risk modelling.

3

Modelling Credit Risk

Unlike market risk, the modelling of credit risk is a very difficult task because credit risk is not the simple manifestation of one single source or driver of the risky event. Credit risk manifests itself not only in just one instance but, rather, in various seemingly different but actually interrelated forms. Consider a simple and intuitive example: the widening yield spread between a risky debt (eg, a corporate bond) and an otherwise similar Treasury bond is a well-known manifestation of the credit risk associated with the issuer of the corporate bond. The fluctuation in the yield spread between these two bonds reflects the intrinsic creditworthiness of the issuer of the corporate bond in relation to an otherwise default-free Treasury bond. The Treasury bond is, of course, guaranteed by the full faith of the US government and is, therefore, considered impossible to default.*

One important reason, among many others, for the relative widening of the spread is the *perceived* potential deterioration of the credit quality of the corporate bond. The credit quality is, of course, dictated by the creditworthiness of the issuer. The creditworthiness of the issuer is, in turn, decided by a host of other factors such as general economic conditions and industry trends and by specific issuer factors like the issuer's financial well-being, degree of leverage, market value, equity value, asset value and capital structure, and by less tangible things, such as reputation and management skills, etc.

*Although the non-defaultability of the Treasury bond is hard to prove, it is interesting to note that the US government has contingency plans for the collection of taxes and payment of debt obligations in the event of nuclear attack.

Academically, it has been widely argued that the value of corporate debt (and therefore yield spread) and the capital structure of the issuer are interlinked variables. The issuing firm's capital structure, in turn, affects the potential for default and bankruptcy. Hence, at least in principle, it would not be possible to determine the yield spread of a corporate bond to an otherwise default-free Treasury bond without having full knowledge of the issuing firm's capital structure.

Other kinds of corporate debt, such as bank loans, are also saddled with similar manifestation of the credit risk phenomenon. The loan spread (over a base rate, eg, Libor) charged by the bank to the borrower of the loan also undergoes fluctuation, albeit not as often and less pronounced than corporate bonds. Depending on the underlying structure and covenants of the loan, the loan spread charged by the bank is likewise reflective of the perceived creditworthiness of the obligor.

Overall, the creditworthiness of a risky debt dictates the pricing of the instrument and, consequently, the fluctuation of the spread. But to focus solely on the spread alone could lead to erroneous conclusions about the issuer's credit quality since the spread has embedded in it not only credit information but also interest rate uncertainty. Of course, the ideal framework to assess credit quality would be to integrate both credit risk and market risk components. However, this integrated approach to credit risk remains both a theoretical and practical challenge. It is, therefore, also unfair to criticise the regulatory rules, discussed at length in the previous chapters, for conveniently segregating credit risk into three separate compartments – banking book credit risk, trading book credit risk and counterparty credit risk – without suggesting some remedy from an integrated perspective.

ELEMENTS OF CREDIT RISK

In the absence of a brilliant integrated framework for modelling credit risk, we have to decide which elements of credit risk in general are the most important and need to be considered first. The answer was actually decided for us in chapter 2 when we discussed the essential components of an internal credit risk model in light of the fundamental objectives for developing such a model. To reiterate, the primary objective is to introduce risk measures that can facilitate prudential risk management at a portfolio level, and secondly, to support the capital allocation and strategic schemes of the bank in a globally competitive environment.

Prudential risk management is defined here in an enlightened way – in terms of both a defensive mode and the taking of a proactive stance. Given credit and market upheavals that can threaten a bank's survivability, a defensive posture involving the rudimentary measurement of risk is understandable. However, taking a proactive stance that goes beyond the usual elements of loss avoidance and risk measurement is also vital to the continued well-being and prosperity of a bank.

Given the essential components highlighted in Figure 2.1, the elements of credit risk that require the most attention now can be grouped as follows:

Individual risk elements

❑ *Default probability* The probability that the obligor or counterparty will default on its contractual obligations to repay its debt.
❑ *Recovery rates* The extent to which the face value of an obligation can be recovered once the obligor has defaulted.
❑ *Credit migration* Short of a default, the extent to which the credit quality of the obligor or counterparty improves or deteriorates.

Portfolio risk elements

❑ *Default and credit quality correlation* The degree to which the default or credit quality of one obligor is related to the default or credit quality of another.
❑ *Risk contribution and credit concentration* The extent to which an individual instrument or the presence of an obligor in the portfolio contributes to the totality of risk in the overall portfolio.

DEFAULT RISK

The key ingredient of credit risk modelling is default risk. Default risk is the uncertainty regarding a firm's ability to service its debts and obligations. Default, although a deceptively rare event, can be quantified by the so-called default probability, which reflects the extent to which an obligor or counterparty is likely to be able to repay its debt on all its contractual obligations. Generally speaking, the default process is not an abrupt one – that is to say, default does not occur instantaneously out of the blue. There is generally a deterioration of a firm's financial position and asset quality which then leads to the eventual degradation of its creditworthiness. We call this phenomenon "credit migration". Thus, a related and very important matter is the *transition probabilities* which indicate the extent to which the credit quality of a firm is likely to improve or deteriorate. The default probability is, in essence, embedded in the last state of the so-called "transition matrix", which ranges from a successive deterioration of credit quality until such time as the firm is no longer able to repay its debt and thereby reaches the default state. The transition probabilities are the measures that quantify the phenomenon of credit migration.

Where do (or should) these default or transition probabilities come from?

There are two major routes to obtaining transition probabilities:

- ❑ The first route is empirical in nature and requires the existence of some public credit quality rating scheme.
- ❑ The second route is based on an options theory framework.

Lately, in an understandable attempt to be simple, a less defensible route taken by some market participants considers default to be a strictly mathematical phenomenon that can be modelled as a Poisson process. Borrowing from actuarial science, they assume that the number of defaults can be approximated by a simple Poisson distribution, obviating the need for full information on the capital structure of the firm. We will completely ignore this approach in the book.

MEASURING DEFAULT PROBABILITY – EMPIRICAL METHOD

We summarise first the empirical route taken by Standard & Poor's. (For a detailed discussion of the empirical method readers are referred to Standard & Poor's 1997 report.) Using its proprietary historical database of corporate defaults, a static pool of all companies that had outstanding ratings as of a given initial year (1981) is formed. The static pool for the subsequent year (1982) is formed by adding those companies first rated in the year 1981 to the surviving members of that year's static pool. This method of stratified sampling is performed for each year until 1996. Standard & Poor's used 15 years' worth of historical corporate ratings in its analysis.

Annual default rates are then calculated for each static pool – first in units and later as percentages with respect to the number of issuers in each rating category. Finally, these percentages are combined to obtain cumulative default rates for the entire 15 years of historical analysis.

To compute one-year rating transition ratios by rating categories, each company's rating at the end of a particular year is compared with its rating at the beginning of the same year. For instance, all 1981 static pool members still rated at the beginning of 1996 have 16 one-year transitions, while companies rated in 1995 have only one. Table 3.2 on page 77 is an example of a one-year transition matrix.

Each one-year transition matrix displays all rating movements between Standard & Poor's letter categories (AAA, AA, A, BBB, BB, B, CCC, D). Multi-year transitions are also calculated for periods of two to 15 years. Of course, the longer the transition period, the smaller the number of observations. Given the nature of the stratified sampling, a 10-year transition matrix would be deemed less reliable than a one-year transition matrix.

A similar empirical method was employed by Moody's Investor Services (1997) covering the period 1920 to 1996 and using the credit histories of more than 14,000 US and non-US corporate debt issuers. The 77-year time frame decidedly allows comparison of rating change patterns over a variety of business, interest rate and other economic cycles. Readers are referred to the Moody's report for further details and comparisons with the Standard & Poor's report just considered.

One of the more important criticisms of the empirical approach employed by the rating agencies to determine default and transition probabilities is the apparently *static* nature of the resulting *average* historical probabilities. In reality, actual transition and default probabilities are very dynamic and can vary quite substantially over the years, depending on general economic conditions and business cycles. This issue is particularly critical if the analysis horizon is rather long.

Unfortunately, there is no clear-cut solution to this dilemma. If it can be argued correctly that the rating agencies cannot provide useful measures of default and credit quality, the financial industry should completely ignore the ratings produced by both Standard

& Poor's and Moody's. Why, then, does this not happen? On the contrary, a good rating from the agencies is very much sought after for many obvious reasons, ranging from vanity and prestige to the economic benefit of reduced funding costs for the corporation.

A real dilemma perhaps relates to private companies that are neither rated by the agencies nor publicly traded. In most banks private companies constitute a large percentage of the banks' credit portfolios. A substantial proportion of these portfolios, therefore, do not have very clear benchmarks for estimating default and transition probabilities.

Such criticisms have led to a vocal academic call to reduce the assessment of default risk to an elegant, deterministic equation. But is the modelling of default risk, in particular, a strictly scientific and academic endeavour? In defence of the rating agencies, it must be borne in mind that credit rating, like derivatives trading and risk management, is also partly an art. A ratings agency's interviews with the managements of firms and sovereign leaders, its access to information not in the public domain and its knowledge of geography and industry sectors, however subjective they may be, are important components of the ratings and overall assessments of the well-being of firms.

Short of a "magic bullet", a bank must decide what is the most appropriate measure for it to use when measuring default and transition probabilities. To this end, the next section presents a brief discussion of the more academic, and decidedly more elegant, approach to measuring default probability offered by options theory. The options theory approach is not, however, without its own set of shortcomings.

MEASURING DEFAULT PROBABILITY – THE OPTIONS THEORY APPROACH

The recent innovations in structured finance vehicles, such as collateralised bond obligations, have thrown concerns about agency ratings into the limelight again. Because of their static nature, the lack of timeliness in the assessment of agency ratings means that a single rating grade contains a wide range of default probabilities, enabling a well-informed collateral manager to choose only the higher-yielding bonds within the grade. The result is that it is easy to produce, from bonds within the same rating grade, two vehicles, one with twice the default risk of the other.

Furthermore, as credit risk modelling becomes a more critical function of large banks, practitioners are now beginning to observe that the confidence interval for the average historical default rates given by bond default studies often stretches from zero to twice the estimate. This observation has been the battle cry of KMV Corporation in its effort to dissuade market practitioners from using average historical default probabilities published by ratings agencies. Of course, KMV is a profit-making organisation that develops and markets its own proprietary methods for extracting default probabilities, called "expected default frequencies" (EDF), to practitioners who believe that agency ratings are inadequate for their internal use. The jury is still out on this debate.

The academic belief (and also the message preached by KMV) is that the phenomenon of a firm defaulting on its obligations is primarily driven by

- ❑ the market value of the firm's assets;
- ❑ the level of its obligations (ie, its liabilities); and
- ❑ the degree to which its market value changes with large moves in the market.

The argument is simple. The default risk of a firm increases as the book value of its liabilities approaches the value of its assets, until such time as the market value of the assets is no longer sufficient to repay its liabilities and the firm ultimately defaults on the payments of its obligations. The firm's liabilities are, therefore, viewed as contingent claims (ie, options) issued against the firm's assets, with payoffs to the various debt-holders specified by the seniority of the claims and other covenants. This key insight is demonstrated mathematically in Appendix A.

This insight is really nothing new and is definitely not the exclusive intellectual property of KMV – nor, for that matter, of anyone else. No one owns the exclusive bragging rights to this approach. The theoretical foundation was laid for us by Merton in 1974. Right up to the present time, the developing theories surrounding the measurement of default risk advocated by many other academic researchers, consultants and practitioners have been neither revolutionary nor outstandingly different from the fundamental framework laid by Merton more than 25 years ago.

How does one determine the probability of default in this theoretical framework? The answer can also be found in Appendix A, where Merton's approach to the valuation of risky debt is first introduced. Then, in Appendix B, I borrow two new concepts from KMV called the "default point" and the "distance to default". Finally, as an example, I derive the probability of default in Appendix B, and this is followed by a sample calculation.

THEORETICAL EDFs AND AGENCY RATINGS

The previous sections outlined the two leading sources of default and transition probabilities – the empirically derived probabilities from the rating agencies' historical databases and the theoretically inferred expected default frequencies based on the interplay between a firm's assets and its liabilities. The comparison of the two approaches is, however, a very contentious matter.

The numerical example presented at the end of Appendix B highlights the fact that, in practice, even with the use of an arguably sound theoretical foundation such as the Merton approach, everything boils down to a subjective estimation of the input parameters. More importantly, it is often difficult to map the calculated EDF consistently back to the empirically derived agency ratings.

Is this decidedly more theoretical approach, then, really any better than the probabilities derived empirically by the rating agencies from their historical databases?

Since 1993, KMV has provided its proprietary calculation of EDFs for many firms, both public and private. In its analysis KMV found that there is a consistently sharp increase in the slope of the EDF between one and two years prior to default, indicating at least some predictability of the calculated probabilities. Unfortunately, the study of the indicative rise in the slope alone, while necessary, is not sufficient to validate the absolute level of risk rating and, therefore, of the actual probabilities of default. In fact, further studies have shown that the "absolute" level of probabilities assigned by the rating agencies to the different rating classes tend to be clustered around the median, with significant variations of EDFs within each rating class. The average default rate for each class is, however, considerably higher than the default rate of the typical firm. This is due to the observation that a rating class typically contains a small group of firms that have much higher probabilities of default. Because of the exponential change in default probabilities as default risk increases, these firms, which should have been downgraded, are still awaiting news of their imminent downgrade, thereby contaminating the sampling pool.

In short, there are significant differences between the probabilities assigned by the rating agencies and EDFs calculated using the theoretical framework. But no one has yet been able to offer a satisfactory explanation for this. The Crouhy and Mark (1998) paper, referred to in Appendix B, suggests three possible reasons for the discrepancies:

- First, since rating agencies are slow to change their ratings, the historical frequency of staying in a rating class should overstate the true probability of maintaining the same credit quality.
- Second, the average historical probability of default overstates the true probability of default for typical firms within each rating class owing to the difference between the mean and the median default rates.
- Finally, if both the probability of staying in a given rating class and the probability of default are too large, then perhaps the transition probabilities are too small.

So far as an internal credit risk modelling effort is concerned, a bank should be careful to choose a set of transition and default probabilities that is at once defensible, easily explainable and readily implementable.

CREDIT RISK MODELS

In the foregoing discussion of the measurement of the probability of default, we have unavoidably digressed to the Merton (1974) approach to the valuation of risky debt. There are, in fact, more recent variations on the same theme.

Collectively speaking, there are three general classes of credit models for pricing risky debt. While the focus of these models is the valuation of risky debt and its associated credit derivatives, the fundamental principles underlying them are equally applicable to the assessment of credit risk embedded in loan portfolios and to the determination of economic or risk capital in a risk-adjusted performance measurement framework. In fact, other than truly generic pricing issues, as far as the ultimate usage in either the institution's trading book or the banking book is concerned, credit risk models focus on one single important issue – default risk – and its two corollaries: how to price it; and how to measure it.

Many are seduced by the sexiness of the mathematics in credit risk models as they are applied to the trading account of the bank, but such seduction is unwarranted. Although similar credit issues are relevant to market risk and specific risk models for the trading book, the enormity of the banking book relative to the trading book alone is sufficient to warrant more concentrated attention on the potential hazards of credit risk embedded in the banking book. Therefore, our primary objective is not the pricing of credit risk *per se*, but how better risk measures can be constructed to give an understanding of and, thereby, mitigate credit risk in the bank as a whole. In fact, as we see in Appendices A and B, the pricing of credit risk (as encapsulated in the credit spread between the risky and the riskless assets) and the measurement of credit risk in general (as represented by the default and transition probabilities, among others) are, indeed, one and the same issue.

Even though our immediate goal is the measurement aspect of credit risk in the banking book rather than its pricing in the trading book, it is instructive to understand the differences in the general approach to the same problem. This chapter began with the exposition of the general classes of credit risk models and will end by highlighting one of them as the foundation for articulating our goal of risk measurement by introducing risk measures such as expected loss and loss given default.

Taxonomy of credit risk models

The three general classes of credit risk models are summarised briefly below.

"Value of the firm" models (contingent claims on a firm's assets)

This class of models views the firm's liabilities as contingent claims (ie, options) issued against the firm's underlying assets. It was noted earlier that as the book value of a firm's liabilities approaches the value of its assets, its default risk increases until the market value of the assets is no longer sufficient to repay the liabilities. Default, in this class of models, is therefore determined by the time evolution of the firm's assets in relation to the various debt covenants or liability structures of the firm. If these "options" on the firm's assets are taken as the underlying framework for the default process, the probability of default can easily be calculated after some more simplifying assumptions. The mathematical presentation of this class of models is given in Appendix A.

As is explained in the first two appendices, the greatest difficulty in using this class of models lies in the estimation of those of the firm's assets which are neither traded nor readily observable in the market. Furthermore, since the "point of default" (the "default point" introduced in Appendix B) is triggered by the evolution of the firm's assets, publicly available credit ratings information is not used, and this could lead to inconsistency with the imputed default probabilities in the derived model.

Well-known models of the "value of the firm" type are those of Merton (1974), Black and Cox (1976) and Shimko, Tejima and van Deventer (1993), along with their implementation by the KMV Corporation. It should be duly noted that KMV has done an excellent job of melding theory with practice in the absence of complete market information about firms.

"Recovery of promised payoff" models

By redefining the default process as occurring when the firm's asset value breaches some exogenously specified absorbing boundary, this class of models posits that only a fraction of the risky debt – known as the "recovery rate" – can be recovered in the event of default. Depending on the underlying covenants, the risky debt has some promised future terminal payoff. This class of models simplifies the default process of the "value of the firm" models by making the cashflows to the promised payoff of the risky debt contingent on whether or not default occurs prior to the maturity of the debt. The trigger point for default, however, is still dependent on the value of the firm's assets, so these models too do not use publicly available credit ratings information.

Models in this class are Hull and White (1995), Longstaff and Schwartz (1992) and Nielsen, Saá-Requejo and Santa-Clara (1993).

"Instantaneous risk of default" models

The third class of models cleverly combines the two previous approaches. They, too, consider a fractional payoff of the promised debt in the event of default, but the time of default is exogenously modelled by assuming that when the *identical* but unlevered firm's asset value hits some exogenous boundary, default can occur at any time in the levered firm, paying off a fraction of the promised payoff. The default process here is assumed to be independent of the capital structure of the firm. These models are normally referred to as the "instantaneous risk of default" type because default is modelled outside of the capital structure of the firm and could be driven by other exogenous variables.

In fact, this class of models can be modified to overcome the inability of the two previous classes to deal with payoffs that are dependent on public credit ratings. This, however, does not necessarily imply that public credit ratings are always correct. As argued at the beginning of the chapter, publicly available ratings and empirically derived default and transition probabilities – though not perfect – serve as important benchmarks in the market whether one likes them or not. Collectively, this publicly available information functions as an important benchmark in the pricing of both loans and credit derivatives.

Some models in this class are those of Litterman and Iben (1991), Jarrow and Turnbull (1995), Schönbucher (1996), Jarrow, Lando and Turnbull (1997) and Blauer and Wilmott (1998).

Depending on the implementation, all three classes of models can, in practice, be made arbitrage-free.

VALUE OF THE RISKY DEBT

In the mathematical preliminary found in Appendix C a rigorous framework for the valuation of risky debt is presented. The approach is based on the instantaneous risk of default class of models developed by Jarrow, Lando and Turnbull (1997). The value of the risky debt, $v(t, T)$, given in terms of the risk-free debt, $p(t, T)$, is

$$v(t, T) = p(t, T)[\delta + (1 - \delta)\tilde{Q}_t(\tau^* > T)] \tag{3.1}$$

where the current time of valuation is t, the debt matures at time T and the random variable τ^* denotes the time of default. $\tilde{Q}_t(\tau^* > T)$ is the probability that default occurs after time T. In the event of default, only a fraction δ, where $0 < \delta < 1$, of the debt is recoverable. This fraction is known as the *recovery rate*.

To place the discussion within a sound mathematical framework, debt is represented in Appendix C by the risky or risk-free zero-coupon bonds $v(t, T)$ or $p(t, T)$, respectively. However, in the context of this chapter and without loss of generality, we can treat $v(t, T)$ as loans subject to default and interpret $p(t, T)$ as the value, at the current time t, of a "sure" payment of the contracted obligation at the maturity time T.

Assuming that the default process is simplified and can take only two possible states, S, namely

$$S = \{\bar{D} = \text{No default}; D = \text{Default}\} \tag{3.2}$$

then equation (3.1) is a simple statement that the risky loan is nothing but the value of an assured payment multiplied by the expected payoff, viz:

$$\delta + (1 - \delta)\tilde{Q}_t(\tau^* > T) \tag{3.3}$$

The expected payoff above is the weighted average of a $1 spread between two possible outcomes – the two states of the default process. If default occurs, only the fraction δ can be recovered.

In fact, with this frame of thinking there is a much simpler interpretation of equation (3.1). The next section addresses this insight.

Decomposition of the payoff

Since the risky debt has a simple interpretation as the value of a default-free (ie, assured) payment weighted by the expected payoff of the promised dollar at time t, the two parts of equation (3.3) can be represented by the diagram in Figure 3.1.

The figure shows that cashflows to the payoff of the risky debt, $v(t, T)$, can be decomposed into two components. The first is the *riskless* component. It is riskless because the payoff is always the

Figure 3.1 Riskless and risky payoff

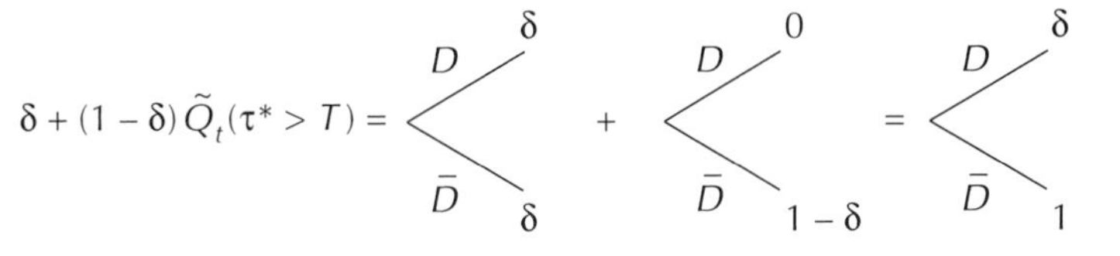

$$\delta + (1 - \delta)\tilde{Q}_t(\tau^* > T) = \left\langle \begin{array}{ll} D & \delta \\ \bar{D} & \delta \end{array} \right. + \left\langle \begin{array}{ll} D & 0 \\ \bar{D} & 1 - \delta \end{array} \right. = \left\langle \begin{array}{ll} D & \delta \\ \bar{D} & 1 \end{array} \right.$$

same amount, δ, regardless of the states of default. The second part of the decomposition is termed the *risky* component since it pays zero in the event of default D and a lesser amount, $1 - \delta$, in the case of no default, $\bar{D}$.

Another insight is illustrated through the following example.

Example 3.1 – Riskless and risky payoff

Note from Figure 3.1 that the riskless component has the expected value given by

$$\delta \times [\text{Prob. of default}, D] + \delta \times [\text{Prob. of no default}, \bar{D}]$$

while the risky component has the expected value

$$0 \times [\text{Prob. of default}, D] + (1 - \delta) \times [\text{Prob. of no default}, \bar{D}]$$

Adding the two components together results in the expression

$$\delta \times [\text{Prob. of default}, D] + 1 \times [\text{Prob. of no default}, \bar{D}]$$

Now, since the probability of no default, $\bar{D}$, before time T is $\tilde{Q}_t(\tau^* > T)$, we have recovered the expected payoff of the sure dollar as given in equation (C.3.5a) of Appendix C:

$$\left[\delta + (1-\delta)\tilde{Q}_t(\tau^* > T)\right] = \tilde{E}_t\left(\left[\delta 1_{\{\tau^* \leq T\}} + 1_{\{\tau^* > T\}}\right]\right) \qquad \textbf{(3.4)}$$

We have thus demonstrated a simple proof of equations (C.3.5a) and (C.3.5b) of Appendix C.

STATES OF THE DEFAULT PROCESS AND CREDIT MIGRATION

The discussions above simplified the default process as a pure *two-state event* – default or no default. In reality, the default process is not a simple binomial process. There is usually a deterioration of credit quality until an unsustainable level is breached and the issuer of the risky debt goes into default mode. In some financial catastrophes the default process can be abrupt indeed. But in most cases there is a transition or migration from one regime to the next before the default state is actually reached. A multi-state default process is called *credit migration*.

Credit migration – or more aptly the change in a firm's credit quality over some time horizon – occurs for a variety of reasons. The first is an improvement or a deterioration of the firm's asset value. The asset value of a firm is the present value of all the expected future cashflows attributable to all the lines of business of the firm. Imposed on its capital structure is a string of liabilities that are the contractual obligations which that firm is obliged to pay at some set point or points in the future. Failure to meet these obligations causes the firm to go into default.

The credit quality of a firm at a specific point in time is measured by the probability that it will be able to pay off its contractual obligations. The first instance of failure to do so is defined as default. Credit risk, therefore, is the manifestation of the probability of default, however unlikely it may be. The point of the matter is that if a firm is not immune to credit migration, it is also not exempt from default.

Depending on the firm's asset and liability structure, credit migration can go three ways: improve; deteriorate; or stay the same. Our main goal, however, is not to explain why and how default occurs but, rather, taking the default process as a given possibility, evaluate the embedded credit risk associated with holding an asset that is subject to credit migration. And, to this end, introduce risk measures that can appropriately quantify the credit risk in the banking book of the institution.

Consider a risky debt with an initial Standard & Poor's rating of A. At the end of the horizon, say one year, there are three possible transition routes the rating can take:

- remain at the current rating A;
- migrate up (eg, to AA) or down (eg, to BBB); or
- default.

Each of these credit migrations has its own associated probability of occurring. Table 3.1 is a tabulation, for a debt with a risk class rating of A, of the probability that it will maintain its rating and its chances of migrating to the different possible ratings over a period of one year.

For example, the table indicates that there is a 89.05% probability that this risky debt, originally rated A, will retain its rating at the end of one year. There is also a 0.03% chance that it will default

Table 3.1 One-year transition probability for a risky debt with a Standard & Poor's rating of A

Risk rating	Transition probability (%)
AAA	0.27
AA	1.59
A	89.05
BBB	7.40
BB	1.48
B	0.13
CCC	0.06
Default	0.03

within one year. Observe that the probability of this highly rated debt defaulting on its obligation is not zero.

Table 3.1 tells us that, with probabilities of 0.27% and 1.59%, the debt may migrate upwards to ratings AAA or AA, respectively. Conversely, the chances of a downgrading to ratings BBB, BB, B or CCC are 7.40%, 1.48%, 0.13% and 0.06%, respectively. These percentages, which represent the likelihood of migrating up or down to a particular state, are known as *transition probabilities*. The lowest state for a downward migration is default. Thus, the number 0.03% represents the chance of the debt defaulting, and we call this number the *default probability*. As discussed earlier in the chapter, these transition and default probabilities can be calculated empirically from historical observations or they may be determined analytically using an options theory framework.

Observe that the percentages in the table sum to 100%, as they should, since they are probabilities of transition from the current state to *all* possible states in the credit migration and default process. The laws of probability dictate that they sum to unity.

To account for all possible transitions (within a one-year horizon) from all possible states and not just from state A, we need an expanded version of Table 3.1. CreditMetrics has conveniently tabulated the so-called "one-year transition matrix" presented here as Table 3.2. The data in the table are modified after transition probabilities calculated by Standard & Poor's from historical observations (*S&P CreditWeek*, April 1996).

By conservation of probability, all the rows in Table 3.2 sum to unity. Unfortunately, depending on the source of historical data

Table 3.2 One-year transition matrix (%)

Initial rating	Rating at the end of one year AAA	AA	A	BBB	BB	B	CCC	Default
AAA	87.74	10.93	0.45	0.63	0.12	0.10	0.02	0.02
AA	0.84	88.23	7.47	2.16	1.11	0.13	0.05	0.02
A	0.27	1.59	89.05	7.40	1.48	0.13	0.06	0.03
BBB	1.84	1.89	5.00	84.21	6.51	0.32	0.16	0.07
BB	0.08	2.91	3.29	5.53	74.68	8.05	4.14	1.32
B	0.21	0.36	9.25	8.29	2.31	63.89	10.13	5.58
CCC	0.06	0.25	1.85	2.06	12.34	24.86	39.97	18.60

Source: Keenan and Carty (1998).

and the time period used in the empirical calculation, the actual percentages in the table can differ significantly. Furthermore, as explained earlier in this chapter, the probabilities calculated by KMV also show significant variations from those derived empirically by the rating agencies. These probabilities should, therefore, never be quoted and used blindly without a full understanding of their impact on the internal credit modelling effort.

In principle, the assessment of credit risk extends beyond the one-year horizon because most risky debts have maturities that are relatively long. This, therefore, requires *multiperiod* transition matrices that extend out to the life of the risky debt. Using its own historical database, Standard & Poor's has tabulated matrices that extend to a horizon of at least 15 years. Moody's has published similar tables. In the epilogue I discuss some problematic issues associated with multi-year transition matrices tabulated by the credit rating agencies.

Throughout this book, we will adhere to the simplistic two-state view of the default process. Generalisation to the multi-state case, though not difficult, is cumbersome.

In the previous section, the probability measure $\tilde{Q}_t(\tau^* > T)$ was conveniently interpreted as a simple two-state process – namely, default or no default. It can easily be extended to the multi-state case by using multiperiod transition matrices discussed in the previous section. This is, however, beyond the scope of the book and we shall be content with only a brief synopsis.

Appendix D addresses the theoretical framework required for the incorporation of a multi-state default process.

Expected loss

In the event of a default, how much does the holder of the risky debt stand to lose? We can answer this question easily by rearranging equation (3.1) as follows:

$$v(t,T) = p(t,T)[\delta + (1-\delta)\tilde{Q}_t(\tau^* > T)]$$

$$= p(t,T)[\delta + (1-\delta)\{1 - \tilde{Q}_t(\tau^* \le T)\}]$$

$$= p(t,T)[1 - (1-\delta)\tilde{Q}_t(\tau^* \le T)] \quad \textbf{(3.5)}$$

where $\tilde{Q}_t(\tau^* \le T)$ is the probability that default occurs before the maturity time T.

Or, equivalently, we have

$$p(t,T) - v(t,T) = p(t,T)(1-\delta)\tilde{Q}_t(\tau^* \le T)] \quad \textbf{(3.6)}$$

The left-hand side of equation (3.6) is the difference between the "assured" value (ie, riskless, given no default) and the risky value of the promised debt. This difference is the amount which the holder of the debt expects to lose in the event of default. The right-hand side is, therefore, called the *expected loss* (EL), ie,

$$EL = p(t,T)(1-\delta)\tilde{Q}_t(\tau^* \le T)] \quad \textbf{(3.7)}$$

The expected loss is the amount that, on average, the holder of the risky debt expects to lose in the event of default.

Loss given default

In the event of default, only a fraction, δ, of the risky debt, $v(t,T)$, can be recovered. In the credit market the convention is to ask how much of the promised debt is *lost* in the event of default rather than how much is *recovered*.

Following this market convention, we need to introduce the concept of *loss given default* (LGD), which is nothing but

$$LGD \equiv 1 - \delta \quad \textbf{(3.8)}$$

Thus, the loss given default is that portion of the risky debt which is not recoverable during the bankruptcy process. We can now rewrite the expected loss in equation (3.7) as

$$EL = p(t,T) \times \text{LGD} \times \tilde{Q}_t(\tau^* \leq T) \tag{3.9}$$

or, in simple words,

Expected loss =
Assured payment at maturity time T × Loss given default ×
Probability that default occurs *before* maturity T **(3.10)**

In a multi-state default process in which credit migration is permissible, defining the expected loss of a risky asset is somewhat problematic. The quantity of concern is the probability of default, which needs to be altered as the probability of migrating to a lower risk class rating than the current one. For each of these possible credit migrations, there is an associated payment structure that is different from the default state and a potential *loss given downgrade* that is different from the loss given default. This undoubtedly makes the analysis more complex. For an institution's banking book, however, we are more interested in the circumstances surrounding the potential for default, although admittedly the downgrade scenarios are equally important for risk management purposes. It is for this reason that I have chosen to use the simplistic two-state default process as the underlying theme throughout this book. Appendix A of the epilogue discusses the multi-state default process.

Decomposition of risky debt

As in Figure 3.1 and using the concept of loss given default, we have another way of viewing the decomposition of the expected payoff of the debt in terms of a risky and a riskless component. This is shown in Figure 3.2.

The expected payoff is, of course, equal to $(1 - LGD) + LGD \times \tilde{Q}_t(\tau^* > T)$, which is the same as equation (3.4). This shows that a contingent payoff of the risky debt which pays $1 - LGD$ in the event of default and \$1 otherwise is equivalent to two cashflows:

- ❑ one that is indifferent to the possible states of default (the riskless component); and

Figure 3.2 Decomposition of risky debt

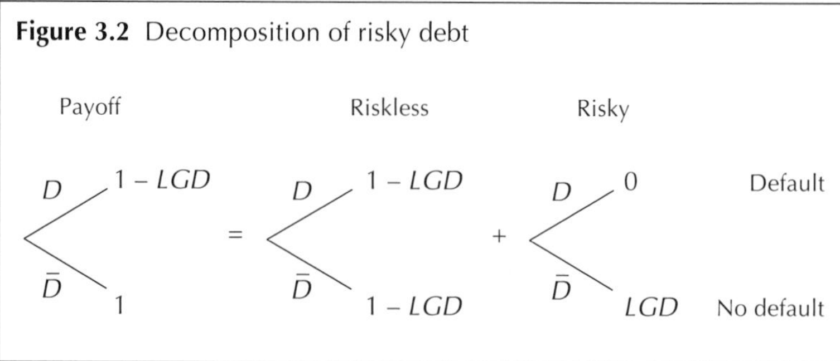

❑ another that is a stream of two payouts weighted by the probabilities of defaulting or not (the risky component).

With this foundation behind us, we can now proceed to discuss in greater detail what is meant by an "expected loss". This is done in the next chapter.

APPENDIX A – MERTON'S OPTIONS THEORY APPROACH TO RISKY DEBT

Following Merton's 1974 formulation for the valuation of corporate securities, consider the *simplified* case of a firm whose risky assets have a current market value of V_0. The asset value, V, is assumed to be uncertain due to factors such as general economic conditions, business risk, foreign exchange risk, industry risk, etc. Assume further that the returns on the firm's assets are instantaneously normal, with constant drift μ and constant asset volatility σ, so that the dynamics of the asset value for all times t obeys a geometric Brownian motion given by

$$\frac{dV_t}{V_t} = \mu dt + \sigma dz \tag{A.3.1}$$

Consequently, the value of the firm's assets for all times t is lognormally distributed and is given by

$$V_t = V_0 \exp\left\{\left(\mu - \frac{\sigma^2}{2}\right)t + \sigma\sqrt{t}Z_t\right\} \tag{A.3.2}$$

where the initial value of the assets is V_0 specified at time $t = 0$. The expected value of the firm's risky assets is $E[V_t] = V_0\exp(\mu t)$. The assumption of lognormality for corporate assets is generally invoked even though, by construction, fixed-income assets will not follow geometric Brownian motion.

In the presence of perfect markets free of transaction costs, taxes and informational differences between market participants, the value of the firm is independent of its capital structure and is simply given by the sum of the debt and equity values (Modigliani–Miller theorem, 1958). This means that the firm has a very simple capital structure and is strictly financed only by equity S_t and by one zero-coupon bond (constituting the firm's debt obligation or liabilities) maturing at time T with principal value F.

Assume that all the assets of the firm can be converted into cash at time T without any liquidity constraints or associated costs. If the terminal value, V_T, of the firm's assets at time T is greater than the principal value, F, of the debt obligation or liabilities, all of the firm's debt will be paid off in full; otherwise the debtors receive the firm's assets. The value of the firm's equity at time T is, therefore, given by

$$S_T = \max[V_T - F, 0] \qquad \textbf{(A.3.3)}$$

which is a call option on the assets of the firm with a strike price equal to the book value of the liabilities of the firm.

Assuming that the assets of the firm can easily be traded (or are at least replicable), the solution to equation (A.3.3) for the firm's equity value is the familiar Black–Scholes call option pricing formula on an asset with initial value V_0, asset volatility σ, remaining time to maturity τ, strike price F, and constant risk-free rate r:

$$S = V_0 N(d_1) - Fe^{-r\tau}N(d_2) \qquad \textbf{(A.3.4)}$$

where

$$d_1 = \frac{\ln\left(\dfrac{V_0}{Fe^{-r\tau}}\right) + 0.5\sigma^2\tau}{\sigma\sqrt{\tau}}$$

and

$$d_2 = d_1 - \sigma\sqrt{\tau}$$

and $N(*)$ is the cumulative normal distribution function.

Since under equilibrium conditions the initial value of the firm, V_0, consists only of debt, D, and equity, S, the value of the risky debt is simply given by

$$D = V_0 - S = V_0 N(-d_1) - Fe^{-r\tau} N(d_2) \tag{A.3.5}$$

Now, the yield on the risky debt D with face value F is

$$r_D = -\frac{1}{\tau}\ln(D/F) \tag{A.3.6}$$

so that the "credit spread", defined as the difference between the yield on the risky debt and the risk-free rate r, is given by

$$\text{Credit spread} = r_D - r \tag{A.3.7}$$

Inspection of equations (A.3.5) and (A.3.6) shows clearly that the credit spread is a function of the asset value, the volatility of the assets, the remaining maturity of the debt and the face value of the debt. More specifically, therefore, credit risk (or default risk for that matter) is a function of the financial structure (debt-to-asset ratio) of the firm, as given by its leverage ratio $Fe^{-r\tau}/V_0$, the asset volatility and the term to maturity of the underlying debt.

In summary, the preceding discussion demonstrates the insight that the creditworthiness of a firm is dependent on three important ingredients, as given by the functional relationship

$$\text{Credit risk} = f(\text{Leverage ratio, Asset volatility, Debt maturity}) \tag{A.3.8}$$

where the leverage of the firm is the ratio of the present value of its debt obligations to its current asset values. The discussion also tacitly assumes that information about the equity of the firm, as given by equation (A.3.4), can either be directly implied from the market or can be obtained in some objective form elsewhere. This can be quite problematic in the case of private firms whose equities are not traded in the market.

APPENDIX B – DEFAULT PROBABILITY, THE DEFAULT POINT AND THE DISTANCE TO DEFAULT

If all the pertinent inputs are to hand, the Merton approach to default risk is quite easy to implement. Because of the lognormal assumption given by equation (A.3.1), it is very convenient in this framework to determine the probability of default and the transition probability. We first illustrate the implementation for the case of default probability.

The diagram in Figure B.3.1 is a graphical summary of the theoretical constructs presented in Appendix A. The figure shows the distribution of the firm's asset value at terminal time T.

Recall that the debt obligation, or liabilities, of the firm has a face value of F. Based on the discussion in Appendix A, if the terminal value, V_T, of the firm's assets at time T is greater than the principal value F, then all the firm's debt will be paid off in full; otherwise the firm defaults and the debtors receive the firm's assets. The probability of default is, therefore, given by the shaded region below F in Figure B.3.1 Mathematically, we would write the probability of default, Q, as

$$Q = \Pr[V_T \leq F] \tag{B.3.1}$$

But is this sufficient? Not quite! KMV Corporation has observed from a sample of several hundred companies that firms are gener-

Figure B.3.1 Terminal distribution of the firm's asset value

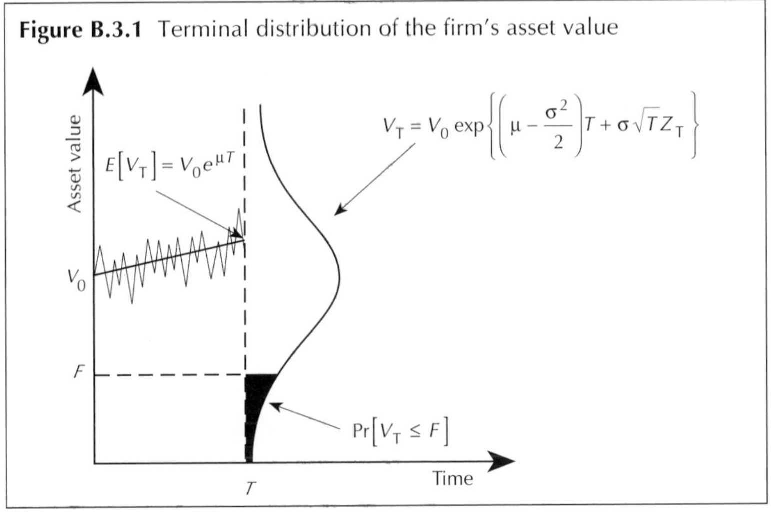

ally more likely to default when their asset values reach a certain critical level somewhere between the value of total liabilities and the value of short-term debt. Therefore, in practice, using F alone as the threshold in the tail distribution might not be an accurate measure of the actual probability of default. KMV implements an additional step and refers to this critical threshold for defaulting as the *default point*.

In the theoretical Merton framework default is synonymous with bankruptcy, and this implies that a firm defaults or goes into bankruptcy when its asset value falls below the value of its liabilities. In practice, however, the bankruptcy of a firm results in the liquidation of its assets. This is distinct from the default phenomenon, which is universally defined in the financial industry as the failure of a firm to make a payment on a coupon or reimburse its debt. There is therefore a degree of "softness" surrounding the threshold level that triggers a default event.

The *default point* (DPT) is not a very precise concept and is loosely defined by KMV as the "book value" of the firm's liabilities. This is roughly approximated by the sum of all the short-term debt (STD) and one-half of all the long-term debt (LTD) of the firm:

$$DPT = STD + 0.5LTD \tag{B.3.2}$$

In addition, an index called the *distance to default* (DD) is defined as the distance between the expected asset value of the firm at the analysis horizon, H, written as $E[V_H]$, and the default point, normalised by the standard deviation, σ, of the future asset returns. Formally, we write

$$DD \equiv \frac{E[V_H] - DPT}{\sigma} \tag{B.3.3}$$

In other words, the distance to default is the number of standard deviations between the mean of the terminal distribution of the asset value and the critical threshold, DPT, for defaulting.

Probability of default

Mathematically, what is the distance to default in the current framework? In addition, how is this related to the probability of default?

To answer these questions, we need to look first at a refined, but more practical, version of the previous diagram. In this diagram (Figure B.3.2), observe that if the future distribution of asset values at the horizon H were known, the default probability would simply be the likelihood that the asset value at the horizon, V_H, falls below the default point, DPT_H, at the analysis horizon. This tail region is shaded in the figure. Notice also that the distance to default is the normalised distance between the mean of the distribution and DPT. Therefore, instead of equation (B.3.1), we write the default probability, Q, more appropriately as

$$Q = \Pr[V_H \leq DPT_H] \qquad \textbf{(B.3.4)}$$

Under the "risk-neutral" probability measure, the expected return on all securities is the risk-free rate, r; therefore the risk-neutral probability of default as given by equation (B.3.4) is equal to

$$\begin{aligned} Q &= \Pr[V_H \leq DPT_H] \\ &= \Pr\left[\ln V_0 + \left(r - 0.5\sigma^2\right) H + \sigma\sqrt{H} Z_H \leq \ln DPT_H\right] \end{aligned}$$

Figure B.3.2 Distance to default and default point

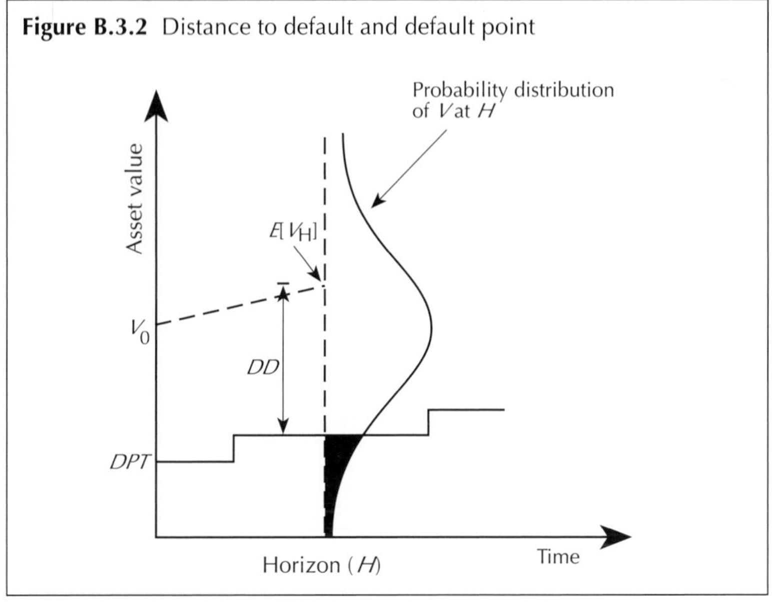

$$= \Pr\left[Z_H \le -\frac{\ln\left[V_0 / DPT_H\right] + \left(r - 0.5\sigma^2\right) H}{\sigma\sqrt{H}} \right]$$

$$= N\left(-d_2^*\right) \qquad \textbf{(B.3.5a)}$$

where $N(*)$ is the standard cumulative normal distribution and

$$d_2^* = \frac{\ln\left[V_0 / DPT_H\right] + \left(r - 0.5\sigma^2\right) H}{\sigma\sqrt{H}} \qquad \textbf{(B.3.5b)}$$

Given the result in equation (B.3.5a), the quantity d_2^* is obviously the distance to default – ie:

$$DD \equiv \frac{\ln\left[V_0 / DPT_H\right] + \left(r - 0.5\sigma^2\right) H}{\sigma\sqrt{H}} \qquad \textbf{(B.3.5c)}$$

Observe that d_2^* is very similar to d_2 in equation (A.3.4) with the following replacements:

$$F \to DPT_H \quad \text{and} \quad r \to \mu \qquad \textbf{(B.3.6)}$$

The similarity is not an accident and is the result of a relationship between the "risk-neutral" probability and the "actual" probability. The actual probability uses the expected return, μ, of the asset in its drift term, while the risk-neutral probability uses the risk-free rate, r. In both the Merton (and therefore KMV's) formulation of default risk, the actual probability is used, which we refer to as the expected default frequency (EDF) throughout this book. Hence

$$EDF \equiv N(-d_2) \qquad \textbf{(B.3.7)}$$

In fact, following Crouhy and Mark (1998), it can be easily shown that because of

$$-d_2 + \frac{(\mu - r)\sqrt{H}}{\sigma} = -d_2^* \qquad \textbf{(B.3.8)}$$

we have

$$Q = N\left(-d_2^*\right) = N\left[-d_2 + \frac{(\mu - r)\sqrt{H}}{\sigma}\right]$$

$$= N\left[N^{-1}(EDF) + \frac{(\mu - r)\sqrt{H}}{\sigma}\right] \qquad \textbf{(B.3.9)}$$

Since $\mu \geq r$, it follows that $Q \geq EDF$, so the risk-neutral probability of default (after adjusting for the price of risk) is greater than the actual probability of default.

For a variety of practical reasons that are articulated in the Crouhy–Mark paper, KMV estimates the risk-neutral *EDF* using available bond data and the functional form

$$Q = N[N^{-1}(EDF) + \rho S H^{\theta}] \qquad \textbf{(B.3.10)}$$

where ρ is the correlation between the asset return and the market return, S denotes the market Sharpe ratio (ie, the excess return per unit of market volatility for the market portfolio) and θ is a time parameter which, in practice, is not really ½. The actual distribution used in practice is also non-normal in nature.

Example B.3.1 – Calculating default probabilities

For simplicity, all calculations in this example will use the "actual" probability measure. We have the following information about the firm:

Analysis horizon, H	1.0 year
Current market value of assets, V_0	\$1,000
Net expected growth of assets per annum, μ	20%
Annualised asset volatility, σ	25%
Short-term liability, STD	\$400
Long-term liability, LTD	\$400

Thus, the default point at the horizon is

$$DPT_{\mathrm{H}} = STD + 0.5LTD = 600$$

Using equation (B.3.5c), the distance to default is

$$DD = \frac{\ln\left[V_0 / DPT_H\right] + \left(\mu - 0.5\sigma^2\right) H}{\sigma\sqrt{H}} = 2.72$$

so that the probability of default (ie, the expected default frequency) can now be calculated as

$$EDF = N(-DD) = 0.0033 = 0.33\% \text{ or } 33 \text{ basis points}$$

The distance to default calculation shows that the firm is 2.72 standard deviations away from its default point. From Table 3.2, the theoretically obtained *EDF* of 33 basis points implies a Standard & Poor's risk rating of somewhere between BBB and BB for the firm.

What the above example highlights is that even using a sound theoretical foundation such as the Merton approach, everything, in practice, still boils down to a subjective estimation of the input parameters. More importantly, it is often difficult to map the expected default frequencies consistently back to the empirically derived agency ratings.

So, are the results given by this decidedly more theoretical approach really any better than the probabilities empirically derived by the rating agencies from their historical databases? Perhaps one can only suggest that in either case one should heed the maxim: "Beware, use with caution and an open mind".

The example here demonstrates the calculation of default probability. A more complicated, albeit not difficult but taxing, procedure exists for obtaining transition probabilities from one rating class to another.

APPENDIX C – MATHEMATICAL PRELIMINARY

Some formalities

Consider a frictionless economy with a finite horizon $[0, \tau]$. Let $p(t, T)$ be the price of a default-free zero coupon at time t paying a sure dollar at time T, where $t \leq T \leq \tau$. The default-free spot rate is denoted by $r(t)$. Let the money market account accumulate at the spot rate and denote it by

$$B(t) = \exp\left(\int_0^t r(s)\,ds\right) \qquad \textbf{(C.3.1)}$$

Under the assumption of arbitrage-free and complete markets, the default-free bond prices are the expected, discounted value of a sure dollar received at time T, viz:

$$p(t,T) = \tilde{E}_t\left(\frac{B(t)}{B(T)}\right) \qquad \textbf{(C.3.2)}$$

where the expectation is taken under the unique equivalent martingale measure $\tilde{Q}$.

Recovery rate

Following Jarrow, Lando and Turnbull (1997), let $v(t, T)$ be the time t price of a risky zero-coupon bond promising to pay \$1 at time T, where $t \le T \le \tau$. If the firm that issues the promised dollar defaults at time T, the firm pays only a fraction $\delta <$ \$1. The fraction δ is called the "recovery rate" and can depend on the liability structure of the firm.

Suppose that default occurs at the random time τ^*. Then the value of the risky zero-coupon bond is given by

$$v(t,T) = \tilde{E}_t\left(\frac{B(t)}{B(T)}\left[\delta 1_{\{\tau^* \le T\}} + 1_{\{\tau^* > T\}}\right]\right) \qquad \textbf{(C.3.3)}$$

where the indicator function means

$$1_{\{\tau^* \le T\}} = \begin{cases} 1, \tau^* \le T \\ 0, \tau^* > T \end{cases} \qquad \textbf{(C.3.4)}$$

The previous expression shows that the risky zero-coupon bond's price can be interpreted as the expected, discounted value of a "risky" dollar received at time T.

We can also interpret the value of the risky zero-coupon bond as the expectation, under the equivalent measure $\tilde{Q}$, of the two possible states, S, of the default process, symbolically represented by

$$S = \{\bar{D} = \text{No default};\ D = \text{Default}\}$$

where the two states of the default process are denoted by the stochastic variable S.

Decomposition of risky debt

Writing the corresponding values of the risky debt as $v(t, T, S)$, it is clear that we have the situation shown in Figure C.3.1. The decomposition in the figure corresponds to the two possible values that the risky debt, $v(t, T)$, can assume. The expectation in equation (C.3.3) is simply taken over the sum of these two possible outcomes in accordance with the two possible states of default, $S = \{\bar{D}, D\}$.

Figure C.3.1 Decomposition of risky debt

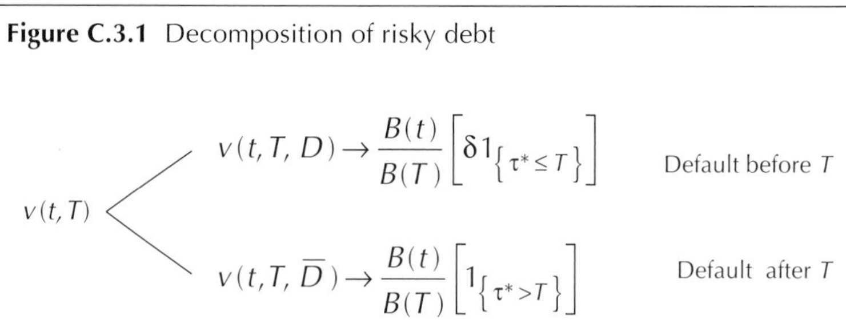

If we make the further assumption that the default-free spot rates, $r(t)$ for $t \leq T \leq \tau$, and the default process, as represented by τ^*, are statistically independent under $\tilde{Q}$, then the expectation is multiplicative, viz:

$$v(t,T) = \tilde{E}_t\left(\frac{B(t)}{B(T)}\right)\tilde{E}_t\left(\left[\delta 1_{\{\tau^* \leq T\}} + 1_{\{\tau^* > T\}}\right]\right) \quad \textbf{(C.3.5a)}$$

$$= p(t,T)\left[\delta + (1-\delta)\tilde{Q}_t\,(\tau^* > T)\right] \quad \textbf{(C.3.5b)}$$

where $\tilde{Q}_t(\tau^* > T)$ is the probability under $\tilde{Q}$ that default occurs *after* time T.

APPENDIX D – THE MULTI-STATE DEFAULT PROCESS AND THE PROBABILITY MEASURE $\tilde{Q}_t(\tau^* > T)$

In the instantaneous risk of default class of models, the crux of the problem is to model the probability distribution for the time of default, $\tilde{Q}_t(\tau^* > T)$, under the equivalent martingale measure $\tilde{Q}$. The distribution for the default time can be modelled as a discrete, time-homogeneous Markov chain in a finite-state space $\Omega = \{1, 2, 3, \ldots, K\}$, representing the possible credit classes, with Class 1 (ie, the equivalent of AAA in the Standard & Poor's rating) as the highest credit rating and Class K as the default class.

Under this representation, Jarrow, Lando and Turnbull (1997) constructed the probability that default occurs after time T:

$$\tilde{Q}_t^i(\tau^* > T) = \sum_{j \neq k} \tilde{q}_{ij}(t, T) = 1 - \tilde{q}_{iK}(t, T) \qquad \textbf{(D.3.1)}$$

where the superscript i refers to the credit rating class the firm is currently in. The martingale transition probabilities, $\tilde{q}_{ij}$, are given in terms of Standard & Poor's or Moody's transition probabilities, q_{ij}, as follows,

$$\tilde{q}_{ij}(t, t+1) = \pi_i(t) q_{ij} \qquad \text{for all } i \neq j \qquad \textbf{(D.3.2)}$$

where $\pi_i(t)$, representing the risk premia, is a deterministic function of time such that

$$\tilde{q}_{ij}(t, t+1) \geq 0, \qquad \forall i, j, i \neq j$$

and

$$\sum_{j=1, j \neq i}^{K} \tilde{q}_{ij}(t, t+1) \leq 1 \qquad \text{for } i = 1, 2, 3, \ldots, K$$

In matrix form, the statements above can be condensed as

$$\tilde{Q}_{t,t+1} - I = \Pi(t)[Q - I] \qquad \textbf{(D.3.3)}$$

where I is the $K \times K$ identity matrix and the risk premium

$$\Pi(t) = \text{diag}\{\pi_1(t), \ldots, \pi_{K-1}(t)\}$$

is a $K \times K$ diagonal matrix.

Q is the familiar empirical transition matrix from either Standard & Poor's or Moody's, viz:

$$Q = \begin{pmatrix} q_{11} & q_{12} & \cdots & \cdots & q_{1K} \\ q_{21} & q_{22} & \cdots & \cdots & q_{2K} \\ \vdots & & & & \vdots \\ q_{K-1,1} & q_{K-1,2} & \cdots & \cdots & q_{K-1,K} \\ 0 & 0 & \cdots & 0 & 1 \end{pmatrix} \quad \textbf{(D.3.4)}$$

where by necessity, we require that

$$q_{ij} \geq 0, \qquad \forall i, j, i \neq j$$

and

$$q_{ii} \equiv 1 - \sum_{j=1, j \neq i}^{K} q_{ij}$$

so that Q is indeed a transition matrix.

Excellent details on how the martingale transition matrix $\tilde{Q}$ can be inferred from the empirical and publicly available transition matrix Q can be found in Jarrow, Lando and Turnbull (1997).

4

Loan Portfolios and Expected Loss

What makes a bank asset risky is that holding the asset over some time horizon is associated with considerable uncertainty. An important role whereby a bank provides value to the market is in acting as a financial intermediary. In fulfilling its function, however, the bank must inevitably take highly illiquid assets – for example, loans and other receivables – into its balance sheet. Although recent innovations in the capital markets such as credit derivatives and asset securitisation allow a bank either to shorten the duration of its illiquid portfolio or to unload some of these uncertain cashflows into the capital markets, for the most part these illiquid assets continue to remain within the bank until maturity. In fact, under current regulatory constraints many such assets continue to be classified as "hold-to-maturity" in the bank's balance sheet instead of being appropriately marked-to-market.

We shall henceforth refer to a collection of these illiquid assets which an institution holds in its banking book by the generic term "loan portfolio". In its generalised meaning, a loan portfolio contains risky assets that are subject to credit risk owing to the probable occurrence of default.

In view of this, it is very important for the bank to come up with some means of quantifying the *unanticipated* change in the value of a single risky asset. We shall later generalise the concept to the portfolio case. For the most part, the riskiness of the asset can be largely attributed to the risk of default, and it is therefore necessary to devise measures that can capture this risk adequately. However, since quantifying the embedded credit risk alone is not sufficient to mitigate risk, it is also necessary to devise tools which can accurately measure the return of the asset in some risk-adjusted framework. Hence, we are motivated by two main objectives – namely, to:

❑ quantify the measures of credit risk; and
❑ devise risk-adjusted return measures.

The determinants of risk-adjusted return measurement are similar to the measures of credit risk. We have already encountered one such measure of credit risk. We called it *expected loss* in the previous chapter. To answer the question "What really is expected loss from a loan portfolio perspective?", we need first to interpret what such loss means for one risky asset in the portfolio.

EXPECTED LOSS

The expected loss (EL), which was defined earlier in equation (3.10) as

$$\begin{gathered}\text{Expected loss} = \\ \text{Assured payment at maturity time } T \times \\ \text{Loss given default} \times \\ \text{Probability that default occurs } \textit{before} \text{ maturity } T\end{gathered} \tag{4.1}$$

In practice, because we are not dealing primarily with bonds (zero-coupon or otherwise) or other trading instruments but with credit-related bank assets such as loans (in a very broad sense of the word), we need to be more precise as to what is meant by an "Assured payment at maturity time T".

For bond-like instruments, the payments are often a stream of cashflows that includes the promised repayment of principal at maturity. For the most part, there are fewer complicated indentures, covenant structures and tax and accounting treatments with bond-like instruments than for, say, a commercial bank loan. In concept, however, loans are really par bonds whose valuation depends on some loan forward curves imbued with upgrade or downgrade characteristics and a loan recovery rate to the amount of the principal in the event of default.

Returns to loans are more complex than, for example, stock returns. Loan returns are highly non-symmetric because there is no upside potential as with a stock. If a firm improves its performance (ie, if its credit quality improves), the lending bank usually does not benefit from the improvement since the borrowing firm can always refinance its debt at a far more attractive lower rate.

Conversely, if the credit quality of a loan deteriorates, the bank is generally not compensated for taking on the increased risk because the loan pricing does not change. As the loan deteriorates further into the non-performing stage, accrued interest is reversed and any new payments are applied to principal. If the credit position worsens further and goes into workout, the lending bank is unlikely to recover the substantial legal and administrative fees incurred in the process.

And, of course, since a corporate loan portfolio is significantly less liquid than a fixed-income bond portfolio, it is more difficult to liquidate a loan portfolio during market downturns. As a consequence, the lending bank is normally forced to hold on to the loan portfolio. If the bank sells a loan at less than book value, it immediately incurs a loss equal to the difference between the market and the book value of the loan. In addition, because of liquidity constraints, most loans do not have current market prices, so the market value in reality is the price the market will bear – whatever it is.

The crux of the situation described above can be summarised by the question: "How much credit exposure does a bank have in the event of default or credit rating migrations?"

Because of these somewhat unique characteristics associated with the credit-related assets of the bank, the quantity "Assured payment at maturity time T" should be replaced by the more appropriate quantity (and nomenclature) *exposure*. We then need to ask: "In the event of default, how much exposure does the bank have to its borrower and how much of this exposure is the bank likely to lose or be unable to recover?" The determination and quantification of the risk of loss in the bank's exposure to its obligors is what we are ultimately seeking.

There are two major parts to this determination exercise:

- the calculation of expected loss; and
- an estimation of unexpected loss.

Turning first to the expected loss, let us suppose that the bank has an exposure to a borrower. Then, the amount the bank stands to lose at the time of default is

$$\text{Exposure} \times \text{Loss given default}$$

Multiplying this by the probability of default gives the expected loss:

$$EL = \text{Exposure} \times LGD \times \text{Probability of default} \quad \textbf{(4.2)}$$

This definition is consistent with our original definition and discussion leading to equation (3.10) and also that expressed in equation (4.1).

Over a period of time the bank can expect to lose, *on average*, the amount of its exposure equal to the expected loss. However, during the same period, either due to market conditions or other economic trends, the fluctuation can swing either side of the average expected loss. In the next sections we will discuss this deviation from the average, which is called *unexpected loss*. From a risk management perspective, it is this quantity that should concern us most. It is because of the unexpected loss, representing uncertainty, that a lending bank must set aside enough economic capital to buffer itself against insolvency.

Before we proceed any further with expected loss, we need to find out what is meant by the term *exposure* or, more appropriately, the *adjusted exposure*. But first, we must introduce two important quantities: *outstandings* and *commitments*. Associated with commitments are embedded optionalities called *covenants*.

ADJUSTED EXPOSURE: OUTSTANDINGS AND COMMITMENTS

Let the value of the bank asset, at current time t_0, be denoted by V_0. The asset is primarily composed of two major parts: outstandings (OS); and commitments (COM); so that

$$V_0 = OS + COM \quad \textbf{(4.3)}$$

Outstandings is a generic term referring to that portion of the bank asset which has already been extended to the borrowers (in the case of loans and bonds) and also to other receivables in the form of contractual payments which are due from its customers. By definition, in the event of default such that the borrowers are unable to repay their contractual obligations and the receivables fail to come in, the bank is exposed to the *entire* amount of the outstandings.

Examples of our generalisation of outstandings are term loans, credit cards, bonds and receivables.

Commitments, on the other hand, normally refer to loans and consist of two portions: drawn and undrawn. A commitment is an amount the bank has committed to lend, at the borrower's request, up to the full amount of the commitment. Should the borrower encounter financial difficulties, it is in its best interest to draw on this committed line of credit. If the borrower eventually defaults, the commitment would also be subject to loss, in addition to all the outstandings the obligor has already received from the bank.

The *drawn portion* of the commitment should be treated as part of the amount currently borrowed (ie, the outstandings). Since it is exactly like a term loan, the entire drawn portion is, therefore, subject to risk of loss upon default. The *undrawn portion* of the commitment, on the other hand, has an embedded contingent claim (a call option, in fact) which the borrower can exercise at any time and draw upon whenever it encounters financial distress. It is, therefore, not entirely a term loan, and should be treated differently when considering the exposure of the bank.

Examples of our generalisation of commitments are stand-by letters of credit (LC).

COVENANTS

Bank assets, such as commitments, normally grant a variety of options to the borrowers. They contain terms and provisions in the form of *covenants,* which are either options the bank reserves to itself or options granted to the obligor. We have just encountered one of these in the discussion of the undrawn commitment, where the obligor has the unrestricted right to draw up to the full amount of the commitment at any time.

Consider a committed facility *without* covenants. Suppose that the amount of the commitment is \$COM, denominated in US dollars. On encountering financial distress, the borrower is likely to draw on the commitment, possibly to the full amount permitted. Hence, in the event of default, an unrestricted commitment of \$COM has the same exposure as a term loan of $\alpha \times$ \$COM, where $0 < \alpha \leq 1$ is the percentage of draw-down.

As a prudent measure to mitigate loss, the bank may impose covenants on the commitment. The covenants may permit:

- a reduction of the maximum percentage of draw-down under the commitment;
- an increase in the seniority of the borrowing;
- an increase in collateral requirement; and/or
- repricing of the loan.

Once these covenants are in place, the loss given default for the exposure should be based strictly on the expected recovery rate assuming an increase in seniority or collateral requirement. This, of course, assumes that the covenants would be initiated and used prior to the event of default.

All this leads us to return to consideration of the adjusted exposure, referred to earlier. This is the totality of the credit risk exposure to which the bank is subject, some fraction of which the bank therefore runs the risk of losing in the event of an obligor's default.

ADJUSTED EXPOSURE

Again, let the value of the bank asset, at current time t_0, be denoted by V_0. In the case of no default prior to the analysis horizon, t_H, the value of the asset remains at V_0. However, if there is default prior to the horizon t_H, then a fraction, say α, of the undrawn portion of the commitments is likely to be drawn.

Only the fraction of the commitment COM that is drawn down upon default (including the outstandings part) stands to lose value. Therefore, as usual, there are two parts to this asset value at the horizon: the risky part and the riskless part.

Let the value of the bank asset at the horizon t_H be denoted by V_1. Then V_1 consists of two parts, as shown in Figure 4.1. It is clear that the entire amount of the outstandings, *OS*, is affected by default, while the portion of the asset value not affected by default

Figure 4.1 Risky and riskless parts of an exposure

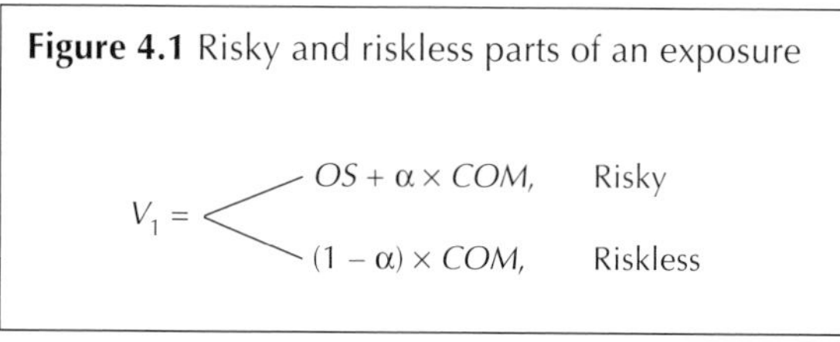

is given by $(1 - \alpha) \times COM$. The value of the asset at the horizon, V_1, is in fact the "exposure upon default", and only the risky part of this asset is subject to loss. In the market, the risky part of V_1 is known as the "adjusted exposure".

The percentage loss in value, as we have seen earlier, is the so-called "loss given default". Equation (4.2) for the expected loss should now more appropriately be rewritten as

$$EL = \text{Adjusted exposure} \times LGD \times \text{Probability of default} \quad \textbf{(4.4)}$$

Later on, we shall derive this mathematically as equation (4.7).

USAGE GIVEN DEFAULT

In practice, we have seen that the commitment is not always fully drawn in the event of default. Hence, the risk of loss on the commitment is less than the risk of loss of the total outstanding. It is necessary, therefore, to estimate the amount of the draw-down, α, if we are to have a better idea of the adjusted exposure as the obligor undergoes credit deterioration. To this end, we introduce another name for the fraction α of the commitment that is likely to be drawn in the event of a default and call it the *usage given default* (or UGD).

Credit optionality

The usage given default is a contingent claim owned by the obligor. It is a "credit option" that is granted by the bank to the obligor in exchange for a premium known as the "commitment fee". As part of the credit process, the bank is paid a commitment fee amounting to some percentage of the commitment granted to the obligor. Depending on the covenants contained in the commitment, the obligor has the right to draw, for a fixed period of time, on the commitment whenever it meets with financial distress during that time frame.

The permissible percentage of draw-down or UGD, given by the variable α in Figure 4.1, is normally stipulated in the covenant. One thing is clear, however: historically, there is very strong evidence to show that an obligor's draw-down rate on a committed credit line tends to increase rapidly as the obligor's credit quality deteriorates. One possible explanation could be that the reduced availability of

Table 4.1 Average usage given default for borrowers with different credit ratings

Credit rating	UGD (%)
AAA	69
AA	73
A	71
BBB	65
BB	52
B	48
CCC	44

Source: Asarnow and Marker (1995).

alternative and cheap funding sources ensuing from credit deterioration forces the obligor to maximise its draw-down on existing credit lines. The credit option is, in fact, the obligor's insurance against the inability to fund its business.

In practice, the option premium or the fee charged to the obligor is not determined very economically or scientifically. In principle, the rate of draw-down, α, or UGD follows some indeterministic process, but it is quite difficult to treat the draw-down rate as a stochastic variable. Each commitment, along with its attached covenants, makes the draw-down rate unique to that specific credit line. Therefore, faced with a problematic impasse, practitioners in the market treat the uncertain draw-down rate as a known function of the obligor's end-of-horizon credit class rating.

The often quoted publicly available source of UGD information is a paper published by Asarnow and Marker (1995). They based their empirical study on Citibank's historical data on defaults on corporate loans and estimated the average draw-down of normally unused commitment in the event of default. Their results are summarised in Table 4.1. These indicate, for example, that an obligor with a initial risk class rating of BBB at the beginning of the analysis horizon will, on average, tend to draw down 65% of its previously undrawn commitment in the event that it has defaulted by the end of the horizon.

The foregoing discussion points very strongly to the fact that the adjusted exposure, which is the amount the bank is exposed to in the event of default, is not a completely deterministic quantity and should therefore be estimated with great care.

Figure 4.2 Expected loss

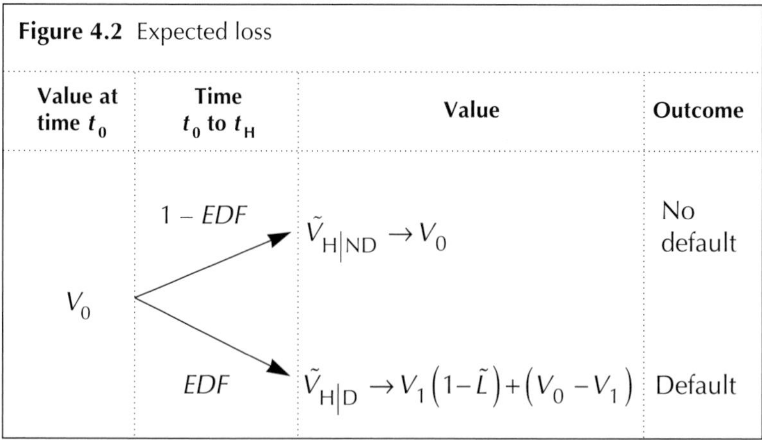

LOSS GIVEN DEFAULT AND THE RISKY PART OF V_1

Recall that the adjusted exposure is the risky part of V_1, where V_1 is the value of the asset at the horizon. What, then, is the relationship between the loss given default and adjusted exposure?

In the event of default prior to the horizon t_H, only the risky part of the asset value V_1 is subject to loss. Denote the loss percentage by loss given default, *LGD*. Then, in the event of default prior to time t_H, the asset held by the bank loses value and reaches a level given by

$$V_1(1 - LGD) + (V_0 - V_1) = V_0 - V_1 \times LGD$$

The portion $(V_0 - V_1)$, which equals $(1 - \alpha) \times COM$, is the riskless part. A schematic representation of the discussion just presented is given in Figure 4.2.

MATHEMATICAL DERIVATION OF EXPECTED LOSS

We can now formally derive an expression for expected loss. The diagram in Figure 4.2 helps to put things into perspective.

Denote by the bracket $<\tilde{X}>$ the expectation of the random variable $\tilde{X}$, and let the loss variable be denoted by $\tilde{L}$, with expectation $<\tilde{L}> \equiv LGD$. The probability of default before the horizon t_H is $\tilde{Q}_t(\tau^* \le t_H)$. With a slight abuse of notation, we write

$$<\tilde{Q}_t(\tau^* \le t_H)> = EDF \tag{4.5}$$

for the *expected default frequency* (EDF), which is another name for the probability of default.

From Figure 4.2 we observe that there are two possibilities for the value of the asset at the horizon t_H, namely $\tilde{V}_{H|D}$ and $\tilde{V}_{H|\bar{D}}$, corresponding to the simplified states of the default process – default, D, and no default, $\bar{D}$, respectively.

The expected loss, EL_H, at the horizon t_H is

$$\begin{aligned} EL_H &= \text{Expected value of the asset at } t_H \text{ given no default} - \\ &\quad \text{Unconditional expected value of the asset at } t_H \\ &= \langle \tilde{V}_{H|\bar{D}} \rangle - \langle V_H \rangle \\ &= V_0 - \langle \tilde{Q}[V_1(1-\tilde{L}) + (V_0 - V_1)] + (1-\tilde{Q})V_0 \rangle \end{aligned} \tag{4.6}$$

which on simplification yields

$$ELH = V_1 \times LGD \times EDF \tag{4.7}$$

Of course, this result is exactly identical to equations (3.10) and (4.4), as it should be.

Observe that in the second term of equation (4.6), the unconditional expected value of the asset at time t_H is simply the weighted average of the two parts (risky and riskless) of V_1, where the weights are the probabilities of default, $\tilde{Q}$, and no default, $(1 - \tilde{Q})$, respectively.

It must also be clear in equation (4.7) that only the risky part of V_1 is subject to loss upon default. To this end, it might be advisable to revise the notation in the equation for expected loss to read as follows:

$$EL_H = AE \times LGD \times EDF \tag{4.8}$$

where *AE* is the *adjusted exposure*, which is the risky part of the asset value at the horizon subject to default risk.

The calculation of the expected loss of a risky asset is demonstrated below using a simple example. We assume, for simplicity, that all the non-deterministic variables such as *UGD* and *LGD* are known with certainty and can be inferred from historical data or some other source.

Table 4.2 Calculation of expected loss

COM	Commitment	\$10,000,000
OS	Outstanding	\$5,000,000
RC	Internal risk rating	3
	Maturity	1 year
	Type	Non-secured
UGD	Unused draw-down on default for $RC = 3$	65%
AE	Adjusted exposure on default $AE = OS + (COM - OS) \times UGD$	\$8,250,000
EDF	1-year default probability for $RC = 3$	0.15%
LGD	Loss given default for non-secured asset	50%
EL	Expected loss $EL = AE \times EDF \times LGD$	\$6,188

Example: Calculation of expected loss

Consider a one-year loan facility, internally rated as risk class 3 (equivalent to a Standard & Poor's senior unsecured debt rating of BBB), with the characteristics listed in Table 4.2. The calculated adjusted exposure is \$8,250,000, and this is the amount the bank is exposed to in the event of default. Observe that not all of the commitment and outstanding are exposed. Specifically, only the risky portion of the asset value at the horizon is exposed, viz:

$$\text{Outstanding} + UGD \times \text{Undrawn part of the commitment}$$

From Table 4.2, the one-year average draw-down in the event of default for a risk class rating of BBB is $UGD = 65\%$.

The loss given default for a non-secured asset is assumed to be 50% for the horizon, which implies that this non-secured asset has a recovery rate of 50% if default occurs within one year.

For assets that are secured either by collateral or for which some other guarantees are in place (as indicated in the covenants), the recovery rates need to be modified to reflect the appropriate level of security required by the bank.

Finally, the calculated expected loss is \$6,188, which is 0.075% (or 7.5 basis points) of the adjusted exposure. This is the amount that the bank should set aside as a *loan loss reserve*. It is also the break-even amount that the bank needs to generate as revenue from the obligor for taking this facility into its banking book.

PARAMETERISING CREDIT RISK MODELS

Without an actual numerical example it is not easy to understand the practical difficulties associated with "parameterising" a credit risk model. Credit risk modelling is definitely not a bystander sport. The mathematics is in fact quite simple, but the paucity of hard data for estimating the model parameters is lamentable. The nuances and subtle difficulties do not show up in the mathematics until the actual implementation of the model. In fact, it would be quite naïve to assume at the outset that most of the required elements in credit risk models can easily be inferred from the market or are even calculable from historical data. Now that we have completed our first numerical calculation using the simplest component – expected loss – it is advisable to pause and consider the important implications surrounding the use of proper parameters in the credit risk modelling process. Although we shall not repeat this soul-searching process again in succeeding chapters, we will, however, continue to be cognisant of the ever present dilemma – *parameterise at your own risk.*

The ingredients necessary for estimating the expected loss of a single risky asset in a two-state default process are:

- ❑ Adjusted exposure
  - ❑ Outstandings
  - ❑ Commitment
  - ❑ Usage given default
- ❑ Loss given default
  - ❑ Secured or unsecured
- ❑ Expected default frequency
- ❑ Maturity
- ❑ Internal risk class rating.

Obviously, the first step in the process requires the bank's information system to be sound and robust and capable of collecting all the appropriate outstanding and commitment amounts for the loan facility. In addition, a "drill-up" mechanism must be in place to allow the different facilities applicable to the same obligor to be rolled up to the obligor level. Later, when we introduce more risk measures on an aggregated portfolio basis, we will see that the role of the obligor in the top parent hierarchy becomes vital to the analysis (see chapter 6).

The only parameter needed for the calculation of adjusted exposure is the usage given default. The UGD, in turn, depends on the risk rating of the facility. Most banks have their own internal risk rating systems, but one needs to consider whether they are sufficiently accurate – for example, a check could be made against publicly available agency ratings. In fact, most of the time internal risk ratings are inconsistent with agency ratings such as Standard & Poor's and Moody's. Furthermore, the agencies rate only publicly traded firms whereas, in most banks, half the loan portfolio consists of private firms for which financial statements are scant and unreliable. Assuming that the internal risk rating is sound, the UGD has to be estimated to take into account the percentage and likelihood of drawn-down in the event of default.

The loss given default, or, conversely, one less the recovery rate, is another difficult parameter to estimate. In practice, the LGD is dependent on the risky asset's seniority in claim and the collateral guaranteed by the asset. It becomes important to distinguish whether the asset is secured or not and by what. Studies of recovery rates implied from corporate bonds have been made, but the results so far are inconclusive. Also, individual banks have attempted to estimate LGD from their own historical experience (which can lead to myopia) and there are organisations that attempt to collect statistics (which can lead to mass hysteria). The jury is still out in this regard.

So, studies of loss given default are plentiful if rather inconclusive. A group that studied the loss experience of corporate bonds, sovereign debt and municipals includes: Altman (1989), Standard & Poor's (1995), Moody's Investor Services (1996), Carty (1996), McDonald and Van de Gucht (1996) and Altman and Saunders (1998). A more recent, separate group which studied bank loan defaults and loss experience includes: Asarnow and Edwards (1995), Carty and Lieberman (1996b) and Altman and Suggitt (1997). The studies by this second group, however, included either default or severity of loss but not both.

Two primary studies of recovery rates for corporate bonds – those by Altman and Kishore (1996) and Carty and Lieberman (1996a) – arrived at similar estimates. Parts of the comparison are reproduced in Table 4.3, as quoted from the CreditMetrics Technical Document (Gupton, Finger and Bhatia, 1997). The recov-

Table 4.3 Recovery rates for corporate bonds

Seniority class	Carty and Lieberman (1996a) Number	Average ($)	σ ($)	Altman and Kishore (1996) Number	Average ($)	σ ($)
Senior secured	115	53.80	26.86	85	57.89	22.99
Senior unsecured	278	51.13	25.45	221	47.65	22.71
Senior subordinated	196	38.52	23.81	177	34.38	25.08
Subordinated	226	32.74	20.18	214	31.34	22.42
Junior subordinated	9	17.09	10.90	n.a.	n.a.	n.a.

ery rates are based on a par value of $100 and are ranked according to seniority class.

For bank loans there are, again, only two publicly available primary studies, and the results of these studies of bank loan loss severities offer conflicting evidence. Carty and Lieberman (1996b) found a unimodal distribution with more than half of the loan loss severities at 30% or less, whereas Asarnow and Edwards (1995) found a bimodal distribution. A graph summarising the second authors' results can be found in their paper or as Chart 7.1 of Gupton, Finger and Bhatia (1997).

More than half of non-financial corporate debt is issued privately. A recent paper (Carey, 1998) analysed the difference between privately placed and publicly issued bonds and compared their default rates, loss severity (ie, LGD) and average loss rates. The results showed "that ex ante riskier classes of private debt perform better on average than public debt. Both diversification and the riskiness of individual portfolio assets influence the bad tail of the portfolio loss distribution." A presentation of my own research and simulation of loss distributions in chapters 9, 10 and 11 also demonstrates the influence of portfolio size, concentration and composition on the tail region of the loss distribution.

Tables 4.4 and 4.5 reproduce the results of the Carey (1998) study. The sample used in the study was data for 13 life insurance companies for the years 1986 through 1992. Their aggregate share of all private placements outstanding was approximately 25% of the universe. Even though the results are indicative for private debt only, they also shed light on public debt, at least from a comparative perspective.

Table 4.4 LGD by year

Year	Average portfolio loss rate (%)	Average LGD (%)
1986	0.32	41
1987	0.21	24
1988	0.17	40
1989	0.26	40
1990	0.35	47
1991	0.66	43
1992	0.47	26
All	0.37	36

Table 4.4 gives the results for the average portfolio loss rate, which is the percentage loss per dollar exposed for the total sample during the year in question. For instance, in 1986 the aggregate of participating portfolios lost an average of 32 cents per $100 invested. The average loss severity (or average LGD) is the percentage of exposed dollars lost on assets that experienced some type of credit event, such as default, but it also includes restructuring and distress sales.

Table 4.5 displays the loss experience by credit risk rating. The abbreviation "n.a." means that no credit event occurred for risk rating AAA.

Table 4.5 LGD by credit risk rating

Most recent rating	Average portfolio loss rate (%)	Average LGD (%)
AAA	n.a.	n.a.
AA	0.03	76
A	0.02	24
BBB	0.24	33
BB	1.50	39
B	2.16	38
<B	4.36	55
Unknown	0.42	32
All	0.37	36

Finally, the crucially important probability of default expressed by the EDF or *expected default frequency* needs to be addressed. Both Moody's and Standard & Poor's have published estimates based on their own historical compilations, but they include only publicly traded firms. KMV Corporation has its Credit Monitor, which applies the "value of the firm" class of model to estimate default probabilities using both public and private financial statements. (The theoretical framework has been outlined in Appendix A of chapter 3, and how these probabilities can be calculated has been demonstrated in Appendix B of chapter 3.) However, a comparison of the absolute numerical values of the default probabilities leaves more nagging doubt than enlightenment. Currently, there is no publicised effort to standardise the numerical values of these default probabilities.

And, yet, this is only the beginning. The parameterisation of credit risk models can be problematic and cumbersome as we head into portfolio aggregation. The most prudent way, it seems, is to parameterise the internal credit risk model in a manner that is commensurate with the risk tolerance of the bank. Further down the road, the regulatory bodies should intervene and set forth consensus-driven parameters to which all banks would have to conform, just like the internal value-at-risk models for market risk capital adequacy.

5
Unexpected Loss

In the previous chapter we observed that a bank which acts as a financial intermediary in the market must inevitably take illiquid assets into its balance sheet. The accumulation of these risky assets in the bank's generic loan portfolio has at least one unpleasant consequence: the bank expects, and will therefore anticipate, some level of deterioration in their value. The risk of loss in the value of these risky assets should, therefore, represent the bank's cost of doing business.

As we have seen, the measure that quantifies the anticipated aspect of the loss on a risky asset is the so-called "expected loss". The expected loss was derived previously as that portion of the risky asset which the bank is exposed to, on average, in the event of default and the loss of which the bank is expected to bear as a consequence of undertaking its role as a financial intermediary in the market. Hence, as a first line of defence against insolvency, the bank should set aside a *loan loss reserve* provision equal to the expected loss. In addition, any targets for returns on assets used by the bank to measure the relative performance of its business units must be correspondingly increased by an amount equal to the provision for expected losses.

The tone of the previous chapter also implied that there is an *unanticipated* loss in the value of the risky asset corresponding to the *anticipated* loss in value. Indeed, there is. There we called the anticipated loss the *expected loss*, and in this chapter we shall call the unanticipated loss the *unexpected loss*.

In fact, most of the time the obligor will probably not default and the actual realised loss from the risky asset will be zero, which is less than the expected loss. In this satisfactory circumstance the

Figure 5.1 Expected loss and unexpected loss

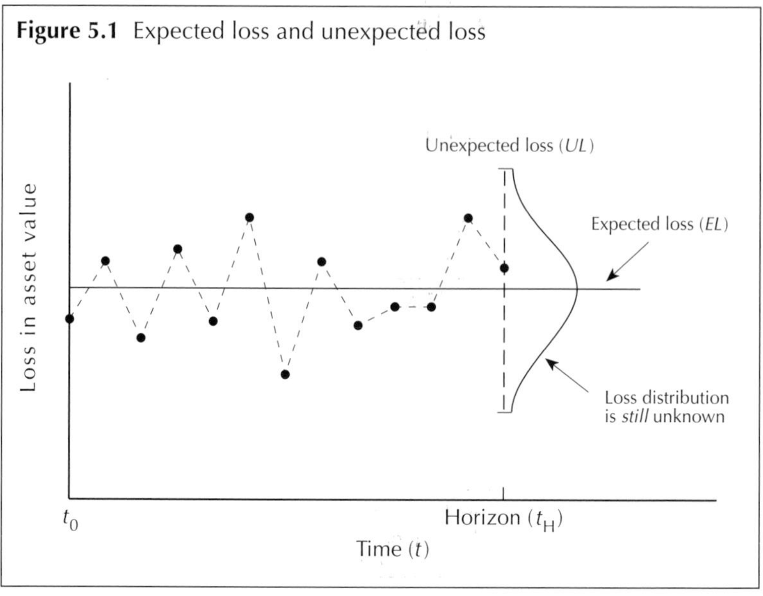

bank can consider itself fortunate (or wise) in having decided to hold the asset, and the loan loss reserve previously set aside can either be rolled over to the next analysis horizon if the asset has not yet matured or, if it has matured, declared as income.

However, every so often, as market conditions or the business cycle head for a downturn, the obligor will default. Depending on the amount of the outstandings and the usage given default of the commitments by the obligor, the actual realised loss in value of the risky asset may be significantly larger than the expected loss. To protect itself from insolvency, the bank needs to set aside sufficient capital for this uncertain event. Even though the realised loss is unanticipated, and therefore unreserved for, the bank needs to be cognisant that under extreme market conditions a confluence of unforeseen factors, including the intrinsic composition of the portfolio of which this risky asset is a part, can lead to losses far in excess of what has been reserved for.

The situation can be summarised as shown in Figure 5.1, which shows the mean (or expected loss) of the possible losses in the value of the risky asset over the analysis horizon as a single straight line. It is a straight line because, on average, the losses over the horizon are represented by a constant number.

However, over time the unanticipated losses are uncertain and may, therefore, deviate from the average or expected loss. At each time point before the analysis horizon the losses can fluctuate about the expected loss (EL). The fluctuations may be above or below the average loss, and they may be small or large. This deviation from the average is called the unexpected loss (UL) and is represented in the diagram as a jagged line. Because it is an uncertain phenomenon, the unexpected loss has a probability distribution, of unknown form, associated with it. We represent this as yet unknown distribution by a hump. As we shall see in later chapters, establishing the shape of the loss distribution raises very thorny theoretical and practical issues.

Building on our earlier discussion of the concept of expected loss, the primary goal in this chapter is, first, to quantify the unanticipated risk of loss of a single risky asset in the event of default. This unanticipated risk of loss is represented by a new measure, mentioned above, called the *unexpected loss*. Following on from the discussion here, the next chapter focuses on the effect of a single risky asset on the bank's overall portfolio and then considers its relationship to extreme, though not improbable, events.

We begin with a discussion of what causes uncertainty in the value of risky assets in a credit portfolio.

CAUSES OF UNANTICIPATED RISK

The uncertainty in the risk of loss at the horizon arises from the unanticipated change in the value of the risky asset. What causes this unanticipated change in value?

There are two primary sources of unanticipated risk:

- ❑ the occurrence of default; and
- ❑ unexpected credit migration.

Historically speaking, even for assets ranked in the highest credit rating category, the occurrence of default, though unlikely, is not an improbable event. This is demonstrated by very small probabilities of default, which are, nevertheless, non-zero. And if default does occur, there is going to be a significant change in the terminal value of the risky asset at the horizon.

The extent of the change in asset value is the difference between the actual realised value and the expected value at the horizon.

Default, of course, devalues the risky asset. Although it is not easy to predict the occurrence of default, a probability of default or an expected default frequency can always be attached to the asset. This can be done either on the basis of historical information (the route taken by rating agencies such as Standard & Poor's and Moody's) or through analytical methods based on options theory (for example, the "value of the firm" class of models used by the KMV Corporation). These alternatives were discussed at length in chapter 3. But, to recap briefly, rating agencies collect information on publicly rated firms, stratify the sample, apply statistical techniques and estimate the firms' probabilities of default and credit migration over a period of time. The analytical approach, on the other hand, is based on the theoretical premise that a firm will default on its debt obligation if the value of its assets falls below a critical threshold level of the book value of its liabilities.

The second cause of devaluation of a risky asset is an unanticipated change in its credit quality. This is known as "credit migration". For instance, if an obligor undergoes financial crisis during the period up to the analysis horizon, this can cause the credit quality of the asset to deteriorate. Such deterioration can significantly reduce the value of the asset, albeit not to the same extent as default. Conversely, a significant improvement in the financial condition of an obligor can bring about a dramatic increase in credit quality.

UNEXPECTED LOSS

The expected loss of an asset is the *average loss* the bank can expect to lose on its asset over the period up to a specified horizon; during that time the asset can fluctuate in value due to the two main sources of unanticipated risk mentioned above. The risk at the horizon can be conveniently measured using the standard deviation of the value at the horizon. We shall call this quantity the *unexpected loss*. In other words, unexpected loss is the estimated volatility of the potential loss in value of the asset around its expected loss.

As defined, the unexpected loss, UL_H, of the asset value V_H at the horizon t_H is simply the standard deviation of the *unconditional* value of the asset at the horizon:

$$UL_{\mathrm{H}} \equiv \sqrt{\mathrm{var}[V_{\mathrm{H}}]}$$

$$= \left\langle V_{\mathrm{H}}^2 \right\rangle - \left\langle V_{\mathrm{H}} \right\rangle^2 \quad \textbf{(5.1)}$$

From hereon the subscript H will be omitted. It will be implicitly assumed that we are referring to the value at the horizon, t_{H}, and that our analysis covers the period up to the horizon, $[t_0, t_{\mathrm{H}}]$, where default has some non-zero probability of occurring.

It is shown in Appendix A that the *unexpected loss* in the value of the risky asset is given by

$$UL = V_1 \times \sqrt{EDF \times \sigma_{LGD}^2 + LGD^2 \times \sigma_{EDF}^2} \quad \textbf{(5.2)}$$

where the variance of the default frequency, *EDF*, is given by

$$\sigma_{EDF}^2 = EDF \times (1 - EDF) \quad \textbf{(5.3)}$$

Equation (5.3) is simply the variance of a binomial distribution since the default process is assumed to be a two-state event (ie, binomial in nature) – that is, one consisting of default, D, or no default, $\bar{D}$. Keep in mind that if we assume a multi-state default process and allow the possibility of credit migration, the expression for the unexpected loss becomes much more complicated. Appendix A of the epilogue (see pages 269–73) contains a brief discussion of the multi-state default process.

Observe in equation (5.2) that the unexpected loss of the asset is *some fraction* of the risky part (ie, the *adjusted exposure*, *AE*) of the exposure amount V_1, attesting to the fact that the uncertainty in the risk of loss, as captured by the standard deviation of the asset value at the horizon, translates only to that portion of the adjusted exposure that could not be recovered by the bank in the event of default. This observation is in keeping with the earlier formulation of expected loss given by equation (4.7), as it should be.

Again, for consistency with the definition of expected loss given in the previous chapter and recognising that only the risky portion of V_1, ie, *AE*, is actually affected by default, we rewrite equation (5.2) more appropriately as

$$UL = AE \times \sqrt{EDF \times \sigma^2_{LGD} + LGD^2 \times \sigma^2_{EDF}} \quad \textbf{(5.4a)}$$

As evident from this equation, the multiplier, given by

$$\sqrt{EDF \times \sigma^2_{LGD} + LGD^2 \times \sigma^2_{EDF}} \quad \textbf{(5.4b)}$$

is dependent on the probability of default, *EDF*, and the loss given default, *LGD*, and their corresponding variances, σ^2_{EDF} and σ^2_{LGD}. If there were no uncertainty in default (ie, $\sigma^2_{EDF} = 0$) and no uncertainty in the recovery rate (ie, $\sigma^2_{LGD} = 0$), both of these variances would be identically zero, rendering *UL* also zero. In this case there is no uncertainty in the value of the asset at the horizon.

Assumptions

Explicit in the derivation of unexpected loss above is the assumption that the random risk factors contributing to an obligor's default (resulting in the default probability, *EDF*) are statistically independent of the severity of loss (as given by the loss given default, *LGD*). The reader is referred to Appendix A at the end of the chapter for clarification on this point.

If the risk factors contributing to the expected default frequency and loss given default were not independent, the multiplier in equation (5.4b) would contain covariance cross-terms owing to the nature of the variance calculation. However, in practice it is not clear whether or not the assumption of statistical independence is well justified. Our conjecture is that statistical dependence would require only a small corrective modification to the expression for unexpected loss.

We have reached the point where a simple example is necessary. The following example continues from the one in chapter 4, where the expected loss was calculated numerically (page 103).

Example – Calculation of unexpected loss

Consider a one-year loan facility, internally rated as risk class 3 (equivalent to a Standard & Poor's senior unsecured debt rating of BBB), with the characteristics listed in Table 5.1.

In contrast to the expected loss example considered in the

Table 5.1 Calculation of unexpected loss

COM	Commitment	\$10,000,000
OS	Outstanding	\$5,000,000
RC	Internal risk rating	3
	Maturity	1 year
	Type	Non-secured
UGD	Unused draw-down on default for $RC = 3$	65%
AE	Adjusted exposure on default $AE = OS + (COM - OS) \times UGD$	\$8,250,000
EDF	1-year default probability for $RC = 3$	0.15%
σ_{EDF}	Standard deviation of *EDF*	3.87%
LGD	Loss given default for non-secured asset	50%
σ_{LGD}	Standard deviation of *LGD*	25%
UL	Unexpected loss $UL = AE \times \sqrt{(EDF \times \sigma^2_{LGD} + LGD^2 \times \sigma^2_{EDF})}$	\$178,511

previous chapter, there are now two new items in the model: the standard deviation of *EDF* and the standard deviation of *LGD*. With a simplistic two-state default process, calculation of the former is trivial; however, the same cannot be said of the standard deviation of *LGD*. For illustrative purposes, we use $\sigma_{LGD} = 25\%$ in this example.

The calculated unexpected loss is \$178,511 or 2.16% of the adjusted exposure. An unanticipated loss of 216 basis points for just one facility is no laughing matter. Just imagine the cumulative loss from thousands of such facilities whose defaults are correlated to some degree. The unexpected losses can accumulate at a very rapid pace to the detriment of the bank.

In contrast, the expected loss for the same facility is only \$6,188 or 0.075% of the adjusted exposure. This example draws attention to how the unexpected loss can significantly exceed the expected loss and should therefore be a cause for concern in credit portfolio management.

ECONOMIC CAPITAL AND UNEXPECTED LOSS

If the unexpected loss is the uncertainty or unanticipated change in the value of the asset at the horizon, what then is the relationship between unexpected loss and economic capital?

Since the unexpected loss is the estimated volatility of potential loss in the value of the asset around its expected loss, it is imperative that the bank, which owns this asset, put aside sufficient capital to sustain the uncertain and potential loss and thereby be in a position to conduct business as usual should this loss in value be realised. The required capital reserve – which acts a buffer against insolvency for the bank in the event of default by an obligor – is known as *economic capital*. In the context of a risk-adjusted performance measure, it is also the issues surrounding economic capital that we are most concerned with when dealing with unexpected loss.

Observe from the foregoing discussion that the unexpected loss fluctuates with the value of the risky asset, so it stands to reason that the economic capital – as a measure of capital adequacy for the bank – will also fluctuate with the market value of each and every single risky asset held by the bank in its portfolio.

We shall return to this important topic when we address in detail the issues surrounding loss distribution and extreme value theory in chapters 8 and 10.

APPENDIX A – DERIVATION OF UNEXPECTED LOSS (UL)

Let the stochastic loss variable $\tilde{L}$ be distributed according to some density function $f(\tilde{L})$. At this point we do not need to know what the density of loss is. We shall, however, need to estimate its shape (more specifically, its tail) when it comes to determining the economic capital requirement. This will be discussed in more detail in chapters 8 and 10.

The following general statements are true:

$$\int f(\tilde{L})d\tilde{L} = 1 \qquad \text{Conservation of probability} \tag{A.5.1a}$$

$$<\tilde{L}> \equiv \int \tilde{L}\, f(\tilde{L})d\tilde{L} = LGD \qquad \text{Expectation of } \tilde{L} \tag{A.5.1b}$$

$$<\tilde{L}^2> \equiv \int \tilde{L}^2 f(\tilde{L})d\tilde{L} = \sigma_{\tilde{L}}^2 + LGD^2 \tag{A.5.1c}$$

Using the relationships above, we derive

$$\langle V_H \rangle = (1-EDF)V_0 + EDF\int f(\tilde{L})\left[V_0 - V_1\right]d\tilde{L}$$

$$= (1-EDF)V_0 + EDF\left[V_0 - V_1 \times LGD\right]$$

$$= V_0 - EDF \times V_1 \times LGD \qquad \textbf{(A.5.2)}$$

Note that the decoupling of *EDF* from the integral is possible only if one assumes that the random risk factors contributing to the default process are independent of the loss variable $\tilde{L}$. The same assumption is made in the derivations that follow here.

Similarly, we have

$$\langle V_H^2 \rangle = (1-EDF)V_0^2 + EDF\int f(\tilde{L})\left[V_0 - V_1\tilde{L}\right]^2 d\tilde{L}$$

$$= (1-EDF)V_0^2 + EDF\int f(\tilde{L})\left[V_0^2 - 2V_0V_1\tilde{L} + V_1^2\tilde{L}^2\right]d\tilde{L}$$

$$= (1-EDF)V_0^2 + EDF \times$$

$$\left[V_0^2 - 2V_0V_1 \times LGD + V_1^2\left(\sigma_{\tilde{L}}^2 + LGD^2\right)\right]$$

$$= V_0^2 - 2 \times EDF \times V_0V_1 \times LGD + EDF \times V_1^2\left(\sigma_{\tilde{L}}^2 + LGD^2\right)$$

(A.5.3)

Thus, the variance of the terminal asset value, V_H, is given by

$$\text{var}[V_H] = \langle V_H^2 \rangle - \langle V_H \rangle^2$$

$$= V_1^2 \times \left[EDF \times \sigma_{\tilde{L}}^2 + LGD^2 \times (EDF - EDF^2)\right]$$

$$\equiv V_1^2 \times \left[EDF \times \sigma_{\tilde{L}}^2 + LGD^2 \times \sigma_{EDF}^2\right] \qquad \textbf{(A.5.4)}$$

using the fact that the default process is assumed to be a two-state binomial process and that its variance is given by

$$\sigma^2_{EDF} = EDF \times (1 - EDF)$$

Hence, we have that the standard deviation of the terminal value of the asset is given by

$$\sigma_{V_H} = V_1 \times \sqrt{EDF \times \sigma^2_{\tilde{L}} + LGD^2 \times \sigma^2_{EDF}} \qquad \textbf{(A.5.5)}$$

This, as explained in the main text and illustrated in Figure 5.1, is the unexpected loss.

6

Portfolio Effects: Risk Contribution and Unexpected Loss

I begin this chapter with a comparison of expected loss and unexpected loss and use the insights gained to show how these two risk measures relate to an aggregate of risky assets in a *portfolio* context.

Default risk, unlike market risk, cannot be conveniently hedged away – even with the use of innovations in the capital markets such as credit derivatives or the ongoing impetus to asset securitisation. Interest rate movements, one of the driving forces behind market risk, can in principle be "netted out" by structuring, say, an equal and opposite position to neutralise the movements. Default risk, as a primary constituent of credit risk, is more subtle because it is driven primarily by the well-being of a firm and by its ability to fulfil its liabilities and contractual obligations, which of course is determined by market conditions in general.

Credit derivatives and asset securitisation programs are merely schemes to shift as much default risk away as possible, but, in the end, someone will be left holding the bag. The good news is that, although it cannot be hedged away, default risk can be reduced and managed through *diversification*. This is nothing new considering that portfolio theory has been around for more than 45 years and banks have been managing loan portfolios for many decades.

The aim of this chapter is to pave the way for a look at risky assets on an aggregate basis. To this end, we need to reformulate our thinking on how the unexpected loss in the value of a single asset should be reconsidered in a portfolio context.

Figure 6.1 *EL* and *UL* for *LGD* = 50%

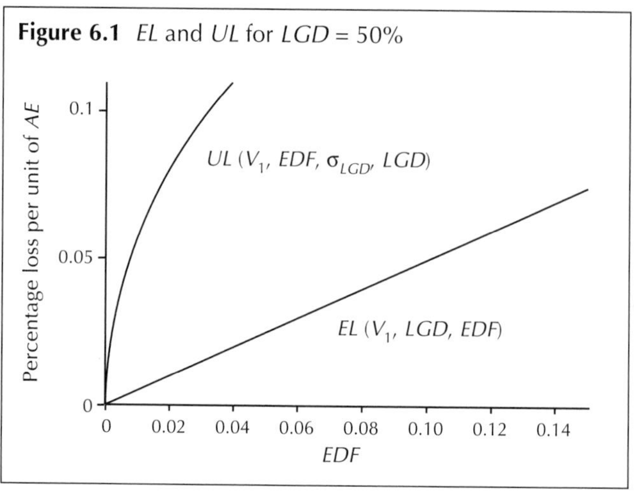

COMPARING EXPECTED LOSS AND UNEXPECTED LOSS

Using a simplistic two-state default process of either default or no default over a fixed horizon, we tackled separately in chapters 4 and 5 the loss characteristics of a single risky asset due to credit risk and introduced two risk measures, *expected loss* and *unexpected loss*. Interestingly, a comparison of the two equations

$$EL = V_1 \times LGD \times EDF \tag{4.7}$$

$$UL = V_1 \times \sqrt{EDF \times \sigma^2_{\text{LGD}} + LGD^2 \times \sigma^2_{\text{EDF}}} \tag{5.2}$$

shows that they depend on the exactly the same variables, except that the expression for *UL* contains additional second-order standard deviation statistics.

Unexpected loss represents the volatility or standard deviation of loss, whereas expected loss represents the average loss over the same fixed horizon. The loss, as usual, refers to the adjusted exposure, which is the risky portion of the value of the asset at the horizon. Figure 6.1 is a graphical display of the relationship between *EL* and *UL* as a function of the expected default frequency, *EDF*, for fixed values of V_1 = \$1.00, σ_{LGD} = 25% and *LGD* = 50%. The *x*-axis is *EDF* in percentage terms and the *y*-axis is the percentage loss per unit of the adjusted exposure.

Using a lower value for *LGD* of 25%, we obtain Figure 6.2.

Figure 6.2 *EL* and *UL* for *LGD* = 25%

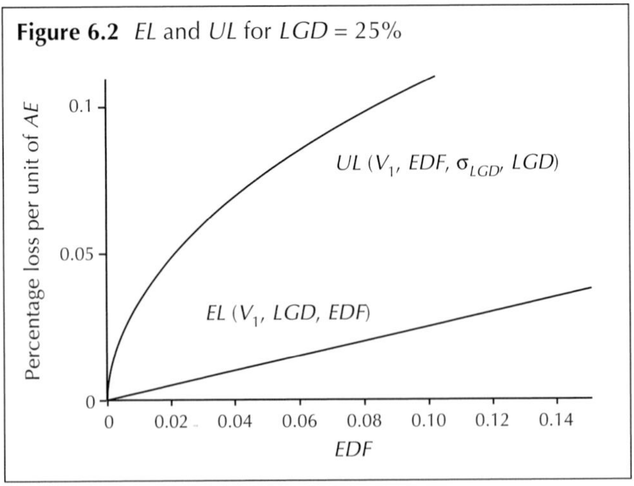

Comparing the two charts, we observe the following obvious intuitive points:

- The higher the recovery rate (ie, the lower the *LGD*), the lower is the percentage loss for both *EL* and *UL*.
- *EL* increases *linearly* with decreasing credit quality (ie, with increasing *EDF*).
- *UL* increases much faster (and *non-linearly*) than *EL* with increasing *EDF*.

THE ANALYSIS HORIZON AND TIME TO MATURITY

The points highlighted above are direct observations of the unexpected loss and expected loss under the assumption that, within a fixed time horizon, there are only two possibilities in the default process – default or non-default. No account has been taken of implicit credit migrations during this period. Unanticipated loss of asset value, however, can also arise as a consequence of credit migration. Therefore, in the period up to the analysis horizon, variation in asset value due to both default and credit migration can conceivably contribute to the volatility of loss. A simple explanation can be found in Appendix A.

This raises an important point concerning the estimation of unexpected loss for assets with varying terms to maturity and the fixed horizon that is chosen (one year being the standard) to analyse their embedded credit risk. The "time" issue also raises a question on the analysis of an aggregate of risky assets with different maturities. The longer the term to maturity, the greater the variation in asset value due to changes in credit quality, which may possibly result in a larger *UL*. In fact this can be inferred from the simple explanation of asset variation due to time effects given in Appendix A.

The internal credit risk models currently used by most banks tend to follow the simple two-state default process paradigm. This inherently ignores the credit losses associated with defaults that occur beyond the analysis horizon. Although the maturity differentials of the assets in the portfolio are important in practice, the risk of default takes precedence over the risk of credit migration in the overall pecking order of things. This explains why two-state default credit risk models are more widely used than full-blown multi-state migration models. And, as has already been pointed out, a two-state default model is decidedly easier to implement than a multi-state migration model.

To mitigate some of these maturity effects that relate to periods beyond a one-year analysis horizon, most banks attempt to alleviate the dilemma in two clever ways:

- *Adjusting a risky asset's internal credit class rating in accordance with its term to maturity* By assigning a lower internal risk rating to a longer-term asset than to a shorter-term asset, effectively banks have been able to assign a higher default probability to longer-term assets over the horizon, thereby increasing the variation in loss.
- *Use of several analysis horizons* Although the common standard of using one year as the analysis horizon is in line with risk-based capital standards and capital adequacy guidelines for market risk, many banks have opted to use several sequential horizons longer than one year. Depending on the confidence they place in their measurements, the most conservative results are chosen for planning or strategic purposes, including capital attribution.

The points considered in this section emphasise yet again the importance of sound and reliable internal risk class rating systems that are capable of distinguishing nuances due to maturity as well as other subtleties; and the unreliability of default probabilities over the longer horizon, whether these are inferred from historical information (as is done by the rating agencies) or whether they are theoretically calculated using "value of the firm" type models (as provided by some vendors). Appendix A of the epilogue provides a lengthy discussion of the issues surrounding multi-year analysis horizons.

With these "time" issues behind us, we can now proceed to our intended discussion on the effects of portfolio aggregation on credit loss.

PORTFOLIO EXPECTED LOSS

The concept of expected loss was discussed in the previous chapter as a measure for quantifying the average loss in value of a single risky asset. What is the expected loss for *two* risky assets?

It does not actually matter whether the two risky assets relate to the same obligor or to different obligors. In either case, the expected loss grows linearly with some attribute of the "credit event", as exemplified by the expected default frequency. Therefore, two different risky assets, A and B, that suffer average losses due to a credit event at some time during the analysis horizon have an aggregate average loss equal to the sum of the two average losses. Mathematically, we write the aggregate expected loss for the two assets as

$$EL_{\mathrm{P}} = EL_{\mathrm{A}} + EL_{\mathrm{B}}$$

or, more generally, for N risky assets indexed by $i = 1,2,\ldots,N$, we have

$$EL_{\mathrm{P}} \equiv \sum_i EL_i = \sum_i \left(AE_i \times LGD_i \times EDF_i \right) \qquad \textbf{(6.1)}$$

where EL_{P} is the expected loss for the portfolio. Again, the adjusted exposure, AE_i, refers only to the risky portion of the terminal value of the ith asset to which the bank is exposed in the event of default.

The portfolio expected loss, EL_{P}, then, is a simple sum of the individual expected losses from all the risky assets in the portfolio. Because of this linear and additive relationship, the topic needs little further discussion here.

Important convention All the formulas given here for EL and UL are measured in units of the adjusted exposure, which is denominated in currency terms – for example, US dollars. In practice, both measures are quoted in terms of some basis points of the adjusted exposure, ie:

$$\frac{EL}{AE} \quad \text{and} \quad \frac{UL}{AE}$$

In this case the portfolio expected loss, measured as a percentage of the adjusted exposure, is the *weighted* sum of the individual expected losses:

$$\frac{EL_P}{AE_P} = \sum_i \omega_i EL_i \tag{6.2a}$$

where the weights are defined as

$$\omega_i = \frac{AE_i}{\sum_i AE_i} \equiv \frac{AE_i}{AE_P} \tag{6.2b}$$

PORTFOLIO UNEXPECTED LOSS

In chapter 5 unexpected loss was discussed in the context of the volatility of loss in value of a *single* asset. In reality, the bank is exposed to a portfolio of risky assets that are each subject to default risk of varying degrees and severity. Therefore, in an aggregate portfolio context, it is imperative that we re-examine unexpected loss at two different levels:

- at the level of the single asset; and
- within the portfolio as a whole.

The two levels are *not* similar in nature!

In chapter 5 we saw that the unexpected loss of a single asset is defined as the volatility (or standard deviation) of the asset's loss of value around its average or expected loss.

For N risky assets indexed by $i = 1, 2, \ldots, N$, equation (B.6.4) in Appendix B of this chapter shows that the portfolio unexpected loss, denoted by UL_P and denominated in currency terms, is given by

$$UL_P = \left[\sum_i \sum_j \rho_{ij} UL_i UL_j \right]^{\frac{1}{2}} \qquad \textbf{(6.3a)}$$

where the individual unexpected losses are given by

$$UL_i = AE_i \times \sqrt{EDF_i \times \sigma^2_{LGD(i)} + LGD_i^2 \times \sigma^2_{EDF(i)}} \qquad \textbf{(6.3b)}$$

and ρ_{ij} denotes the correlation of default between asset *i* and asset *j*. (We shall deal with the issue of correlation of default in the next chapter.)

It is obvious from equation (6.3a) that

$$UL_P \neq \sum_i UL_i \qquad \textbf{(6.4a)}$$

This means that the portfolio unexpected loss is *not* equal to the linear sum of the individual unexpected losses of the risky assets that make up the aggregate portfolio. Because of diversification effects (benefits really!), the portfolio unexpected loss is very much smaller than the sum of the individual unexpected losses:

$$UL_P << \sum_i UL_i \qquad \textbf{(6.4b)}$$

This implies that only a portion of each asset's unexpected loss actually contributes to the portfolio's total risk of loss. This portion is called the *risk contribution*.

RISK CONTRIBUTION

How much *incremental* risk does a single risky asset contribute to the portfolio as a whole?

This is a very important question for two simple reasons:

- The first, obvious, reason comes from equations (6.4a) and (6.4b), which show that, unlike expected loss, individual unexpected losses do not add up to the total unexpected loss for the portfolio. The sum of these is actually much larger than the total risk in the portfolio. Therefore, when assessing the risk and return characteristics of a single risky asset in a portfolio context, it becomes necessary to ask how much risk this asset contributes to the whole portfolio and what kind of return can be expected of this asset for the level of risk it contributes to the portfolio.

- The second reason is a corollary of the first. In an economic downturn such as a recession the incidence of default is more frequent. Most banks, by virtue of their expertise, are quite specialised in particular industry sectors and, therefore, suffer from concentration risk. That is to say, most bank loan portfolios are highly concentrated in terms of their exposure to specific types of industry and are, therefore, highly susceptible to correlated default and credit migration events. To continue their roles as financial intermediaries in the market, banks need a better tool to measure the extent of diversification in their portfolios and thereby make good use of this knowledge for strategic purposes.

Risk contribution is that measure which can properly answer the question posed above. In fact, from a portfolio management perspective, risk contribution is the single most important risk measure for assessing credit risk.

The *risk contribution* of a risky asset, denoted by *RC*, to the portfolio unexpected loss is defined as the incremental risk that the exposure of a single asset contributes to the portfolio's total risk. Mathematically, we write the risk contribution of asset i as

$$RC_i \equiv UL_i \frac{\partial UL_{\mathrm{P}}}{\partial UL_i} \tag{6.5a}$$

Observe that the risk contribution of asset i is measured in terms of the units of unexpected loss of asset i, or UL_i.

From equation (6.5a), we can see that the risk contribution of asset i, RC_i, is a sensitivity measure, as represented by the partial derivative, of the portfolio unexpected loss with respect to the unexpected loss of asset i. Furthermore, by performing the actual differentiation on equation (6.3a), it can easily be shown that

$$RC_i = \frac{UL_i \sum_j UL_j \rho_{ij}}{UL_{\mathrm{P}}} \tag{6.5b}$$

This is the equation that is used in practice. However, in the presence of many industry groupings the indexing scheme in Appendix C may be easier to implement.

UNDIVERSIFIABLE RISK

The risk contribution is a measure of the *undiversified risk* of an asset in the portfolio. It is the amount of credit risk which cannot be diversified away by placing the asset in the portfolio. The best way to view risk contribution is to consider it as the smallest unit of credit risk in a given portfolio – a unit that is no longer decomposable into smaller units. The sum of all these small risk contributions, of course, is the totality of the portfolio unexpected loss. This is shown below in equation (6.6).

Knowledge of the risk contribution of a single asset, therefore, allows us to modify the risk profile of the portfolio by changing the risk characteristic of this asset. In addition, knowing the smallest unit of risk also facilitates a better measurement of the return on the asset. That is why risk contribution is the most important risk measure in credit portfolio management. Returning to the question posed at the beginning of the preceding section, this highlights the first reason given for the importance of knowing the incremental risk to the portfolio.

In fact, by summing equation (6.5b) over the index i, one can easily demonstrate the relationship

$$UL_{\mathrm{P}} = \sum_{i} RC_i \tag{6.6}$$

Equation (6.6) states that the sum of all the risk contributions from all the assets in the portfolio is, indeed, the portfolio unexpected loss. This is no accident – equation (6.5a) was defined with this objective of summability in mind.

RISK CONTRIBUTION AND CORRELATION OF DEFAULT

In line with the second reason given for the importance of the incremental risk contribution of an asset to a portfolio, we need to know how the risk contribution is related to the correlation of default and how this relationship affects concentration risk in the credit portfolio. We shall tackle this important issue in the next chapter, although Appendix C at the end of this chapter gives a preview of the difficulty.

In practice, given the size of a bank's typical credit portfolio, it is quite difficult to determine the individual correlation of default between two assets (ie, between two obligors). It is, therefore, also

Table 6.1 Data for two-asset portfolio example

Exposure 1		
COM_1	Commitment	\$10,000,000
OS_1	Outstanding	\$5,000,000
RC_1	Internal risk rating	3
	Maturity	1 year
	Type	Non-secured
UGD_1	Unused draw-down on default for $RC = 3$	65%
AE_1	Adjusted exposure on default $AE = OS + (COM - OS) \times UGD$	\$8,250,000
EDF_1	1-year default probability for $RC = 3$	0.15%
σ_{EDF_1}	Standard deviation of EDF_1	3.87%
LGD_1	Loss given default for non-secured asset	50%
σ_{LGD_1}	Standard deviation of LGD_1	25%
EL_1	Expected loss $EL = AE \times EDF \times LGD$	\$6,188
UL_1	Unexpected loss $UL = AE \times \sqrt{(EDF \times \sigma^2_{LGD} + LGD^2 \times \sigma^2_{EDF})}$	\$178,511
Exposure 2		
COM_2	Commitment	\$2,000,000
OS_2	Outstanding	\$1,500,000
RC_2	Internal risk rating	5
	Maturity	3 years
	Type	Secured
UGD_2	Unused draw-down on default for $RC = 5$	48%
AE_2	Adjusted exposure on default $AE = OS + (COM - OS) \times UGD$	\$1,740,000
EDF_2	1-year default probability for $RC = 5$	4.85%
σ_{EDF_2}	Standard deviation of EDF_2	21.48%
LGD_2	Loss given default for secured asset	35%
σ_{LGD_2}	Standard deviation of LGD_2	24%
EL_2	Expected loss $EL = AE \times EDF \times LGD$	\$29,537
UL_2	Unexpected loss $UL = AE \times \sqrt{(EDF \times \sigma^2_{LGD} + LGD^2 \times \sigma^2_{EDF})}$	\$159,916

Table 6.2 Calculations for two-asset portfolio example

Portfolio = Exposure 1 + Exposure 2		
ρ	Default correlation between the two exposures	3.00%
EL_P	Portfolio expected loss	\$35,724
	$EL_P = EL_1 + EL_2$	
UL_P	Portfolio unexpected loss	\$243,212
	$UL_P = \sqrt{(UL_1 \times UL_1 + UL_2 \times UL_2 + 2\rho \times UL_1 \times UL_2)}$	
RC_1	Risk contribution from Exposure 1	\$134,543
	$RC_1 = UL_1 \times (UL_1 + UL_2 \times \rho)/UL_P$	
RC_2	Risk contribution from Exposure 2	\$108,669
	$RC_2 = UL_2 \times (UL_2 + UL_1 \times \rho)/UL_P$	
Sums of *RC* and *UL*		
	$RC_1 + RC_2 = UL_P$	\$243,212
	$UL_1 + UL_2 \gg UL_P$	\$338,427

quite difficult to calculate the individual risk contributions incorporating pairwise correlation of default among all the obligors in the portfolio. For a relatively small portfolio of $N = 100$ obligors, there are 4,950 possible pairs of default correlation to consider. Imagine the amount of work needed for a moderately large portfolio of $N = 3{,}000$ obligors!

Appendix C shows how risk contribution can easily be calculated by broadly classifying assets under some standard industry groupings, effectively reducing the number of pairwise correlations. For implementation purposes, it is advisable to follow the equations derived in that appendix.

At this point it would be beneficial to pause for some numerical calculations. Using the building blocks introduced so far, let us consider a sample portfolio containing only two risky assets.

Example – Calculation of EL, UL and RC for a two-asset portfolio
This example provides another opportunity to sharpen our calculation skills for single asset expected loss and unexpected loss. The portfolio consists of two risky assets, Exposure 1 and Exposure 2. We need to determine the risk contribution of each asset to the portfolio as a whole. Details of the assets are given in Table 6.1 and the calculations are set out in Table 6.2.

The computations are self-explanatory and there is little further to discuss. Observe that the sum of the two *UL* for the two exposures is much larger than the portfolio *UL*. How much larger depends entirely on the degree of correlation of default between the two obligors. In contrast, as we would expect, the sum of the two *RC* add up to the portfolio *UL*. It is important that readers figure out for themselves why the portfolio *EL* is so much smaller than the portfolio *UL*. If this were not the case, the loan loss reserves (equal to the portfolio *EL*) required of the bank would be astronomically burdensome.

APPENDIX A – VARIATION IN ASSET VALUE DUE TO TIME EFFECTS*

We want to show that the value of a risky asset, over time, can demonstrate a great deal of volatility (or variation) due to two major time effects: default and credit migration.

Consider, for simplicity, the value of a loan commitment with a current outstanding or notional amount denoted by A. The current value of the loan can easily be valued by discounting the various cashflows as follows:

$$V = \sum_{k=1}^{M} \frac{C_k}{(1+r_k)^k} + \frac{A + C_M}{(1+r_M)^M} \tag{A.6.1}$$

where C_k is the cash payment for the kth period, M is the maturity of the loan, and r_k is the yield of the loan for the kth period, which depends on the credit rating, R.

For pedagogical purposes and without loss of generality, assume that the payment frequency is annual, although payment frequency is somewhat irrelevant to this discussion. Suppose that we choose an analysis horizon of one year. At the end of one year the loan may have migrated to another credit rating class or it might already have defaulted. Thus, the expected value, V_1, of the loan at the end of one year is the probability-weighted value of all possible values in each rating class R:

$$V_1 = AC + \sum_R p_R (V_R - \Delta_R) \tag{A.6.2}$$

*This appendix is based on an internal note written by Weixiong Li.

These values are denoted by V_R, where the index R runs over all possible risk classes or states.

What are the other quantities in the equation? The first term, AC, represents the accrued cash payments compounded to the end of analysis horizon (ie, their future value). The sum is over all the possible ratings, and p_R is the migration or transition probability associated with risk class R. The quantity Δ_R represents the expected amount of additional draw-down of the commitment given a downgrade in credit rating. It also represents the additional pay-down (ie, repayment) of the loan if there is an upgrade. Obviously, if U is the unused portion of the commitment, the restriction $-A \le \Delta_R \le U$ holds. In general, Δ_R is positive when there is a downgrade and negative when there is an upgrade.

Notice that V_R should be calculated using the one-year forward yield curve corresponding to the credit rating R, with the amount Δ_R added to the notional amount of the commitment and the cash-flow properly adjusted. This results in

$$V_R = \sum_{k=1}^{M-1} \frac{C'_k}{(1+r_{1k})^k} + \frac{A+\Delta_R+C'_{M-1}}{(1+r_{1,M-1})^{M-1}} \tag{A.6.3}$$

where r_{1k} is the one-year forward yield for risk rating R and is, therefore, a function of the risk rating R. C'_k is the adjusted cashflow due to change in the outstanding by an amount Δ_R.

At the one-year analysis horizon, the variance of V_1 about the mean, representing the variation or volatility of the change in asset value, can then easily be calculated as

$$\sigma_1^2 = \sum_R p_R (V_R - \Delta_R)^2 - \left[\sum_R p_R (V_R - \Delta_R)\right]^2 \tag{A.6.4}$$

Observe that, inherently in equation (A.6.4), the variation in the loan value contains information associated with both the probability of default and the probability of migration to all the possible risk rating classes. In addition, the variation also depends on the additional draw-down of unused commitments (in the case of downward migration) and on the pay-down of the current outstanding (in the case of upward migration).

Expression (A.6.4) for the variance of the expected value of the loan at the end of one year assumes that there is no further uncertainty in the valuation of the loan. This, however, is not true, as there may be other sources of randomness. For example:

- In the case of default, the percentage of loss given default has some uncertainty and we usually assume that a bell-shaped distribution with a mean and standard deviation suffices.
- Additionally, the amount of draw-down on migration (more appropriately, the usage given migration in contrast to the usage given default) is actually a random variable that has different probability distributions depending on the rating to which the loan migrates at the end of the one-year analysis horizon.

If it can be assumed that all the other random variables are statistically independent, we can generalise the expression for variance as

$$\sigma_1^2 = \sum_R p_R \left[(V_R - \Delta_R)^2 + S_R^2 \right] - \left[\sum_R p_R (V_R - \Delta_R) \right]^2 \qquad \textbf{(A.6.5)}$$

where S_R^2 is the sum of all the variances arising from other sources of randomness. In a practical implementation of an internal credit risk model, it is usual to include only the randomness in loss given default.

APPENDIX B – DERIVATION OF PORTFOLIO *UL*

Recall from the Appendix A of chapter 5 that the variance of the terminal value of a single risky asset at the horizon, t_H, is given by

$$\begin{aligned} \text{var}\left[V_H\right] &= \left\langle V_H^2 \right\rangle - \left\langle V_H \right\rangle^2 \\ &\equiv V_1^2 \times \left[EDF \times \sigma_{LGD}^2 + LGD^2 \times \sigma_{EDF}^2 \right] \end{aligned} \qquad \textbf{(B.6.1)}$$

For N risky assets indexed by $i = 1, 2, \ldots, N$, we now need the variance of the weighted sum of these asset values at the horizon, viz:

$$\text{var}\left[\sum_i \omega_i V_i\right] = \left\langle \left(\sum_i \omega_i V_i \right)^2 \right\rangle - \left\langle \left(\sum_i \omega_i V_i \right) \right\rangle^2 \qquad \textbf{(B.6.2)}$$

The subscript H, denoting the value at the horizon, has been intentionally suppressed in the equation above.

As in Appendix A of chapter 5, we need not know at this point in time the density function, $f(\tilde{L})$, of the loss distribution corresponding to the stochastic loss variable $\tilde{L}$. The expectations $<*>$ in equation (B.6.2) can easily be integrated with respect to this distribution function to yield the standard deviation given by

$$UL_P \equiv \sqrt{\mathrm{var}\left[\sum_i \omega_i V_i\right]} = \left[\sum_i \sum_j \omega_i \omega_j \rho_{ij} UL_i UL_j\right]^{\frac{1}{2}} \qquad \textbf{(B.6.3)}$$

where ρ_{ij} denotes the correlation of default between asset i and asset j, and ω_i is the portfolio weight for asset i such that $\sum_i \omega_i = 1$.

Convention Since equation (B.6.2) is calculated in terms of weighted average, the portfolio unexpected loss, UL_P, in equation (B.6.3) is measured in units of percentage of the portfolio adjusted exposure, AE_P – that is, UL_P/AE_P. In currency terms (say, US dollars) and for consistency with the units used in previous chapters, the proper equation to use in practice is

$$UL_P = \left[\sum_i \sum_j \rho_{ij} UL_i UL_j\right]^{\frac{1}{2}} \qquad \textbf{(B.6.4)}$$

APPENDIX C – DERIVATION OF RC_k

Using the definition of risk contribution and applying it to asset k, from equation (6.5a) we have

$$RC_k \equiv UL_k \frac{\partial UL_P}{\partial UL_k}$$

$$= UL_k \times \frac{1}{2UL_P}\left[2UL_k + 2\sum_{i \neq k} UL_i \rho_{ik}\right]$$

(denote all UL quantities hereon by U)

$$= \frac{U_k}{U_P}\left[U_k + \sum_i U_i \rho_{ik} - U_k \rho_{kk}\right]$$

$$= \frac{U_k}{U_P}\left[U_k(1-\rho_{kk}) + \sum_i U_i \rho_{ik}\right]$$

The indices in the equations above refer to assets. In a practical implementation the number of pairwise correlations can be reduced by categorising the assets into the appropriate standard industry groupings.

To incorporate industry correlation, we introduce two industry indices, α and β, using the schema

$$k \rightarrow \text{ind}\,\alpha \quad \text{and} \quad i \rightarrow \text{ind}\,\beta \tag{C.6.2}$$

With the industry schema, we have

$$RC_k = \frac{U_k}{U_P}\left[U_{k\in\alpha}\left(1-\rho_{\alpha\alpha}\right) + \sum_{\beta}\left(\sum_{j\in\beta}U_j\right)\rho_{\alpha\beta}\right] \tag{C.6.3}$$

This completes the derivation of the risk contribution due to asset k.

Finally, by multiplying both sides by U_P, we recover the portfolio unexpected loss:

$$\begin{aligned} U_P^2 &= U_P \times \sum_k RC_k \\ &= \sum_k U_k \times \left\{U_{k\in\alpha}\left(1-\rho_{\alpha\alpha}\right) + \sum_{\beta}\left(\sum_{j\in\beta}U_j\right)\rho_{\alpha\beta}\right\} \end{aligned} \tag{C.6.4}$$

For implementation purposes, we use equations (C.6.3) and (C.6.4) for *RC* and *UL* rather than the general equations for these terms given in the main text of the chapter (6.5b for *RC* and 6.6 for UL_P).

7

Correlation of Default and Credit Quality

In the previous chapter, we observed that the pairwise correlation of default, ρ_{ij}, between asset i and asset j is very important when assessing the totality of portfolio risk. We learned earlier that the totality of the credit risk embedded in the portfolio can be quantified by the so-called portfolio unexpected loss, UL_P. More specifically, in the context of proactive risk management and risk mitigation, the intrinsic risk embedded in the portfolio needs to be considered with respect to the risk contribution, RC_i, of the individual asset to the whole portfolio. The correlation of default is the glue that binds all of the risk contributions of the individual assets to the portfolio as a whole.

As a consequence of the statements above, from a credit risk management and measurement perspective, the following three issues are one and the same:

- Correlation of default
- Concentration risk
- Diversification.

The close link between the three items above is a direct consequence of the relationship between the portfolio unexpected loss and the risk contribution of the individual assets to the portfolio's overall risk characteristics. The glue that ties the risk contribution of a risky asset to the totality of the portfolio is default correlation. In turn, an aggregate of risk contributions from several risky assets dictates the level of concentration risk in the portfolio. Finally, the level of concentration risk decides on the degree of diversification in the portfolio.

But, unfortunately, however important its role in the bigger scheme of things, the correlation of default is by far the most problematic of all parameters in credit risk modelling – default correlation cannot be measured directly!

In this chapter I will discuss the major elements of incorporating correlation into the credit risk modelling process. The main chapter focuses on default correlation, but Appendix D discusses at length the joint movement of credit quality. The first two sections of the chapter distinguish the correlation of default with the correlation of credit quality, followed by a sample calculation of the default correlation between two obligors. Because many of the required elements are not directly inferable from the marketplace, we need to resort to some kind of proxy mechanism. The section "Industry index and asset correlation" discusses how this proxy can be achieved. The final section of the chapter extends the framework to a multifactor case.

Diversification in the banking book (eg, the credit portfolio) of an institution is not as easily achievable as in the trading book since credit risk cannot be readily hedged away like market risk. Admittedly, without a careful plan on how the correlation of default can be parameterised in a credit model, it would be impossible to assess the level of concentration and the degree of diversification in the portfolio.

CORRELATION OF CREDIT QUALITY

Although we talk only about default correlation, there are actually two levels to consider when addressing issues related to the general topic of correlation:

- ❏ Correlation of default
- ❏ Correlation of credit quality.

The two are related but not the same. In a two-state default process of either default or non-default during a fixed analysis horizon, the only important consideration is how well correlated are defaults between two obligors during the horizon. In other words, "How does the default of one obligor affect the financial well-being (or default status) of other obligors in the portfolio?" In a multi-state default process where credit migration is permissible, it is very important to ask a different but related question: "How does the credit quality movement of one obligor affect the credit quality of the other obligors in the portfolio?"

In general, the higher the degree of correlation in either case, the greater is the volatility in the portfolio value attributable to credit risk. Using a portfolio of rated corporate bonds as an example, a recent study by Moody's[1] showed there is ample evidence that a positive credit quality correlation among the issuers affects the distribution of the future value of a portfolio, suggesting the significant impact of credit quality correlation on the general risk profile of a portfolio. Furthermore, credit quality correlation is determined, in part, by factors specific to both the issuer's industry and geographic classification. Therefore, the country of domicile and the obligor's specific industry classification (or compositions, in the case of multinationals) are also relevant factors affecting correlation.

The Moody's study includes the credit histories of over 14,000 US and non-US corporate debt issuers for the years 1920–1996. The following results are direct quotes from the summary of the study:

- "Over the past 77 years sudden large changes in credit quality have been very infrequent. Of all ratings since 1920, only 11% involved changes of more than one rating category."
- "Higher ratings have been generally less likely than lower ratings to be revised over any time period from one to 15 years."
- "When the higher-end investment-grade ratings have changed, they have demonstrated a greater propensity for downward movement than upward."
- "There is evidence that movements in credit qualities of different issuers are correlated with each other and that the strength of this correlation is determined, in part, by macroeconomic, industrial, geographic, and temporal factors. The extent to which the changes in credit quality among different issuers in a portfolio are or are not correlated can have a significant impact on the overall volatility of that portfolio."

The results above strengthen our conviction that correlation effects need to be considered carefully in the risk management and measurement of credit portfolios. More importantly, it is absolutely vital that the parameterisation of any internal credit risk models properly take into account the factors mentioned earlier.

CORRELATION OF DEFAULT

If it can be argued that the fortunes of individual obligors are linked together via the condition of their specific industry and the condition of the general economy, to a very large extent all obligors must, therefore, suffer or prosper together. This is what the correlation of default is all about.

When using the term "correlation of default" in practice, however, what exactly does it mean? Correlation of default is really a very strong statement: "If Obligor A defaults, and Obligor B has a joint probability of defaulting at the same time, what is the correlation of these two default events?" In other words, the question asks about the likelihood of one obligor's defaulting on its contractual obligations that could affect the contemporaneous defaults of other obligors.

A weaker, albeit much better, statement should read: "If Obligor A's credit quality deteriorates, how well does the credit quality of Obligor B correlate to Obligor A?" Implicit in this version of the question is one thorny aspect of credit migration. Although this is a very difficult question to answer, there are some empirical observations on the matter. They are based on Moody's Investors Services historical data from 1970 through 1993 and reported in the article by Lucas (1995). Briefly, the important findings can be summarised as follows:

❑ *Default correlations are generally low although they decrease as ratings increase.* Default correlations among highly rated obligors are very small since defaults for these obligors, besides being rare events, are typically the result of obligor-specific problems. Lower-rated obligors on the cusp of default are more susceptible to downturns in the economy and are, therefore, more likely to default *en masse* in line with shifts in the state of the general economy.

❑ *Default correlations generally increase initially with time and then decrease as the horizon extends longer.* The explanation given in the article is that the occurrence of defaults over a shorter horizon is necessarily random in nature and the decrease over longer time periods may be caused by the relationship of the time period studied to the average business cycle.

❑ *Default among and between specific industries are inconclusive.*

It is advisable to compare the points articulated above with the analytical conclusions reached in Appendix B.

In general, default correlation can be estimated in one of three ways:

- Given two obligors' asset volatilities and their variance–covariance structure, calculate analytically their joint probability of default and impute the default correlation.
- Use Monte Carlo simulation on a specific choice of risky debt model from chapter 3 and impute the covariance structure.
- Use historical default data and statistically calculate pairwise correlation of default.

The historical data "brute force" approach does not capture any obligor-specific information so the results can be difficult to interpret. Monte Carlo simulation is not a practical solution given its lack of speed and enormous number-crunching requirements. This leaves us with the first alternative: impute default correlation from obligor-specific information – namely, the asset volatilities and their market-implied asset correlation.

Fortunately, although market-driven information on default correlation is not available, information about asset correlation is, in fact, available. Pairwise correlation of default needs to be either mathematically calculated or implied assuming some joint-default distribution. The joint-default distribution is probably normal – but who knows?

The correlation of default between two assets, i and j, is derived in Appendix A. The mathematical expression is restated below for reference:

$$\rho_{ij} = \frac{P\left(D_i \cdot D_j\right) - EDF_i \cdot EDF_j}{\sqrt{EDF_i\left(1-EDF_i\right)} \cdot \sqrt{EDF_j\left(1-EDF_j\right)}} \qquad \textbf{(7.1)}$$

where the joint probability of default, $P(D_i \cdot D_j) = EDF_i + EDF_j - P(D_i + D_j)$ and $P(D_i + D_j)$ is the probability that at least one obligor has defaulted.

There are two mathematical statements in equation (7.1): both default; and at least one of them defaults. Thus, there are two possible routes to take:

- ❑ Compute the joint probability of default, $P(D_i \cdot D_j)$, by making some assumptions about the distribution of the jointedness; or
- ❑ Calculate the probability, $P(D_i + D_j)$, that at least one default has occurred.

Given a pair of obligors, all the quantities in equation (7.1) are known except for the joint probability of default, $P(D_i \cdot D_j)$. Additional assumptions are required on the joint distribution of pairwise default. It is by no means a trivial exercise.

For our practical purpose in the example below, I shall take the first route and make the bold assumption that the joint probability of default is normally distributed. Appendix B takes the second route and gives a much more precise result based on a so-called first-passage time model but at the expense of introducing more parameters that are difficult and inherently subjective to estimate.

Appendix D extends the two-state default process to a more general multi-state default process that allows the possibility of credit migration.

I first illustrate some correlation of default calculations invoking the first route and using a simple example below. An example for the multi-state default process is given in Appendix D.

Example 7.1 – Correlation of default
Suppose that each default probability is assumed to be standard normal, then $P(D_i \cdot D_j)$ is jointly bivariate standard normal. The following MathCad file demonstrates the calculation.

Suppose the asset correlation between Asset A and Asset B is $\rho := 0.19$. The respective default probabilities for Asset A and Asset B are given by

$$EDF_a := 0.0062 \qquad \text{and} \qquad EDF_b := 0.0025$$

and the asset volatilities are

$$S_a := 0.3 \qquad \text{and} \qquad S_b := 0.6$$

The respective upper limits of integration for the joint probability of default are the inverse normals given by

$$D_a := \text{qnorm}(EDF_a, 0, S_a), \qquad D_a = -0.75$$

$$D_b := \text{qnorm}(EDF_b, 0, S_b), \qquad D_b = -1.404$$

Thus, the joint default probability, *JDP*, can be calculated as

$$JDP := \int_{-10}^{D_b}\int_{-10}^{D_a} \frac{1}{\left(2\cdot\pi\cdot S_a\cdot S_b\cdot\sqrt{1-\rho^2}\right)}\times$$

$$\exp\left\{-\frac{1}{2}\cdot\frac{1}{1-\rho^2}\cdot\left[\left(\frac{x}{S_a}\right)^2 - 2\cdot\rho\cdot\left(\frac{x\cdot y}{S_a\cdot S_b}\right)+\left(\frac{y}{S_b}\right)^2\right]\right\}dx\,dy$$

resulting in

$$JDP = 6.504\times 10^{-5}$$

Hence, using equation (7.1), the default correlation between A and B is

$$Default\ \rho_{ab} := \frac{JDP - EDF_a \times EDF_b}{\sqrt{EDF_a\left(1-EDF_a\right)\times EDF_b\left(1-EDF_b\right)}}$$

$$= 0.013$$

Observe from the equations above that the integral is invariant under a scale transformation of x and y variables by the asset volatilities, σ_A and σ_B, respectively. In effect, the integration can be simplified to a standardised *unit* bivariate normal without using the asset volatilities at all.

DEFAULT CORRELATION MATRIX AND SOME IMPORTANT OBSERVATIONS

Here are some observations and comments regarding the default correlation matrix.

- The calculated default correlation of 0.013 is at least an order of magnitude smaller than the asset correlation, 0.19. Indeed, there is very strong empirical evidence supporting this observation.
- There is a common myth that the typical range of default correlation is between 1% and 5%, but this is more an "average". Correlations within the same industry tend to be significantly higher than this range. In Appendix C the default correlation matrix for industry groups demonstrates the point. The sample

correlation matrix was calculated in a manner similar to the example above.

- Is the correlation between obligors belonging to the *same* industry group equal to 1.0? The answer is obviously not; otherwise, the answer to the following question would also be yes: "If General Motors defaults, does Ford Motors and everyone else in the automobile industry group default?" An affirmative answer is, of course, silly. Therefore, the correlation between obligors within the same industry group must be much less than 1.0!

For a large credit portfolio consisting of many obligors, it is quite cumbersome to consider all possible pairwise default correlations. A portfolio consisting of just 100 obligors requires almost 5,000 pairs of default correlations. To this end, we can resort to short cuts by lumping obligors into industry-specific groupings.

Appendix C is the resulting default correlation matrix as implied from an asset correlation matrix. With some assumptions regarding obligor-specific risk, the calculations are very similar to those presented in Example 7.1 above. The industry groupings used in the calculations are official Standard & Poor's industry classifications. The next few sections will elaborate further on some caveats and the rationale in the industry classification as part of our attempt to be practical when deriving correlation information.

INDUSTRY INDEX AND ASSET CORRELATION

In principle, pairwise default correlations between obligors need to be calculated, but this is not practical given the number of pairs to consider and also given the paucity of correlation information between individual assets. For a credit portfolio containing $N = 100$ obligors, there are 4,950 possible pairs of correlations to consider. For a bank credit portfolio of moderate size, say $N = 2{,}000$ obligors, there are 1,999,000 possible pairs of default correlations that need to be calculated. It is clearly impractical to incorporate a full-blown default correlation calculation between all possible pairs of obligors. What should one do in this situation?

In previous sections, we saw some indications that industry- and geography-specific information can play an important role in the co-movement of defaults between obligor pairs in the portfolio. Therefore, as an approximation – albeit a good one – we resort to indexing all the obligors in the portfolio by industry group and then calculating only the default correlation between industry groups. The practical implication is that default correlation among obligors simply becomes a "look-up" of the industry default correlation matrix. Only one unique industry code is assigned to each obligor. Not only does this cut down on the number of required pairwise correlations but, in fact, in the bigger scheme of things, our implementation shows that it actually does not result in any significant loss of material information. As an added bonus to grouping by industry, the resulting covariance matrix also exhibits "block structure" and is certainly easier to handle.

It was also explained earlier in the previous chapter that default correlation, concentration risk and diversification are one and the same issue. To this end, our scheme to use industry groupings in lieu of a full-blown pairwise default correlation has two fundamental objectives:

- ❑ to minimise the number of default correlation calculations; and
- ❑ to highlight the risk of concentration effects using industry-specific groupings as a point of discussion.

In principle, however, geography-specific concentration risk also needs to be highlighted, but we shall consider this aspect a trivial corollary of our current effort.

To determine default correlation between industry indexes as outlined above, we need to determine first the *asset correlation* among industry indexes. The next section presents the methodology and a simple example.

ESTIMATING ASSET CORRELATION

Following JP Morgan's CreditMetrics, we use S&P index correlation as a proxy for asset correlation between industries. For consistency, the original S&P index matrix is downloaded from JP Morgan's website at http://www.creditmetrics.com.

Suppose we wish to calculate the correlation of default between two obligors, A and B. What should we do if only the following public information is available to us?

- ❑ Equity returns of the obligors can be explained by some given percentage of the returns of some Standard & Poor's industry indexes.

- ❑ A given percentage of the equity returns of the obligors can be explained only by company-specific movements.
- ❑ Company-specific movements are largely independent of industry-specific movements.
- ❑ Returns of the Standard & Poor's industry indexes have derivable and stable standard deviations.

The claim is that, given the information above, it is sufficient to determine an *approximate* default correlation between the two obligors.

To this effect, consider the following notations. Let Obligor A and Obligor B be indexed by industry groups α and β, respectively, and let $\rho_{\alpha\beta}$ be the industry correlation between indexes α and β.

Let us start with the simplest discussion and allow room for a generalisation later. Suppose that the *asset return*, r^A, of Obligor A is the weighted average of two returns, *industry return*, r_α, and *obligor-specific return*, $\hat{r}^A$:

$$r^A = \omega_1^A r_\alpha + \omega_2^A \hat{r}^A \qquad \textbf{(7.2a)}$$

The practical interpretation of equation (7.2a) is that the asset return of Obligor A can be sufficiently explained by the index return of the industry classification to which the firm belongs, with a residual part that can be explained solely by information unique and specific to the firm. The obligor-specific information may involve both qualitative and quantitative statements about the firm's senior management, financial condition, leverage ratios, etc.

Similarly, the asset return for Obligor B can be written as

$$r^B = \omega_1^B r_\beta + \omega_2^B \hat{r}^B \qquad \textbf{(7.2b)}$$

where again, there are two parts, namely, one related to the industry β and the other representing the obligor-specific return $\hat{r}^B$.

The obligor-specific returns are also known as "idiosyncratic returns" for the respective obligors. We now make an assumption that the idiosyncratic returns are independent – ie, $\rho(\hat{r}^A, \hat{r}^B) = 0$. Using this assumption, we can now easily determine the correlation of asset returns between Obligor A and Obligor B:

$$\rho(A, B) = \omega_1^A \times \omega_1^B \times \rho_{\alpha\beta} \qquad \textbf{(7.3)}$$

In the context of this chapter, equation (7.3) shall, henceforth, be called the "asset correlation". It is this asset correlation number, $\rho(A, B)$, in addition to the standard deviations of the two index returns, that were used in chapter 6 to impute the default correlation.

There is empirical evidence to show that, on average, a typical asset correlation across a portfolio is somewhere in the range of 20% to 35%.

Observe that in equation (7.2) the industry-specific returns can be generalised to multi-industry returns. In this case, the resulting framework is then similar to a multifactor macroeconomic regression analysis. I shall briefly touch on this generalisation later on in the chapter.

OBLIGOR-SPECIFIC RISK

The first weight, $\omega_1^{A \text{ or } B}$, in equation (7.2) is easily determined once the composition of a firm's business and industry classifications (notice the plurality of industry classifications) is known and can be indexed to the standard Standard & Poor's industry classification. How to determine the second weight is a different story.

"How does one determine the second weight associated with an obligor's specific and idiosyncratic return?" To answer this question requires the answer to the query: "How much of the obligor's asset return is explained by the obligor-specific return, namely $\omega_2^{A \text{ or } B}$?"

Obligor-specific risk can generally be considered to be a function of company asset size. Larger companies tend to have smaller firm-specific risk because their behaviour tends to be more like the overall market in which they make up part of the benchmarks. Smaller companies, on the other hand, tend to have larger firm-specific risk since they are more likely to behave independently of broad market trends and indexes and are, thus, less likely to be components of market indexes. Using this argument, the obligor-specific risk can, therefore, be considered as a *decreasing* function of asset size, as indicated in Figure 7.1.

The following logistic curve for the obligor-specific risk comes from JP Morgan's CreditManager:

$$ObligorSpecificRisk = \frac{1}{2(1 + Assets^{\gamma} e^{\lambda})} \tag{7.4a}$$

Figure 7.1 Obligor-specific risk

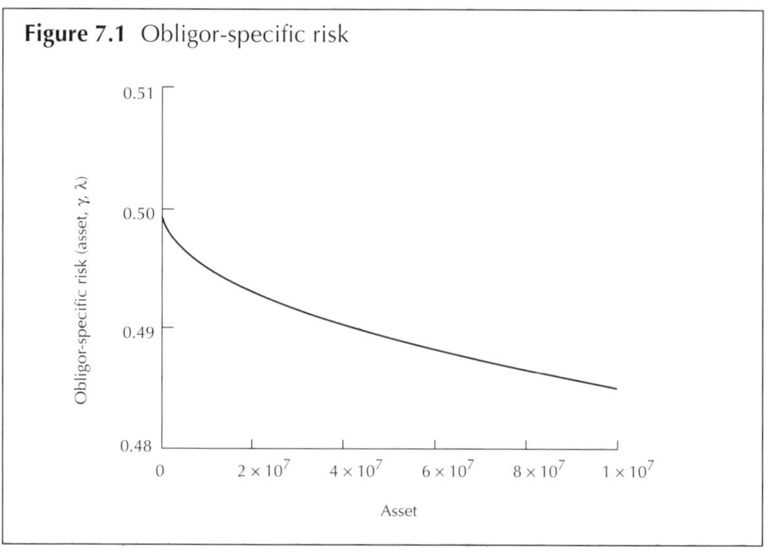

where *Assets* = total assets in US dollars, and the estimated parameters are

$$\gamma = 0.4884 \qquad \text{and} \qquad \lambda = -12.4739 \tag{7.4b}$$

A graph of obligor-specific risk as a function of asset size is presented as Figure 7.1. Although the general shape is probably correct, the parametric fit needs to be analysed further. We shall not make any attempt in this book to justify the functional fit of this curve rigorously, except to remark that more improvements are definitely needed down the road. For now, we will take it as given.

Example 7.2 – Calculation of asset correlation

Consider for instance, when *Assets* are in the \$100 million range, *ObligorSpecificRisk* using the logistic form given above is approximately equal to 48.5%. This is somewhat a very rough estimate. Consequently, for obligors with this range of asset sizes, we can therefore approximately use an industry weighting of $\omega_1^{A \text{ or } B}$ = 51.5%, resulting in a very crude approximate asset correlation of

$$\rho(A, B) \approx 51.5\% \times 51.5\% \times \rho_{\alpha\beta} = 0.27\rho_{\alpha\beta}$$

expressed in terms of the industry index correlation $\rho_{\alpha\beta}$.

Hence, once the industry index correlation is estimated from publicly available information, the default correlation between two obligors can be easily calculated using the equation (7.1) in the previous section.

In practice, it might be prudent to choose an exceedingly large asset size, say \$100 billion. The corresponding *ObligorSpecificRisk* is approximately 25%, so that the industry weight is $\omega_1^{A \text{ or } B} = 75\%$. The resulting asset correlation is about 56% of the index correlation.

Notice that the asset size in this large range practically covers the bulk of all obligors in question. At such a wide range, this estimate of asset correlation can be considered to be quite conservative.

FURTHER GENERALISATION TO THE MULTIFACTOR CASE

The discussion above – specifically equations (7.2a) and (7.2b) – can be generalised to a multifactor framework. However, the amount of calculations needed also increases proportionately.

In general, an obligor's firm-wide structure may be an aggregate of several related, or otherwise unrelated, industry groups. The movement of the asset return of this obligor should, therefore, be explained by more than one industry index. Specifically, if the obligor engages in the industries indexed by $I \equiv \{\alpha, \beta, \gamma, \delta, \ldots\}$, the obligor's asset return is the weighted average:

$$
\begin{aligned}
r^{\text{obligor}} &= \omega_\alpha r_\alpha + \omega_\beta r_\beta + \omega_\gamma r_\gamma + \cdots + \omega \hat{r}^{\text{obligor}} \\
&= \sum_I \omega_I r_I + \omega \hat{r}^{\text{obligor}} \qquad (7.5)
\end{aligned}
$$

where the last term refers to the obligor's specific or idiosyncratic return with weight w.

Again, we need to assume statistical independence between the industry indexes and the obligor's specific return.

Suppose that the returns on the industry indexes have volatilities given by $\sigma_I \equiv \{\sigma_\alpha, \sigma_\beta, \sigma_\gamma, \sigma_\delta, \ldots\}$ and correlations given by $\rho_{IJ} \equiv \{\rho_{\alpha\beta}, \rho_{\alpha\delta}, \ldots\}$, then the volatility of the obligor's weighted industry index is

$$
\sigma^{\text{obligor}} = \sqrt{\sum_I \omega_I^2 \sigma_I^2 + 2 \sum_{I,J} \omega_I \omega_J \rho_{IJ} \sigma_I \sigma_J} \qquad (7.6)
$$

We now need to rescale the obligor's weights in each respective industry so that, *in toto*, the industry indexes explain only a fraction of the volatility obligor's standardised return. The rest, of course, can be explained by the obligor's firm-specific idiosyncratic component. This means that the obligor-specific weight must satisfy the relationship

$$w = \sqrt{1-\Gamma^2} \qquad (7.7)$$

where the fraction Γ is defined by

$$\omega_I = \Gamma \cdot \frac{\omega_I \sigma_I}{\sigma^{\text{obligor}}}$$

$$\text{over the index set } I \equiv \{\alpha, \beta, \gamma, \delta, \ldots\} \qquad (7.8)$$

The scaling process above guarantees that the industry indexes (in aggregate) explain only Γ percentage of the total standardised return of the obligor. The rest of the weight can be attributed to the obligor-specific return.

Clearly, the correlations between related industry indexes become very important. Section 8.5.2 of the CreditMetrics technical document (Gupton, Finger and Bhatia, 1997) contains examples on how the weights in this generalisation can be calculated. Readers, however, should be forewarned that there is more art than science in all these default correlation calculations.

Generally speaking, the method outlined briefly in this section could, in principle, also be extended to incorporate sovereign or country risk. A global covariance structure containing the countries, their respective traded indexes (eg, the ASX, CDAX, FTSE, Hang Seng, etc), and their respective industry groupings would need to be constructed to capture all these multifaceted nuances. CreditMetrics has conveniently provided this free service in its website for easy download. The KMV Corporation has similarly collected this kind of information on a global scale, which is available for a price. It is called the "Global correlation model", and is part of their proprietary system. For countries that do not have index families, some major indexes could be prudently used as proxies.

SOME COMMENTS AND SUGGESTIONS

The dilemma surrounding default correlation is not an issue of methodology, of mathematics or of its effects on portfolio concentration and diversification. The main difficulty is the absence of direct empirical observation of "simultaneous defaulting events" from the market over a reasonable period of time.

As there is *very* strong evidence (see Moody's Investor Services, 1997, for instance) that movements in credit quality of different obligors are correlated, it is not prudent to set all correlations to zero, ignoring their implications for portfolio credit risk management. It must be kept in mind that the higher the degree of correlation, the greater is the volatility (ie, unexpected loss) of a portfolio's value attributable to credit risk. Hence, portfolio management of credit risk cannot be performed in isolation without understanding the full impact of default correlation on the portfolio.

Faced with these dilemmas – the paucity of correlation data and the necessity of incorporating default correlation – I suggest, at the very least, that some fixed, *constant* level of correlation be used in the internal credit risk model. The schema introduced earlier in the chapter regarding groupings by industry, country and other indexes to get round the paucity of data and the onerous number-crunching requirements, in many senses, uses the prudent idea of some fixed levels of constant correlations. In retrospect, it may be wiser to do this than to use zero correlation.

APPENDIX A – CORRELATION OF DEFAULT

Let D_i and D_j denote the events that Obligor *i* and Obligor *j* default before the horizon, respectively. The corresponding probabilities of default are

$$P(D_i) = EDF_i \qquad \text{and} \qquad P(D_j) = EDF_j \tag{A.7.1}$$

From the definition of covariance, the correlation between the default events D_i and D_j is given by

$$\rho_{ij} = \frac{\sigma_{ij}}{\sigma_i \sigma_j} \tag{A.7.2}$$

where σ_{ij} is the covariance between the two default events and σ_i and σ_j are the standard deviations of events i and j.

Assuming that the default process is a two-state event, the default events D_i and D_j are binomial in nature, and their corresponding standard deviations are

$$\sigma_i = \sqrt{P(D_i)\left[1-P(D_i)\right]} \quad \text{and} \quad \sigma_j = \sqrt{P(D_j)\left[1-P(D_j)\right]} \tag{A.7.3}$$

Now, the covariance is

$$\begin{aligned}\sigma_{ij} &= E[D_i \cdot D_j] - E[D_i]E[D_j] \\ &= P(D_i \cdot D_j) - P(D_i)P(D_j) \\ &= P(D_i \cdot D_j) - EDF_i \cdot EDF_j \end{aligned} \tag{A.7.4}$$

Hence, using equation (A.7.2), the correlation between the two default events is

$$\rho_{ij} = \frac{P\left(D_i \cdot D_j\right) - EDF_i \cdot EDF_j}{\sqrt{EDF_i\left(1-EDF_i\right)} \times \sqrt{EDF_j\left(1-EDF_j\right)}} \tag{A.7.5}$$

where the joint probability of default $P(D_i \cdot D_j) = EDF_i + EDF_j - P(D_i + D_j)$, and $P(D_i + D_j)$ is the probability that either obligor has defaulted.

APPENDIX B – FIRST-PASSAGE TIME MODEL OF DEFAULT CORRELATION

All the results for this appendix are taken from the paper by Zhou (1997). Zhou's model of default correlation between two obligors, Firm 1 and Firm 2, makes the following assumptions.

Assumption 1 Let V_1 and V_2 denote the asset values of Firm 1 and Firm 2, which obey the stochastic process

$$\begin{bmatrix} d\ln(V_1) \\ d\ln(V_2) \end{bmatrix} = \begin{bmatrix} \mu_1 \\ \mu_2 \end{bmatrix} dt + \Omega \begin{bmatrix} dz_1 \\ dz_2 \end{bmatrix} \tag{B.7.1}$$

where μ_1 and μ_2 are constant drift terms, z_1 and z_2 are two independent standard Brownian motions and Ω is a constant 2×2 matrix such that

$$\Omega \cdot \Omega' = \begin{bmatrix} \sigma_1^2 & \rho\sigma_1\sigma_2 \\ \rho\sigma_1\sigma_2 & \sigma_2^2 \end{bmatrix} \tag{B.7.2}$$

is the covariance matrix. The constant ρ represents the asset correlation between the two firms.

Assumption 2 Following the "value of the firm" class of risky debt model, allow the default of a firm to be triggered by the decline of its asset value. For each firm i, there exist two positive constants, K_i and λ_i, such that the firm i defaults on all of its contractual obligations instantaneously as soon as $V_i(t) \le e^{\lambda_i t} K_i$.

By the second assumption, determining the default event of a firm is equivalent to finding the first passage time of the firm's asset value breaching the trigger level.

The major contribution of Zhou's paper was to show that the probability that at least one default has occurred by the time t is given by

$$P(D_1 + D_2) = 1 - \frac{2r_o}{\sqrt{2\pi t}} \cdot e^{-\frac{r_o^2}{4t}} \cdot \sum_{n=1,3,5,\cdots} \frac{1}{n} \sin\left(\frac{n\pi\theta_o}{\alpha}\right) \times$$

$$\left[I_{\frac{1}{2}\left(\frac{n\pi}{\alpha}+1\right)}\left(\frac{r_o^2}{4t}\right) + I_{\frac{1}{2}\left(\frac{n\pi}{\alpha}-1\right)}\left(\frac{r_o^2}{4t}\right) \right] \tag{B.7.3}$$

where $I_\nu(z)$ is the modified Bessel function with order ν and $Z_i = b_i/\sigma_i$. The other quantities of interest are

$$\theta_o = \begin{cases} \tan^{-1}\left(\dfrac{Z_2\sqrt{1-\rho^2}}{Z_1 - \rho Z_2}\right) & \text{if } (*) > 0 \\[2ex] \pi + \tan^{-1}\left(\dfrac{Z_2\sqrt{1-\rho^2}}{Z_1 - \rho Z_2}\right) & \text{otherwise} \end{cases} \tag{B.7.4a}$$

$$r_o = \frac{Z_2}{\sin(\theta_o)} \tag{B.7.4b}$$

$$\alpha = \begin{cases} \tan^{-1}\left(-\dfrac{\sqrt{1-\rho^2}}{\rho}\right) & \text{if } \rho < 0 \\ \pi + \tan^{-1}\left(-\dfrac{\sqrt{1-\rho^2}}{\rho}\right) & \text{otherwise} \end{cases} \tag{B.7.4c}$$

and

$$b_1 = \ln\left[\frac{V_1(0)}{K_1}\right]$$

$$b_2 = \ln\left[\frac{V_2(0)}{K_2}\right] \tag{B.7.4d}$$

The parameters that require estimation are asset values, asset volatilities, asset correlations and the point of default, K.

Some prominent conclusions from this first-passage model of default correlation are:

- Default correlation and asset correlation have the same sign. The higher the asset correlation, the higher is the default correlation.
- Default correlations are generally small over a shorter horizon. They first increase and then decrease slowly with time. (Note that this analytical result agrees with the empirical findings of Lucas, 1995.)
- Default correlations among higher credit quality obligors tend to be lower.
- The time to reach peak default correlation depends on the credit quality of the obligors. The higher the credit quality, the longer it takes to reach the peak. (This analytical result is again consistent with the empirical finding of Lucas, 1995.)
- Default correlations are, in general, very dynamic.

APPENDIX C – INDUSTRY DEFAULT CORRELATION MATRIX

The default correlation matrix for industry groups is given on the facing page.

Table C.7.1 Industry default correlation matrix (%)

S&P index	1	2	3	4	5	6	7	8	9	10	11	12	13	14	15	16	17	18	19	20	21	22
1 Automobiles (.SPAUTO)	11.0																					
2 Financial (.SPF)	1.0	13.9																				
3 Building materials (.SPBULD)	1.1	2.1	10.6																			
4 Chemicals (.SPCHEM)	1.1	2.2	1.7	13.0																		
5 Electronics (instrumentation) (.SPELCHI)	0.6	1.5	0.8	1.1	11.1																	
6 Energy (.SPEN)	0.3	1.6	1.2	1.6	0.5	10.2																
7 Entertainment (.SPENTE)	0.5	2.5	1.2	1.6	1.1	0.7	11.3															
8 Foods (.SPFOOD)	0.1	2.4	0.5	0.9	1.0	1.0	2.2	11.8														
9 Health care (.SPHC)	0.1	3.1	0.6	0.9	1.4	1.0	2.7	5.4	15.8													
10 Insurance composite (.SPINS)	0.3	5.6	1.1	0.9	0.5	0.8	1.2	1.5	1.4	7.9												
11 Machinery (diversified) (.SPMCHD)	2.6	1.9	2.3	3.1	1.2	1.4	1.4	0.6	0.4	0.9	12.0											
12 Manufacturing (diversified) (.SPMAND)	1.7	4.0	2.9	4.3	1.7	1.2	2.2	1.7	1.5	2.1	4.0	12.8										
13 Metals mining (.SPMETL)	1.2	1.0	1.0	2.7	1.2	0.4	0.9	0.1	0.0	0.3	2.5	2.3	17.0									
14 Oil & gas (refining & marketing) (.SPENRM)	0.8	0.9	1.1	1.8	1.1	2.0	1.1	0.4	0.3	0.4	2.2	1.8	1.0	14.2								
15 Paper & forest products (.SPPAPR)	1.3	0.8	1.2	2.8	0.7	0.3	0.7	0.1	0.0	0.3	2.7	2.0	2.8	0.8	11.7							
16 Publishing (.SPPUBL)	0.4	1.8	0.9	1.3	0.8	0.7	1.9	1.5	1.7	1.1	0.8	1.9	0.7	0.9	0.6	13.3						
17 Technology (.SPTK)	0.8	1.8	1.2	1.4	3.8	0.3	2.0	1.0	1.8	0.8	2.1	2.6	1.5	1.4	1.0	0.9	11.5					
18 Telecommunications (long distance) (.SPTELC)	0.4	2.0	0.4	0.6	0.6	0.8	1.4	1.6	1.3	1.7	0.5	1.0	0.6	0.7	0.5	1.7	0.7	14.6				
19 Textiles (apparel) (.SPTEXT)	0.3	0.8	0.5	0.6	0.0	0.3	0.5	0.6	0.3	0.2	0.6	0.9	0.7	0.3	0.5	0.3	0.5	0.3	10.6			
20 Transport (.SPT)	2.2	3.5	3.0	3.8	2.0	1.5	2.3	1.1	1.5	1.4	3.8	5.0	2.7	2.1	3.1	2.1	2.6	1.0	0.9	14.4		
21 Utilities (.SPU)	0.2	3.1	0.6	0.4	0.4	1.4	0.9	2.1	1.4	2.1	0.4	1.2	0.0	0.5	0.1	1.0	0.3	2.2	0.2	1.4	10.0	
22 Other	2.0	2.0	2.0	2.0	2.0	2.0	2.0	2.0	2.0	2.0	2.0	2.0	2.0	2.0	2.0	2.0	2.0	2.0	2.0	2.0	2.0	2.0

The S&P industry groupings and their calculated default correlations are meant for illustrative purposes only. In practice, there are several more industry indexes to incorporate into the correlation matrix.

APPENDIX D – CORRELATION OF JOINT CREDIT QUALITY MOVEMENT

Our needs for credit risk modelling go beyond the estimation of default correlations. In fact, a better framework must incorporate the joint likelihood of all the possible combinations of credit quality migration. In addition to the more restrictive two-state credit process (ie, default or no default only scenarios), the credit quality of the obligor should also be allowed to either improve or deteriorate to many other different states within the analysis horizon.

For instance, suppose we are given an eight-state default process classified by the risk ratings AAA, AA, A, BBB, BB, B, CCC and default, D. There are 64 possible joint states of likelihood between any two given obligors. The example below illustrates all the possible pairwise relationship between their respective credit qualities.

Example D.7.1 – Two obligors in an eight-state default process

Consider two obligors with initial credit ratings of BBB and AA, respectively. In an eight-state default process, there are 64 possible pairwise combinations between their credit quality and migration possibilities, as illustrated in Figure D.7.1. The different likelihoods take into account the joint movements of credit quality, including upgrades, downgrades and default.

Given a typical portfolio in the banking book, the task of imputing the joint probabilities given by the possible risk rating scenarios in this example is, admittedly, a very daunting one. We are saddled not only by the practicalities of pure number-crunching capability but also by the paucity of empirical data with which to impute these joint likelihoods.

For the lack of a brilliant scheme, we need to resort to an *indirect* approach using asset information instead. In the case of a two-state default process, the indirect approach was discussed extensively earlier in the main chapter (pages 142–5 and example 7.2), whereby we indirectly imputed the correlation of default between pairs of obligors using their respective asset correlation.

As usual, we invoke the fundamental Merton "value of the firm" framework, which proposes that the underlying process that drives a firm's default (and appropriately extended to credit rating change) is the firm's own asset value. In the two-state default pro-

Figure D.7.1 Illustration of possible combinations of credit rating migration from their initial state for two obligors

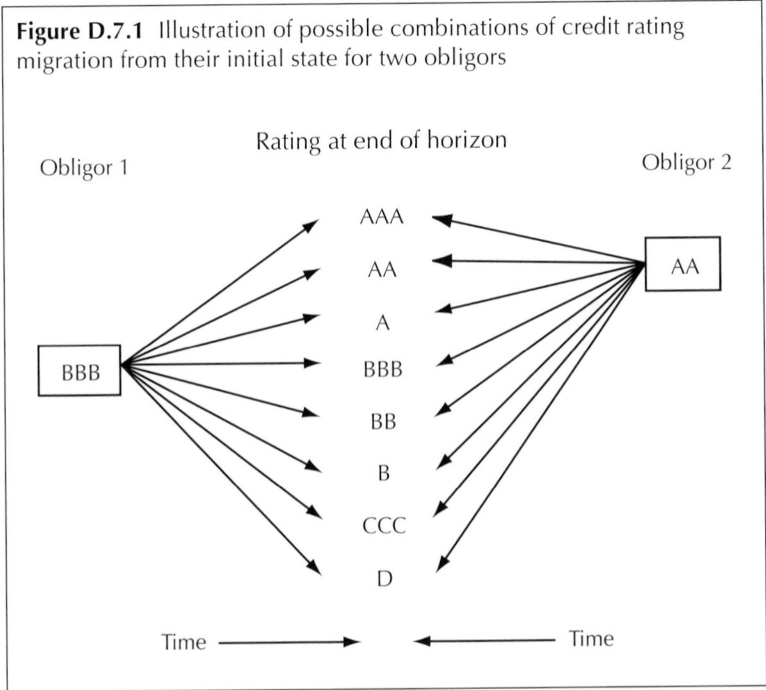

cess used throughout this book, it was sufficient to know that once a firm's asset value fell below a critical threshold, it would not be able to meet the timely payment of its debt obligations. In a multi-state default process, however, the associated change in portfolio value, given a pairwise change in credit quality between two obligors, also needs to be properly taken into account.

More specifically, following the arguably more practical philosophy espoused in the "value of the firm" framework as implemented by CreditMetrics, we assume that there exists a series of levels of the firm's asset value which determine the credit rating of the firm. Recall that in the two-state default process, there is only one such level – given by the critical threshold level of asset value – for which the firm will default on its debt obligation once its asset value falls below this critical threshold. In particular, for a multi-state default process, the level of asset values (within the series of all possible levels) attained by the firm at the analysis horizon determines the firm's credit risk rating at the end of the same period.

Figure D.7.2 Mapping of asset value to credit rating

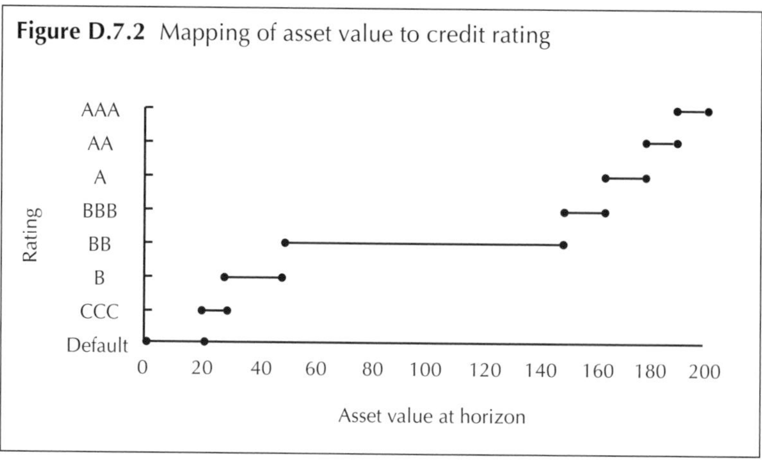

In Figure D.7.2 (reproduced from Chart 8.1 of the CreditMetrics technical document by Gupton, Finger and Bhatia, 1997), we illustrate these threshold levels of a firm's asset values at the analysis horizon. Each level of the threshold reached by the firm's asset value determines its credit rating. A change in threshold level allows the possibility of credit rating migration. For instance, an asset value of between \$50 million and \$150 million places the firm at the BB rating.

The tacit implication of such an indirect approach linking asset value threshold levels to the firm's credit rating is that the changes in a firm's asset value ultimately decide the evolution of the firm's creditworthiness. Purists might balk at this approach, but would they themselves be able to propose a better and more practical alternative? I think not.

Assuming that asset returns, denoted by the symbol R, are normally distributed with mean μ and standard deviation σ, the generalisation concerning the firm's credit quality immediately translates to the slicing of the asset returns distribution into distinct bands. Each band, representing the different threshold levels of asset returns, can be mapped one-to-one to the credit migration frequencies in the transition matrix. A typical transition matrix is the one-year transition matrix that we previously encountered as Table 3.2 of chapter 3.

In Figure D.7.3 (reproduced from Chart 8.2 of Gupton, Finger and Bhatia, 1997), we illustrate the different bands of the asset

Figure D.7.3 Asset return distribution and Z-thresholds for a firm with a current rating of BB

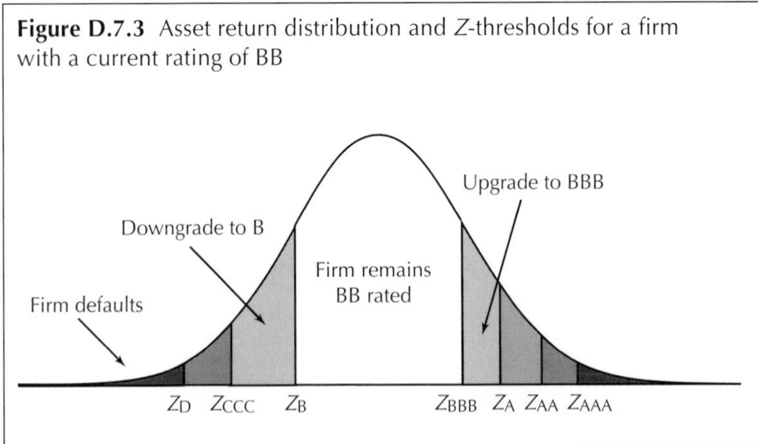

return distribution of a firm that is currently rated as BB. The bands corresponding to the asset return thresholds are denoted by the variable Z and subscripted appropriately by the risk ratings.

In Example 7.1 of the main chapter it was mentioned that, in the two-state default process, the actual mean and standard deviation of the asset return distribution are irrelevant.[2] Therefore, all the pertinent calculation hereon can be based on a *standardised* normal distribution with mean of zero and a standard deviation of one.

From Figure D.7.3, we observe that the probability of the firm defaulting, expressed in terms of its asset return distribution, is given by

$$\text{prob}\{\text{Default}\} = \text{prob}\{R < Z_{\text{D}}\} = N(Z_{\text{D}}) \qquad \textbf{(D.7.1)}$$

where N(∗) is the cumulative normal distribution function.

Similarly, the probability that the obligor's credit rating is downgraded to CCC is given by

$$\begin{aligned}\text{prob}\{\text{CCC}\} &= \text{prob}\{Z_{\text{D}} < R < Z_{\text{CCC}}\} \\ &= N(Z_{\text{CCC}}) - N(Z_{\text{D}}) \qquad \textbf{(D.7.2)}\end{aligned}$$

If we use the *empirically observed* transition matrix from Standard & Poor's or Moody's (like that in Table 3.2), we can also associate these transition probabilities with empirically assigned Z threshold

Table D.7.1 Transition probabilities and asset return thresholds for Obligor 1 (initial BBB rating)

Rating	Probability (P_i)	Threshold	Range $Z(I)$
AAA	0.02%		
AA	0.33%	Z(AA)	3.540
A	5.95%	Z(A)	2.696
BBB	86.93%	Z(BBB)	1.530
BB	5.30%	Z(BB)	−1.494
B	1.17%	Z(B)	−2.179
CCC	1.12%	Z(CCC)	−2.748
Default	0.18%	Z(D)	−2.912

values. For instance, suppose that Obligor 1, with an initial rating of BBB, has a default probability of 0.18%, then the asset return threshold for default can be easily calculated as

$$Z_{\mathrm{D}} = N^{-1}[\mathrm{prob}\{\mathrm{Default}\}]$$

$$= N^{-1}[0.0018] = -2.912$$

Likewise, since Obligor 1 has a 86.93% probability of retaining its initial BBB rating, its asset return threshold can be calculated as

$$Z_{\mathrm{BBB}} = N^{-1}[\mathrm{prob}\{\mathrm{BBB}\}] = 1.53$$

The rest of the Z thresholds for Obligor 1 can be found in Table D.7.1.

Suppose, in addition, that there is another firm called Obligor 2 which has an initial credit rating of A. Table D.7.2 displays all the pertinent transition probabilities and the calculated Z thresholds.

Given the two tables we are now ready to tackle the case when there are two different obligors, each of which initially starts out with its own credit rating and then both ratings are allowed to migrate before the analysis horizon. The main question we need to ask now is: "What is the correlation of credit quality evolution between these two obligors?" In other words, how do the asset return thresholds between the two obligors (as given by their respective Z thresholds) affect their credit ratings when they move in some joint fashion?

Table D.7.2. Transition probabilities and asset return thresholds for Obligor 2 (initial A rating)

Rating	Probability (Q_j)	Threshold	Range $Z'(j)$
AAA	0.09%		
AA	2.27%	Z'(AA)	3.12
A	91.05%	Z'(A)	1.98
BBB	5.52%	Z'(BBB)	−1.51
BB	0.74%	Z'(BB)	−2.30
B	0.26%	Z'(B)	−2.72
CCC	0.01%	Z'(CCC)	−3.19
Default	0.06%	Z'(D)	−3.24

Joint credit quality movement

Similar to the two-state default case, we use equity returns as proxies for asset returns because asset returns are not directly observable in the market. The proxy mechanism has the implicit assumption that all the firm's activities are financed by equities. This, of course, is generally not true.

Our goal is to derive the joint probability, P_{ij}, that best describes the joint movement of credit quality between the two obligors in the portfolio. Since the respective asset return of each obligor is assumed to be a standardised normal distribution, the joint movement is a bivariate normal distribution with density given by

$$\mathrm{f}(x, y, \eta) = \frac{1}{2\pi\sqrt{1-\eta^2}} \exp\left[-\frac{1}{2\left(1-\eta^2\right)}\left(x^2 + y^2 - 2\eta x y\right)\right] \tag{D.7.3}$$

where η represents the asset correlation between the two obligors.

Generally speaking, if the asset returns are not assumed to be normally distributed *a priori*, the joint distribution given in equation (D.7.3) need not be bivariate normal. The choice of the joint density $\mathrm{f}(x, y, \eta)$ is best left to individual banks themselves, if at all possible.

The asset correlation, in practice, can be approximated by

$$\eta = \alpha \times \mathrm{corr}(Ind\,1, Ind\,2) \tag{D.7.4}$$

where $Ind1$ and $Ind2$ refer to the Standard & Poor's industry indexes to which the two obligors, respectively, belong. The quantity $\text{corr}(Ind1, Ind2)$ is the correlation of the asset returns of the two obligors as proxied by equity index returns. The numerical factor α plays the role of effectively *reducing* the asset correlation proxied by equity index returns. The rationale for introducing such a reducing factor is motivated by the somewhat negative response to the question considered earlier in the chapter (page 142): If General Motors' credit quality changes or if the company defaults, does Ford Motors suffer the same fate, both being in the same industry grouping?[3]

Given the joint bivariate distribution, the joint probability of credit quality movement is given by

$$P_{ij} = \int_{Z_{i-1}}^{Z_i} \mathrm{d}x \int_{Z'_{j-1}}^{Z'_j} \mathrm{d}y\, \mathrm{f}(x, y, \eta) \qquad \textbf{(D.7.5)}$$

where the limits of integration, Z_{i-1} and Z_i, with respect to the x variable, represent the band for the threshold levels. The same convention is true for the y variable. To impute the joint movement of credit quality for all possible states in the eight-state default process given in Example D.7.1, the quantity $P_{ij} - P_i Q_j$ needs to be calculated for all the states indexed by $i, j = 1, 2, 3, \ldots, 8$. There are 64 possible combinations. The following example illustrates the calculation of one such combination.

Example D.7.2 – Joint probability of credit quality movement
Suppose that the asset correlation is known to be $\eta = 30\%$ and we wish to find the joint probability that Obligor 1 has migrated to the state $i = 2(\text{AA})$ while Obligor 2 has remained at its initial state $j = 3(\text{A})$. We need to compute the quantity

$$P_{23} - P_2 Q_3 = \int_{2.696}^{3.54} \mathrm{d}x \int_{-1.51}^{1.98} \mathrm{d}y\, \mathrm{f}(x, y, 0.30) - [0.33\% \times 91.05\%]$$

$$= -1.41 \times 10^{-4}$$

The limits of integration are readily available from Tables D.7.1 and D.7.2 above.

In practice, the double integrals are calculated outside of the core model itself so that their numerical values can be looked up more conveniently later in the form of a cross-reference table.

1 *Rating Migration and Credit Quality Correlation, 1920–1996*, published in July 1997.
2 The *normalised* asset return is given by

$$R = \frac{\ln\left(\frac{V_1}{V_0}\right) - \left(\mu - 0.5\sigma^2\right)t}{\sigma\sqrt{t}}$$

where V_0 and V_1 are the asset values at time zero and at the analysis horizon, respectively.
3 This is probably not a very good example as both Ford and General Motors are not strictly classified as automotive in nature. In fact, no mega-conglomerates are engaged solely in one classificatory type of industry.

8

Loss Distribution for Credit Default Risk

We first encountered the issue surrounding the determination of loss distribution in chapter 5 when considering the concept of unexpected loss. While all the derived equations regarding unexpected loss relied on the existence of a loss density function, $f(\tilde{L})$, where $\tilde{L}$ is the stochastic loss variable, it was not necessary at that time to assume an explicit distribution for the loss variable.*

In a portfolio context, however, the portfolio unexpected loss of the aggregate of bank assets is the estimated volatility of potential loss in portfolio value. It is, therefore, important to know the confidence level with which this estimated volatility is derived.

Furthermore, the so-called economic capital necessary to cushion the bank's risk of unexpected credit default losses is a multiple of the portfolio's unexpected loss. Hence, the determination of this "capital multiplier" is crucial in assessing the level of confidence with which the volatility estimate is made. The need to capture the likelihood of "extreme losses" via the tail of the loss distribution is consequently of paramount importance. The choice of the loss distribution is, however, yet another contentious task that always leads to very strong and emotional disagreement.

Unfortunately, too, for banking portfolios, which predominantly contain credit-related assets by nature, the loss distribution is also decidedly non-normal. As we shall see later, the loss distributions for these banking credit portfolios tend to be highly skewed and leptokurtic; therefore, *the usual market-based assumption of a normal distribution for credit portfolios is not appropriate.*

*Observe that in Appendix 5.1 the functional form for the density $f(\tilde{L})$ need not be known explicitly *a priori* in any of the derivations for the unexpected loss.

In this chapter I shall discuss the importance of choosing an appropriate loss distribution that is suitable for practical use. We begin with a simple choice as exemplified by the so-called *beta distribution*. In a series of examples, we attempt to fit the tail of the simulated loss distribution to the analytical beta distribution so that the parameters of the distribution can be estimated with some confidence. Once the tail section of the loss distribution is fitted, we impute the capital multiplier, which represents the number of standard deviations (as measured by the portfolio unexpected loss) necessary to protect the bank from insolvency, given any desired level of confidence.

CHOOSING THE PROPER LOSS DISTRIBUTION

There are many possible choices of probability distributions to fit these extreme "tail events". The important piece of information is not the "hump" (ie, the location of the mean) of the distribution but, rather, the tail of the distribution. The choice of distributions can range from a beta distribution to other, more esoteric, extreme value theory-type distributions, such as the Cauchy, Gumbel or Pareto distributions. Later, in chapter 10, I shall discuss extreme value theory in greater detail.

Given only the two statistical or risk measures about the credit portfolio – the portfolio expected loss and portfolio unexpected loss – and no tail information whatever, it is not possible to construct a complete picture of the loss distribution without making all sorts of *silly* assumptions. Figure 8.1 highlights the dilemma in choosing an analytical loss distribution that fits the risk profile of the portfolio. Depending on the choice of probability distributions, the overall shape differs and, more importantly, the tail region also differs dramatically from one distribution to the next.

What should one do? Perhaps the only sensible tail-fitting procedure might be to combine *both* analytical loss distributions with numerically derived Monte Carlo simulations. This will be the continuing theme in the chapters to follow.

Figure 8.1 shows three representative examples of portfolio loss distributions, each imbued with its own statistic, such as mean and standard deviation. These two main statistics can be interpreted, respectively, as the portfolio expected loss and unexpected loss. However, these two statistics can be vary quite differently from one

Figure 8.1 Choosing the loss distribution

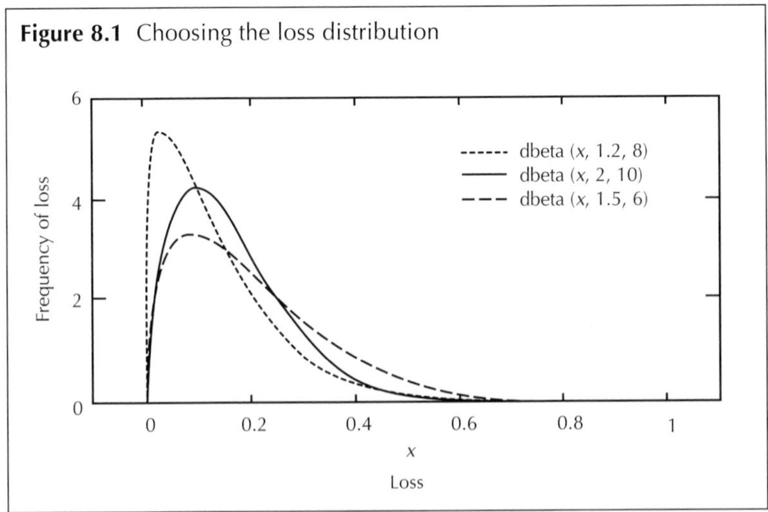

distribution to another depending on the shape of the distribution. In addition, depending on the shape of the distributions, the tail sections are also different in the way in which they extend further out into the higher loss region. In other words, how each distribution is skewed also varies significantly.

The big question is: "Given some potential choice of loss distribution, which should be chosen to represent the possibility of extreme losses in portfolio value?" When confronted with this serious question, we must further elucidate on our findings and proceed with a simple demonstration of the tail-fitting process to a beta distribution. I begin with a discussion of the beta distribution in the next section.

THE BETA DISTRIBUTION

The beta distribution is a family of parametric probability distributions with two degrees of freedom and with support defined on the interval $[0, 1]$. The *density function* is given by

$$f(x, \alpha, \beta) = \begin{cases} \dfrac{\Gamma(\alpha+\beta)}{\Gamma(\alpha)\cdot\Gamma(\beta)} x^{\alpha-1}(1-x)^{\beta-1}, & 0 < x < 1 \\ 0, & \text{otherwise} \end{cases} \tag{8.1}$$

for some fixed constant parameters $\alpha > 0$ and $\beta > 0$. The two constants are generally known as the *shape parameters*, and they control

Figure 8.2 The beta distribution

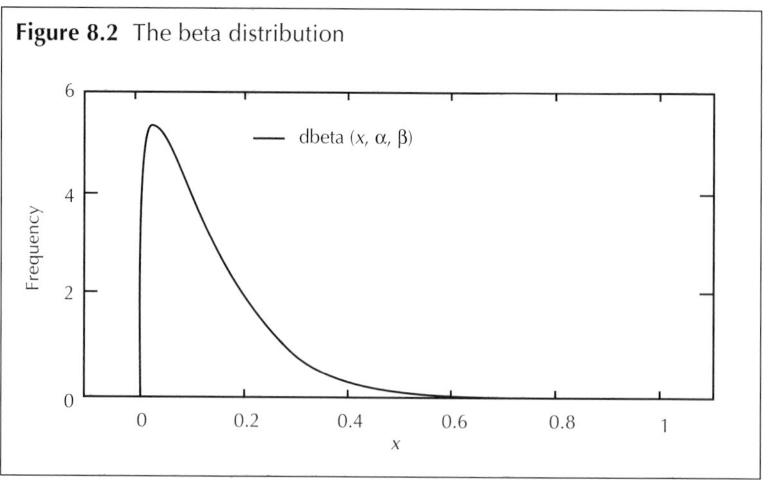

the *steepness* of the hump and the *fatness* of the tail, respectively. The mean, μ, and variance, σ^2, of the beta distribution are, respectively, given by

$$\mu = \frac{\alpha}{\alpha+\beta} \quad \text{and} \quad \sigma^2 = \frac{\alpha \cdot \beta}{(\alpha+\beta)^2 \cdot (\alpha+\beta+1)} \tag{8.2}$$

For the special case when $\alpha = \beta = 1$, the beta distribution degenerates into a *uniform distribution* on the interval $0 < x < 1$.

Figure 8.2 is a MathCad graph of the beta distribution, denoted by $\text{dbeta}(x, \alpha, \beta)$. The distribution is plotted for the chosen parameter values $\alpha := 1.2$ and $\beta := 8$. It is obvious from the graph that the two parameters (as seen from the mean and variance) control the steepness of the hump and the fatness of the tail of the beta distribution.

The cumulative beta distribution

The cumulative beta distribution gives the cumulative probabilities for the distribution. The *cumulative function*, which is denoted by $\text{pbeta}(x, \alpha, \beta)$, is the probability that a quantity which follows a beta distribution with parameters α and β will be less than or equal to x. Alternatively, we write

$$\text{pbeta}(x, \alpha, \beta) = \int_0^x \text{f}(t, \alpha, \beta)\,\text{d}t \tag{8.3}$$

Figure 8.3 Cumulative beta distribution showing graphical representation of cumulative function pbeta(x, α, β)

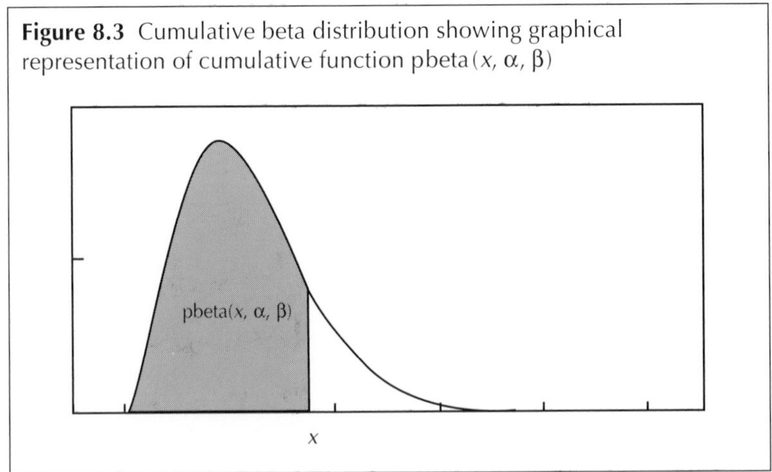

Graphically, the cumulative function pbeta(x, α, β) is the area under the distribution curve shown in Figure 8.3 to the left of the point x, given a chosen set of distribution parameters.

A graph of the cumulative function pbeta(x, α, β) is presented as Figure 8.4, where the parameters α and β are as for Figure 8.2.

Since the support of the beta distribution is defined only on the interval $x \in [0, 1]$, observe that as $x \to 1$ the probability accumulates rapidly towards the point pbeta$(x, \alpha, \beta) = 1$. With this in mind, the tail of the distribution can readily be analysed by observing, instead, the accumulation of probability as it approaches unity.

Figure 8.4 Cumulative beta distribution

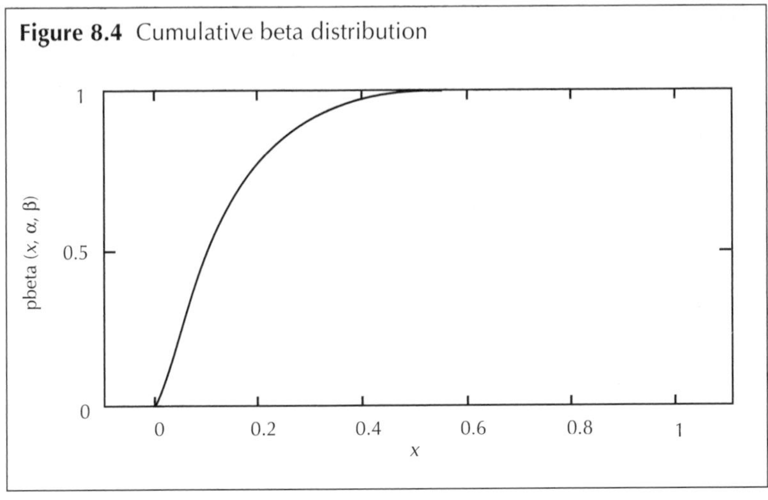

Before we proceed, we need to understand which part of the tail corresponds to the probability of loss. The next section addresses this aspect.

ECONOMIC CAPITAL AND PROBABILITY OF LOSS

Earlier, I mentioned that the amount of capital needed to buffer against the bank becoming insolvent due to default risk is a multiple of the bank portfolio's unexpected loss. This capital is called the *risk capital* or *economic capital*. To achieve the proper capitalisation for any line of business, it is necessary for the bank to identify a confidence level that is consistent with the bank's desired credit rating. This is because a desired debt rating for the bank corresponds to a given probability of capital exhaustion.

The distribution that determines the probability of loss is important because it determines the number of standard deviations of unexpected losses necessary to achieve, say, a 99.97% confidence level for a desired AA rating. The following table gives an indication of the confidence levels required for the desired debt rating of the firm.

Desired rating	Confidence level
AAA	99.99%
AA	99.97%
A	99.90%
BBB	99.70%

The confidence levels listed above are merely indicative of the average historical default probabilities corresponding to a particular risk rating. In reality, these averages fluctuate with business cycles and with time.

The pertinent question to ask at this point is: What minimum level of economic capital should the bank hold to protect itself from unexpected losses? We can rephrase this mathematically as: If X_T is the random variable for loss and z is the percentage probability (ie, confidence level), what is the quantity, v, of *minimum* economic capital needed to protect the bank from insolvency at the horizon time T such that

$$\text{prob}\{X_T \leq v\} = z \tag{8.4}$$

Figure 8.5 Required economic capital

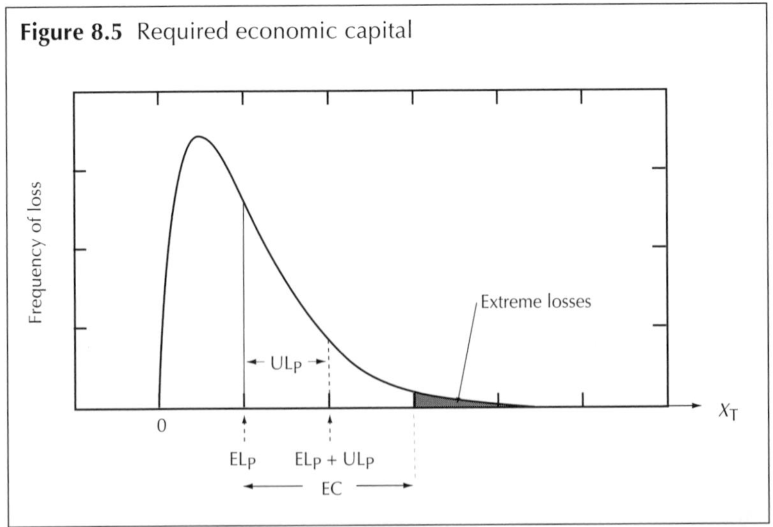

The quantity z, as mentioned earlier, also refers to the desired debt rating of the bank – for example, 99.97% for an AA rating. Figure 8.5 presents a graphical illustration of the meaning of the required economic capital.

With reference to Figure 8.5 and using the risk measures introduced thus far – portfolio expected loss, EL_P, portfolio unexpected loss, UL_P, and economic capital, EC – we ask the related question: Given a desired level of confidence, z, what is EC such that

$$\text{prob}\{X_T - EL_P \leq EC\} = z \tag{8.5a}$$

Since the economic capital is some *capital multiplier*, *CM*, times the portfolio unexpected loss – ie

$$EC = CM \times UL_P$$

– we can rewrite the question posted in equation (8.5a) as

$$\text{prob}\left[\frac{X_T - EL_P}{UL_P} \leq CM\right] = z \tag{8.5b}$$

We shall return to a more thorough discussion and practical application of equation (8.5b) in the examples at the end of the chapter.

EXTREME EVENTS: FITTING THE TAIL

At this juncture it is important to realise that the exercise of capital attribution, which by itself is a simple corollary of determining the proper loss distribution, has largely been reduced to the art of "tail-fitting". That is to say, given an *assumed* probability distribution for the loss in portfolio value, how well does the tail of the distribution explain the extreme or tail events associated with the unexpected losses due to default? This exercise is, however, neither simple nor trivial.

Two examples are given below to illustrate the subtleties and difficulties, and also to provide some interesting insights.

Example 8.1: Fitting the beta tail (initial trial)

The portfolio used in this example consists entirely of corporate loans, but the conclusions reached are equally applicable to any portfolio subject to default risk. Here are some facts about the sample portfolio:

Total number of facilities	2570
Commitments	\$62.4 billion
Current outstanding	\$17.5 billion
Adjusted exposure, *AE*	\$47.3 billion

Without loss of generality, a zero asset covariance structure is first used for this example. Specifically, the asset correlations are all set at a constant level of 0%. Also, for simplicity, the loss given default, *LGD*, is set at 50% and 35% for secured and unsecured facilities, respectively. Again, for simplicity and tractability, the standard deviations for *LGD* are all set to zero.

In addition, a Monte Carlo simulation for the portfolio losses was conducted for each facility in the portfolio. (Chapter 9 includes a thorough discussion of the Monte Carlo simulation technique for generating loss distributions.) There were 15,000 trials in all. The simulated losses from the trials were sorted into bins and their corresponding frequencies were counted. A beta distribution was then fitted to the tail of the resulting distribution of simulated losses.

For comparison, the results of the calculations from an internal analytical model and a simulation exercise are set out below. The numbers in parenthesis are percentages of the adjusted exposure.

	Internal model	**Simulation**
Expected loss	\$71.3 million (0.15%)	\$75.3 million (0.16%)
Unexpected loss	\$30.1 million (0.064%)	\$30.2 million (0.064%)

The results of the simulation and the tail-fitting exercise are given in Table 8.1 (overleaf), where the first column is the loss, denoted by x_i; the second column is the frequency with which the losses occurred; the third column is the cumulative distribution of simulated losses, denoted by y_i; and the fourth column is the analytic cumulative beta distribution, denoted by $\beta(x_i)$.

The shaded region in the table indicates where the beta tail-fitting was performed. More specifically, short of any scientific prescription at this early point in our experiment, we have naïvely chosen to fit the tail section given by $Loss \in [190, 480]$. Later we shall see that the choice of the tail section has important implications.

Best-fit calibration The criterion for "best fit" is decided by minimising the sum of the least-square errors given by

$$\chi^2 \equiv \sum_i \left[\frac{y_i - \beta(x_i)}{y_i} \right]^2$$

which is iteratively solved for the best-fit parameters of the beta distribution.

Using the chosen tail region in Table 8.1, the calibrated parameters for the fitted beta distribution are $\alpha = 1.02$ and $\beta = 1273$, where the convergence criterion was achieved for a least-squares error of $\chi^2 = 8.21 \times 10^{-6}$.

The mean and standard deviation of the fitted beta distribution are, respectively, $\mu = 0.080\%$ and $\sigma = 0.079\%$, which are quoted in units of percentage of the adjusted exposure.

Cumulative distribution The resulting cumulative distribution of the fitted beta distribution is also graphed here (Figure 8.6) for clarity.

Capital multiplier Under the assumed beta distribution and appropriately calibrated to the bank's desired credit rating or confidence

Table 8.1 Results of simulation and tail-fitting – Example 8.1

Loss ($ million) x_i	Simulation Frequency	Cumulative % y_i	Beta Cumulative % $\beta(x_i)$
0	0	0.00	0.00
10	0	0.00	22.63
20	7	0.04	40.52
30	168	1.11	54.35
40	795	6.13	65.00
50	1703	16.90	73.18
60	2514	32.80	79.47
70	2701	49.88	84.28
80	2346	64.72	87.97
90	1764	75.87	90.80
100	1248	83.77	92.96
110	900	89.46	94.62
120	591	93.20	95.88
130	352	95.42	96.85
140	231	96.88	97.60
150	156	97.87	98.16
160	86	98.41	98.60
170	74	98.88	98.93
180	56	99.23	99.18
190	37	99.47	99.37
200	18	99.58	99.52
210	8	99.63	99.63
220	11	99.70	99.72
230	6	99.74	99.79
240	5	99.77	99.84
250	5	99.80	99.88
260	3	99.82	99.91
270	2	99.84	99.93
280	3	99.85	99.94
290	1	99.86	99.96
300	5	99.89	99.97
310	3	99.91	99.98
320	1	99.92	99.98
330	4	99.94	99.99
340	1	99.95	99.99
350	0	99.95	99.99
360	0	99.95	99.99
370	1	99.96	100.00
380	2	99.97	100.00
390	1	99.97	100.00
400	1	99.98	100.00
410	1	99.99	100.00
420	1	99.99	100.00

and so on...

Figure 8.6 Cumulative distribution – Example 8.1

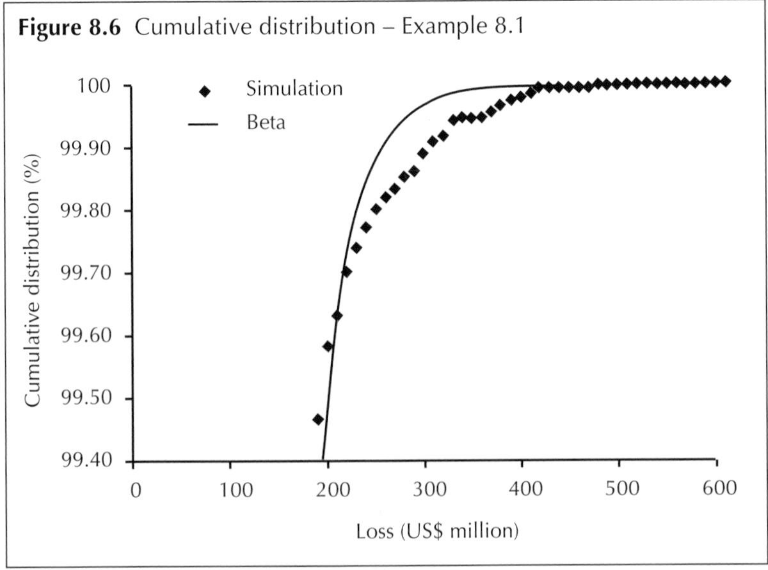

interval, we need to determine the number of standard deviations required to achieve this confidence level.

For example, to achieve a AA debt rating – corresponding to a 99.97% confidence level – one has

$$\text{pbeta}(x_{max}, \alpha, \beta) = 99.97\%$$

which, on solving for the *beta inverse*, yields $x_{max} = 0.640\%$. From equation (8.5b), the number of standard deviations required is therefore given by

$$\frac{x_{max} - \mu}{\sigma} = \frac{0.640 - 0.080}{0.079} = 7.057$$

This implies that the bank would have to set aside 7.057 times the portfolio unexpected loss of its portfolio to achieve a desired Standard & Poor's debt rating of AA. Henceforth, the number 7.057 shall be called the "capital multiplier".

The economic capital required for the bank to remain solvent in extreme loss situations is

$$\textit{Capital multiplier} \times \textit{Portfolio unexpected loss} = \$863{,}800{,}000$$

What if we change the region of the tail for fitting extreme events – will it change the shape of the assumed loss distribution, thereby changing the required capital multiplier? The answer is: it depends. The next example tackles this question more carefully.

Example 8.2: Fitting the beta tail (an improvement?)
Using the same portfolio and simulation method, we can choose where the tail-fitting begins. Suppose we choose a section further out in the extreme tail region. What will happen to the tail-fitting? The shaded area in Table 8.2 indicates the new chosen region. More specifically, we choose the region $Loss \in [270, 480]$ for the current tail-fitting exercise.

The resulting least-squares minimisation yields the best-fit parameters $\alpha = 0.92$ and $\beta = 1050$. This results in a mean and standard deviation for the fitted beta distribution of $\mu = 0.088\%$ and $\sigma = 0.091\%$, respectively, as percentages of the adjusted exposure.

As in the previous example, the cumulative distributions of the simulation and the beta tail-fit are plotted in Figure 8.7 for comparison. At least visually, there is a reasonably better fit in the section beyond $Loss > 270$ than in that example (Figure 8.6). This region is also further out on the tail than the region used in Example 8.1.

Figure 8.7 Cumulative distribution – Example 8.2

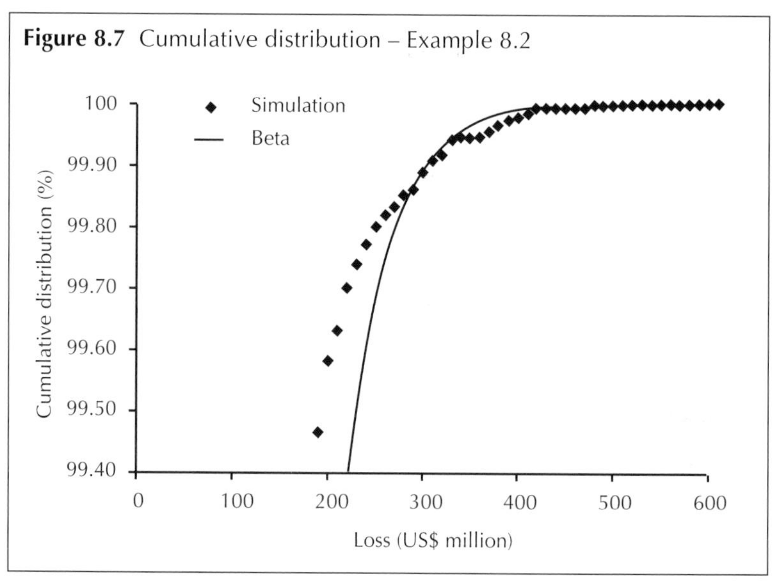

Table 8.2 Results of simulation and tail-fitting – Example 8.2

Loss ($ million) x_i	Simulation Frequency	Simulation Cumulative % y_i	Beta Cumulative % $\beta(x_i)$
0	0	0.00	0.00
10	0	0.00	23.30
20	7	0.04	39.89
30	168	1.11	52.63
40	795	6.13	62.55
50	1703	16.90	70.34
60	2514	32.80	76.47
70	2701	49.88	81.32
80	2346	64.72	85.16
90	1764	75.87	88.20
100	1248	83.77	90.61
110	900	89.46	92.53
120	591	93.20	94.05
130	352	95.42	95.26
140	231	96.88	96.23
150	156	97.87	96.99
160	86	98.41	97.60
170	74	98.88	98.09
180	56	99.23	98.48
190	37	99.47	98.79
200	18	99.58	99.03
210	8	99.63	99.23
220	11	99.70	99.38
230	6	99.74	99.51
240	5	99.77	99.61
250	5	99.80	99.69
260	3	99.82	99.75
270	2	99.84	99.80
280	3	99.85	99.84
290	1	99.86	99.87
300	5	99.89	99.90
310	3	99.91	99.92
320	1	99.92	99.94
330	4	99.94	99.95
340	1	99.95	99.96
350	0	99.9S	99.97
360	0	99.95	99.97
370	1	99.96	99.98
380	2	99.97	99.98
390	1	99.97	99.99
400	1	99.98	99.99
410	1	99.99	99.99
420	1	99.99	99.99

and so on...

Figure 8.8 Simulated loss distribution

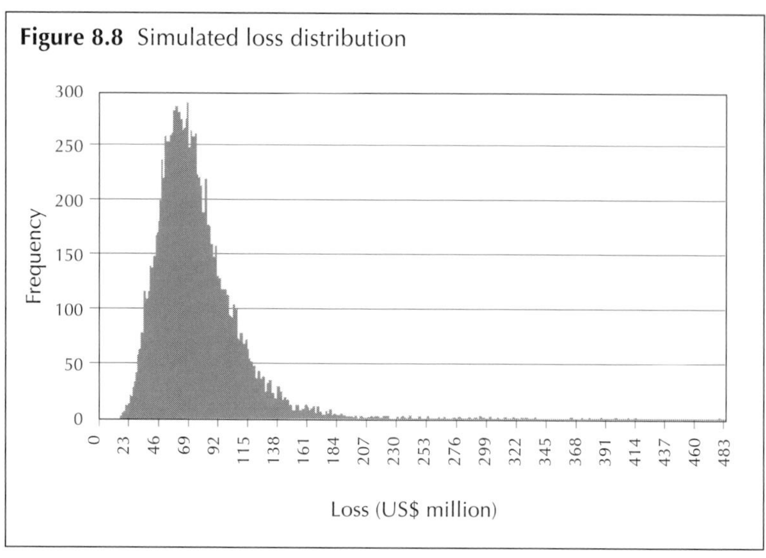

The implied capital multiplier corresponding to a 99.97% confidence level is calculated to be 7.246, which is slightly larger than the previous multiplier of 7.057.

Further comments on the two tail-fitting examples

Shape of the simulated loss distribution

It is also interesting to plot a frequency diagram of the simulation data given in the second column of both tables. The histogram plot of the simulated losses is presented as Figure 8.8. Observe that the loss distribution is evidently highly skewed and definitely non-normal, as we asserted earlier. Generally speaking, the shape of the loss distribution varies widely between different portfolios and is highly dependent on the composition of the portfolio, specifically:

- the risk ratings of the facilities or instruments in the portfolio;
- relative exposure sizes;
- the covariance structure; and
- diversification and concentration by industry and country classification.

From an analytical perspective, it is the tail region which is of utmost interest. The factors listed above contribute significantly to both the fatness or heaviness (ie, the extent) of the tail region. Therefore, any simulation schemes must be thought out and performed with great care. This is the scope of the next chapter. Before we proceed to that chapter, there are some lessons to be learned from these two simple examples.

Comparison of the two examples – some important observations

The main features of examples 8.1 and 8.2 are summarised in Table 8.3. The second example covered a sector further into the extreme tail region and, therefore, used significantly fewer loss events than the first. As seen from the table, neither the parameters (α and β) of the beta distribution nor the resulting statistics (μ and σ) of the parametric fit differ significantly from one another. Consequently, the resulting capital multipliers – though dissimilar – are also not significantly different in the two examples.

Table 8.3 Comparative data for the two tail-fitting examples

	Example 1	Example 2
Tail region	[190, 480]	[270, 480]
Number of loss events	121	28
α	1.02	0.92
β	1273	1050
μ (%)	0.080	0.088
σ (%)	0.079	0.091
Capital multiplier	7.057	7.246

We can therefore conclude that:

- ❑ With a beta distribution it is quite difficult to match exactly the statistics (eg, the mean and standard deviation) of the simulated portfolio if the objective is to fit the tail of the distribution. In fact, with just about any choice of loss distribution it is not a trivial task to match both statistics and tail simultaneously.
- ❑ A beta distribution with only two degrees of freedom is perhaps insufficient to give an adequate description of tail events in the loss distribution.
- ❑ It is perhaps feasible to go deeper into the extreme tail region and use only a few carefully chosen loss events to describe the entire tail region completely.

The examples are, in fact, pointing to an even more powerful area of statistical research known as "extreme value theory". This is the scope of the next few chapters.

9

Monte Carlo Simulation of Loss Distribution

In the previous chapter two simple examples were used to demonstrate how to estimate the tail of the loss distribution using a combination of Monte Carlo simulation and analytical tail-fitting to a beta distribution. In fact, my own research has shown that this combination of simulation and tail-fitting might be a more sensible way to study extreme events associated with an *unknown* loss distribution due to credit risk. Of course, the same thing is also true for market risk. This chapter addresses the simulation technique, while the following chapter demonstrates the use of extreme value theory as a departure from the beta distribution.

The beta distribution was naïvely chosen in the previous chapter as a representative of portfolio loss without giving it much analytical thought other than merely to observe that the generic features of the two-parameter beta family of distributions are somewhat similar to the loss distribution for an actual portfolio. Beginning with this chapter and following up on some insights gained from the previous chapter, we need to tighten some loose ends up a bit and introduce more analytical machinery and rigour into the original thought processes. We shall begin first with a detailed description of the simulation process.

SIMULATING THE LOSS DISTRIBUTION

There are several steps in generating a portfolio loss distribution. Many refinements can be made to the simulation technique, but they are best left to the reader's imagination. The more enterprising reader can certainly think of other clever enhancements to improve on the generic scheme presented below. The following is a brief outline of how the loss distribution of a credit portfolio can be simulated using Monte Carlo methods.

- *Estimate defaults and losses* The default probability for each facility is assigned according to its internal facility risk rating (or some industry credit rating from Standard & Poor's or Moody's). For simplicity, the mean of the loss given default is set to an industry average of, say, 35% for secured transactions and 50% for unsecured transactions. The standard deviation of the LGD also requires some estimation. In practice, there could be further granularity in the LGD depending on the type of collateralisation that is applicable to the credit facilities in the portfolio. It is interesting to note that both CreditMetrics and KMV Corporation hinted at the possibility of using the beta distribution to model loss given default.
- *Estimate asset correlation between obligors* If it is not feasible to incorporate pairwise asset correlation between obligors, it is important to approximate the asset correlation matrix by industry groupings as discussed in chapter 7.
- *Generate correlated default events*
  - First, generate a set of random numbers drawn from a standard normal distribution to simulate the asset values of all the obligors in the portfolio.
  - Second, perform a decomposition (eg, Cholesky, singular value or eigenvalue) on the asset correlation matrix to transform the independent set of random numbers obtained in the preceding step into a set of correlated asset values. It is important to note that the asset correlation matrix need not be positive definite in practice.
  - Third, calculate the default point of each obligor using the standard normal distribution and the known default probability for the obligor.
  - Finally, check obligors' asset values against their simulated default points; if an obligor's asset value in a particular scenario falls below the simulated default point, a default event is said to occur.
- *Generate random loss given default* Whenever a default event occurs, a random number is drawn from a uniform distribution

Figure 9.1 Flow diagram of portfolio loss simulation

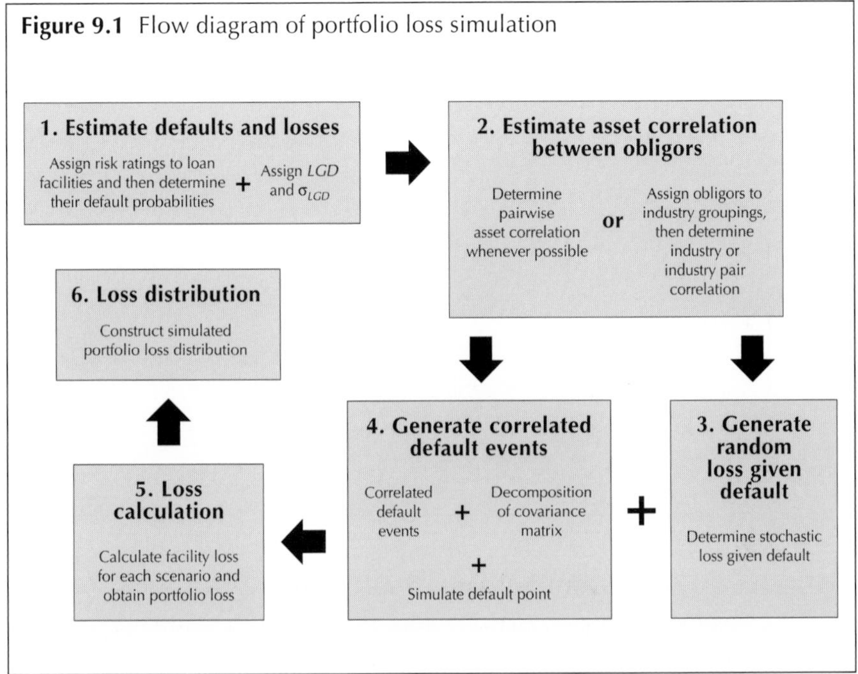

that matches the mean and standard deviation of the LGD given in the first step. This step provides the amount of loss given default.

- *Loss calculation* For obligors that have defaulted in a particular scenario, set $Loss = Exposure \times LGD$; for obligors not in default in the same scenario, set $Loss = 0$. The portfolio's total loss is the simple sum of all the losses for each obligor in the portfolio.
- *Loss distribution* A single total portfolio loss number is produced for each scenario. By repeating all the preceding steps, say, 100,000 times, we obtain 100,000 different scenarios of portfolio loss. The resulting histogram of these portfolio losses is the simulated loss distribution of the portfolio due to default risk.

A simple flow diagram is presented in Figure 9.1 to illustrate the components of the simulation just described. Mathematical details of the simulation process can be found in Appendix A. The example that follows demonstrates the results of a sample simulation using the steps outlined above.

Figure 9.2 Simulated loss distribution

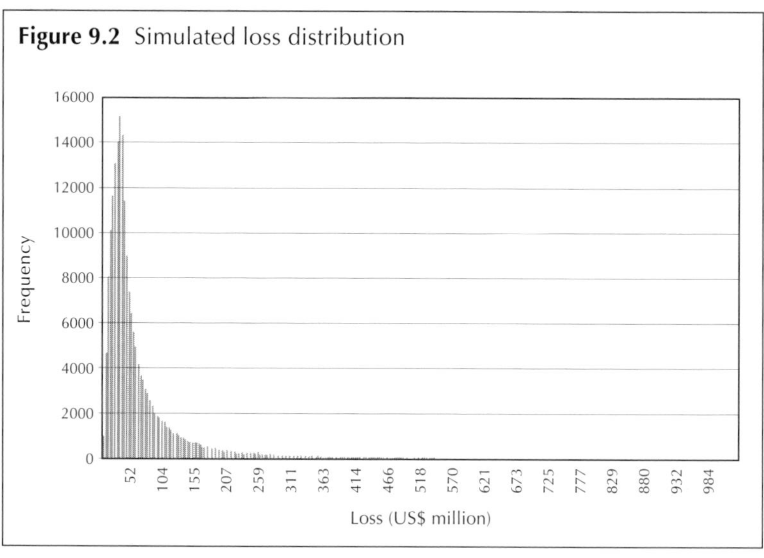

Example 9.1: Simulation and the tail

Consider a sample portfolio with the following characteristics:

Total number of facilities	2165
Commitments	\$56.0 billion
Current outstanding	\$15.1 billion
Adjusted exposure	\$42.2 billion

For convenience, the internal risk ratings of the facilities are mapped to Standard & Poor's credit ratings so that default probabilities can be assigned to them. Each facility is appropriately identified as being secured or unsecured so that the loss given default percentages can also be assigned. In addition, every single facility is mapped one-to-one to one of the available Standard & Poor's standard industry classifications to facilitate construction of the covariance matrix. Asset correlations among the different obligors are proxied by their corresponding Standard & Poor's industry index return correlations according to the procedure prescribed in chapter 7.

Once the portfolio has been properly prepared for analysis, the technical details of the Monte Carlo simulation of the portfolio loss distribution follow very closely the steps outlined in Appendix A. The simulated loss distribution is displayed in Figure 9.2.

Figure 9.3 Tail of the loss distribution

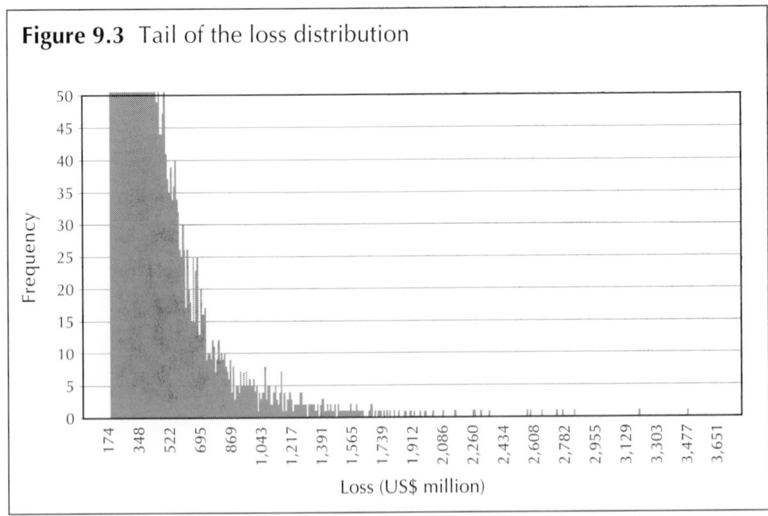

One can immediately observe how highly skewed and leptokurtic the distribution is. The tail is also quite stretched out into the high-loss region towards the right end of the chart. For the more statistically inclined reader, it is very tempting to perform a thorough statistical analysis of the simulated loss distribution so that the higher-order statistics can be calculated. Furthermore, the error bounds for the simulation exercise can also be determined. This, however, is not the intent here.

The next chart, Figure 9.3, zooms in on the tail and highlights the frequency count in this section of the distribution. Observe that there are many non-zero losses in the tail section, so the loss distribution exhibits a very fat, heavy tail.

The Monte Carlo simulation that generated the two charts on these pages used a total of 200,000 scenarios, incorporating default correlations between industry groupings and using a historical mean LGD of 35% for secured facilities and 50% for unsecured facilities. The standard deviations of the LGD were 21% and 28% for the secured and unsecured facilities, respectively.

The mean and standard deviation of the simulated loss distribution are \$65.2 million and \$97.6 million, respectively. The capital multiplier corresponding to a 99.97% confidence was calculated to be 14.4. But would this be the correct capital multiplier to use in practice? To answer this question we need to perform an additional tail-fitting exercise. This is followed up in the next example.

Figure 9.4 Tail-fitting

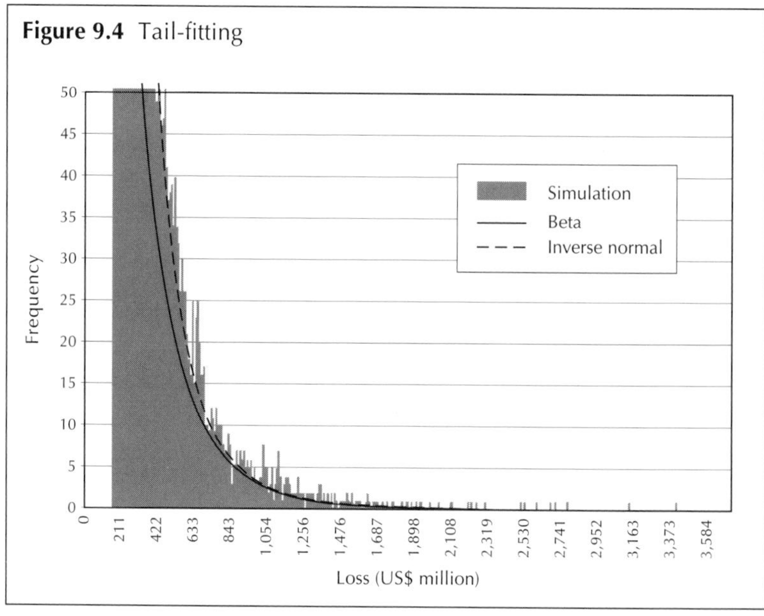

Example 9.2: Another tail-fitting

In this example we attempt to fit the tail of the simulated loss distribution using the beta distribution and the so-called *inverse normal distribution* advocated by KMV Corporation.

The inverse normal is a two-parameter family with a cumulative distribution defined by

$$Q(x, p, \rho) \equiv N\left[\frac{1}{\sqrt{\rho}}\left(\sqrt{1-\rho}N^{-1}(x) - N^{-1}(\rho)\right)\right]$$

where x is a standard normal variable and the parameters are $0 < p$, $\rho < 1$. The function $N(*)$ denotes the standard cumulative normal distribution.

The calibration to these two analytical distributions (beta and inverse normal) produced capital multipliers of 16.16 and 14.28, respectively.

Figure 9.4 shows the parametric tail-fit with a beta distribution and KMV's inverse normal distribution. Observe that both analytical distributions have excellent parametric fit in the chosen tail region corresponding to the percentile between 99.5% and 99.92%, or $Loss \in [618, 1136]$, but disagree away from this region. Therefore,

Figure 9.5 Cumulative distribution – tail region

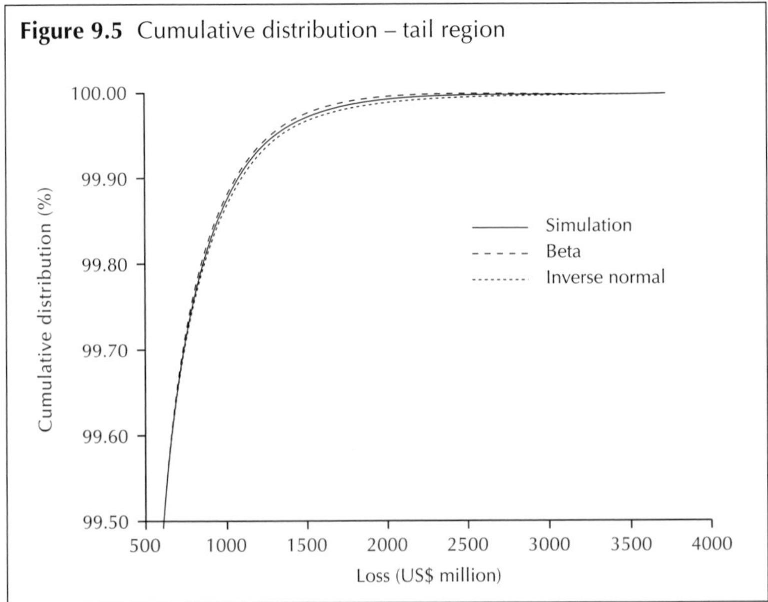

we can already expect ahead of time that the mean and standard deviation calculated directly from these fitted loss distributions will not agree with either the results from the simulation or from our internal model calculation.

Admittedly, even with the "snugness" of the tail-fit, it is still quite difficult to form any objective conclusion on the correctness of the choice of multiplier and, therefore, of loss distribution.

The cumulative distributions in the tail region corresponding to the two parametric tail-fits and the simulation are plotted in Figure 9.5.

Figure 9.6 (overleaf) shows the cumulative distribution of the entire loss profile. As expected, the fit is not good away from the tail region since our focus was on extreme tail events. Therefore, there is no reason to expect agreement with the simulated expected loss and unexpected loss.

SOME OBSERVATIONS FROM THE EXAMPLES

The simulation exercise above coupled with the analytical tail-fitting shows how difficult and non-scientific the determination of extreme events can be. Simply using simulation alone could result in very large economic capital requirements that would be quite

Figure 9.6 Cumulative distribution – entire region

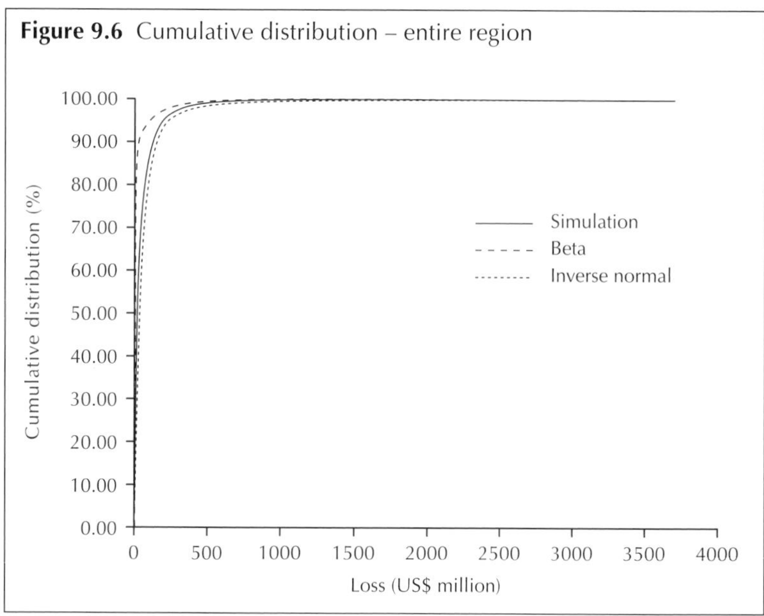

uneconomical from a bank's perspective. It is my opinion that a naïve assessment of the confidence levels using any one method alone can be quite misleading and is probably incorrect for all practical purposes. To remedy this, I shall introduce the notion of extreme value theory, or EVT, in the next section.

A comparison of the results from the two previous examples and our own internal calculation (labelled "Portfolio") is made in Table 9.1, where all data are in units of millions of US dollars.

Observe that, as expected, the mean, μ, and standard deviation, σ, of the analytical parametric fits do not agree with each other, and they also do not agree with either the simulation or the internal model calculation. The simple reason is that the analytical distributions were deliberately fitted only to a specifically chosen section of the tail region and were not subject to the constraint of fitting to the actual mean and standard deviation of the simulated loss distribution nor of the internal model.

WHY EVT AND NOT JUST SIMULATION?

As a precursor to the next chapter on extreme value theory, we need to ask why we cannot just perform a Monte Carlo simulation to arrive at the unknown loss distribution.

Table 9.1 Comparison of the examples

	Portfolio	Simulation	Beta	Inverse normal
Expected loss	65.7	65.2		
μ			19.8	54.9
Unexpected loss	135.0	97.6		
σ			87.5	102.8
Capital multiplier		14.5	16.2	14.3

In fact, simulation, while powerful, has its weaknesses. It is not the entire loss distribution that one is interested in when determining economic capital requirements. We are interested only in the extreme regions of the tail section where infrequent but potentially huge or even catastrophic losses might occur. It is also precisely the same regions where Monte Carlo simulation is unreliably weak. With two separate simulation runs, it is conceivable that two entirely different tail sections could result. Nevertheless, a simulation framework allows one a better glimpse of the region *close* to the extreme tail section. It is this "near-tail" region which is needed to extrapolate into the extreme tail section. Colloquially speaking, we need the "good" region of the near-tail section that is obtainable only through simulation while the simulated signals are still good.

APPENDIX A – MATHEMATICS OF LOSS SIMULATION*

The first three steps of the Monte Carlo simulation process are:

- ❑ estimate defaults and losses;
- ❑ estimate asset correlation between obligors; and
- ❑ generate correlated default events.

The first two, preliminary, steps involving parameterisation are assumed to have been done at this point. The next step is to generate correlated default events among all the obligors in the portfolio.

We start the discussion immediately by using a mathematical formalism. For each instrument in the portfolio of N obligors, we generate a random number to determine whether a specific obligor

*This appendix is based on an internal note written by Stevan Maglic. The author also wishes to thank S. Maglic for performing extensive portfolio simulation using Matlab.

is in default or not. To this end, we populate an N-dimensional vector with N independent *standard normal* random variables:

$$\varepsilon = \begin{bmatrix} \varepsilon_1 \\ \varepsilon_2 \\ \vdots \\ \varepsilon_N \end{bmatrix} \tag{A.9.1}$$

where $\varepsilon_i \sim N(0,1)$ for all i.

To generate a vector of random variables that are mutually correlated, we must perform a transformation:

$$\varepsilon'_u = \sum_{p=1}^{N} m_{up} \varepsilon_p \tag{A.9.2}$$

or, when expressed in matrix form:

$$\varepsilon' = M\varepsilon \tag{A.9.3}$$

The task is to find the transformation matrix M. For an appropriately chosen matrix, M, the random vector ε' can be made into one that has a *multivariate normal* distribution with some specified covariance structure. We shall focus on this issue next.

To specify the covariance structure of ε', note that the correlation coefficient between two correlated variables is given by

$$\rho_{jk} \equiv \left\langle \varepsilon'_j \cdot \varepsilon'_k \right\rangle = \sum_{p,q}^{N} m_{jp} m_{qk} \left\langle \varepsilon_j \cdot \varepsilon_k \right\rangle \tag{A.9.4}$$

where the bracket <*> represents the expectation operator over many scenarios. Since the average is taken over normally distributed variables, the second bracket in equation (A.9.4) simplifies to

$$\left\langle \varepsilon_j \cdot \varepsilon_k \right\rangle = \delta_{jk} \tag{A.9.5}$$

where δ_{jk} is the Kronecker delta function defined by

$$\delta_{jk} = \begin{cases} 1, & j = k \\ 0, & j \neq k \end{cases} \tag{A.9.6}$$

Thus, the correlation in equation (A.9.4) becomes

$$\rho_{jk} = \sum_{q}^{N} m_{jp} m_{qk} \tag{A.9.7}$$

or, in matrix form, the correlation matrix (or more appropriately the covariance matrix) is given by

$$\Sigma = M^t M \tag{A.9.8}$$

Notice the notation in component form, $(\Sigma)_{jk} \equiv \rho_{jk}$. Also, observe that

$$\begin{aligned} \text{var}[\varepsilon'] &= \langle (M\varepsilon)^2 \rangle - \langle M\varepsilon \rangle^2 \\ &= \langle M^t \varepsilon\varepsilon^t M \rangle - \langle M\varepsilon \rangle^2 \\ &= M^t \langle \varepsilon\varepsilon^t \rangle M - M^t \langle \varepsilon \rangle^2 M \\ &= M^t I M = M^t M \end{aligned} \tag{A.9.9}$$

since the random vector ε is normally distributed, $<\varepsilon\varepsilon^t> = I$ and $<\varepsilon> = 0$. Hence, from equation (A.9.9) we have recovered that the variance of the correlated vector ε' is equal to the covariance matrix $\Sigma = M^t M$ in equation (A.9.8), as it should be.

To implement the approach set out above, we start with the covariance matrix Σ as given and then generate correlated random numbers using equation (A.9.3). To do this we must take equation (A.9.8), perform the decomposition, and then take the "square root" of Σ to get the transformation matrix M. Once M has been obtained, the correlated random vector ε' can be constructed from equation (A.9.3).

Recall that the *empirical* covariance matrix (ie, the asset correlation matrix based on Standard & Poor's industry groupings) has already been calculated in Appendix C of chapter 7. All that remains, therefore, is the problem of determining the transformation matrix, M, in equation (A.9.8).

Obtaining the square root of a matrix

The square root of a matrix may be obtained in several ways. Two general approaches will be outlined here. The most straightforward method is to use a *Cholesky decomposition*. This, unfortunately, does not work effectively if the matrix is singular or not positive definite. Here the *singular value decomposition* and *eigenvalue decomposition* approaches are more effective, but at the expense of greater computational complexity and longer computing times.

Cholesky decomposition

The scheme of a Cholesky decomposition is to decompose a given positive definite matrix, Σ, into the form

$$\Sigma = A^t A \tag{A.9.10}$$

where the matrix elements, $(\Sigma)_{ij} = s_{ij}$, of the decomposition are only non-zero along the diagonal and upper or lower triangle. Explicitly, for a 3×3 matrix the decomposition looks like this:

$$\begin{pmatrix} s_{11} & s_{12} & s_{13} \\ s_{21} & s_{22} & s_{23} \\ s_{31} & s_{32} & s_{33} \end{pmatrix} = \begin{pmatrix} a_{11} & 0 & 0 \\ a_{21} & a_{22} & 0 \\ a_{31} & a_{32} & a_{33} \end{pmatrix} \begin{pmatrix} a_{11} & a_{12} & a_{13} \\ 0 & a_{22} & a_{23} \\ 0 & 0 & 0 \end{pmatrix} \tag{A.9.11}$$

where the matrix A has elements along the diagonal and on the upper triangle. When expressed in this way, it can easily be shown that the matrix elements in A are related to Σ by

$$a_{ii} = \left[s_{ii} - \sum_{k=1}^{i-1} a_{ik} \right]^{\frac{1}{2}} \tag{A.9.12a}$$

along the diagonal of A and by

$$a_{ij} = \frac{1}{a_{ii}} \left[s_{ij} - \sum_{k=1}^{i-1} a_{ik} a_{jk} \right]^{\frac{1}{2}} \tag{A.9.12b}$$

off-diagonal of A.

These recursive relationships allow the equations to be solved easily with a computer and have the advantage of being simple and straightforward. As just mentioned, however, the Cholesky scheme does not work if the matrix is singular or not positive definite. For example, in equation (A.9.12b), when the a_{ii} term in the denominator is either zero or close to zero, a_{ij} diverges. In this case other algorithms are needed.

Eigenvalue decomposition

This approach exploits the similarity with the well-known eigenvalue problem in matrix theory. The eigenvalue equation is

$$\Sigma U = U\Lambda \tag{A.9.13}$$

where Σ is a given matrix and Λ is a matrix with only diagonal elements which are the eigenvalues of the matrix Σ. The matrix U must be determined.

Rearranging equation (A.9.13), we obtain

$$\Sigma = U\Lambda U^{-1} \tag{A.9.14}$$

Equation (A.9.14) is the well-known *similarity transformation*, which diagonalises Σ. Because Λ is diagonal, it is easy to take the square root of the matrix by simply taking the square root of each of the elements in Σ. We then rewrite equation (A.9.14) as

$$\begin{aligned} \Sigma &= U\Lambda^{1/2}\Lambda^{1/2}U^{-1} \\ &\equiv Q^t Q \end{aligned} \tag{A.9.15}$$

where $Q \equiv \Lambda^{1/2}U^{-1}$. Observe that, for this to be true, the matrix U must necessarily be orthogonal, ie, $U^t = U^{-1}$.

Using the matrix Q as the required transformation, we can now generate the required correlated random numbers from initially uncorrelated random numbers, viz:

$$\varepsilon' = Q\varepsilon = \Lambda^{1/2}U^{-1}\varepsilon$$

It can easily be checked that the variance of the correlated vector ε is indeed the covariance matrix, ie, $\mathrm{var}[\varepsilon'] = Q^t Q = \Sigma$.

Singular value decomposition

For covariance matrices that are singular or numerically close to being singular, we need to resort to a different kind of decomposition called the *singular value decomposition* (SVD). Briefly, the SVD of a *square* covariance matrix is given by

$$\Sigma = VDV^t \tag{A.9.16}$$

where V is an orthogonal matrix such that $V^t = V^{-1}$ and D is a diagonal matrix with the singular values of Σ along the diagonal and zeros elsewhere. Again, owing to its diagonality, the square root of matrix D can be extracted easily. The required correlated random numbers can, therefore, be obtained from the initially uncorrelated random numbers using the transformation $\varepsilon' = D^{1/2} V^{-1} \varepsilon$. As usual, it can easily be checked that $\text{var}[\varepsilon'] = VDV^{-1} = \Sigma$, as it should.

Calculating the default point

Using the previous steps, correlated asset values that are normally distributed can be generated for each of the constituent instruments of the portfolio. The word "instruments" is used very generically here to refer to loan facilities, bonds or other receivables which are subject to default risk. Associated with each instrument is a normally distributed and correlated random variable, ε'_i, with a mean of zero and a standard deviation of one. In the simulation process, this association will be used to determine whether the obligor associated with the instrument is in default or not. Note that a more complex indexing scheme needs to be introduced for the case when multiple instruments are associated with the same obligor.

At this point, the following things are known:

- The correlated asset value is constructed to be normally distributed, ie, $\varepsilon'_i \sim N(0, 1)$.
- The corresponding probability of default, given by EDF_i, is known.

The *default point* threshold, *DP*, of the *i*th obligor can be defined as $DP_i \equiv N^{-1}(EDF_i, 0, 1)$, where $N^{-1}(*)$ is the inverse cumulative normal distribution. Thus, the criterion of default for the *i*th obligor can be constructed as follows:

$$\begin{array}{ll} \text{If } \varepsilon'_i < DP_i, & \text{then } \textit{Default} \\ \text{If } \varepsilon'_i \geq DP_i, & \text{then } \textit{No default} \end{array} \tag{A.9.17}$$

If a number is drawn that generates an asset value below the default point threshold, the instrument is in default. This process is continued for each instrument in the portfolio until the instruments that are in default for a single scenario have been determined.

Figure A.9.1 Default point

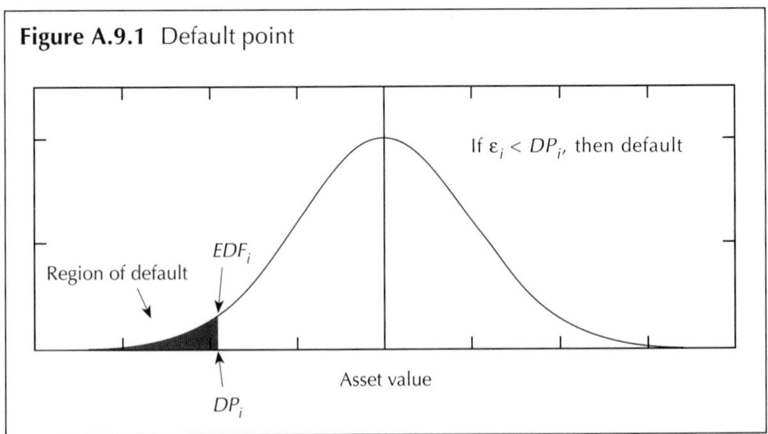

Appendix B of chapter 7 and this chapter give a theoretically better description of the default point. Appendix B of chapter 3 also contains a lengthy discussion of the default point. The default point is best illustrated in Figure A.9.1, where the criterion (A.9.17) is demonstrated graphically.

Generate loss given default

To every obligor that is simulated to be in default in the previous step it is necessary to assign a loss given default (LGD). Because of the embedded covenant structures, uncertainty is associated with the LGD. Indeed, in principle, the LGD is a stochastic variable with an unknown distribution. A random number should therefore be generated to simulate this stochastic variable as well. Both CreditMetrics and KMV hinted at using a beta distribution to model LGD stochastically.

In our example we assume that the loss given default and its uncertainty, as characterised by the standard deviation σ_{LGD}, are as shown in Table A.9.1. The numbers in the table are for indicative purposes only.

Table A.9.1 Loss given default

	Recovery rate (%)	***LGD*** (%)	σ_{LGD} (%)
Secured	65	35	21
Unsecured	50	50	28

Using the delineation (secured or unsecured) of each instrument, we determine the "average" historical LGD from Table A.9.1 and then draw a *uniform* random variable $z \in [0,1]$. In essence, the data in the table are used as an historical average for all the instruments in the portfolio.

We can now generate the random LGD_i of the ith instrument by using the approximate relationship given by

$$LGD_i = LGD^S + f_i \times \sigma_{LGD}^S \qquad \textbf{(A.9.18)}$$

where f_i is drawn from a uniform distribution whose range is selected so that the resulting loss given default has a standard deviation that is consistent with historical observation. The superscript "S" in the equation is an indicator of whether the instrument is secured or not. The resulting distribution of *LGD* is, of course, by construction consistent with the average historical uncertainties given in Table A.9.1.

Table A.9.1 represents the simplest case of assigning loss given default percentages. Depending on the seniority structure and other embedded covenants, it needs to be expanded to take other nuances into account.

Calculation of loss

Once defaults have been determined for a particular scenario, it is necessary to determine the loss in value of the portfolio. This is easily performed by summing all the simulated losses from one single scenario:

$$\text{Loss} = \sum_{\substack{\text{Obligors}\\ \text{in default}}} \text{Adjusted exposure}_i \times LGD \qquad \textbf{(A.9.19)}$$

Simulated loss distribution

The simulated loss distribution is obtained by repeating the processes above from 10,000 to 1,000,000 times, recording the loss calculation for each scenario. A histogram is then generated which shows the number of events that fall in a range of bins. The result of such a simulation is shown in Figure A.9.2.

Figure A.9.2 Simulated loss distribution

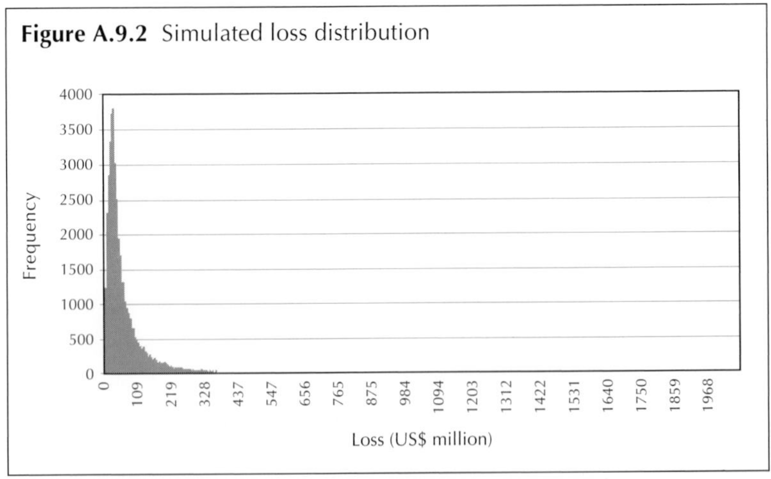

APPENDIX B – SIMULATING DEFAULT AND THE DEFAULT POINT

Using Assumptions 1 and 2 in Appendix B of chapter 7 as background, we use the "value of the firm" class of risky debt model and allow the default of a firm to be triggered by the decline of its asset value below some given threshold called the *default point*.

Following the first-passage time implementation of Zhou (1997), assume that for each firm i there exist two positive constants, K_i and λ_i, such that firm i defaults on all of its contractual obligations instantaneously as soon as $V_i(t) \leq e^{\lambda_i t} K_i$. The constant K_i is known as the *default point threshold*.

For simplicity and without loss of generality, set $\lambda_i = \mu_i$ to prevent the drift terms from clogging the mathematics. Denote

$$\tau_i \equiv \min_{t \geq 0} \{ t \mid e^{-\lambda_i t} V_i(t) \leq K_i \}$$

as the first time that firm i's asset value reaches its default point threshold, K_i. Then, the event $D_i(t)$ that firm i defaults before $t > 0$ can be expressed as $D_i(t) = \{\tau_i \leq t\}$ A direct application of Harrison (1990) gives the expression for the probability of default:

$$P\left(D_i(t)\right) = P(\tau_i \leq t) = 2 \times N\left(-\frac{Z_i}{\sqrt{t}}\right) \qquad \textbf{(B.9.1)}$$

The quantity Z_i, defined by

$$Z_i \frac{\ln\left[V_i(0)/K_i\right]}{\sigma_i} \tag{B.9.2}$$

can be considered as firm i's "normalised" *distance to its default point*. Notice that since only the losing tail of the loss distribution is of interest, the factor of two in equation (B.9.1) is not necessary.

Note Observe the similarity between the more theoretically precise discussion here and the default point defined in the simulation exercise in Appendix A. It will be left to the readers to convince themselves that the two formalisms are, indeed, exactly identical. The reader is also advised to refer back to Appendix B of chapter 3 for a loose definition of the default point as implemented by KMV Corporation and its comparison with a more theoretical definition.

10

Extreme Value Theory

The primary issue risk managers have always been interested in is assessing the *size* – more so than the *frequency* – of losses. This desire led market participants to develop the so-called "worst-case scenario" approach for risk assessment. In the value-at-risk (VAR) framework for market risk capital adequacy, it is easier by far than for credit risk capital adequacy to assume a "normal-like" distribution when determining confidence levels although market returns have relatively long and fat tails. When assessing credit risk in conjunction with economic capital allocation, it takes an incredible stretch of imagination to rely solely on normal-like loss distributions. As we have seen through our simulation effort in the previous chapters, the loss distribution for the credit portfolio is highly skewed and, therefore, has an extremely long, fat tail.

I have also demonstrated in earlier chapters that using either Monte Carlo simulation or analytical distributions in isolation is very impractical and misleading. To estimate tail events it is necessary to combine both simulation techniques with analytical tail-fitting. However, in spite of this combination, it is still difficult to come up with an objective criterion that can conclusively determine the *capital multiplier*. In this chapter I propose the use of a very well-established tool in actuarial statistics called extreme value theory, or, simply, EVT, as another viable combination of alternatives.

Extreme value theory, as the name implies, focuses on extreme events and their associated *tail probabilities*. The problem of estimating the tail of the loss distribution considered in the previous chapter is one instance where EVT could be very useful. In fact, EVT offers precisely the methodology for characterising these rare, *but not impossible*, occurrences of losses.

FUNDAMENTAL REGIMES OF LOSSES

From a risk management and risk measurement perspective, we have seen in previous chapters that there are three fundamental regimes of loss:

- *Expected loss* The losses a bank is expected to bear as a consequence of undertaking its day-to-day business activities.
- *Unexpected loss* The unanticipated, though predictable, loss which a bank must be able to absorb in the normal course of doing business.
- *Extreme loss* The highly rare, though not improbable, loss that the bank, in extreme, distressed conditions, must be able to survive and remain solvent.

The first two regimes of loss, the expected and the unexpected, have been clearly quantified in earlier sections of the book. It is the last and the most difficult regime – the extreme case – that requires the full power of EVT.

Extreme value theory, as an actuarial science, offers the appropriate solution to quantify the boundaries between these three regimes of losses. This is the main topic of this chapter.

There are many bibliographical references for extreme value theory. Some of the more useful are: Reiss and Thomas (1997); Embrechts, Resnick and Samorodnitsky (1998); Embrechts, Kluppelberg and Mikosch (1997); McNeil and Saladin (1997); and McNeil (1998).

EXTREME VALUE THEORY – SOME BASICS

Extreme value theory is actually quite simple. Mathematically, EVT can be summarised briefly as follows. Suppose we have a sequence of independent, identically distributed observations $\{X_1, X_2, \ldots, X_n\}$ drawn from a common but yet *unknown* distribution, F. If the sequence represents losses, the most extreme case within the data sequence concerns the largest loss, symbolised by

$$M_n = \max\{X_1, X_2, \ldots, X_n\} \qquad \textbf{(10.1)}$$

More generally, we might be interested in the behaviour of a subset of the k largest losses, but in many practical situations the data sequence is incomplete. Thus, for a given confidence level α, we may have to extrapolate beyond the range of the given data sequence. We are, therefore, primarily interested in the *excess losses* over some high threshold u_α, where the index α denotes the confidence level. This means, for a *small* α, determine the threshold u_α such that

$$P(X > u_\alpha) = 1 - F(u_\alpha) = \alpha \tag{10.2}$$

For example, the economic interpretation of equation (10.2) goes something like this:

> If the random variable X represents the loss variable associated with credit default risk, then u_α corresponds to the minimum amount of economic capital the bank needs to set aside in order to survive (with some confidence level α) an extreme loss in portfolio value due to default.

Of course, once the threshold is fixed, one would need to estimate the size of potential losses beyond this level. Therefore, we would also need to be able to estimate the conditional probability of excesses, viz:

$$F_{u_\alpha}(x) \equiv P(X - u_\alpha \le x \mid X > u_\alpha) \tag{10.3}$$

The simple interpretation of equation (10.3) is:

> Given that there is a loss beyond the threshold u_α, the conditional probability that the excess loss $X - u_\alpha$ is no bigger than some level x is $F_{u_\alpha}(x)$, with some confidence level α.

For reference purpose later, the probability in equation (10.3) can also be rewritten as

$$\begin{aligned} F_{u_\alpha}(x) &\equiv P\left(X - u_\alpha \le x \middle| X > u_\alpha\right) \\ &= \frac{P\left(X - u_\alpha \le x, X > u_\alpha\right)}{P\left(X > u_\alpha\right)} \\ &= \frac{F_{u_\alpha}\left(x + u_\alpha\right) - F_{u_\alpha}\left(u_\alpha\right)}{1 - F_{u_\alpha}\left(u_\alpha\right)}, \qquad x \ge 0 \end{aligned} \tag{10.4}$$

From the basic theory outlined above, observe immediately that there are two practical generalities to consider regarding the information required for extreme value analysis:

- *Sufficient data* If there are sufficient data above the threshold, the estimate of the conditional probability $F_{u_\alpha}(x)$ involves only those losses above the threshold which are contained in the data sequence $\{X_1, X_2, \ldots, X_n\}$. This is, therefore, a trivial case.
- *Insufficient data* In the case of insufficient data above the threshold (which is normally the case in practice), it is necessary to find a suitable approximation for the conditional probability. The distribution $F_{u_\alpha}(x)$ is, in this case, truly unknown, especially along the tail region.

From the practical perspective of risk management and the measurement of credit risk, one of the main goals of EVT should be to provide answers to the second case. In the next section we begin with a very large class of suitable EVT distributions under the heading "generalised Pareto distribution".

Before we proceed, however, the reader may first wish to peruse the panel on pages 212–13, which contains a reprint of a non-mathematical article by A. McNeil entitled "History Repeating". The essay is a hypothetical story based on the historic black Monday crash of October 19, 1987, when the S&P500 index closed down 20.4% of its opening value, sending shock waves around the global financial world. The simple message is that extreme value theory might have a sensible role to play in the risk management of extreme phenomena.

GENERALISED PARETO DISTRIBUTION

The distribution, $F_{u_\alpha}(x)$, of excesses can be approximately modelled by the class of generalised Pareto distributions, among many other possible distributions. The generalised Pareto distribution (GPD) is a family with three degrees of freedom, parameterised by

$$G_{\xi,\mu,\psi}(x) = \exp\left\{-\left(1+\xi\cdot\frac{x-\mu}{\psi}\right)_+^{-\frac{1}{\xi}}\right\} \quad \text{for } \xi \neq 0 \qquad \textbf{(10.5a)}$$

where the three parameters are the *scale* parameter, $\psi > 0$, the *location* parameter, $\mu \in R$, and the *shape* parameter, $\xi \in R$. The subscript "+" means $y_+ \equiv \max[0, y]$. The special case when $\xi = 0$ is to be interpreted as the limiting form given by

$$G_{0,\mu,\psi}(x) = \exp\left\{-\exp\left(-\frac{x-\mu}{\psi}\right)\right\} \tag{10.5b}$$

In practice, instead of using equation (10.5a), it is also not uncommon to use the simpler functional form given by

$$G_{\xi,\mu,\psi}(x) = 1-\left(1+\xi\cdot\frac{x-\mu}{\psi}\right)_+^{-\frac{1}{\xi}} \quad \text{for } \xi \neq 0 \tag{10.5c}$$

Observe that both equations (10.5a) and (10.5c) have asymptotically the same limiting form. Therefore, it does not matter which functional form is chosen for practical implementation.

The generalised Pareto family of distributions (10.5a) subsumes three other well-known distributions:

- $\xi = 0$ the *Gumbel* or *double exponential*;
- $\xi > 0$ the *Fréchet*, which has unbounded support to the right; and
- $\xi < 0$ the *Weibull*, which has unbounded support to the left.

Representative distributions of the generalised Pareto family are shown in Figure 10.1, which was prepared using *Mathcad* software.

Figure 10.1 Distributions of the generalised Pareto family

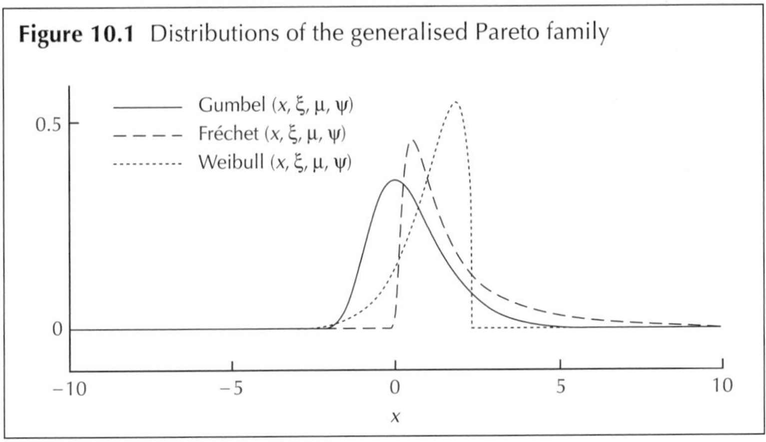

At this juncture it would be instructive to pause for a simple example. Example 10.1 is based on the same loan portfolio used throughout the book. A generalised Pareto distribution was used to fit the tail of the distribution. Recall that earlier we naïvely employed a beta distribution and an inverse normal distribution coupled with Monte Carlo simulation.

Example 10.1: Tail-fitting using generalised Pareto distribution
The graph in Figure 9.3 accompanying Example 9.1 in the previous chapter is a zoom-in view of the tail region of the simulated loss distribution of the portfolio. Table 10.1 focuses on the region of the tail that we wish to fit.

The first column is the simulated loss (in millions of US dollars). The second column is the percentile of the total simulated portfolio. The region to be fitted with a generalised Pareto distribution is the percentile range from 99.5% to 99.92%, corresponding to a portfolio loss in the range $Loss \in [618, 1136]$, denominated in millions of dollars. The third column displays the cumulative probability of the fitted Pareto distribution.

The tail-fitting process, again using the minimisation of least-squares error, results in the best-fit parameters ψ (the scale parameter) = 0.00256, μ (the location parameter) = −0.00693, and ξ (the shape parameter) = 0.15998.

A graph of the cumulative distribution of the tail-fit versus the simulated loss distribution is displayed as Figure 10.2 (on page 204). Clearly, there is a remarkably tight fit – overall a much better fit than is obtained with a beta distribution – demonstrating the usefulness of using extreme value theory in determining the tails of loss distributions due to default risk. But what does this really mean?

Capital multiplier It is interesting to note that the associated capital multiplier (for an AA rating) obtained with this GPD tail-fit is 14.77. What if we had used a different criterion for setting up capital requirements?

Table 10.2 (also on page 204) gives the capital multipliers corresponding to the different classes of desired debt rating for the bank. The table compares the results for two cases: the Pareto tail-fit and the simulation exercise.

Table 10.1 Data for tail-fitting example

Loss (US$ million)	Cumulative probability Simulation	Pareto
618	0.995010	0.995163
621	0.995085	0.995232
625	0.995160	0.995301
629	0.995275	0.995369
633	0.995355	0.995435
636	0.995430	0.995501
640	0.995555	0.995565
644	0.995595	0.995628
647	0.995660	0.995690
651	0.995760	0.995751
655	0.995835	0.995812
658	0.995900	0.995871
662	0.995935	0.995929
666	0.996015	0.995986
670	0.996085	0.996043
673	0.996165	0.996098
677	0.996230	0.996152
681	0.996315	0.996206
684	0.996360	0.996259
688	0.996400	0.996311
692	0.996430	0.996362
695	0.996480	0.996412
699	0.996520	0.996462
703	0.996570	0.996510
707	0.996615	0.996558
710	0.996645	0.996605
...		
1088	0.999040	0.999044
1091	0.999040	0.999055
1095	0.999055	0.999065
1099	0.999075	0.999076
1102	0.999100	0.999086
1106	0.999135	0.999096
1110	0.999140	0.999106
1113	0.999140	0.999116
1117	0.999160	0.999126
1121	0.999160	0.999135
1124	0 .999165	0.999145
1128	0.999165	0.999154
1132	0.999170	0.999163
1136	0.999180	0.999173

Figure 10.2 Graphical comparison of cumulative distributions for tail of simulated loss distribution and Pareto fit

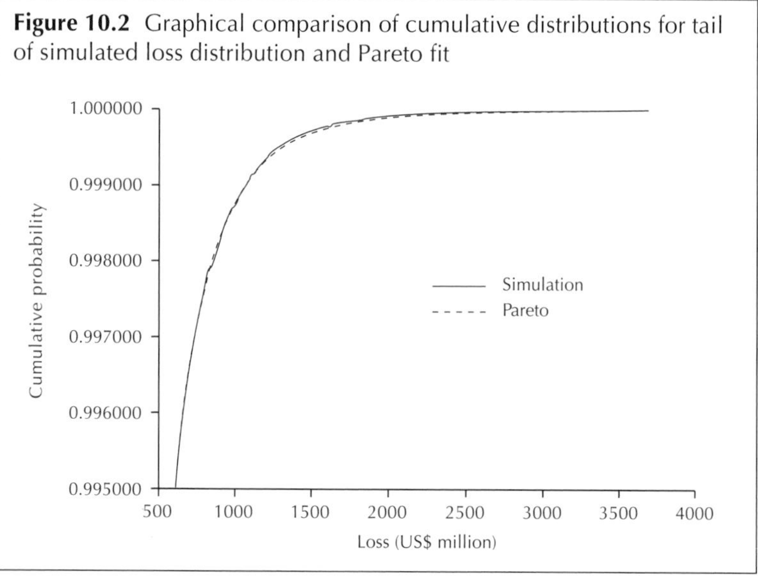

Observe that the capital multipliers resulting from a GPD tail-fit agree remarkably well with our simulation results. Note also from Table 10.2 that as one moves further away from the most extreme tail (ie, a lower rating), the capital multiplier for both the GPD tail-fitting and pure simulation decreases, indicating a lower economic capital requirement associated with a lower level of confidence.

Although this example demonstrates the power of using extreme value theory to fit the distribution of extreme losses, it is still important to justify the application of EVT and to understand the conditions under which the tail-fit is meaningful. The next two sections address issues concerning convergence criteria, the choice of threshold (ie, the range over which the tail-fitting should occur) and other analytical tools.

Table 10.2 Capital multipliers

Debt rating	Pareto tail-fit (99.95%–99.92%) Percentile	Max loss	CM	Pure simulation – no fitting Percentile	Max loss	CM
AAA	99.99	1,982	19.64	99.99	1,883	18.63
AA	99.97	1,506	14.77	99.97	1,470	14.39
A	99.90	1,073	10.32	99.90	1,071	10.31
BBB	99.70	744	6.95	99.70	745	6.97

Max loss: maximum loss, millions of US dollars; CM: capital multiplier.

By necessity, the topic of convergence requires some maths. For non-mathematical readers, the sections that follow can be read without paying too much attention to the mathematical details but, rather, to the contents and their implications.

CONVERGENCE CRITERIA

The practical application of extreme value theory requires rigorous justification. This section summarises the known results regarding EVT. There are three fundamental results to consider. They are:

- *Convergence of the empirical distribution to the generalised Pareto family* This is guaranteed by the Fisher–Tippett theorem.
- *Criterion for the tail of the extreme losses to be in the domain of applicable extreme value distributions* This is answered by the Gnedenko theorem and similar results.
- *Criterion for choosing a high threshold* This is guaranteed by the Picklands–Balkema–de Haan theorem.

The first of these important results is the well-known Fisher–Tippett theorem. This plays the same role as the central limit theorem in the statistical study of sums. The theorem describes the limiting behaviour of appropriately normalised maxima. The theorems mentioned above will be quoted without proofs. The mathematical details are widely available in the references cited earlier. I shall enumerate the theorems and comment on their practical implications.

THEOREM (Fisher–Tippett, 1928) *Suppose that the sequence of data* $\{X_1, X_2, \ldots, X_n\}$ *is* i.i.d. *with a common but unknown distribution function, F, for which an* empirical *but incomplete distribution* $F^{\text{empirical}}$ *exists. Suppose further that sequences of real constants,* a_n *and* b_n*, can be found such that* $(M_n - a_n)/b_n$*, the sequence of normalised maxima, converges in the distribution, viz:*

$$P\left(\frac{M_n - a_n}{b_n} \le x\right) = F^{\text{empirical}}\left(a_n x + b_n\right) \to G(x) \quad \text{as } n \to \infty \tag{10.6}$$

$x \in R$ *for some non-degenerate limit distribution G. Then G is one of the generalised Pareto classes* $G_{\xi,\mu,\psi}(x)$.

Maximum domain of attraction

If the condition given by equation (10.6) holds, we say that F is in the *maximum domain of attraction* (MDA) *of* G, and we write

$$F \in \text{MDA}\{G\}$$

Interpretation of the Fisher–Tippett theorem

In other words, the content of the Fisher–Tippett theorem can be summarised simply as follows:

$$F \in \text{MDA}\{G\} \Rightarrow G \text{ is of the type } G_{\xi,\mu,\psi}(x) \text{ for some } \xi, \mu, \psi \tag{10.7}$$

Hence, if we know that suitably normalised maxima converge in the distribution, the limiting distribution must be an extreme value distribution for some carefully chosen parameters ξ, μ, ψ. This is a very revealing insight. The implication is that if we were able to choose a reasonably adequate number of sample points from some empirical experiment that are properly normalised and that appear to have some limiting behaviour, the limiting distribution must be one of the generalised Pareto classes.

For most practical uses in financial risk management the Fréchet case, corresponding to $\xi > 0$, is the most important. The Fréchet case has unbounded support on the positive real axis. The following theorem gives necessary and sufficient conditions for the distribution F to be in the maximum domain of attraction of G for the case $\xi > 0$.

THEOREM (Gnedenko, 1943) *For the Fréchet case* $\xi > 0$, *we have*

$$F \in \text{MDA}\{G\} \Leftrightarrow 1 - F(x) \sim x^{-1/\xi} L(x) \tag{10.8}$$

for some slowly varying function $L(x)$.

This theorem shows that if the tail of the distribution $F(x)$ decays as a power function, the distribution is in the maximum domain of attraction of the Fréchet distribution. Similar results hold for the other classes subsumed under the generalised Pareto family.

Examples of generalised Pareto distributions

A few readers might be surprised to learn that some very familiar probability distributions are theoretically classified as generalised Pareto distributions. The list below gives examples of well-known distributions in the maximum domain of attraction of the generalised Pareto family.

- ❑ *Fréchet class* Ordinary Pareto, Burr, log-gamma, Cauchy and Student's t, along with combinations of these
- ❑ *Gumbel class* Normal, exponential, gamma, and lognormal
- ❑ *Weibull class* Beta and uniform distributions

In earlier sections I demonstrated the tail-fitting of extreme losses to the beta distribution without making clear, at the time, the full power of extreme value theory. It should now be obvious why, although the fits were not very exact, visually they look very good and promising.

THRESHOLDS REVISITED

In the beta tail-fitting exercise it was not clear how the threshold could be chosen objectively. Our criterion at that time was that the bank's debt rating should be maintained at AA, corresponding to a 99.97% confidence level. The next theorem guarantees that the distribution function of the excesses above the threshold converges in the limit to the generalised Pareto distribution.

THEOREM (Picklands, 1975; Balkema–de Haan, 1974) *Let x_0 be the finite or infinite right end-point of the distribution F, ie,*

$$x_0 = \sup\{x \in R : F(x) < 1\} \leq \infty$$

Let the distribution of the excesses over the threshold u_a be given by

$$F_{u_a}(x) \equiv P(X - u_a \leq x \mid X > u_a) \qquad \text{for } 0 \leq x < x_0 - u_a \tag{10.9}$$

Then, $F \in$ MDA$\{G\}$ if and only if G is the generalised Pareto distribution as the threshold tends to the right end-point. That is, there exists a positive measurable function $\psi(u_a)$ such that

$$\lim_{u_\alpha \to x_0} \sup_{0 \leq x < x_0 - u_\alpha} \left| F_{u_\alpha}(x) - G_{\xi,\mu,\psi(u_\alpha)}(x) \right| = 0$$

if and only if $F \in$ MDA$\{G\}$.

This theorem suggests that for sufficiently high thresholds u_a, the distribution function of the excesses, F, may be well approximated by the generalised Pareto distribution, $G_{\xi,\mu,\psi}$, for some suitable parameters ξ, μ, ψ. The theorem gives us theoretical grounds to expect that if a sufficiently high threshold is chosen, the data beyond that point will exhibit generalised Pareto behaviour. The statistical implication is that it is theoretically sound to fit the generalised Pareto distribution to data that exceed high thresholds.

THE MEAN EXCESS FUNCTION

"How does one choose the threshold?" This is a very important and practical question. Our choice for the threshold during the beta tail-fitting exercise was dictated by the desired debt rating of the bank. There are, however, a variety of more scientific ways.

Most of the methods are visual or graphical. Some are listed below.

- *Quantile–quantile or QQ plots* A concave or convex departure from the straight line indicates a heavier or shorter-tailed empirical distribution.
- *Hill estimator* This is nothing but the inverse of the average of the log ratios of ordered statistics in the data sequence. The estimator is used to approximate the Pareto shape index, ξ^{-1} for $\xi > 0$.
- *Mean excess function* A graphical method and also the easiest.

The mean excess function is defined as

$$\hat{e}(u) = \frac{\sum_{i=1}^{n} (X_i - u)_+}{\sum_{i=1}^{n} 1_{\{X_i > u\}}} \qquad \textbf{(10.10)}$$

which is the sum of the excesses above the threshold u divided by the total number of data points which exceed that threshold. In other words, the mean excess function is an empirical estimate of the expected overshoot of a threshold given that exceedance occurs.

Mathematically, the mean excess function $\hat{e}(u)$ is an *empirical* estimate of the actual expectation of exceedances given by

$$e(u) \equiv E[X - u \mid X > u] \qquad \textbf{(10.11a)}$$

For the generalised Pareto family, the expectation can easily be calculated as

$$e(u) = \frac{\psi + \xi \cdot u}{1 - \xi} \qquad \textbf{(10.11b)}$$

where $\psi + \xi \cdot u > 0$. Observe that for the generalised Pareto distribution, the expected exceedances is a *linear* function of the threshold level u. This implies that a criterion for choosing the region above the threshold for tail-fitting can easily be established. More specifically, if the *empirical* plot of the mean excess function follows a reasonably straight line (or at least with positive gradient) above a certain threshold u, this is indicative that the exceedances beyond the threshold u follow a generalised Pareto distribution with a positive shape parameter. The positive gradient is a sure sign of heavy-tailed behaviour.

We demonstrate this insight using a simple illustration in Example 10.2.

Example 10.2: Mean excess plot

The example that follows is a plot of the *empirical* mean excess function against values of the threshold – ie, $(u, \hat{e}(u))$ – using the simulated loan portfolio data from previous sections. For consistency the threshold, on the abscissa, is denominated in units of percentage loss (ie, loss in US dollars divided by total portfolio adjusted exposure).

The two square points in the plot (Figure 10.3) represent the chosen points corresponding to the thresholds $u_{99.31\%}$ and $u_{99.98\%}$, and to loss levels of 1.3% and 3.7%, respectively. The percentages 99.31% and 99.98% represent the percentiles of the simulated loss data below the thresholds.

Observe from the plot that the region between these two thresholds has *positive gradient* and is a promising candidate for GPD tail-fitting. The region above the upper threshold, $u_{99.98\%}$, is sparsely populated and will not be incorporated into the tail-fitting exercise. As such, whatever resulting distribution is fitted to the region between the two chosen thresholds will automatically subsume the exceedances beyond the higher threshold.

Figure 10.3 A mean excess plot

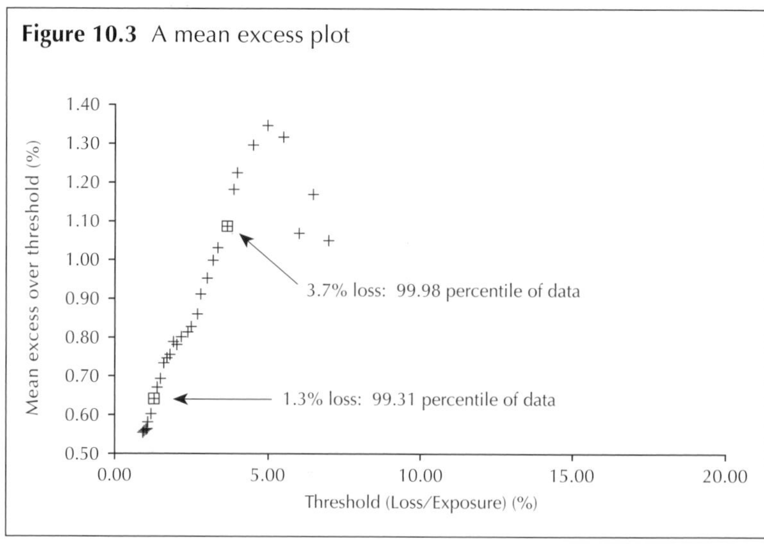

The results of the GPD fit have already been presented. Judging from the mean excess plot, it is not, therefore, just a coincidence that there was such an excellent tail-fit to the generalised Pareto family.

Indications of longer and fatter tails The particular portfolio used in this example does not have an unusually long and heavy tail like other portfolios we have considered. Depending on the composition of the portfolio analysed and the associated tail characteristics, the region above the upper threshold might contain only very few data points. Also, the upper threshold need not be located very deep inside the tail section as in this example.

For instance, the plot in Figure 10.4 for a different portfolio has a chosen upper threshold at $u_{99.93\%}$ and the region beyond that is very thinly populated. In this case, the tail region chosen for GPD fitting is from 99.47% to 99.93%, where the mean excess function has a positive gradient.

The "best fit" using least-squares minimisation gives a Pareto shape index of $\xi = 0.577$, which is much larger than in the first example ($\xi = 0.159$). Observe from the chart that there are more outlying points at much higher thresholds than in the previous example. As to the size of ξ, there are two possible conclusions:

Figure 10.4 Another example of a mean excess plot

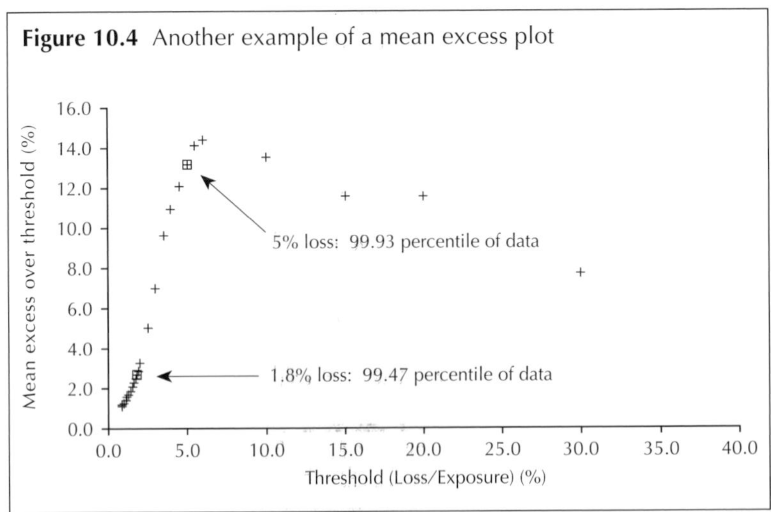

- Using Monte Carlo methods to fit the loss distribution beyond the upper threshold, $u_{99.93\%}$, is not reliable and the results should be ignored; or
- This is an indication of a longer and fatter tail.

We know from the frequency diagrams for the two portfolios that the second definitely has a much longer tail – the Pareto shape index confirms this. However, both portfolios exhibit a negative gradient beyond the upper threshold. This is an indication of either a rapidly shortening tail beyond the upper threshold or that the extreme tail sections are not excessively fat or heavy in nature. Because – unlike insurance claims – there are insufficient real-world data for portfolio loss, we need to take the more conservative path. Extreme value theory, as applied in these examples and for capital purposes, provides that level of conservatism.

HISTORY REPEATING*

Alexander McNeil

Swiss Re Research Fellow, Department of Mathematics, ETH Zurich

It is the early evening of Friday, October 16, 1987. An unusually turbulent week in the equity markets has seen the S&P500 index fall by 9.21%. On that Friday alone the index is down 5.25% on the previous day, the largest one-day fall since 1962. A young employee at a major bank's risk management division is asked to calculate a worst-case scenario for a future fall in the index. He has at his disposal all daily closing values of the index since 1960 and can calculate from these the daily percentage returns. Fresh out of university, where he followed a course in extreme value theory as part of his mathematics degree, he decides to undertake an analysis of annual maximal percentage falls in the daily index value.

He reduces his data to 28 annual maxima, corresponding to each year since 1960 and including the current unusually large percentage fall. To these data he fits a distribution known as the Fréchet and attempts to calculate estimates of various return levels. A return level is an old concept in extreme value theory, popular with hydrologists and engineers who must build structures to withstand extreme winds or extreme water levels. The 50-year return level is a level which, on average, should only be exceeded in one out of every 50 years.

Our employee uses his Fréchet model to calculate return levels. Having received a good statistical education, he also calculates a 95% confidence interval for the return levels. He recognises that he is using only 28 data points and that his estimates of the parameters of the Fréchet model are prone to error and tabulates his results for the 50-year return level. The most likely value is 7.4, but there is much uncertainty in the analysis and the confidence interval is approximately [4.9, 24].

Being a prudent person, it is the conservative value of 24% that the employee brings to his supervisor as a worst-case fall in the index. He could, of course, have calculated the 100- or 1,000-year return levels, but somewhere a line has to be drawn and a decision has to be taken. His supervisor is sceptical and points out that 24% is more than three times as large as the previous record daily fall since 1960. The employee replies that he has done nothing other than analyse the available data with a natural statistical model and give a conservative estimate of a well-defined rare event.

On Monday, October 19, 1987, the S&P500 closed down 20.4% on its opening value.

*This item first appeared in *Risk* (January, 1998) and is republished here with the kind permission of the author.

To the best of our knowledge the above story never took place, but it could have. There is a notion that the crash of October 19, 1987, represents an event that cannot be reconciled with previous and subsequent market price movements. According to this view, normal daily movements and crashes are things of an entirely different nature (see, for example, Zangari, 1997). One point of the above story, however, is to show that a process generating normal daily returns is not necessarily inconsistent with occasional crashes. Extreme value theory (EVT) is a branch of probability theory that focuses explicitly on extreme outcomes and provides a series of natural models for them. Long used in engineering, it is now finding a role in risk management. The return level calculated in the story is an example of a risk measure: the reader may have detected an element of hindsight in the choice of the 50-year return level so that the crash lay near the boundary of the estimated confidence interval. Before the event, the choice of level would, however, have been a risk management decision. We define a worst case by considering how often we could tolerate its occurrence; this is exactly the kind of consideration that goes into the determination of dam heights and oil rig component strengths. But, of course, the logical process can be inverted. We can imagine a scenario which we believe to be extreme – a 20% fall in the value of something, say – and then use EVT to attempt to quantify how extreme, in the sense of how infrequent, the scenario might be.

EVT offers other measures of risk not touched upon in the story but described in the main text: for example, the value-at-risk (ie, the high quantile of a return distribution), and the shortfall or beyond-VAR risk measure, the amount by which VAR may be exceeded in the rare event that it is exceeded.

There is a further important point embedded in the story, and that is the necessity of considering uncertainty on various levels. Only one model was fitted: a Fréchet model for annual maxima. The Fréchet distributional form is well supported by theoretical arguments, but the choice of annual aggregation is somewhat arbitrary; why not six-monthly or quarterly maxima? This issue is sometimes referred to as "model risk" and would be addressed in a full analysis. The next level of uncertainty is parameter risk. Even supposing the model in the story is a good one, parameter values could only be established roughly, and this was reflected in a wide range of values for the return level.

In summary, one can say that EVT does not predict the future with certainty. It is more the case that EVT provides sensible and natural models for extreme phenomena and a framework for assessing the uncertainty that surrounds rare events; in finance, these could be pressed into service as benchmarks for measuring risk.

11

Risk-Adjusted Performance Measurement

Beginning with chapter 3, the basic foundation for quantifying and measuring credit risk in the banking book was carefully laid down. Specifically, important risk measures such as *expected loss* and *unexpected loss* were first introduced at the level of the individual loan facility. The building blocks for these risk measures were discussed extensively in chapters 4 and 5. To assess the credit risk embedded in the overall portfolio, practical methods for determining the *correlation of default* and the joint movement of credit quality were introduced in chapter 7. Correlation effects are the glue that binds the individual credits in the portfolio together. So that the influence of a single credit facility on the overall portfolio can be adequately assessed, chapter 6 introduced the concept of the *risk contribution* of an individual facility to the aggregate portfolio.

Once the credit risk in an aggregate portfolio can be adequately measured, we need to ask: "How much capital does a bank need to buffer itself against unanticipated losses in the credit portfolio?" Chapter 8 responded with the concept of *economic capital*, which is dependent on the *tail*, or *extreme events*, of the loss distribution. Since tail events are notoriously difficult to predict, chapters 8 and 9 advocated combined analytical and simulation techniques to approximate such events. Chapter 9 concentrated on the techniques of Monte Carlo simulation as applied to the distribution of portfolio losses and demonstrated some analytical tail-fitting procedures. This was followed by a presentation in chapter 10 of the basic foundation for an actuarially based statistical tool called *extreme value theory* (EVT). EVT was viewed in the chapter as a supplementary tool for the approximation of tail events.

With the basic building blocks for credit risk measurement in place, we are now ready to tackle some of the most important questions concerning the measurement of returns. This chapter gathers the strands from all the previous chapters by concentrating on this aspect. After all, why take risk if there is no reward? However, to provide a more equitable reward mechanism, a suitable framework for measuring returns must first be established. This is the main goal of the current chapter.

In a collective response to the highly inadequate risk-based capital requirement policies promulgated in the Basle Capital Accord in 1988, banking organisations have, over the past several years, begun in earnest to develop their own internal capital allocation systems. Since credit risk is a significant part of the overall risk faced by banking institutions, it also behoves these banks to develop their own internal credit risk models swiftly. These two developmental efforts eventually converged as one mandate that is now generally known as "risk-adjusted performance measurement", or RAPM. RAPM is considered by many risk managers to be the pinnacle of risk/return measurement and to represent the ultimate achievement for enterprise-wide risk management.

There are a variety of ways of defining performance measures using a risk-adjusted framework. The issue of performance measurement, however, cannot be addressed in isolation. How a bank chooses its risk-adjustment process is dependent on the intended application of these internally concocted performance measures. From a shareholder perspective, the bank may opt for the so-called *shareholder value analysis* (SVA). If the focus is on value creation, the bank may choose to adopt *economic value added* (EVA)[1] types of performance measures. Other lines of approach are being followed in the market, as summarised by Matten (1997).

Because a bank is not a charitable organisation, whatever performance measures are formulated should not deviate from the fundamental premise that, for the bank to take risk, it must be duly compensated for its actions. Any performance measure that fails to heed this wisdom is meaningless.

Internally developed capital allocation schemes are the basis on which a bank measures the profitability of the various lines of business it engages in. These schemes are then, in turn, used as evaluation measures in rewarding "good" business performances that meet the bank's expected hurdle rates. Risk and reward are, indeed, intertwined, as they should be. Furthermore, the rapid development of internal credit risk models and economic capital allocation schemes have also been driven largely by the day-to-day risk management needs of most banks. These risk management processes originally began in earnest in the *trading book* of the bank – the *banking book* being traditionally the more passive business. The general acceptance by the regulators in early 1998 of internal models for market risk capital adequacy also stimulated rapid development on the credit risk side.

To put things in the proper perspective, the discussion in this chapter addresses risk measurement from two fronts:

- the allocation of economic capital; and
- performance evaluation in conjunction with the level of risk-taking involved.

The first perspective is necessary so that each business unit in the bank is capitalised in a manner consistent with the bank's desired debt rating (eg, AA). The allocation scheme must, therefore, take into account the business unit's inherent "stand alone" risk and any internal diversification benefits provided by the unit to the overall bank portfolio. The aim of capital allocation is to force the bank to behave like a portfolio manager, thereby facilitating an efficient *enterprise-wide risk management* programme at the holding company level.

A key element in the emerging rationale of risk-based performance measurement is the assignment of economic capital to the different lines of business. The purpose is twofold, namely:

- first, equity capital usage and returns ultimately drive shareholder value;
- second, capital attribution is required to express the riskiness of the business that is being measured.

With these objectives, capital is clearly the common denominator of risk and return. If there were no risk-taking activities, there would really be no need for capital; therefore, risk is captured through capital needs. We have seen in earlier chapters that, other things being equal, the higher the volatility (as quantified by the unexpected loss), the greater the need for economic capital. Hence, accurately measuring performance requires that risk be taken into account. Regardless of the activities of the lines of business, risk needs to be measured *and* priced. Only then are the different business lines measurable on a level playing field.

The performance evaluation perspective is required so that the bank can determine the economic value added by each business unit. Ultimately, the performance evaluation should transcend the level of the business unit and extend to the assessment of individual credits. Therefore, the objective of performance evaluation is to provide a *comparable* benchmark for the measurement of a business unit's contribution to shareholder value and, as a consequence, also provide an effective capital budgeting process and incentive compensation programme.

In its October 1995 issue, *Euromoney* announced: "A RORAC [Return On Risk-Adjusted Capital] type system will increasingly become a necessity for all banks .... Calculating how much capital a bank needs has suddenly become the hot topic in banking." Indeed, many banks have employed a variety of performance measurement systems of varying complexity and sophistication to address the dual issues of performance measurement and capital attribution. The purpose of this chapter is to present some simple performance measures.

RISK-ADJUSTED PERFORMANCE MEASUREMENT

With these two broad perspectives above and their associated objectives in mind, it is now easy to incorporate the risk-adjustment function into the credit modelling process. This can be done in a variety of ways. The most generic risk-adjusted performance measure can be defined simply as

$$RAPM = \frac{Revenues - Costs - Expected\ losses}{Value\text{-}at\text{-}risk} \qquad \textbf{(11.1)}$$

The numerator of this performance measure consists of revenues generated,[2] less the costs of doing business, and, finally, an adjustment by the expected losses. The expected loss, as we have seen in earlier chapters, is equivalent to the loan loss provision the bank needs to set aside as part of carrying on its daily business activities. Statistically speaking, it is the credit losses that are *expected* in the course of doing business. Because it is anticipated, the expected loss is really not a risk measure *per se*.

In making the adjustments set out above, the return measure is adjusted by the risk involved in generating that return – the balancing act between risk and return being the key focal point. The denominator, the value-at-risk, is the amount of operating capital needed to cushion the bank against unexpected losses, operating risk, market risk and other conceivable risks. This value-at-risk is generally interpreted in the industry as the risk capital or economic capital.

Perhaps the concept of a risk-adjusted performance measurement can best be illustrated by a simple example.

Example 11.1: A CEO's dilemma – which proposal to choose?
This example is based on one given by Allen (1996). It is annual budget time and capital is scarce. The chief executive officer of the bank is faced with a dilemma as two of her business unit managers have approached her with similar requests.

The lending manager says: "I can make another $1 million over the year if you increase the limit of my loan book by $200 million." The trading manager says: "I can also make another $1 million over the year if you can increase my position limit by $10 million."

There is not enough capital to fulfil both requests. What is the CEO to do? How can a meaningful comparison be made between the two proposals?

Clearly, the CEO should choose the alternative that offers the higher return on capital but which introduces the least risk to the bank. To do so would require a good knowledge of how much economic capital is necessary to support each proposal and how much incremental risk each proposal introduces to the bank holding company.

The dilemma does not end there. At the end of the year it is annual bonus time and both managers have achieved their targets. The CEO is now obliged to determine how much to reward the two managers. How would she do that?

This example illustrates the importance of comparability when faced with the need to choose between several alternatives. To be able to conduct a fair comparison of return performance requires that the comparison be done on a level playing field. RAPM is one such measure that allows comparability in terms of the delicate balance between risk and reward.

RAROC DEFINED

A clear, simple and intuitive approach amongst all risk-adjusted performance measures is RAROC – the acronym for risk-adjusted return on capital. It is also known by other acronyms such as RORAC (return on risk-adjusted capital) and RARORAC (risk-adjusted return on risk-adjusted capital). Semantics aside, they all mean the same thing – the only difference being where the risk adjustments are done. Therefore, I shall use the term RAROC in the remaining chapters in a somewhat generic manner.

As the name implies, the risk adjustment is taken on both the revenue and capital components of the equation. On the revenue side, the "cost or expenses" of doing business needs to be taken into account. The "cost", from a credit default risk perspective, is the expected loss of engaging in the credit-generating business activity. Recall in earlier chapters we argued for the expected loss to be treated as the loan loss reserve that banks must set aside as part of doing their daily business. But from a business expense perspective (eg, salaries, bonuses, information systems infrastructure, and other expenses incurred in doing business), it would be ideal if the bank had some internal cost allocation scheme that could systematically attribute the different expenditures to each business unit.

Other "expenses" may also include tax provisions and transaction expenditures. There is a school of thought which advocates that the cost associated with tied-up capital also needs to be subtracted from the numerator. Refer to Appendix A for a brief discussion of a revised version of RAPM.

Capital in the denominator is appropriately replaced with risk capital or economic capital. Observe from previous chapters that we have decidedly incorporated the unexpected loss component (under extreme loss conditions) into the capital determination exercise. Since the bank, as a holding company, also engages in activities other than those which induce credit risk, the capital must, in principle, also incorporate other risks such as market risk, operational risk, etc. Our focus in this book is centred more on credit risk; nevertheless, other forms of risk can easily be included without any loss of generality.

Simply put, the ingredients for the RAROC equation can be defined very clearly as shown in Figure 11.1.

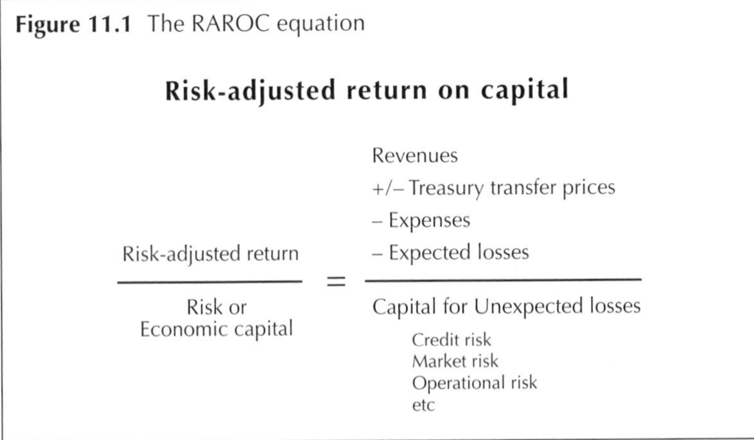

Figure 11.1 The RAROC equation

DISSECTING THE RAROC EQUATION

The best way to understand the RAROC calculation is to dissect the equation into its constituent parts. The RAROC equation has two major components: risk-adjusted return as the numerator; and risk capital or economic capital as the denominator.

We will start by examining the numerator and then consider the denominator.

The numerator, which represents the return component, consists of revenue information, "expenses" in the broadest sense, transfer pricing amongst the different business units, and the expected losses associated with engaging in the different lines of business.

The schematic diagram in Figure 11.2 (overleaf) shows in detail the subcomponents of the numerator. The diagram clearly highlights some quantities that should be familiar by now. All the quantities in the diagram that are amenable to mathematical modelling have been modelled, with appropriate caveats, in earlier chapters.

The denominator, on the other hand, represents the amount of capital the bank needs to sustain a desired credit rating commensurate with the level of risk it is taking. This capital cushion is called risk capital or economic capital.

Figure 11.3 is a schematic diagram of the constituents that make up the risk or economic capital in the denominator. Observe from the diagram that the denominator is the most difficult aspect of the modelling effort. Both practical and theoretical issues abound in the determination of quantities such as pairwise default correlation,

Figure 11.2 The numerator of the RAROC equation

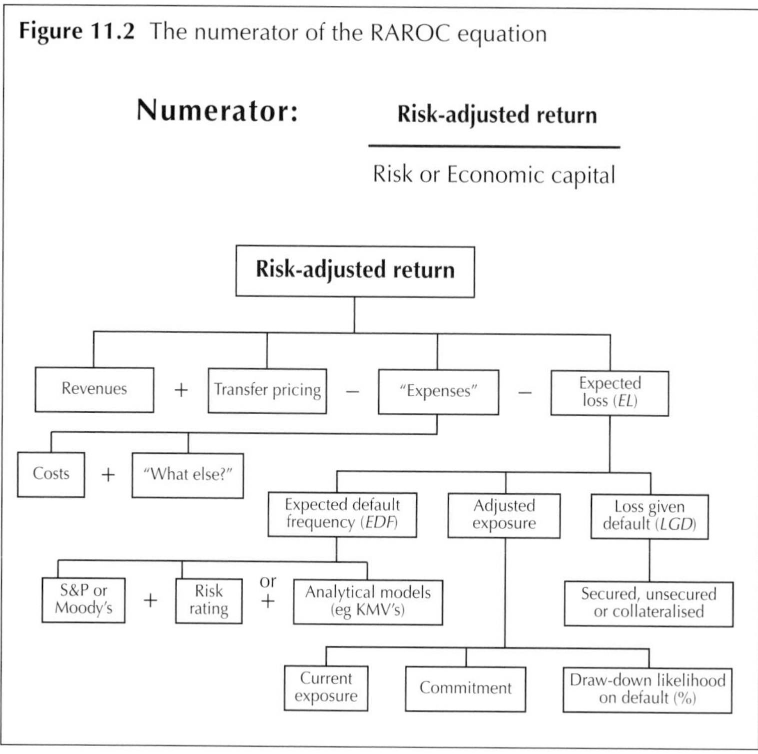

an obligor's idiosyncratic risk as represented by the industry index, the standard deviation of *LGD*, the confidence level in the loss distribution, and many others.

Previous chapters have presented the results of some theoretical research efforts to quantify the risk measures delineated in Figures 11.2 and 11.3. Perhaps more importantly, we considered practical techniques for modelling credit risk with the goal of establishing the most *sensible*, *reasonable*, and *practical* solutions for implementation, especially in the case when theory can no longer be stretched beyond its fundamental assumptions.

After all, the results of any modelling process that cannot be articulated and explained *in simple terms* to both senior management and regulatory supervisors do not have a chance of being fully accepted, let alone implemented, throughout the enterprise. One of the great challenges in writing this book is to satisfy the practical constraints that we must impose on our internal model of clarity, transparency and ease of implementation.

Figure 11.3 The denominator of the RAROC equation

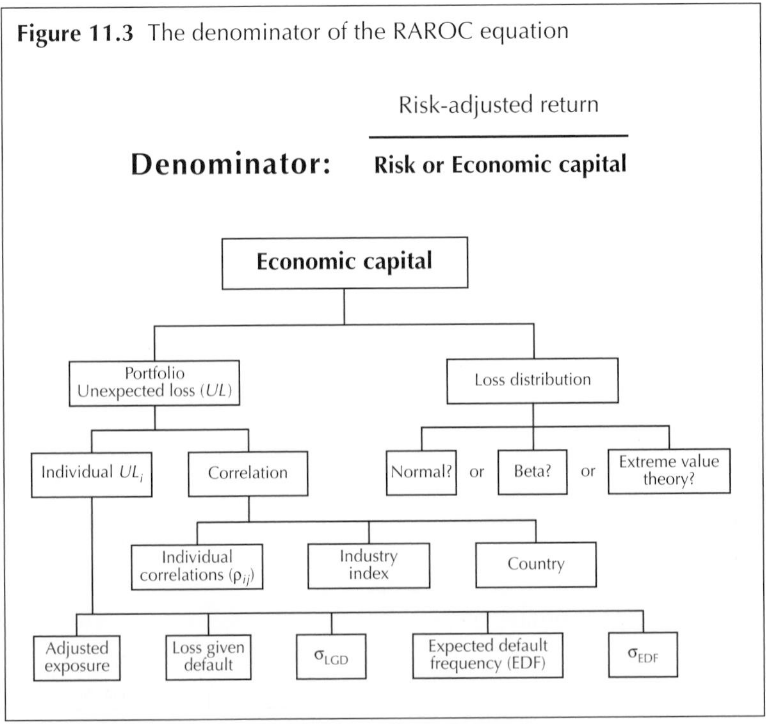

APPROACHES TO MEASUREMENT: TOP-DOWN OR BOTTOM-UP?

The previous section has presented a general template for determining the proper measure of return given the level of risk assumed, to the extent that the risk measures in the diagrams are quantifiable and, therefore, acceptable to both senior management and regulatory supervisors. How a bank decides to use the risk and return measures dictates at what aggregate levels these measures need to be calculated. Depending on the intended application of a risk-adjusted performance measure, there are two general, but inseparable, approaches to measurement to consider:

- a top-down (strategic) approach; or
- a bottom-up (tactical) approach.

The two approaches are complementary and are inextricably linked with the comprehensive, enterprise-wide risk management function of the entire bank. It is unwise to prefer one over the other owing

Figure 11.4 Hierarchies in top-down and bottom-up approaches

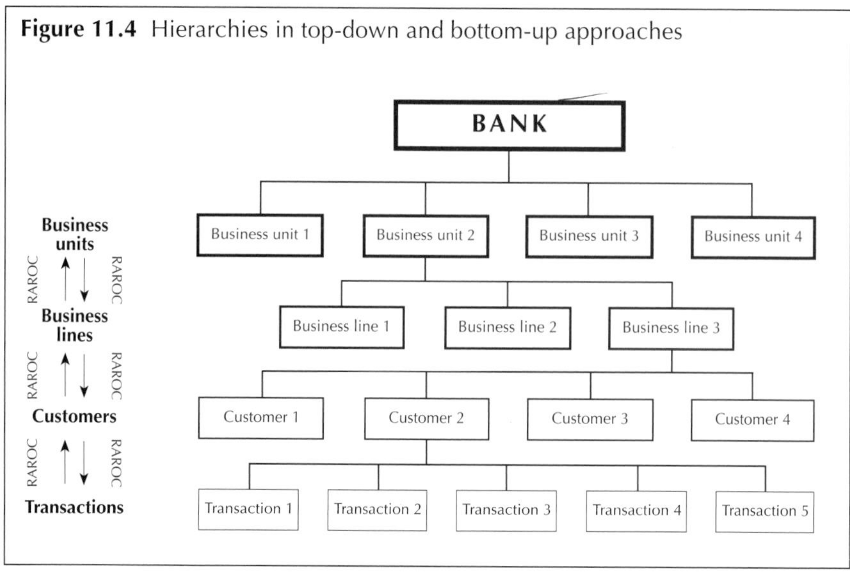

to their complementary nature, but it will become clear later that the bottom-up or tactical approach is quite difficult to implement across the board without unduly taxing the existing systems infrastructure of the bank and, thereby, incurring very large capital expenditure.

Figure 11.4 illustrates the hierarchical levels in a typical bank. The strategic, top-down approach in performance measurement concentrates primarily on the returns at business unit level and their effect on the strategic well-being of the bank as a whole. The more tactical, bottom-up approach requires a detailed transactional level performance measurement, including comparative analysis of returns from the bank's customers. The latter can then be used to decide which of these customers and their associated transactions are truly beneficial to the bank. Clearly, even though the lowest level of performance measurement makes extreme demands on the bank's information systems infrastructure, the granularity it is capable of providing is the most desirable.

The first perspective illustrated in Figure 11.4, the top-down or strategic approach, is driven primarily by the requirements of senior management at the level of the bank holding company, whose primary focus is on the "big picture" – a medium- to long-term view of the enterprise:

- ❑ How should the bank strategically position different lines of business in the most profitable and *de minimis* risk prospects in line with projected market developments over the next business cycle?
- ❑ How do the different lines of business compare in their returns in conjunction with the level of risk they assume from one planning period to the next?
- ❑ How should business units be compensated for the returns they generate and for the incremental risks they bring into the bank's overall portfolio?
- ❑ What are the projected ranges of profits and losses over the next planning horizon?
- ❑ What is the impact of operating costs relative to earnings and returns – ie, the efficiency ratio?
- ❑ What are the chances of encountering a debilitating loss during the next few horizons?
- ❑ How should the bank strategically acquire or divest itself of lines of business over the long term?

From the objectives delineated above one can see that, from a senior management perspective, the strategic top-down approach attempts to infer some measure of the totality of risk and return on *aggregated* or broadly defined business categories. Some banks have opted to use peer analysis and benchmarking to arrive at their own internal targets instead of painstakingly deriving the aggregates from their own bottom-up experience. Such an approach has both pros and cons. The point is that the aggregated top-down approach for strategic usage is a simple corollary of the bottom-up approach. In principle, if a bank can overcome the obstacles in its management information systems infrastructure, it would be able to perform these risk and return calculations from a very low level and should, therefore, succeed in aggregating the results to a higher and broader level – albeit somewhat myopically.

The bottom-up or tactical perspective, in contrast, is driven primarily by such short-term day-to-day concerns as:

- ❑ How to assess the risk and return profile of the trading book from one day to the next.
- ❑ In credit committee deliberations, how to structure and approve loan facilities to specific obligors in light of the existing portfolio in the banking book.

- ❏ The "fair" price to charge for transactions in either book as compensation for taking risks into the bank portfolio in accordance with the bank's set hurdle rates.
- ❏ If the hurdle rate for a business unit cannot be met with the risk-adjusted pricing of a new transaction, where else to make up the difference.

Tactical measures of risk and return allow the business units to undertake risk-adjusted pricing, thereby providing them with adequate information about "fair" pricing in relation to the bank's existing portfolio, set hurdle rates and purported risk appetite. A bottom-up approach, therefore, requires credit risk to be quantified at a very low level – for example, at a loan facility level or on a credit default swap. The key point is that low-level aggregations would eventually lead to business unit sub-portfolios and, once the covariance structure of the different business units is known, the aggregation can be done at the level of the bank holding company. This is, of course, easier said than done.

With these discussions behind us, we can now proceed to the next chapter on implementing the internal credit risk model (and, ultimately, RAROC) across the enterprise.

APPENDIX A: REVISED RAPM

There is a school of thought which advocates that the "costs" associated with tied-up capital also need to be subtracted from the numerator of the RAPM equation. Correspondingly, we need to amend equation (11.1) to read

$$RAPM' = \frac{\textit{Net revenues} - \textit{Expected losses} - \textit{Cost of tied-up capital}}{\textit{Value-at-risk}} \tag{A.11.1}$$

where the prime symbol on *RAPM* signifies the revised measure and

$$\textit{Net revenues} = \textit{Gross revenues} - \textit{Financing costs} - \textit{Tax} - \textit{Salaries and bonuses} - \textit{Etc}$$

The tied-up capital is either the regulatory capital the bank is required to set aside (based on BIS rules) or the internally calculated economic capital. Either way, capital is tied up as a non-performing asset and, therefore, has an associated cost. This cost can be approximately described as the missed opportunity to generate a required rate of return (called the "hurdle rate") that might be obtained if the capital were allowed to be utilised to fund some business activity. Approximately, we can write

$$\textit{Cost of tied-up capital} = \textit{Hurdle rate} \times \textit{Tied-up capital}$$

This school of thought asserts that the capital amount needs to be subtracted from the net revenues as part of the cost of conducting business.

As a special case, if the tied-up capital is equal to the risk capital (ie, the value-at-risk), we have

$$\begin{aligned} \textit{RAPM}' &= \frac{\textit{Net revenues} - \textit{Expected losses} - \textit{Hurdle rate} \times \textit{Risk capital}}{\textit{Value-at-risk}} \\ &= \frac{\textit{Net revenues} - \textit{Expected losses}}{\textit{Value-at-risk}} - \textit{Hurdle rate} \\ &= \textit{RAPM} - \textit{Hurdle rate} \end{aligned} \qquad \textbf{(A.11.2)}$$

Clearly, the goal of an internal risk-adjusted performance measurement scheme is to ensure that

$$\textit{RAPM} > \textit{Hurdle rate}$$

so that the overall return measure, RAPM′, remains positive.

1 EVA is a registered trademark of Stern Stewart & Co. This metric was originally conceived by G. Bennett Stewart III in his book, *The Quest for Value* (New York: Harper Collins, 1991).

2 More appropriately, it is the projected or *expected* revenue at the end of the analysis horizon that is the required input.

12

Implementing the Internal Model Across the Enterprise

There are various information systems-related challenges when an internal RAROC model is implemented even on a localised scale, let alone one that encompasses the entire enterprise. The implementation of any internal model under the aegis of a risk-adjusted performance measurement framework requires a considerable amount of information from across all business units of the bank. Especially if the goal is to do a "bottom-up" approach at the transaction level, the scope of the systems infrastructure required to undertake the onerous task of amassing pertinent information from both the banking and the trading books can be quite daunting.

While it is not the intent of this chapter to address these difficult systems issues and the more practical problem of data gathering, it must, however, be recognised that these issues are very real and important to the implementation process. Ultimate success or failure in implementing an internal model of this nature across the enterprise is directly related to the bank's ability to collect the necessary information. This is neither – by any stretch of the imagination – easy nor cheap. It is not, however, an impossible task.

Throughout the remainder of the book I shall use the acronym "RAROC" synonymously with "internal model". Although the focus of the book has been on credit risk, the other pertinent major sources of risk to the bank – for example, market risk and operational risk – can be accommodated easily within a generic RAPM framework such as RAROC.

By way of example, we shall use a sample credit portfolio from the banking book similar to that used in the previous discussion of the simulation and tail-fitting of loss distributions.

SAMPLE PORTFOLIO

The sample credit portfolio has the following initial characteristics:

Total number of facilities	2165
Commitments	$56.0 billion
Current outstanding	$15.1 billion
Total regulatory capital	$1.5 billion

The RAROC model calculations result in:

Adjusted exposure (AE)	$42.2 billion
Expected loss	$ 65.7 million (or 0.16% of AE)
Unexpected loss	$135.0 million (or 0.32% of AE)

All the calculations done here using the internal model arbitrarily used a one-year planning horizon. In principle, subject to the quality of default probabilities and other parameters, the calculations can be extended to longer horizons.

Since not all of the committed amounts will be drawn upon default, observe that by using the definition of *adjusted exposure*, the internal RAROC model calculation results in a much smaller AE amount of $42.2 billion, instead of the totality of either the outstanding or the commitments in isolation. In reality, the bank's likely overall exposure in the event of default is capped at the AE level.

Of this adjusted exposure amount (and given the composition of the current credit portfolio), the bank needs to set aside *loan loss reserves* equal to the *expected loss*. The internal model calculates it at $65.7 million, which is 0.16% of the adjusted exposure amount. In contrast, the volatility of the portfolio as measured by its *unexpected loss* is 0.32% of the adjusted exposure.

In order to maintain some desired debt rating for the institution (or, equivalently, some confidence level of remaining solvent in the event of obligor defaults), the bank needs to prudently set aside a multiple of the unexpected loss amount as *risk capital* or *economic capital*. The multiple, as we have discussed in earlier chapters, is called the *capital multiplier*. This number is dependent on the bank's desired debt rating for the overall institution and comes from the loss distribution assumed for the portfolio. Generally speaking, the economic capital the bank requires to protect itself against insolvency is given by

Economic capital = (*Capital multiplier*) × (*Portfolio unexpected loss*)

Broken down further by internal risk ratings, Table 12.1 (overleaf) highlights the results of the RAROC calculation. The first column is the internal risk class rating, which can easily be mapped to, say, a Standard & Poor's rating (see the footnote to the table). For strategic planning purposes, the expected and the unexpected losses are normally quoted in terms of percentage of the adjusted exposure. These are shown in columns 6 and 8. The last two columns of the table display the required economic or risk capital and the regulatory capital.

From the results given in Table 12.1 one can easily calculate the risk-adjusted return numbers in the RAROC scheme discussed in chapter 11. For instance, once the revenue information (including operating expenses and transfer-pricing information) is known, the "net revenue" less expected loss divided by the risk capital gives the RAROC number. The following example demonstrates some simple calculations.

Example 12.1: Calculation of returns using RAROC
Consider, for illustration, the return for risk code 3. Suppose that the "net revenue" is $150 million for the entire class; then the return based on the RAROC framework is

$$\frac{\text{Net revenue} - EL}{\text{Risk capital}} = \frac{\$150.0 - \$12.5}{\$465.8} = 30\%$$

indicating an excellent risk-adjusted return of 30% for BBB-rated credits.

In contrast, the risk-adjusted return on *regulatory* capital is

$$\frac{\text{Net revenue} - EL}{\text{Regulatory capital}} = \frac{\$150.0 - \$12.5}{\$846.0} = 16\%$$

which is smaller.

Of course, the reverse is true for risk codes 5, 6 and 7, where the regulatory capital is lower than the risk capital.

Also, observe that the sample portfolio requires an overall total of $1.5 billion for regulatory capital in contrast to a lower economic capital of $0.979 billion, alluding to the fact that there is a very good arbitrage opportunity between economic and regulatory capital.

Table 12.1 Results of the RAROC calculation

Risk code	Commitment ($ million)	Outstanding ($ million)	Adjusted exposure ($ million)	Expected loss (% of AE)	EL/AE	Risk contribution ($ million)	RC/AE	Risk capital ($ million)	Regulatory capital ($ million)
1	7,015	1,334	5,367	0.2	0.00	4.1	0.08	30.0	36.1
2	12,587	1,242	9,297	1.5	0.02	14.6	0.16	106.1	230.8
3	28,247	8,003	21,162	12.5	0.06	64.3	0.30	465.8	846.0
4	6,565	3,572	5,128	19.7	0.38	32.9	0.64	238.5	354.5
5	353	218	283	4.7	1.66	3.7	1.33	27.2	17.6
6	58	58	58	4.4	7.53	2.1	3.61	15.2	4.5
8	52	41	41	18.6	45.66	2.4	5.86	17.3	3.2
A	16	16	16	0.0	0.01	0.0	0.09	0.1	–
B	1,075	595	844	3.7	0.44	10.4	1.24	75.7	26.2
NR	46	–	27	0.4	1.60	0.4	1.63	3.2	–
Total	56,013	15,078	42,223	65.7	0.16	135.0	0.32	979.1	1,518.9

The numerical internal risk ratings map to Standard & Poor's ratings as follows: 1, AAA or AA; 2, A; 3, BBB; 4, BB; 5, B; 6, CCC; 7, CC; 8, C. Risk code A (equivalent to a Standard & Poor's rating of A) refers to entities in the OECD countries category, while risk code B (equivalent to a Standard & Poor's rating of BB) covers entities from non-OECD countries. NR (not rated) refers to those facilities which do not have internal ratings for various reasons.

Such arbitrage could take the form of asset securitisation programmes, the use of credit derivatives or other mechanisms in the capital markets.

Observe that in this framework of risk and return measurement, it is quite easy to incorporate market risk and operational risk into the RAROC equation. For instance, the associated economic capital requirement for market risk is the value-at-risk number calculated from the internal market risk model and appropriately scaled up to the analysis horizon.

Table 12.1 also displays the *risk contribution* of each risk class to the entire portfolio. Recall from chapter 6 that risk contribution is the measure that quantifies the incremental risk of a single risky asset in relation to the portfolio. From the table, observe that even though risk code 8 has a sizable expected loss, its risk contribution to the total portfolio is a modest $2.4 million. But, relative to its adjusted exposure of $41 million, its risk contribution is a significant 5.86%. Interestingly, risk code 8 also consumes almost eight times more economic capital than is indicated by the BIS-based regulatory capital. We can only imagine the kind of mediocre returns that loans in this particular risk class provide to the overall portfolio. This issue will be addressed in the next few sections.

These simple types of *relative* comparison between risk classes that we have just performed can provide the bank with very good strategic insights into the necessary course of action to take. If the implementation of the internal model follows a bottom-up approach, the relative comparison can also be done at even lower levels – at obligor level, facility level or transactional level. Keep in mind, however, that in contrast to the regulatory capital as a measure, a meaningful relative comparison can only be adequately achieved if the bank has developed an internal model.

NEGATIVE RAROC

It is also very clear from example 12.1 that RAROC can be a *negative* number. (Refer also to Appendix A of chapter 11 on the issue of negative returns.) Consider for instance, the case when the net revenue is smaller than the expected loss; then the numerator of the RAROC equation is negative:

$$RAROC < 0 \qquad \text{if } \mathit{Net\ revenue} < EL$$

reflecting the fact that not enough revenue was generated to cover both internal operating expenses and the expected losses from potential credit defaults. If the RAROC for a loan facility is negative, it is very likely that the bank will be at the losing end of the game in the event of default because not enough spread was generated to compensate for holding that level of risk. In short, a negative RAROC is indicative of a situation in which the bank is not properly compensated for the risk it takes, signalling a perilous imbalance between risk and return – unless of course the bank can generate other non-loan revenues from the client through its trading operations in the capital markets or cash management activities. An internal risk-adjusted return framework certainly allows the bank to do this kind of internal soul-searching. Later on, in chapter 13, we shall address the important issue of "fair" pricing and required spread.

PARAMETERISING AND CALIBRATING THE INTERNAL MODEL

In the last section ("Parameterising credit risk models") of chapter 4, we discussed at length the importance of properly calibrating the internal model. In order to have senior management and regulatory support for an internal modelling effort, the model is initially calibrated to "benchmark"* parameters that are known in the market. Over the long haul, it is also important to use proprietary parameters inferred from internal experience, but in doing so the bank is well advised to provide sufficient justification and internal documentation to back up its own calibration and experiences.

The default probabilities used in the sample internal RAROC calculations are those corresponding to the published Standard & Poor's default probabilities for 1998. These are all listed in Table 12.2, which also gives the usage given default information according to risk codes.

In principle, one can also use the EDFs (expected default frequencies) provided by vendors like KMV Corporation, although it must be borne in mind that, for the most part, the default proba-

*There are really not too many tangible benchmarks to extract from the market. For the most part, credit portfolios in the financial industry's banking books are very opaque. Pertinent information, such as losses, charge-offs, draw-downs, credit quality, etc, are always deemed proprietary and are, therefore, not openly shared in the market.

Table 12.2 Standard & Poor's default probabilities – one-year default probability table

Risk code	Default probability (%)	Usage given default (%)
1	0.01	71
2	0.04	71
3	0.15	65
4	0.95	52
5	4.85	48
6	19.25	44
7	100.00	0
8	100.00	0
A	0.04	71
B	0.95	52
C	4.85	48
0	4.21	58.50
X	4.21	0.00

Usage given default is draw-down percentage of unused commitment in the event of default.

Table 12.3 Loss given default table

Secured	LGD (%)
Yes	35
No	50

bilities differ from public rating agencies in their absolute levels. We have already seen this in chapter 3 (in the section "Theoretical EDFs and agency ratings"). For private firms which are not rated by public agencies, the default probabilities can also be inconsistent with internal risk ratings. As a good portion of a bank's credit portfolio contains non-publicly rated private firms, it must be prepared to make an astute choice.

The loss given default percentages used for the sample portfolio are given in Table 12.3. This tabulation is, however, only meant for expediency and for pedagogical purposes. Whenever necessary, the loss given default table should be expanded to incorporate a finer gradation if, internally, the bank distinguishes the different quality of colateralisation and other guarantees in relation to its own internal risk-rating schemes.

In practice, a bank that has an internal view of how default-related quantities such as EDF, UGD and LGD are assigned could parameterise its internal model to suit its own needs. The standard deviations of these items are also required.

In addition, the default correlations implied by asset correlations need to be carefully considered since the issue of correlation lies at the very heart of portfolio concentration and diversification.

Furthermore, the joint probability distribution of default requires some assumption and justification. The macroeconomic analysis required to decide on the obligor-specific risk and the industry and country composition of an obligor needs careful planning since this, in turn, affects the covariance structure of the internal model. All of these vital issues have been discussed in chapter 7.

For capital adequacy purposes, it is important to use a capital multiplier that is consistent with the real unexpected risk of loss of portfolio value and the desired debt rating of the bank. The original impetus of the BIS Capital Accord of 1988 was agreed on so that banks under BIS regulatory supervision would be placed on a level playing field in regard to capital adequacy. The confidence intervals used, therefore, for determining the amount of required capital must be set at defensible levels and must be completely devoid of arbitrariness – banks that go in for higher levels of risk-taking activity should be subject to higher levels of capital adequacy requirement. In chapters 8, 9 and 10, I discussed extensively how to use a combination of tools and simulation methods to arrive at the proper capital multiplier. We are humbled by the fact that although this is not a trivial exercise, careful and sensible approximations are feasible.

Stress-testing and back-testing

A value-at-risk (VAR) market risk model is definitely more amenable to *back-testing* than other kinds of risks. It is also a regulatory requirement, as provided for in the Amendment to the Capital Accord (1996), to both stress-test and back-test an internal VAR model. However, unlike market risk VAR, it is actually quite problematic to back-test an internal credit risk model.

In contrast to a scaled-up *one-day* assessment of market risk in an internal VAR model, the internal credit risk model estimates the probability of credit loss over a longer time horizon – at least one year. Back-testing, with a high degree of confidence, the unexpected loss due to credit default over at least the one-year horizon stretches the boundary of prudent mathematical analysis. Two dilemmas arise immediately:

- ❑ The time frame needed to collect annual loss experiences to achieve a desired level of confidence generally measures in the impractical zone of dozens of years.

- In addition, the credit portfolio is very sensitive to credit cycles. Thus, in principle, it might take a back-test process through several instances of credit cycles before conclusions can be drawn.

It seems, at least for now, that a full-blown Monte Carlo simulation might be a better substitute, although a full-blown simulation of a modestly large credit portfolio takes many, many hours and so could not be performed more frequently. Monte Carlo simulation, furthermore, is not without its own set of shortcomings.

In practice, there are not that many critical parameters to consider in an internal credit risk model. Thus, as a control mechanism by way of *stress-testing*, it is prudent to analyse the sensitivities of the model to various shocks to the parameters. This also allows the analysis to gauge the effect of fat and heavy tails in the loss distribution. Provided that the bank's systems infrastructure is properly in place, stress-testing is easy to perform and takes very little time. Parameters that are inferred from market averages can be shocked either way – up or down – to gauge how the credit portfolio might react to incorrect parameterisation. In addition, through a judicious choice of scenarios – either *extremes* or *historical* – model parameters can be shocked to extreme or historical levels to gauge the breaking point, parametric sensitivities and performance of the internal model.

Although it is clear that many of the model parameters and benchmarks are difficult to infer from the market, and some of the intrinsic assumptions may be difficult to justify, this book attempts to model credit risk and its attendant capital adequacy issues in a simple, clear, transparent and consistent manner. The hope is that, in the final analysis, simplicity will redeem itself.

However, short of very clear and precise regulatory guidance and directives, the bank therefore also runs the risk of being myopic if it exclusively uses its own internal default experience to calibrate its internal model. Once again, it is necessary to warn: "Parameterise at your own risk".

When an internal model has been successfully implemented as described above, one can start interpreting some of the results. The remainder of this chapter concentrates on the topic of interpretation, thereby facilitating the proactive use of these results to manage and mitigate risk.

INTERPRETING THE RESULTS OF RAROC

Having discussed the implementation of risk-adjusted performance measures (RAPM) across the enterprise and the many issues that surround the parameterisation and calibration of the internal model, we find that the problem does not stop here.

As with any risk measurement tool, it is very important to interpret the results of the RAROC calculations properly, especially if the results are to be used at bank holding company level for strategic senior management purposes. The calibration and interpretation of the results from an internal model are interrelated topics. They must also be *iterative* processes. A better understanding of one's own experience in relation to the general market experience only serves to enhance and improve on the calibration and interpretation of the internal model. A misguided and myopic use of RAROC is, therefore, unconscionable.

Why does a bank need to apply risk-adjusted performance measures, such as RAROC, in its business activities? The intended usage dictates how one interprets the results of an internal model which, in turn, refines recursively how it should be used properly. Since models are imperfect, usage and interpretation are linked, iterative processes. There are three simple but important answers to the question posed above. They are:

- To measure *risk-adjusted* profitability.
- To facilitate *portfolio* risk management.
- To streamline the *allocation* of economic capital.

All these reasons, of course, have significant implications for the overall strategic and tactical decisions which the bank needs to make to ensure its continued existence and solvency in the event of catastrophe. The emphasis on the key words *risk-adjusted, portfolio* and *allocation* is in line with the fundamental function of an internal model in supporting the bank's risk-taking activities.

At the core of the RAPM philosophy is that, as a performance evaluation tool, RAROC gives bank management the ability to apply risk-adjusted measures when comparing business lines that are quite dissimilar in their risk-taking activities. The return measures, as calculated by RAROC, say, therefore enable management to set hurdle rates in a consistent manner across the enterprise. In so doing, management can assess the trade-off between risk and reward, and thereby refine its business strategies to be consistent with the risk appetite of the bank as a whole.

The commonality in risk measurement provided by an RAPM framework allows the bank to establish a common language to communicate risk. And, more importantly, because RAROC is founded on a portfolio framework of assessing risk, the results can be used by management and business units to identify, evaluate and measure portfolio risk, thereby providing an integrated view of market, credit, operational and liquidity risk policies.

ENTERPRISE-WIDE RISK MANAGEMENT AND RAPM

Perhaps the most important reason for using any kind of risk-adjusted performance measure is a bank's enlightened desire to achieve a coherent and comprehensive level of *enterprise-wide* risk management. In the financial industry this is the ultimate achievement of any risk manager's career.

Risk management on an enterprise-wide basis sits at the pinnacle of all the business activities of the bank, uniting all the major components of risk affecting it, as shown in Figure 12.1. Risk manage-

Figure 12.1 Major components of risk

Figure 12.2 Enterprise-wide risk management and RAROC

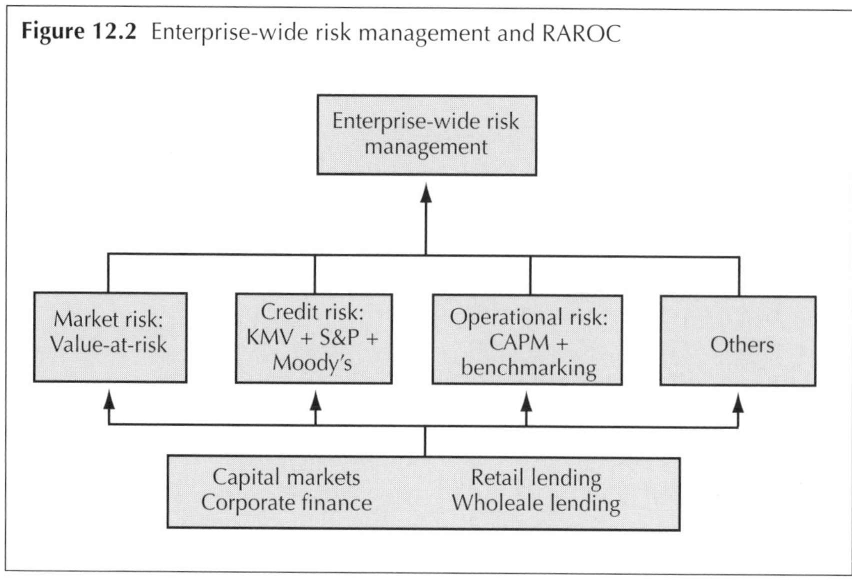

ment on such a basis uses the capital attribution process as the glue to bind all the constituent components of risk together, as graphically displayed in Figure 12.2.

The foregoing discussion of why the bank needs to use some kind of RAPM can be summarised by highlighting the following obvious points:

- *Firm-wide risk management*
  - Provide an integrated view of market, credit, operational and liquidity risk policies
  - Establish a common language to communicate risk
- *Business strategy and corporate risk appetite*
  - Create a link between strategic, operating and risk management objectives and expected return
  - Identify, evaluate and measure portfolio risk
  - Assess the trade-off between risk and reward
- *Performance evaluation*
  - Apply risk-adjusted performance measures to refine business strategies
  - Establish a consistent performance measurement
  - Establish better reward mechanisms through relative merits

Figure 12.3 The role of RAROC

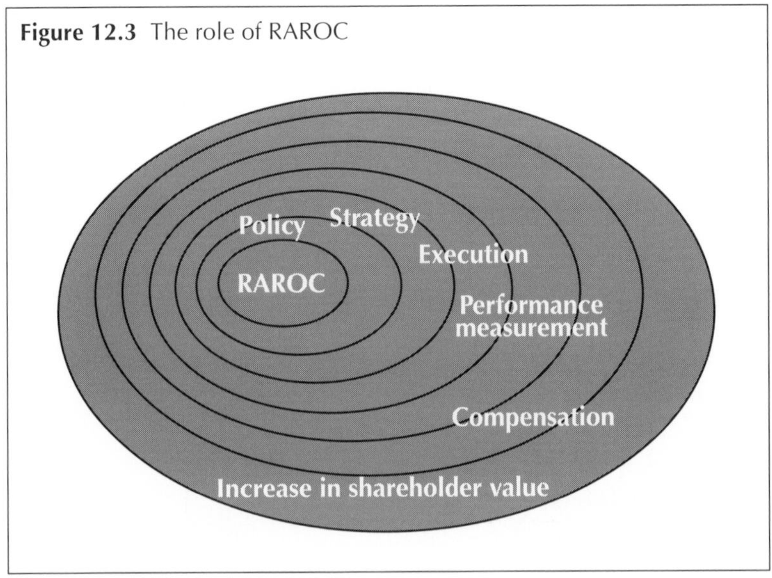

- *Improvement in pricing*
  - Price loans and other credit-embedded transactions on a risk-adjusted basis
  - Define hurdle rates that can be used to evaluate the true profitability of transactions across customers and product lines
- *Arbitrage between economic and regulatory capital*
- *Future regulatory requirement*
  - Prepare for forthcoming regulatory requirements for capital adequacy using risk-adjusted methodologies
- *Better measurement tools for credit derivatives market and asset securitisation activities*

It is clearly evident from these points that any risk-adjusted performance measure such as RAROC sits at the core of an organisation, affecting its internal risk policies and strategic decision function, the execution of these strategies and policies, the measurement of performance, the determination of compensation schemes, and, ultimately, the enhancement of shareholder value, as displayed in Figure 12.3.

Now that the objectives delineated above have been clearly spelt out in a risk-adjusted performance measurement framework, we can conclude by returning to the sample portfolio introduced at the beginning of this chapter and interpret the results from our internal model calculations. This is done in the next section.

SAMPLE CREDIT PORTFOLIO

For illustration, Table 12.4 is a subset of the sample credit portfolio. As usual, all the calculations using the internal model are based on a one-year analysis horizon for convenience. The columns of the table are:

- A Risk-adjusted return as calculated by the RAROC model
- B Return on regulatory capital (ie, net revenue divided by regulatory capital)
- C Expected loss
- D Risk or economic capital
- E Regulatory capital as calculated using BIS rules
- F Net revenue generated from the obligor
- I Obligors 1 through 13
- J Industry designation of obligor
- K Term to maturity of the credit facility
- L Internal risk rating of obligor

Table 12.4 RAROC results for sample credit portfolio

	A RAROC (%)	B Regulatory (%)	C Expected loss ($)	D Risk capital ($)	E Reg capital ($)	F Revenue ($)
1	−2.6	13.8	49,896	1,044,446	168,072	23,247
2	15.6	40.5	36,195	217,199	173,354	70,181
3	31 4	44.6	6,330	130,966	106,616	47,503
4	−30.7	32.9	431,917	983,894	393,333	129,404
5						
6	20.7	6.6	9,113	236,085	874,286	57,884
7	10.4	3.0	10,287	205,707	1,053,333	31,744
8	158.2	26.1	5,046	128,682	800,000	208,621
9	187.9	28.8	14,135	360,607	2,400,000	691,774
10	5.3	2.3	5,680	578,110	1,600,000	36,500
11	67.1	33.3	401	87,887	178,380	59,342
12						
13	13.6	#DIV/0!	15,311	189,952	–	41,111
14	57.4	#DIV/0!	3,525	201,025	–	118,850
15	−1.5	#DIV/0!	9,050	234,440	–	5,520

For explanation of the columns, see text.

M Expected default frequency
N Total outstandings
O Total commitments

Dissecting the risk groups within the portfolio

To facilitate our discussion, we categorise the obligors in Table 12.4 into three main sub-groupings:

- *High risk* – obligors with high numerical internal risk ratings equivalent to Standard & Poor's ratings of B, CCC, D and lower.
- *Low risk* – obligors with medium internal risk ratings equivalent to Standard & Poor's ratings of BBB or better (ie, investment grade or better).
- *Others* – obligors that do not require regulatory capital.

High-risk group

Obligors 1–4 in Table 12.4 belong to the high-risk category. Observe that, on the basis of regulatory capital, overall the returns appear to be very good, but this is misleading. In reality, given the high EDF (18.35%) for Obligor 4, the associated expected loss ($431,917) is quite large relative to the net revenue generated ($129,404).

Table 12.4 (*cont*) RAROC results for sample credit portfolio

	I Customer name	J Industry	K Maturity (years)	L Risk code	M EDF (%)	N Outstanding ($)	O Commitment ($)
1	Obl 1	Financial	1.00	B	0.95	10,504,487	10,504,487
2	Obl 2	Chemical	5.00	5	4.85	2,166,929	2,094,698
3	Obl 3	Financial	2.13	B	0.95	1,332,698	1,332,698
4	Obl 4	RetailW/S	0.95	6	18.35	3,166,667	6,666,667
5							
6	Obl 5	FoodBev	7.98	3	0 15	6,857,143	15,000,000
7	Obl 6	PaperPulp	3.50	3	0.15	11,333,333	15,000,000
8	Obl 7	ConstructR	4.33	3	0.15	8,888,889	10,000,000
9	Obl 8	Manufact	3.33	3	0.15	21,209,498	30,000,000
10	Obl 9	NBF	2.59	2	0.04	–	40,000,000
11	Obl 10	Finance	4.04	1	0.01	10,387,256	11,910,270
12							
13	Obl 11	Media	0.50	4	0.47	–	12,500,000
14	Obl 12	Reg Utility	0.77	2	0.03	–	45,900,000
15	Obl 13	FoodBev	1.00	3	0.15	6,618,243	15,000,000

Obl, Obligor; NBF, NonBankingFinc. For explanation of the columns, see text.

Consequently, after subtracting the expected loss from the revenue, the return (−30.7%) becomes negative, as opposed to the strongly positive 32.9% based on regulatory capital! This shows that the BIS rules do not adequately adjust for the true risk in the portfolio.

Also, observe the difference between columns D and E on capital. Due to the nature of its high risk, the risk capital is significantly larger than the regulatory capital calculated using BIS capital adequacy rules. This points up the inadequacy of using regulatory capital as the benchmark against which to measure return. On average, regulatory capital in this group tends to be much smaller than risk capital.

In the high-risk group, Obligors 1 and 4 have negative returns after risk adjustment. Obligor 3, on the other hand, even though internally it is rated as a risky non-OECD bank, has a smaller expected loss relative to the revenue generated. Consequently, the return on a risk-adjusted basis is also very good.

Low-risk group

Obligors 5–10 belong to this group. Return figures can swing either way depending on the size of the expected loss relative to the revenue generated. On average, however, regulatory capital in this group is significantly much larger than risk capital, highlighting the unfair penalty that BIS rules exact on "good" credits.

Observe that even though Obligor 9 has no current outstandings, it still incurs expected loss. This is because the adjusted exposure, which is the true measure of a bank's exposure, comes from a fraction of the undrawn commitment likely to be drawn on default. Another observation is that returns which are good from a regulatory perspective also tend to be good on a risk-adjusted basis. This is due to the fact that, for good credits, the expected loss is normally quite small.

Others

In certain cases – for instance, a 364-day facility or a collateralised facility – no regulatory capital may be required, but this does not imply that there is no credit risk. From a regulatory capital perspective all the returns are infinite (ie, divided by zero), but this does not mean the returns are excellent. RAROC returns clearly show that it is still possible to generate a negative return, as in the case of Obligor 13. This is because although no regulatory capital is required, it is still necessary to set aside a loan loss reserve equal to the expected loss, which is not zero. If insufficient revenue is generated to cover the risk for less than a one-year period, the risk-adjusted return will appropriately show up unfavourably.

This again demonstrates the incorrect risk assessment of the BIS rules for facilities that are less than one year in maturity. The uneven treatment of regulatory rules allowed many banks to structure loans that are 364-day facilities with annual rollover covenants, defeating the purpose of regulatory risk-based capital adequacy rules.

ON TO THE NEXT STEPS

Risk-adjusted performance measurement (RAPM) is decidedly a philosophy and a way of life. Banks which choose to embrace the philosophy and live in its umbrage have much to gain and little to lose. A bank that strives to manage its risks in an enterprise-wide framework stands a better chance of optimising its efficiency in all the key processes pertaining to risk and return, thereby ensuring longevity and stability both in its human capital investments and in its systems infrastructure investments. The benefits of the ensuing increase in efficiency and reduction in costs are immeasurable. This, after all, is common sense.

But a few first steps need to be taken. Given the size of the banking book, the first step is to begin with an internal credit risk modelling effort, the ultimate goal of which is the integration of the other major forms of risk in a consistent manner. In so doing, the process of capital attribution can be brought into better alignment with the actual risks undertaken by the different business units, thereby facilitating a more accurate measurement of return. Furthermore, a comprehensive assessment of risk and return on a portfolio basis not only increases the transparency of risk to senior management, but it also enables an institution to cut down on the wasteful and unnecessary practices for which behemoth banks are notorious.

In practical terms, I believe strongly that the implementation of a risk-adjusted measure across the enterprise, such as RAROC, also serves as a "cleansing act" for the bank. The information technology challenge associated with such a grand and noble vision of collecting, integrating, massaging and the eventual cleaning up of the various source systems in search of better data and quality information forces the bank to deal head-on with its disjointed and myriad legacy systems – covering both front and back offices. An inability to fix these complex systems-related problems could eventually choke and cripple a bank by gradually limiting its future growth potential. A shoddy quick fix, which many banks are tempted to undertake, also has significant repercussions in terms of ongoing systems stability, curtailing any potential for expansion in the future. Needless to say, a bank that can overcome these seemingly insurmountable obstacles has a greater chance of dominating and determining the market. In the long run, the bank also stands a better chance of surviving catastrophe and enhancing its ability to beat the competition.

A bank's mission, after all, is not to shun risk, but instead to take the risks it is able to manage well and for which it can be adequately compensated, thereby enhancing shareholder value. The mandate on our internal credit risk modelling effort, therefore, does not, and should not, end here. There are more steps to take.

How much should the bank be compensated for taking on credit risk? The next chapter addresses this question. To this end, I shall introduce the so-called "loan pricing calculator" as a mechanism that enables the bank to charge adequately, in risk-adjusted terms, for taking an additional increment of credit risk into its portfolio. In the absence of arbitrage and to the extent that the market would allow this "fair" pricing of credits to occur, I also discuss the phenomenon of what is known as the "credit paradox" as an introduction to the next chapter.

13

Credit Concentration and Required Spread

Banks may be the most efficient generators of loans, but they are among the least effective managers of credit risk. For a variety of reasons, banks normally do not charge a sufficient amount of spread for taking on credit risk into their balance sheets. As the adjusted exposure to a specific obligor increases, the size of the potential loss increases dramatically.

Recall from earlier chapters that the two measures of credit loss – expected loss and unexpected loss – are both proportional to the adjusted exposure, which is the amount of the current outstanding plus a percentage draw-down on the commitment. Therefore, the anticipated loss (ie, portfolio EL) in the course of doing business and the volatility of loss (ie, portfolio UL) depend on the total amount of credit the bank is exposed to with specific obligors.

How much should the bank charge for taking on credit risk from a specific obligor in exchange for some desired risk-adjusted return? In other words, what is the required spread the bank needs to charge given a particular level of risk-adjusted return?

The loan spread required to take on larger amounts of the same credit increases dramatically with concentration. This increasingly greater amount of required spread is necessary to reward the bank for holding larger amounts of credit risk with the same obligor and hence, exposing it to an even larger probability of suffering from the obligor's default.

The phenomenon is known in the market as the *credit paradox*. This phenomenon is counterintuitive to other, non-credit-related areas where, as a result of the economy of scale, it is normally cheaper to do more of the same thing, and not the other way round.

This chapter addresses two topics, namely:

- ❑ The credit paradox
- ❑ The loan pricing calculator

The tool developed here, called the *loan pricing calculator*, is used to determine the required spread the bank needs to charge as compensation for taking on additional credits into an *existing* portfolio given a desired level of risk-adjusted return. Two important points must be borne in mind – the risk-adjusted return, such as RAROC, must be specified *a priori*; and the required spread is calculated *relative* to the existing banking book. We shall begin with a discussion of the credit paradox.

THE CREDIT PARADOX

A credit portfolio that is not well diversified will generally be characterised by an excess in the two portfolio risk measures,expected loss and unexpected loss, relative to a more diversified portfolio of similar size and other characteristics. This is because the credit losses in the portfolio are highly correlated and the risk of default between individual obligors is not sufficiently mitigated by portfolio effects.

Unlike doing volume in market risk, it is normally not "cheaper" to accept more credit risk because an institution needs to charge an increasingly larger credit spread as its exposure to a specific obligor rises. The larger spread is required to compensate the bank for the increase in the expected and unexpected losses associated with the increased exposure to the obligor. However, banks rarely charge more in hopes of retaining the "good relationship" of the borrower. In fact, the opposite is true – relationship managers normally argue for higher levels of exposure as a means of retaining lead bank status with a client or as a hedge to receiving more lucrative business down the road. A problematic paradox hereby exists, resulting in significant concentration risk for the bank.

CAUSES OF CONCENTRATION RISK

The following are some factors that contribute to concentration risk in a credit portfolio.

- ❑ *Specialisation* Most financial institutions, by virtue of their expertise (or lack of it), tend to specialise in specific industries or geographical areas. This causes their credit portfolios to be concentrated on clusters of clients that tend to have similar default characteristics and whose businesses tend to be highly correlated with the economic cycles they are in. This means that specialised institutions can normally operate only within the scope of their natural markets and have a very difficult time matching their origination capacity with their objectives for diversification. Consequently, the more specialised an institution is, the greater the problem posed by concentration risk in the balance sheet.

- *Credit trends* As a consequence of direct issuance of securities to investors and capital-raising in the capital markets, larger corporations have succeeded in bypassing bank financing, leaving a concentration of lower credits that do not have easy access to the capital markets for financing. As a result, some institutions are beginning to have a disproportionate concentration of lower-quality borrowers in their portfolios.
- *Relationships* To preserve a cosy client relationship in the hope of generating more non-credit-related business down the road, many institutions struggle with the dilemma of increasing their commitment to individual borrowers beyond what is considered profitable for them. Consequently, faced with the inability to directly offload the larger credit exposures, many incur substantial concentration risk with specific borrowers.

Given these factors that collectively contribute to the credit paradox phenomenon, financial institutions are quickly turning to the credit derivatives market for solutions. Although the early indications are that banks are not too adept, or profitable, in using the credit derivatives vehicle to alleviate concentration risk, the resulting capital relief, nevertheless, allows them to generate earnings elsewhere. For now it appears that the newly released capital and the new opportunities it creates have adequately compensated for the loss in using credit derivatives.

In tandem with the asset securitisation vehicle, credit derivatives potentially allow a substantial amount of credit risk and its associated concentration effects to be lifted from the balance sheet. The amount of credit relief and capital reduction depends to a considerable extent on the embedded tranches in the asset securitisation and the kinds of credit derivatives that are structured.

It seems that, in the absence of regulatory intervention, financial institutions have at their disposal a considerable arsenal of innovative products wherewith to align their capital structure with the businesses they engage in, while at the same time shifting the credit content of their balance sheets to more favourable positions. In chapter 1, in the section "Game theory: regulatory capital arbitrage", I discussed at some length this unintended, albeit cosmetic, response by big banks to the regulatory risk-based capital requirement.

CREDIT CONCENTRATION AND REQUIRED SPREAD

Figure 13.1 graphically demonstrates the interesting phenomenon discussed above. The curves clearly show that the required spread, plotted as a function of increasing exposure, behaves in an exponentially increasing manner. For illustrative purposes, the data in the figure were calculated on the basis of a desired hypothetical risk-adjusted return of 13%, as represented in RAROC terms.

Figure 13.2, which is a log–log plot to downscale the exponential growth, shows the required spreads for the different risk classes. The data in this figure were calculated for the same risk-adjusted return as in Figure 13.1. Observe here that the higher the risk class rating (corresponding to worsening credits), the sharper is the increase in required spreads relative to an increase in the amount of exposure. In principle, this implies that the bank needs to charge an ever increasing amount of loan spread so that it can be fairly compensated for taking a higher concentration of worse credits into its portfolio. But, in reality, would the bank be able to charge these kinds of spreads in the market? Probably not.

Banks with very large relationships with specific clients suffer most from the credit paradox, but, despite the fact that diversification is a tenet of modern portfolio theory, there is no motivation for these banks to reduce concentrations. Because a reduction in credit concentration lowers revenue from net interest margins, banks which originate loans are reluctant to offload a portion of the concentration. Second, since in most banks credit portfolios are not measured on a risk-adjusted basis (eg, RAROC) but in a regulatory capital framework, banks are not encouraged to seek returns commensurate with the risk they take on in their credit portfolios, even though the BIS rules have been universally promoted as "risk-based" capital standards.

Figure 13.1 Concentration and required spread

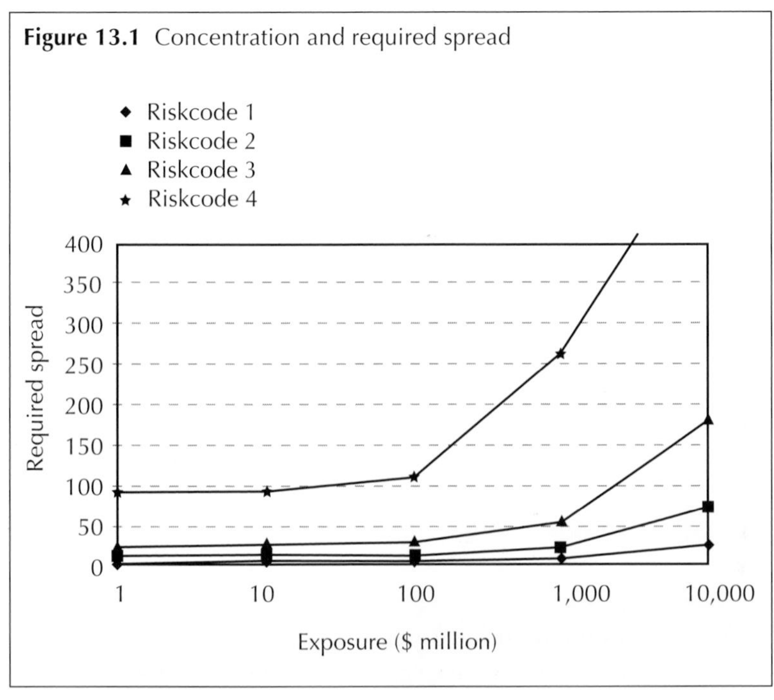

Figure 13.2 Required spreads for different risk classes

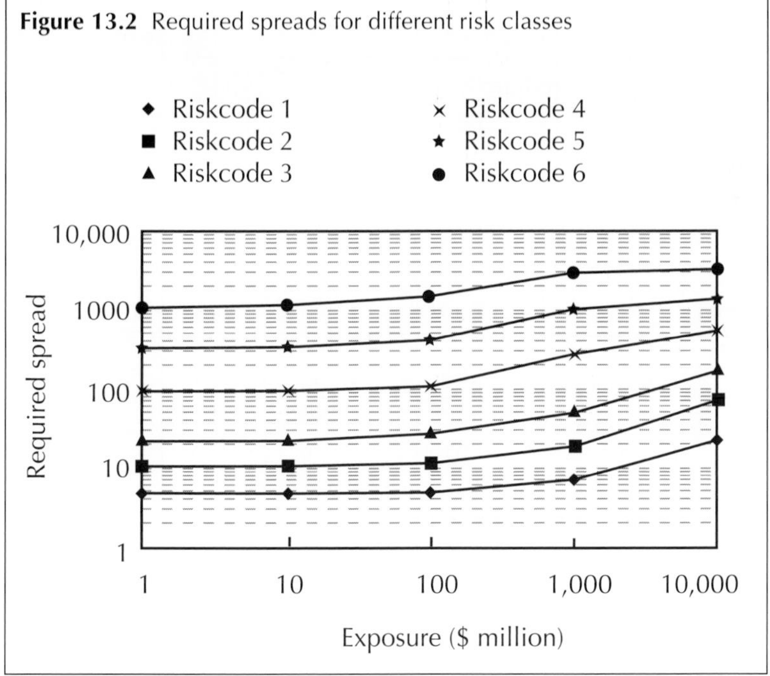

Figure 13.3 The loan pricing calculator – an example

Loan Pricing Calculator (With respect to 31 May 1998 Loan Portfolio)

Enter all input data, Press F9 to calculate

Input: New Facility information						
	Customer no	00184233	Industry SIC code	5122	Internal risk code	4+
	Customer name	DUMMY CORP.				
	Commitment in $	30,000,000	Commitment fee in bp	5	Maturity in years	1.00
	Outstanding in $	10,000,000	Up front fee in $	20,000	Secured?	N

Output			Existing customer number, existing exposure			
	Exposure upon default	21,400,000	Customer name	DUMMY CORP.		
	Expected loss	65,240	Commitment	21,500,000	SIC	5122
	Unexpected loss contribution	131,433	Outstanding	17,766,667	Customer risk rating	B4+
	Capital	952,959	RAROC	–5.27%		

Enter spread, Calculate RAROC for this deal

Input	Loan spread in bp	125		
Output	Revenue	160,000		
	New deal RAROC	9.94%	Customer RAROC	2.76%

Enter target RAROC, Calculate required spread

Input	New deal target RAROC	13.00%		
Output	Required revenue	189,124		
	Required loan spread in bp	154	Customer RAROC	4.58%

In fact, observing some of the sizable required spreads shown in Figures 13.1 and 13.2, it is important to ask whether it is even feasible, in a very competitive and ever-narrowing spreads market, for a bank to charge the spread that is commensurate with the concentration risk it is taking. In practice, although it might not be possible for a bank to charge the required spread, with increasing innovations in asset securitisation (eg, collateralised loan and bond obligations) and credit derivatives, it will become easier for banks to unload or even swap out a portion of this concentration risk so that the credit paradox need not make any difference one way or the other to their portfolios. It is, however, also quite disconcerting to point out that in many asset securitisation programs, the intrinsic credit risks of the securitised assets are, in reality, not completely jettisoned from the banks' balance sheets. These credit risks, for the most part, are still sitting in the residual tranches of the securities, thereby continuing to need economic capital even though regulatory capital has been substantially (and artificially) reduced. It is too early to predict how the market will evolve beyond this point in time. It is also not clear how the regulators need to respond.

Not surprisingly, the credit paradox also exists on a geographic and industry basis when one takes on an increasing concentration of country risk in a specific country or increasing exposure to a specific industry. The credit paradox is, however, strictly a credit phenomenon and is unrelated to market risk.

THE LOAN PRICING CALCULATOR

How much should a bank charge, *in risk-adjusted terms*, for taking an additional increment of credit risk into its portfolio? The answer requires knowledge of the *risk contribution* of this additional increment of credit risk *relative* to the existing portfolio.

The mathematics associated with the derivation of the risk contribution due to the incremental addition of a new credit to an existing portfolio is given in Appendix A. The results are self-explanatory.

In Figure 13.3 an example is given of the effects of adding a new loan facility to an existing portfolio. In the existing portfolio, a hypothetical obligor named Dummy Corporation has a current outstanding of $17.8 million and a commitment of $21.5 million. The corporation is identified as belonging to some standard industry classification (SIC) so that the appropriate correlation effects with the existing portfolio can be taken into account. Dummy Corporation is internally rated as a risk class of 4+ and currently has a negative RAROC of −5.25%. Given these known facts about the obligor, the bank needs to make a decision on whether or not it is economically beneficial for it to extend additional loan structures to this client.

Suppose that a new one-year loan facility of $10 million is being structured for the corporation, with an additional $30 million in commitments. Dummy Corporation will pay the bank an up-front commitment fee of 5 basis points (or $20,000). The loan pricing calculator determines that the adjusted exposure due to this new credit facility will be $21.4 million, an expected loss of $65,240, and a risk contribution of $131,443. Given the risk characteristics of this new facility, the additional economic capital required to sustain the new deal is $952,959.

If the bank charges a loan spread of 125 basis points for the new transaction, the new deal will result in a RAROC of 9.94%. The overall RAROC of Dummy Corp. will therefore be raised to 2.76%. This clearly is beneficial to the bank, erasing the negative RAROC attributable to all the facilities associated with this obligor. But is this sufficient from the bank's perspective?

Suppose the bank decided on an internal risk-adjusted hurdle rate of 13% for this transaction. In this case the calculator determines the required spread to be 154 basis points. If the bank were able to charge this loan spread, the overall RAROC for the obligor would increase to 4.38% – which again is beneficial to the bank. The bank now has sufficient risk measures to make a prudent decision on the extension of additional credits to Dummy Corporation.

By constructing a loan pricing calculator similar to the one we have just demonstrated, the bank can easily decide whether or not to approve additional new credits in light of the current composition of the portfolio. By toggling between a target hurdle rate and the required spread, the bank can make a conscious judgment on whether it is being fairly compensated for the risk it is being asked to undertake. In addition, if for some reason the bank cannot charge the required spread to this obligor, it then behoves the bank to find alternative means of maintaining the target hurdle rate by seeking the spread elsewhere.

Through the prudent use of a loan pricing calculator constructed from all the risk measures we have introduced in the book, the bank would possess a very transparent and explainable mechanism for quantifying incremental credit risk to an existing portfolio. This has always been the goal of this book – to promote transparency in internal credit risk modelling in the market and to facilitate a greater degree of confidence in the modelling efforts on the part of both senior management and regulatory supervisors.

APPENDIX A – MATHEMATICS OF THE LOAN PRICING CALCULATOR

Let the existing portfolio unexpected loss be denoted by U_{P}. Denote the unexpected losses of any two obligors, UL_i and UL_j, by U_i and U_j, respectively. Then, from equation (6.3a), the portfolio unexpected loss is given by

$$U_{\mathrm{P}}^2 = \sum_{ij} U_i U_j \rho_{ij} \tag{A.13.1}$$

where ρ_{ij} is the default correlation between obligors i and j.

Now, suppose we add a new deal to the existing portfolio. Let the new transaction be indexed by k and belong to some industry index γ, and denote its expected and unexpected losses, respectively, by the lower case symbols e and u.

There are two possible cases to consider with respect to the new, additional deal, namely:

- *New customer* The additional deal is made with an entirely new customer of the bank with no prior exposure in the existing portfolio.
- *Old customer* The additional deal is made with a current customer of the bank who is therefore already a part of the existing portfolio.

Case 1: New customer

Let the resulting newly enlarged portfolio (with the addition of this single incremental new deal) have a portfolio unexpected loss denoted by χ; then

$$\chi^2 = \sum_{ij} U_i U_j \rho_{ij} + u^2 + \sum_{i \neq k} U_i u \rho_{i\gamma} + \sum_{j \neq k} u U_j \rho_{\gamma j}$$

$$= U_P^2 + \left[u^2 + 2u \sum_{i \neq k} U_i \rho_{i\gamma} \right]$$

$$= U_P^2 + \left[u^2 + 2u \sum_{\beta} \left(\sum_{i \neq k} U_i \right) \rho_{\beta\gamma} \right]$$

$$\equiv U_P^2 + \left[u^2 + 2u Y_{\gamma}^{\text{Old}} \right] \tag{A.13.2}$$

with the notation

$$Y_{\gamma}^{\text{old}} \equiv \sum_{\beta} \left(\sum_{i \neq k} U_i \right) \rho_{\beta\gamma} \tag{A.13.3}$$

Observe that equation (A.13.3) is the sum of all the *UL* for index γ.

The *risk contribution* of the incremental new deal, in relation to the existing portfolio, is

$$c \equiv u \frac{\partial \chi}{\partial u}$$

$$= u \frac{1}{\chi} \left[u + Y_{\gamma}^{\text{old}} \right] \tag{A.13.4}$$

Thus, the risk or economic capital associated with the incremental new deal is

$$\textit{Economic capital}^{\text{new}, e} = c \times \textit{Capital multiplier}$$

The RAROC of the individual new deal is

$$RAROC^{\text{new}, e} = \frac{\textit{Revenue}^{\text{new}, e} - e}{\textit{Economic capital}^{\text{new}, e}} \tag{A.13.5}$$

Finally, the RAROC for the total "enlarged" portfolio as a result of including this new deal is given by

$$RAROC^{\text{new}} =$$

$$\frac{Revenue^{\text{old}} + Revenue^{\text{new},\,e} - EL^{\text{old}} - e}{Capital\ multiplier \times \chi} \qquad \textbf{(A.13.6)}$$

We now need to consider the case where the new deal is, say, an additional loan facility for an existing customer of the bank and the customer already has a current exposure in the bank portfolio.

Case 2: Old customer

The incremental addition of some loan facility for an old customer to the existing portfolio results in a new portfolio unexpected loss of

$$\chi^2 = \sum_{ij,\, i\neq k,\, j\neq k} U_i U_j \rho_{ij} + (U_k + u)^2 + (U_k + u)\sum_{j\neq k} U_j \rho_{kj} +$$

$$(U_k + u)\sum_{i\neq k} U_i \rho_{ik}$$

$$= \sum_{ij} U_i U_j \rho_{ij} + 2u\sum_{j\neq k} U_j \rho_{kj} + 2uU_k + u^2$$

$$= U_P^2 + 2u\sum_{j} U_j \rho_{kj} - 2uU_k\rho_{kk} + 2uU_k + u^2$$

since the existing portfolio has $U_P^2 = \sum_{ij} U_i U_j \rho_{ij}$.

So that

$$\chi^2 = U_P^2 + 2u\left[\sum_{j} U_j \rho_{kj} + (1-\rho_{\gamma\gamma})U_k\right] + u^2 \qquad \textbf{(A.13.7)}$$

Notice that we have used $\rho_{kk} = \rho_{\gamma\gamma}$ since the new deal is indexed by k and belongs to industry indexed by γ.

Recall that from equation (A.13.3) we have

$$Y_{\gamma}^{\text{old}} \equiv \sum_{\beta}\left(\sum_{i \neq k} U_i\right)\rho_{\beta\gamma} = \sum_{i} U_i \rho_{i\gamma} \qquad \textbf{(A.13.8)}$$

so that equation (A.13.7) finally becomes

$$\chi^2 = U_P^2 + 2u\left[Y_{\gamma}^{\text{old}} + (1-\rho_{\alpha\alpha})U_k\right] + u^2 \qquad \textbf{(A.13.9)}$$

The risk contribution of this new deal with an old customer (in relation to the existing portfolio) is, therefore, given by

$$c \equiv u\frac{\partial\chi}{\partial u}$$

$$= \frac{1}{\chi}\left\{u\left[Y_{\gamma}^{\text{old}} + (1-\rho_{\alpha\alpha})U_k\right] + u^2\right\}$$

$$= \frac{u}{\chi}\left[u + Y_{\gamma}^{\text{old}} + (1-\rho_{\alpha\alpha})U_k\right] \qquad \textbf{(A.13.10)}$$

Comparing equations (A.13.4) and (A.13.10) for the risk contribution in the two cases considered, observe that in the latter there is an extra term, $(1 - \rho_{\alpha\alpha})U_k$, representing the extra contribution of the new deal with an old customer to the existing portfolio. Clearly, the effect of the contribution of this new deal to portfolio risk is purely a play in correlation.

The formulas for the economic capital and the RAROC corresponding to this new deal are the same as equations (A.13.5) and (A.13.6), respectively.

Epilogue

The Next Steps

So now what? We have come to the end of the book. I have achieved my primary objective of discussing the current regulatory capital regime, its fundamental flaws and the need for reform. In so doing, I introduced simple and practical building blocks for measuring credit risk in the banking book, leading to the more important issues of capital allocation and performance measurement. Hopefully I have presented practical, albeit imperfect, solutions for a very difficult subject and paved the way for a more open dialogue in the years to come. But these are just the first steps and the task is by no means complete.

My pen has almost stopped writing, but the task does not end here; this should be only the beginning of the first steps towards transparency and enlightenment. To this end, I offer some recommendations to the two main groups of interested parties: the regulatory supervisors and the banks. Somewhere along the evolutionary path of the process of revamping the current risk-based capital adequacy rules for credit risk, these two main groups of people need to come together in a dialogue and reach agreement on what is the most prudent thing to do.

In addition to what I have already articulated in the book, there are some further important areas that must not be overlooked during the dialogue. Allow me to reiterate them as follows:

- Internal credit risk ratings
- The general opaqueness of credit-related information (eg, loss severity and recovery rates) and the quality of credit data
- Techniques for assessing extreme loss distributions
- The implications of risk-adjusted performance measurement and risk-adjusted pricing

- ❑ The multi-state default process, marking-to-market and multi-year analysis horizons
- ❑ Reconcilable or irreconcilable differences between the credit models offered by various vendors
- ❑ The integration of market risk and credit risk.

In the next few sections I shall briefly discuss each of these points and draw attention to more recent work that has been done in the specific area. From there, it is over to the reader to continue on to his or her own "next steps" towards transparency and enlightenment.

INTERNAL CREDIT RISK RATINGS

First and foremost in the next steps of credit risk modelling are the integrity and robustness of the bank's own internal credit risk-rating system. As we have seen throughout the book, a bank's internal risk rating plays a vital role in assigning risk. An internal risk rating is the bank's front-line defence against default risk. It is the bank's primary indicator of risk for individual credit exposures. Most large banks use internal ratings to guide the loan origination process, portfolio reporting and management reporting. Internal risk ratings are used to provide guidance for setting loan loss reserves, profitability analysis and loan pricing analysis.

Although credit risk ratings are becoming increasingly important in the credit risk management process of large banks, Treacy and Carey (1998) noted in their paper that

> ... banks' rating systems differ significantly from those of the [rating] agencies (and from each other) in architecture and operating design as well as in the uses to which ratings are put. One reason for these differences is that banks' ratings are assigned by bank personnel and are usually not revealed to outsiders ...

rendering the risk-rating systems of banks rather opaque and non-comparable. Furthermore, they argued, "variations across banks are an example of form following function. There does not appear to be one 'correct' rating system. Instead, 'correctness' depends on how the system is used."

Whatever the argument is concerning "correctness" or uniformity or consistency, or the inability to compare and differentiate between banks' internal risk ratings, the truth of the matter is this: the risk-rating system is the bank's only compass, without which the bank is lost amidst the sea of credits. Why, therefore, has sufficient effort not been exerted in the past to strengthen the integrity and consistency of banks' internal risk-rating systems?

Some issues regarding internal risk ratings that require immediate attention are considered in the three subsections that follow.

Granularity of risk ratings

The number of grades on internal risk-rating scales varies considerably across banks. In this book, the experience we gained in the internal credit risk modelling exercise pointed to the importance of refined and clearly distinguishable grades – both in the passing and in the non-passing grades. In addition, so that we could properly distinguish the different levels of risk and return, we saw that it is crucial to have more grades rather than fewer. In fact, perhaps due to their own internal modelling needs, many banks that have redesigned their internal risk-rating systems during the past decade have decided to increase the number of grades on their rating scales (Udell, 1987). Interestingly enough, the majority of the banks interviewed by Treacy and Carey (1998) and Federal Reserve Board supervisory staff "expressed at least some desire to increase the number of grades on their scales and to reduce the extent to which credits are concentrated in one or two grades".

The dichotomy between bank ratings and agency ratings

There continues to be a an unresolved dichotomy between internal bank ratings and agency ratings. As pointed out in the Treacy and Carey paper, agency and bank ratings differ substantially mainly because rating agencies themselves make no risky investments and are, therefore, not a party to transactions between borrowers and lenders. Bank ratings are private and proprietary, whereas agency ratings are sold publicly for a fee. In more ways than one, agency ratings are more likely to incorporate "intangible" but important information – for example, management quality and market conditions – along with the capital structure and financial statements one would expect. Bank ratings, on the other hand, are generally assigned by a "loan review committee" with a membership that normally does not have access to the same extensive information resources that are available to the rating agencies, whose sole function and source of income is the provision of ratings.

Mapping of internal risk ratings to agency grades

When assigning default probabilities (EDF), it is very convenient to map the bank's internal risk ratings to the agency scales because the agencies provide publicly available default information derived from their own database of the historical loss performance of publicly issued bonds. To use data on bond loss experience, however, the bank must be careful when assuming some correspondence (if it truly exists) between agency ratings and its own ratings for loans that need not necessarily have the same default experiences as bonds. Treacy and Carey (1998) identified four potential problems, as set out below:

- ❏ A bank's internal rating system may place loans with widely varying levels of EDF in the same grade and those with similar EDFs in different grades. In this case, grades bear little relation to default probabilities, thereby rendering the mapping inaccurate. Throughout this book we have been very cognisant of this potential problem.
- ❏ EDFs on publicly rated bonds may differ systematically from actual loan default rates.
- ❏ The mapping exercise may simply associate internal grades with the wrong agency grades.
- ❏ The differences arising from a bank's point-in-time assessment of credit risk and the agencies' through-the-cycle rating approach may not be properly taken into account.

Concerning the mapping of internal risk ratings to agency ratings, it is instructive to consult the paper written by Miller (1998), where he describes a methodology for testing whether a quantitative credit rating system (such as one based on the "value of the firm" framework) is a statistically significant improvement (ie, provides additional information) on a broader rating system. To this end, he compares the EDFs generated by KMV Corporation's Credit Monitor system with the Standard & Poor's ratings for US companies. Miller's paper is reproduced in the Appendix to this book.

Readers are also referred to an article by English and Nelson (1998), which followed up on the Treacy and Carey (1998) paper by providing further information on the use of risk ratings by small and medium-sized US banks and by the US branches and agencies of foreign banks. They "investigated on how common is risk rating at all banking institutions in the U.S., what fraction of business loans are assigned ratings, how fine the gradations generally are, and how risk ratings are related to loan price and non-price terms". One of their key findings was that "despite the concerns raised by some observers that banks do not price risk properly, the survey data show that the ratings are reflected in loan pricing and other term loans. Not surprisingly, loan interest rates rise with loan risk."

DATA QUALITY AND OPAQUENESS

By virtue of either benign neglect or extreme myopia over the years, only scant information about loss experiences is normally available internally within a bank. In the parameterisation of the internal model, quantities such as loss given default (and, hence, recovery rates), usage given default (the percentage draw-down of the unused part of the commitment) and the default probabilities themselves are absolutely critical.

The mapping of the bank's internal risk ratings to agency grades alleviates some of the problems stemming from the lack of internal data, although, as articulated in the previous section, mapping can introduce its own problems. However, the framework used in this book to approximate the correlation of default and credit quality was also adopted in direct response to the opaqueness of the financial information provided by firms, particularly the unrated private ones. Although it is pleasing to be able to make a sensible approximation, a greater transparency in the information provided by firms is definitely beneficial to the risk quantification process.

TECHNIQUES FOR ASSESSING EXTREME LOSS DISTRIBUTIONS

There are two general ways of constructing credit loss distributions. The first is to make simplifying assumptions about the portfolio and derive analytical expressions. The second approach is to use full-blown Monte Carlo simulation methods. We have done both in this book. We also combined both methods and used extreme value theory to extrapolate the extreme tail of the loss distributions. Full-blown simulation methods can be very slow, but there are ways of speeding up the simulation for credit modelling purposes. The paper by Arvanitis and Gregory (1999), reproduced in the Appendix to the book, discusses some of these newer methods. In particular, they introduced techniques to deal with the modelling of default correlations without any assumption about the capital structure of the firm. In addition, the authors introduce an approach to "modeling stochastic recovery rates that intuitively links the recovery amount to the severity of default".

RISK-ADJUSTED PERFORMANCE MEASUREMENT AND RISK-ADJUSTED PRICING

A smart bank makes the best use of its capital by allocating it efficiently to the different lines of business. However, the spirit of the 1988 Basle Accord has prevented an accurate measurement of economic capital that reflects the underlying risk characteristics of the banking books undertaken by banks. Consequently, the current regulatory capital framework has led to incentives that are for the most part contradictory with the trade-off between risk and return. An article by Punjabi (1998) continues along the lines of argument set forth in this book. The article, reproduced in the Appendix, discusses the four variants of risk-adjusted return performance measurement (RAPM): ROC (return on capital), RORAC (return on risk-adjusted capital), RAROC (risk-adjusted return on capital), and RARORAC (risk-adjusted return on risk-adjusted capital). The author eloquently contrasts and compares these four performance measures and discusses their applications and implications. The article also provides some guidance on how a bank can choose the performance measure that is most suitable for its needs.

A RAROC-type performance measure is not without detractors. An early criticism of the approach can be found in an article by Wilson (1992; given in the Appendix), who demonstrated the intrinsic bias of the RAROC approach and suggested some modifications.

MULTI-STATE DEFAULT PROCESS, MARKING-TO-MARKET AND MULTI-YEAR ANALYSIS HORIZONS

Two-state and multi-state default processes

To keep the book going at a manageable pace, I have deliberately chosen to emphasise only the two-state default process of achieving either default or no default at the analysis horizon. In reality, however, the default process is multi-state in nature, whereby the intervening stages of credit quality migration are also permissible.

Figure E.1 graphically illustrates the difference between a two-state and a multi-state default process. In a simple two-state default process there are only two possible outcomes at the end of the

Figure E.1 Two-state and multi-state default processes compared

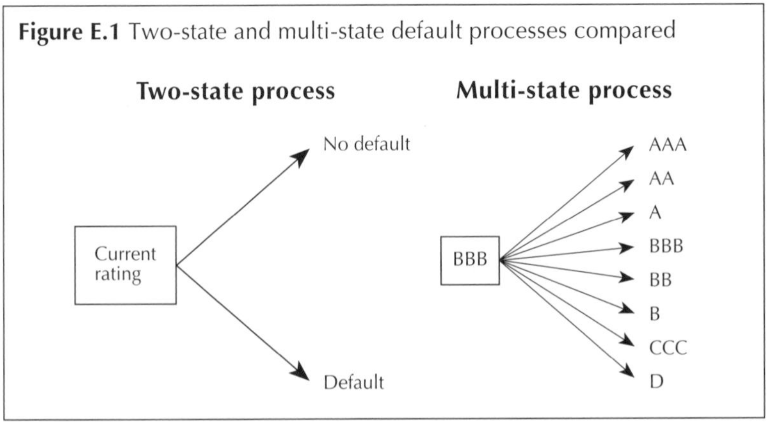

analysis period. In contrast, in the multi-state process, an obligor currently assigned an initial BBB rating can improve on its rating, remain the same, get downgraded or enter into default.

In Appendix A ("Variation in asset value due to time") of chapter 6, it was shown that the value of a risky asset changes with time owing to two major time effects: default and credit migration. We then proceeded to determine the asset's expected value and its standard deviation. Appendix A of this Epilogue continues and expands on that discussion.

Marking-to-market valuation

The specific results of Appendix A, which extend the simple case to a multi-state default process, highlight a very important point I did not have the opportunity to discuss in the book. This concerns the issue of *marking-to-market* valuation. Observe that in Appendix A all the equations containing the value V require a discounting of cashflows to some point in time (the one-year horizon was chosen for convenience). The simple reason is that, associated with any possible state the risky asset could migrate to, there is a corresponding value which the asset must take. Therefore, to arrive at the expected value of the risky asset at the horizon, one must obtain the probability-weighted value of the asset over all the possible paths (ie, risk ratings) it could conceivably take over the period up to the horizon. This is the non-mathematical interpretation of equation (A.E.2).

All the remaining equations, including those for the portfolio expected and unexpected losses, contain an important component of valuation. We call it "mark-to-market" valuation because all the cashflows emanating from the risky asset must be discounted using the appropriate forward curves associated with each credit rating class. An article by Li (1998) explains one approach to building such "credit curves".

Mark-to-market valuation is an important component of credit risk modelling because the value of a risky asset changes with time, and time gives the asset the opportunity to change its credit quality, thereby potentially changing its value.

Multi-year horizons

Tradition dictates that the analysis horizon be one year forward in time. This prevailing "wisdom" can perhaps be traced to an unintended effect of the BIS risk-based capital rules. Regulatory reporting procedures require banks to submit their "call reports" to the banking supervisors once every year. These reports contain, among many other things, information about the banks' solvency ratios and risk-weighted assets. Perhaps as an unintended consequence, banks have become accustomed to focus their attention on regulatory capital and credit risk in the framework of an annual time horizon. But should the credit risk in the banking book be shoehorned into a one-year box? I think not.

Unlike market risk, credit risk certainly entails a much longer time horizon. This makes the analysis of credit risk quite difficult. In earlier chapters of the book we encountered the multi-year transition matrices inferred by the rating agencies from their proprietary databases of historical bond defaults. Currently, there are only two sources of empirical transition matrices that extend to a 15-year horizon – Standard & Poor's and Moody's.

To mathematically incorporate multi-year horizon analysis into our internal credit risk modelling effort is easy – simply replace all probabilities in Appendix A with their corresponding multi-year transition probabilities and calculate the expected loss and the unexpected loss as usual. In principle, therefore, one could calculate all the risk measures associated with the credit portfolio for any desired time horizon. If, for example, one simply uses data from the two multi-year transition matrices from the agencies in the internal model, it produces quite erratic results – too erratic to be of much practical use. Why is that?

A simplifying assumption that is often invoked in financial modelling is the Markov property of financial systems. Very briefly, the Markov property supposes that the evolution in time of a system depends only on the state that preceded it. Implicitly embedded in the agencies' multi-year transition matrices is the initial one-year transition matrix whose evolution from one year to the next must ultimately form the basis for all longer-term transition matrices that are empirically derived by the agencies. Appendix B presents work performed by my colleague S. Maglic in our attempt to understand the time-dependent evolution of credit risk. The conclusion is that: the study is inconclusive! There are many possible initial transition matrices that could fit the empirically derived multi-year transition matrices within the bounds of acceptable optimisation error. More research is definitely needed in this area.

DIFFERENCES BETWEEN VENDOR MODELS

Although the intent of this book is to remain impartial and not to glorify one model nor debase another, it is, however, instructive to understand the subtle differences between the models that are currently available in the market. There are differences – some reconcilable and some irreconcilable – between the models from the various vendors that practitioners and regulators must be aware of. Koyluoglu and Hickman (1998) focus on three representative models for comparison:

- ❑ "Value of the firm"-based: JP Morgan's CreditMetrics and KMV's Portfolio Manager
- ❑ Econometric-based: McKinsey's CreditPortfolio View
- ❑ Actuarial-based: CSFP's CreditRisk+.

Their article, which appears in the Appendix to this book, specifically examines only the default component of portfolio credit risk. The conclusions are that

> ... the models belong to a single general framework, which identifies three critical points of comparison – the default rate distribution, the conditional default distribution, and the convolution/aggregation technique. Differences were found to be immaterial in the last two of these, so that any significant differences between the models must arise from differences in modelling joint-default behavior which manifests in the default rate distribution.

Parameter inconsistency, as I have forewarned many times in the book, is not a trivial issue and is, conceivably, the cause of many of the systematic differences. Koyluoglu and Hickman postulated further that

> ... rather than conclude that parameter inconsistency potentially constitutes irreconcilable differences between the results of these models, this paper concludes that because the models are so closely related, the estimates are complementary and should provide improved accuracy in parameter estimation within the generalized framework as a whole.

Other comparative studies of vendor models are being conducted at the present time.

INTEGRATION OF MARKET RISK AND CREDIT RISK

A final important point I wish to draw attention to is the ongoing need for an integrated view of market risk and credit risk, primarily, and maybe other forms of risk later on. The segregated view we have now is yet another unintended consequence of the risk-based capital rules. The 1996 Amendment to the Basle Accord exacerbated the dichotomy still further by requiring banks to set aside capital specifically to cover market risk in the trading book, and, to a lesser extent, a residual capital requirement for "specific risk" due to individual issuers of the traded securities. In response, the regulated banks began to aggregate their risks into "silos of risks" attributable specifically to market activities and credit activities.

There is something drastically wrong with this picture. First of all, credit risk and market risk are not strictly additive in nature. For regulatory capital purposes, however, they are incorrectly assumed to be so. In reality, both forms of risks are driven by the same fundamental market variables, so both market risk and credit risk are derived from the same market value distributions. As Mark (1995) eloquently explained:

> They have an inverse relationship: market risk is the risk that the market value of the position will decline; credit risk is the risk that the counter-party will default when the market value of the position is positive. Because of their inverse relationship, there are many similarities in the way that credit and market risk are measured.

Owing to the relative hedgeability of market risk as compared to credit risk, there is a difference in the time scales that are used when assessing these two risks – shorter for market risk and much longer for credit risk.

To be able to measure risk and return effectively, it is mandatory to measure both market and credit risk simultaneously as otherwise the additivity rule imposed by the current capital regime will result in an overestimate of required capital. Furthermore, to achieve the greatest efficiencies, banks must superimpose credit risk on top of their market risk models as their portfolios move with the market. In other words, default risk (or risk due to credit migration) should be embedded in the valuation of risky assets and not be considered as a separate add-on – in marked contrast to the approach taken in the BIS guidelines discussed in chapter 1.

Without a doubt, the implementation of a best-practice risk-adjusted performance measure, such as RAROC, will one day *force* the integration of market risk and credit risk into one unified framework, as should be the case. But until that happens, the question that remains is not "how?" but "when?".

APPENDIX A – THE MULTI-STATE DEFAULT PROCESS[1]

This appendix is a continuation of Appendix A of chapter 6. First, we need to repeat some of the equations derived previously.

The current value, V, of a single loan commitment with current outstanding, or notional, amount A can easily be valued by discounting the various cashflows:

$$V = \sum_{k=1}^{M} \frac{C_k}{(1+r_k)^k} + \frac{A + C_M}{(1+r_M)^M} \qquad \textbf{(A.E.1)}$$

where C_k is the cash payment for the kth period, M is the maturity of the loan, and r_k is the yield of the loan for the kth period, which depends on the credit rating, R.

Without loss of generality, we assume that the payment frequency is annual and we choose an analysis horizon of one year. At the end of one year the loan may have migrated to another credit rating class or it might have already defaulted. Thus, the expected value, V_1, of the loan at the end of one year is the probability-weighted value of all the possible values in each rating class, R:

$$V_1 = AC + \sum_R p_R (V_R - \Delta_R) \tag{A.E.2}$$

where we have denoted all these possible values by V_R and where the index R runs over all the possible risk classes or states available, as illustrated in Figure E.1.

The first term in equation (A.E.2), AC, represents the accrued cash payments compounded (ie, their total future value) to the analysis horizon. The sum is over all the possible ratings and p_R is the migration or transition probability associated with risk class R. The quantity Δ_R represents the expected amount of additional draw-down of the commitment given a downgrade in credit rating. It also represents the additional pay-down of the loan if there is an upgrade. If U is the unused portion of the commitment, the restriction $-A \leq \Delta_R \leq U$ holds. In general, Δ_R is positive when there is a downgrade and negative when there is an upgrade.

The quantity V_R should be calculated using the one-year forward yield curve corresponding to the credit rating R, with the amount Δ_R added to the notional amount of the commitment and the cash-flow adjusted appropriately. This results in

$$V_R = \sum_{k=1}^{M-1} \frac{C'_k}{(1+r_{1k})^k} + \frac{A + \Delta_R + C'_{M-1}}{(1+r_{1,M-1})^{M-1}} \tag{A.E.3}$$

where r_{1k} is the one-year forward yield for risk rating R and is, therefore, a function of R. C'_k is the adjusted cashflow due to change in outstanding by the amount Δ_R.

At the one-year analysis horizon, the variance of V_1 about the mean – representing the variation or volatility in the change in asset value – is

$$\sigma_1^2 = \sum_R p_R (V_R - \Delta_R)^2 - \left(\sum_R p_R (V_R - \Delta_R)^2 \right) \tag{A.E.4}$$

Inherent in equation (A.E.4) is the variation in the value of the loan, which contains information associated with both the probability of default and the probability of migration to all possible risk-rating classes. In addition, the variation also depends on the additional draw-down of unused commitments (in the case of downward migration) and on the pay-down of the current outstanding (in the case of upward migration).

Portfolio of risky assets

Now let us consider a portfolio of risky assets, each of whose values can be described by the process delineated above. The goal is to determine the mean and variance of the value of the portfolio at the end of the one-year analysis period. The portfolio mean is rather trivial and is given by

$$V_{\mathrm{P}} = \sum_i AC_i + \sum_i \sum_R p_R (V_R - \Delta_R) \quad \textbf{(A.E.5)}$$

where the index i is summed over all the risky assets in the portfolio.

We are now ready to derive the expected loss and unexpected loss of the portfolio.

Expected loss

Denote by V_i^N (where the superscript N represents no rating change) the value of a commitment at the analysis horizon whose rating remains unchanged from the beginning of the analysis period. Since the sum of all the migration probabilities is equal to one for a given initial rating, the following identity is true:

$$\sum_i V_i^N = \sum_i \sum_R p_R V_i^N \quad \textbf{(A.E.6)}$$

Subtracting this from equation (A.E.5), we obtain

$$V_{\mathrm{P}} - \sum_i V_i^N = \sum_i AC_i + \sum_i \sum_R p_R \left(V_R - \Delta_R - V_i^N\right) \quad \textbf{(A.E.7)}$$

The sum over R on the right-hand side of equation (A.E.7) can be decomposed into three distinct parts:

- The first is when $R = D$, representing default;
- The second is when R is equal to the initial risk rating, R_i, representing no change in rating (ie, no credit migration); and
- The third is when credit migration to other states is allowed.

Observe that when there is no rating change the second part is actually zero, since in general $\Delta_R = 0$ when there is no rating change. Collecting all the non-zero terms in equation (A.E.7), we rewrite it as

$$V_P - \sum_i V_i^N = \sum_i AC_i + \sum_i p_D \left(V_D - \Delta_D - V_i^N\right)$$
$$+ \sum_i \sum_{\substack{R \neq D \\ R \neq R_i}} p_R \left(V_R - \Delta_R - V_i^N\right) \qquad \textbf{(A.E.8)}$$

The left-hand side of equation (A.E.8) is defined as the expected loss of the portfolio over the analysis period. Looking at the right-hand side of equation (A.E.8), we observe that the expected loss includes the cash payment during the first year (the first term), the realised loss due to default (the second term), and the unrealised loss due to migration (the third term).

Note that in the two-state process, when there is no credit migration or fluctuation of credit exposure, the third term is zero. The second term then takes a more familiar form on realising that if no additional draw-down is allowed (that is, $\Delta_R = 0$), we obtain

$$V_D = E_i(1 - LGD_i)$$
$$V_i^N = E_i$$

where E_i is the exposure (or outstanding) and LGD_i is the loss given default. Consequently, the second term becomes $-\sum_i p_D E_i LGD_i$, which is the familiar definition of expected loss given default derived in chapters 3 and 4.

Unexpected loss and correlation

The variance of the value of the portfolio represents the uncertainty in the change in value of the portfolio. The square root of this variance is the unexpected loss of the portfolio.

The variance of the portfolio is related to the standard deviation of each individual credit through the correlation coefficients, viz:

$$\sigma_P^2 = \sum_i \sigma_i^2 + \sum_{i \neq j} \sigma_i \sigma_j \rho_{ij} \qquad \textbf{(A.E.9)}$$

where ρ_{ij} is the correlation between the values of two risky assets i and j at the end of the analysis period. The correlation is given by

$$\rho_{ij} = \frac{\langle V_i U_j \rangle - \langle V_i \rangle \langle U_j \rangle}{\sigma_i \sigma_j} \qquad \textbf{(A.E.10)}$$

where the bracket <$*$> denotes the expectation operator.

The evaluation of $\langle V_i \rangle$ and $\langle U_j \rangle$ has already been discussed above. The calculation of $\langle V_i U_j \rangle$, however, requires knowledge of the joint probability distribution of the two asset values. We have also discussed at length, in chapter 7, the correlation of default and credit quality. In particular, we need to apply the method outlined in Appendix D of chapter 7 to obtain the correlation of joint credit quality movement.

APPENDIX B – MATCHING TRANSITION MATRICES TO HISTORICAL DATA[2]

Introduction

Rating agencies such as Standard & Poor's and Moody's publish statistics that describe the historical performance of companies, which they rate in terms of rating changes and default probabilities. The data are presented in matrix form and indicate the likelihood that a company of given rating will make a transition to a different rating state at the end of a specified period. Table B.E.1, published by Standard & Poor's,[3] is an example of a one-year transition matrix. AAA corresponds to the highest quality and D indicates default. To determine the probability that an A-rated company will

Table B.E.1 Standard & Poor's one-year transition matrix (1997)

Initial state	Final state: AAA	AA	A	BBB	BB	B	CCC	D	NR
AAA	88.77	7.80	0.68	0.05	0.10	0.00	0.00	0.00	2.60
AA	0.69	88.23	7.32	0.56	0.05	0.14	0.02	0.00	2.99
A	0.07	2.25	87.85	4.88	0.61	0.25	0.01	0.05	4.03
BBB	0.03	0.28	5.37	82.97	4.44	1.00	0.11	0.18	5.62
BB	0.02	0.06	0.53	7.12	74.44	7.29	0.79	0.90	8.85
B	0.00	0.08	0.25	0.41	6.15	72.96	3.32	4.72	12.11
CCC	0.16	0.00	0.32	0.81	2.27	9.87	53.08	19.09	14.40

Table B.E.2 Standard & Poor's one-year transition matrix (1997) adjusted for removal of NR category

Initial state	Final state: AAA	AA	A	BBB	BB	B	CCC	D
AAA	91.14	8.01	0.70	0.05	0.10	0.00	0.00	0.00
AA	0.71	90.95	7.55	0.58	0.05	0.14	0.02	0.00
A	0.07	2.34	91.54	5.08	0.64	0.26	0.01	0.05
BBB	0.03	0.30	5.69	87.91	4.70	1.06	0.12	0.19
BB	0.02	0.07	0.58	7.81	81.67	8.00	0.87	0.99
B	0.00	0.09	0.28	0.47	7.00	83.01	3.78	5.37
CCC	0.19	0.00	0.37	0.95	2.65	11.53	62.01	22.30

undergo a downgrade to a BBB rating, one selects the row corresponding to the initial state A and finds the number in the column corresponding to the final state, BBB. The table gives the A to BBB transition likelihood as 4.88% (or, in probability terms, 0.0488).

One feature that is particular to the Standard & Poor's data is the presence of the final state NR, which indicates that the issue is no longer rated. Since this primarily occurs when a company's outstanding debt issue expires, it is not relevant in our analysis. We therefore wish to remove this column and shift the remaining probabilities accordingly. Table B.E.2 shows the same data adjusted for the NR category. Note that if *actual* transition probabilities are required, one must refer back to the original data.

In addition, rating agencies publish the same matrices for two, three or more years. Table B.E.3 summarises the cumulative default probabilities from multi-year matrices.

Unfortunately, because the historical observations represent a limited sample and a limited time of observation, the quality of the statistical data has limitations. For the most part, the broad features of the historical data are consistent with our intuition. However, careful inspection indicates that the historical performances are counterintuitive. For example, we know that in general the cumulative probability of default should increase for longer horizons, but in the table we observe that the CCC rating category exhibits a decreasing cumulative default probability in years 8, 9 and 10. From an intuitive and statistical perspective we know that we can expect this anomalous behaviour because of the limitations of the data.

Table B.E.3 Standard & Poor's cumulative default probabilities for years 1–10 (%)

	Year									
	1	2	3	4	5	6	7	8	9	10
AAA	0.000	0.000	0.060	0.130	0.210	0.390	0.520	0.790	0.900	1.050
AA	0.000	0.020	0.080	0.170	0.310	0.470	0.700	0.920	1.120	1.370
A	0.050	0.140	0.260	0.440	0.650	0.900	1.190	1.560	1.940	2.340
BBB	0.180	0.430	0.710	1.280	1.850	2.490	3.220	3.900	4.510	5.000
BB	0.900	3.060	5.490	7.980	10.570	13.310	15.370	17.210	18.400	19.400
B	4.720	10.030	14.910	18.780	21.780	23.980	25.910	27.190	27.790	28.240
CCC	19.090	26.610	32.620	36.700	40.780	43.480	44.690	43.920	41.610	39.820

For modelling purposes, we are interested in extracting trends established by historical performance rather than the anomalous behaviour of a small number of companies during a certain year. Therefore, we are interested in slightly modifying the historical data to make them more consistent with our intuition. In addition, we know that there are conditions that we may impose to ensure that the data are self-consistent mathematically. The next section outlines several steps that can be taken to improve the data.

Mathematical framework

A property that is frequently invoked in the discussion of financial systems is the idea of the Markov process. Simply stated, the Markov condition exists when the (time) evolution of a system depends only on the state before it. In the context of our one-year transition matrix, it states that the rating at the end of one year depends only on its present rating. We see that the Markov condition is *implicit* in the data that Standard & Poor's supplies.

An interesting property that follows directly from this condition is that an n-period (each period in our case is one year long) transition operator is the nth power of the one-period transition operator. We may state this result mathematically if we represent the original multi-year cumulative transition data by $D_1, D_2, D_3, \ldots, D_n, \ldots, D_N$, where D_n is the transition matrix for the nth year:

$$D_n = D_1^n$$

where the superscript indicates the nth power of that matrix. For example, the first two powers of D are

$$D_2 = D_1^2 = D_1 \times D_1$$

and

$$D_3 = D_1^3 = D_1 \times D_1 \times D_1$$

We therefore wish to impose the Markov condition on the one-year matrix so that it is consistent with the historical multi-year data. To do this we envisage a one-year matrix that is very similar to the original one-year matrix except that successive powers of this matrix show better agreement with the multi-year data. Therefore we combine a matrix, M, with the original one-year matrix, D_1, to obtain a modified matrix

$$\tilde{D}_1 = D_1 + M$$

where $\tilde{D}_1$, by invoking the Markov condition, is chosen to be more consistent with the historical multiple-year transition matrices by using the relation

$$\tilde{D}_n = \tilde{D}_1^n$$

What remains is a computational problem of choosing a matrix M to minimise the difference between $\tilde{D}_n$ and D_n.

Before continuing on to the next section we note that two constraints on D (and $\tilde{D}_n$) must be satisfied:

$$\text{(A)} \quad D_{n\mu\nu} \geq 0$$

$$\text{(B)} \quad \sum_{\nu=1}^{8} D_{n\mu\nu} = 1$$

The subscripts μ and ν on the matrix D indicate the row and column (or initial and final rating states), respectively. These two requirements merely state, (A), that the probabilities must be positive and, (B), that the total probabilities of the final states must sum to 1 or 100%.

Intuitive constraints

As outlined earlier, we must now impose additional constraints on this system to make it reflect our intuition. To distinguish these from constraints (A) and (B) introduced above, we refer to them as "soft" constraints. We make this distinction because, mathematically, we know that the "hard" constraints must be maintained, whereas the soft constraints are imposed by our intuition as a guide.

We summarise the soft constraints we wish to impose as follows:

1 The likelihood of default for higher-rated names is less than for lower-quality credits. Stated mathematically:

$$\tilde{D}_{\mu,\nu}\big|_{\nu=8} \leq \tilde{D}_{\mu+1,\nu}\big|_{\nu=8}$$

2 Transitions that consist of only one rating change are more probable than transitions that involve more rating categories. We may state this mathematically as

$$\tilde{D}_{\mu,\mu+1} \geq \tilde{D}_{\mu,\mu+2} \geq \tilde{D}_{\mu,\mu+3} \geq \ldots,$$

$$\tilde{D}_{\mu,\mu-1} \geq \tilde{D}_{\mu,\mu-2} \geq \tilde{D}_{\mu,\mu-3} \geq \ldots$$

3 For a given horizon, we wish the population distributions in the rating categories to be consistent with what we know is the steady-state distribution of the rating categories. Equivalently, we state that after n periods we would like the relative population distribution of the different ratings to be maintained.

Implementation

With a description of the problem and of the constraints we wish to impose, we are ready to discuss implementation of the formalism that has been outlined. The approach taken is similar to that of the "travelling salesman" or "simulated annealing" problem, where different scenarios are introduced randomly and tested to find an optimal solution. With our problem, the matrix M is modified iteratively with perturbations that are introduced randomly, and an error function is calculated at each iteration. Perturbations are chosen to be in agreement with the constraints and are rejected if the error function is not reduced.

With a relationship between the one-year and n-year matrices, we state mathematically how we wish the fitted n-year matrix to relate to the data for year n. Formally, we wish to minimise the error function

$$\chi^2 = \sum_{\mu\nu} \sum_{n=2}^{N} \left[\frac{\tilde{D}^{n}_{1\mu\eta} - D_{n\mu\nu}}{D_{n\mu\nu}} \right]^2$$

or, perhaps, if we wish to fit exclusively to the cumulative default data, we let $\nu = 8$ and minimise the function

$$\chi^2 = \sum_{\mu} \sum_{n=2}^{N} \left[\frac{\tilde{D}^{n}_{1\mu 8} - D_{n\mu 8}}{D_{n\mu 8}} \right]^2$$

where the μ and ν symbols indicate a sum over each element in the N matrices.

We now consider how the constraints are included in the implementation. To enforce that the hard constraint (A) is maintained, all perturbations are checked to ensure that the resulting probability is not negative. To maintain the hard constraint (B), equal and opposite perturbations are introduced to a given row in pairs. By doing this, all rows sum to one for each iteration. In this case the magnitude of the perturbations is taken to be 0.00001 – ie, much smaller than the total probability of 1. Since soft constraints (1) and (2) are violated with by the original data, we are unable to enforce these conditions rigorously. Therefore the only perturbations that are considered are those which are likely to lessen the violation of these constraints. Soft constraint (3) states that we wish to impose the relative population on the distributions of ratings at a given horizon. Table B.E.4 gives Standard & Poor's data for 1996 indicating the distribution of the companies that it rates.

Table B.E.4 Distribution of companies rated by Standard & Poor's in 1996

	AAA	AA	A	BBB	BB	B	CCC
Number	85	200	487	275	231	87	13
Proportion (%)	6.2	14.5	35.3	20.0	16.8	6.3	0.9

Implementing soft constraint (3) requires that we choose a specific horizon or period. Unfortunately we are unable to exploit the mathematical framework that has been outlined above to help us impose the steady-state distribution. This is because the default state is modelled as an *absorbing* state whereby all firms end in bankruptcy given an infinite amount of time (although this may take hundreds of years). We therefore arbitrarily choose a period of 10 years, after which we impose our steady-state distribution. To enforce this criterion we use an error function similar to that introduced earlier in this section. The two error functions are both normalised and subsequently combined, with equal weights, into one error function.

Results

Table B.E.5 gives the matrix resulting from the simulation along with the original transition matrix. The modified matrix is quite similar to the original matrix.

Table B.E.5 Comparison of modified Standard & Poor's one-year transition matrix (above) with original matrix adjusted for removal of NR category (below; data as Table B.E.2)

Initial state	Final state: AAA	AA	A	BBB	BB	B	CCC	D
AAA	91.43	5.07	1.27	1.26	0.96	0.01	0.01	0.01
AA	1.19	87.15	7.45	3.18	1.01	0.01	0.01	0.01
A	0.63	2.43	91.45	2.62	2.62	0.15	0.05	0.05
BBB	0.45	0.52	3.50	86.05	8.32	0.85	0.12	0.19
BB	0.47	2.39	2.40	6.28	79.98	6.53	0.97	0.99
B	0.37	1.51	1.51	1.51	6.81	79.13	3.78	5.37
CCC	1.14	1.92	1.92	1.93	2.56	7.24	54.55	28.73

Initial state	Final state: AAA	AA	A	BBB	BB	B	CCC	D
AAA	91.14	8.01	0.70	0.05	0.10	0.00	0.00	0.00
AA	0.71	90.95	7.55	0.58	0.05	0.14	0.02	0.00
A	0.07	2.34	91.54	5.08	0.64	0.26	0.01	0.05
BBB	0.03	0.30	5.69	87.91	4.70	1.06	0.12	0.19
BB	0.02	0.07	0.58	7.81	81.67	8.00	0.87	0.99
B	0.00	0.09	0.28	0.47	7.00	83.01	3.78	5.37
CCC	0.19	0.00	0.37	0.95	2.65	11.53	62.01	22.30

Table B.E.6 Comparison of cumulative default probabilities (%): Standard & Poor's data (Table B.E.3); calculated from the original one-year matrix (Table B.E.2) multiplied out; and calculated from the modified one-year matrix (Table B.E.5, part 1) multiplied out

Original Standard & Poor's cumulative default probability data for years 1–10

	Year									
	1	2	3	4	5	6	7	8	9	10
AAA	0.000	0.000	0.060	0.130	0.210	0.390	0.520	0.790	0.900	1.050
AA	0.000	0.020	0.080	0.170	0.310	0.470	0.700	0.920	1.120	1.370
A	0.050	0.140	0.260	0.440	0.650	0.900	1.190	1.560	1.940	2.340
BBB	0.180	0.430	0.710	1.280	1.850	2.490	3.220	3.900	4.510	5.000
BB	0.900	3.060	5.490	7.980	10.570	13.310	15.370	17.210	18.400	19.400
B	4.720	10.030	14.910	18.780	21.780	23.980	25.910	27.190	27.790	28.240
CCC	19.090	26.610	32.620	36.700	40.780	43.480	44.690	43.920	41.610	39.820

Original Standard & Poor's one-year matrix multiplied out for years 1–10

	Year									
	1	2	3	4	5	6	7	8	9	10
AAA	0.000	0.001	0.006	0.015	0.029	0.049	0.076	0.110	0.150	0.198
AA	0.000	0.017	0.049	0.095	0.155	0.227	0.309	0.403	0.508	0.626
A	0.050	0.121	0.217	0.338	0.479	0.638	0.814	1.002	1.206	1.424
BBB	0.180	0.436	0.750	1.111	1.505	1.903	2.286	2.661	3.017	3.366
BB	0.900	2.003	3.130	4.139	4.947	5.749	6.546	7.324	8.075	8.637
B	4.720	8.252	10.687	12.460	13.635	14.442	15.165	15.707	15.973	16.212
CCC	19.090	27.550	31.855	33.468	34.192	35.663	36.753	36.433	34.594	34.174

Modified cumulative default probability data for years 1–10

	Year									
	1	2	3	4	5	6	7	8	9	10
AAA	0.005	0.023	0.058	0.112	0.187	0.282	0.399	0.534	0.685	0.849
AA	0.005	0.030	0.081	0.162	0.275	0.418	0.587	0.779	0.994	1.231
A	0.050	0.141	0.273	0.443	0.642	0.864	1.105	1.356	1.621	1.897
BBB	0.180	0.460	0.823	1.248	1.716	2.185	2.631	3.060	3.457	3.836
BB	0.900	1.993	3.061	3.963	4.635	5.273	5.886	6.465	7.007	7.378
B	4.720	8.279	10.630	12.223	13.159	13.704	14.151	14.424	14.450	14.462
CCC	24.590	33.572	37.081	37.534	37.207	37.873	38.261	37.312	34.949	34.128

Figure B.E.1 Error function smoothly converges with iterations

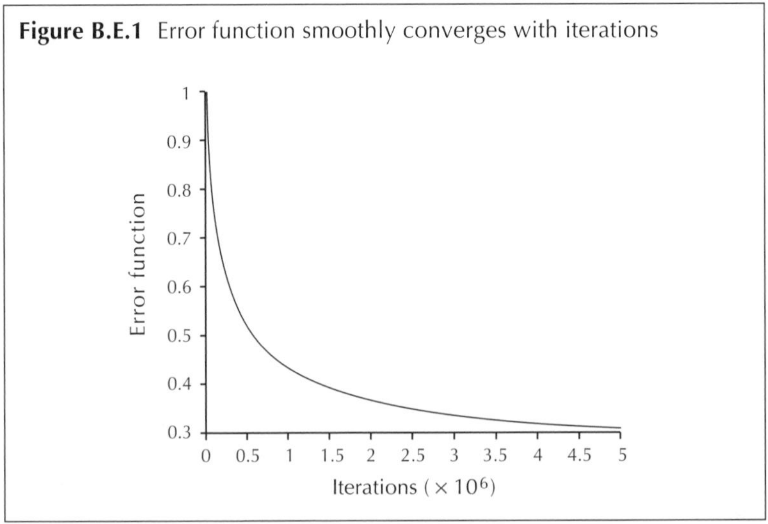

Table B.E.6 compares the cumulative default probabilities from the original data (given earlier in Table B.E.3), from the original one-year matrix multiplied out, and from the modified one-year matrix multiplied out. The modified data are observed to be in better agreement with the historical data.

Finally, a plot is presented to show the convergence of the error function with successive iterations (Figure B.E.1). This is used as a test to ensure that the solution that has been found is computationally stable. We note that the solution that has been obtained is stable.

However, further simulations indicate that the error function exhibits local minima. This means that there are multiple "correct" matrices that one can obtain using different sets of random perturbations. Although these "correct" matrices are all quite similar, it is difficult to establish which is more correct. For this reason, we feel that the problem is non-trivial and requires further investigation beyond the scope of this initial study.

1 This appendix is based on an internal note written by Yang Song and Weixiong Li.
2 This appendix was prepared and written by Stevan Maglic.
3 "Ratings Performance 1997, Stability and transition" (updated August 1998), available from the Standard and Poor's website at http://www.ratings.com.

Appendix

RAROC Remodelled

Thomas C. Wilson, Swiss Re New Markets

One of the most important developments in risk management over the past few years has been the widespread implementation of risk-adjusted performance measurement (RAPM) systems, designed to put the returns of very different risk businesses on a comparable, risk-adjusted basis. The main benefit of such systems is that they help institutions to identify businesses where they have a competitive advantage and make it easier to decide how to allocate capital.

Many transformation rules are used, but the most popular versions either adjust returns directly, for example by loan loss provisions, and then divide by allocated regulatory capital (modified return on equity), or divide unadjusted returns by risk-based capital allocations, like RAROC (risk-adjusted return on capital).

Suppose, for example, that point A in Figure 1 represents the risk and realised return profile for swaps trading. As the left-hand panel shows, it would not be possible to compare A's performance directly with that of other business units without adjusting for risk: while A has generated higher/lower absolute returns than other units, it has also accepted more/less risk.

The right-hand panel in Figure 1 shows the same units' returns adjusted by a risk-adjusted performance measure. In this example the swaps business, A, has outperformed the other business units on a risk-adjusted basis, thereby generating excess returns. Once the unit has been identified as providing excess returns, it should be allocated more equity capital at the expense of the other, non-performing business units. Although additional criteria, such as long-term strategic goals or cross-selling opportunities, will also affect the capital allocation decision, it is nonetheless important to know which units are currently making a net positive (or negative) contribution to the bottom line on a risk-adjusted basis.

But what would happen if the RAPM systems did not correctly adjust for risks? What if its results were fundamentally biased relative to the way that the market actually compensated risks through higher returns? Then risk-adjusted performance evaluations would also be biased, leading the

Figure 1 Risk adjustment

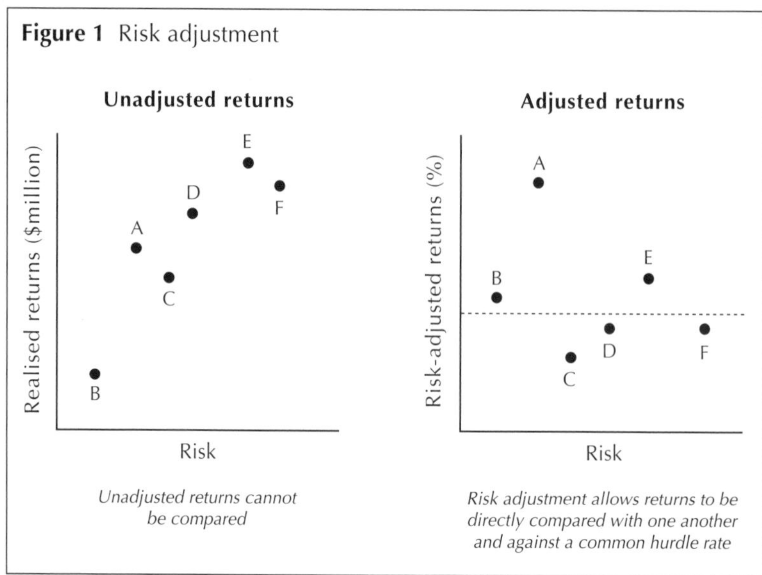

Unadjusted returns cannot be compared

Risk adjustment allows returns to be directly compared with one another and against a common hurdle rate

institution to undercapitalise businesses in which it truly had a competitive advantage and overcapitalise those units with mediocre or even negative performance.

And the market's standard RAPM system – RAROC – *is* fundamentally biased: for most risk portfolios there is a trading strategy which will generate an infinite RAROC. This bias is unfortunate because RAROC is easy both to implement and to communicate and can therefore form the foundation of a strong and pervasive risk management culture. Fortunately, a very simple adjustment to the standard RAROC formula will leave the ease of both implementation and communication largely intact. But the intuition behind the correction requires a different and much more market-oriented way of thinking about the role of equity in financial institutions.

To understand RAROC's bias and its consequences, consider Figure 2, which plots three possible relationships between an expected risk-adjusted return measure and risk. The incentives are such that, under calculation rule A, the risk manager's attention is focused only on low-risk transactions (such as triple-A credits and short-term Treasuries) since these are the transactions with the highest expected risk-adjusted returns, while under calculation rule B his attention is focused only on high-risk transactions like junk bonds and massive exposures to derivatives.

There are two ways of interpreting scenarios A and B: either the risk-adjustment method has correctly identified mispriced transactions, implying that the market is inefficient; or the risk adjustment method is incorrect and falsely biases the risk manager's decisions. In an efficient market with no mispriced transactions the expected risk-adjusted return measure

Figure 2 Implications of RAPM bias

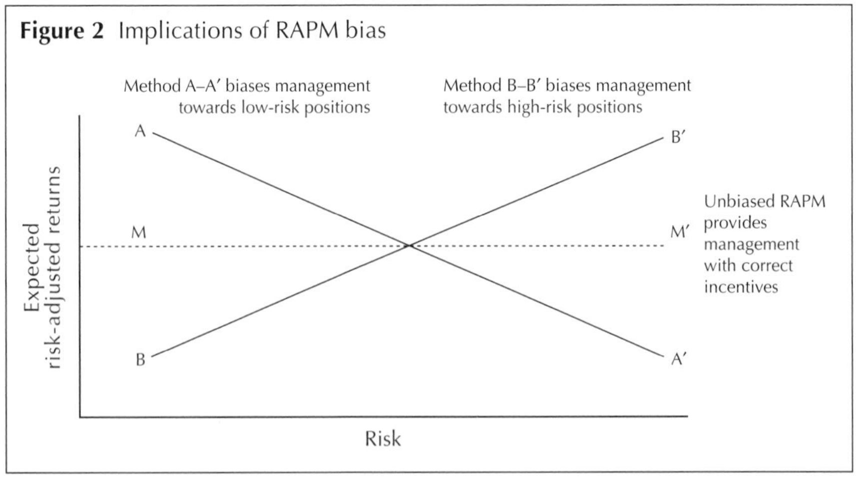

should be flat – like line M–M′ in Figure 2 – implying that it has fully and correctly adjusted for risks, making all risk positions directly comparable.

If, in an efficient market, this line were not flat, risk arbitrageurs would enter the market and take the excess risk-adjusted returns that such mispriced transactions would imply. For the purpose of this article, a biased RAPM system is one that does not make returns comparable, even in efficient markets.[1]

The standard RAROC calculation divides a portfolio's realised returns by its capital at risk in an attempt fully to adjust for risk:

$$RAROC = \frac{Realised\ returns}{Capital\ at\ risk} = \frac{R}{CAR} \tag{1}$$

where capital at risk is defined as the portfolio's maximum possible loss within a given confidence interval over an orderly liquidation period. We assume that the portfolio's capital at risk is correctly calculated, incorporating all the necessary return correlations and relying on the complete return distribution rather than a linear (or delta) approximation. So the bias that we demonstrate does not come from an incorrect calculation of capital at risk.

We further assume that the portfolio's realised returns are correctly calculated (on a change in mark-to-market basis rather than on accrual-based accounting measures). Therefore the bias does not come from non-economic income recognition. In fact, it comes from the RAROC calculation rule itself.

One of the main reasons for RAROC's bias is that it implicitly assumes that only the portfolio's risk capital is compensated, rather than the economic capital invested in the portfolio. It is therefore always possible for the risk manager to achieve an infinite RAROC for any portfolio given two simple conditions: the portfolio has non-zero mark-to-market value, and the risk manager has access to a risk-free asset.

Consider, for example, a portfolio which has a strictly positive mark-to-market value and assume that the risk manager has a risk-free investment opportunity. Under these relatively weak conditions, an infinite positive RAROC can be achieved by liquidating the entire portfolio immediately and investing the proceeds in the risk-free asset. This strategy would generate positive realised returns with no capital at risk – implying an infinite RAROC. The same logic holds true for portfolios with negative initial value.

This bias does not merely produce an inaccuracy of a few basis points which can arbitrarily be dismissed as rounding or estimation error – and it has nothing to do with market inefficiencies. It is a direct consequence of a calculation rule that considers only the position's risk when allocating capital and does not consider the economic capital or market value invested in the position.

Since the results are so strong, these necessary conditions deserve further elaboration. Although the bias is strongest for portfolios with high economic investment, such as the asset/liability portfolio or equity or bond trading portfolios, even pure derivative portfolios will be affected because of their unrealised and undistributed gains or losses. In practice, all portfolios will be affected to some degree.

Furthermore, most risk books do have access to a risk-free asset either directly or through arbitrage relationships (for example, using the put/call parity theorem). But this second condition is not even necessary to prove RAROC's bias. This is proved in Figure 3, which plots expected RAROC against capital at risk for a $1 million investment in Treasuries with different maturities. As anticipated, at zero-risk expected RAROC is infinite. More interesting is the fact that as risk increases, expected RAROC decreases. This demonstrates RAROC's bias for portfolios with non-zero value, independent of whether the risk manager has access to a risk-free investment.

The technical implication is that if RAROC applies at all, it only applies to self-financing, pure risk portfolios, and then only if they have exactly zero value. In other circumstances, an institution's management might wake up one morning to find all its funds invested in overnight Treasuries, which would guarantee the risk managers an infinite RAROC. This is probably not the signal the board wants to send out.

To demonstrate all the sources of RAROC's bias, we will make the simplifying assumption that market price processes are Itô-differentiable[2] and that the performance to be measured is based on single-period returns. The first assumption is consistent with most price processes used for option pricing and allows us to take full advantage of standard mean

Figure 3 Establishing RAROC's bias

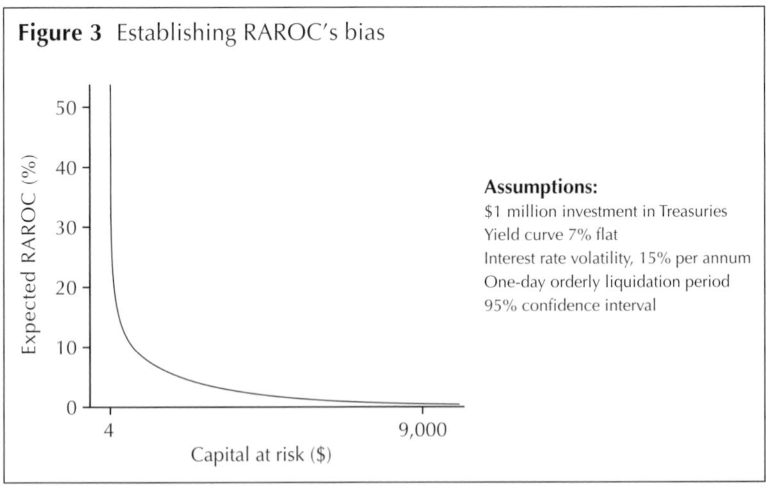

variance techniques in finance.[3] Under this assumption, we can rewrite equation (1) as equation (2):

$$RAROC = \frac{Realised\ returns}{Capital\ at\ risk} = \frac{R}{\alpha \times \sigma_R} \quad (2)$$

where α is the number of standard deviations required to give the arbitrary confidence interval (for example, $\alpha = 2$ implies a 95% confidence interval, $\alpha = 3$ implies a 99% confidence interval, etc), σ_R is the instantaneous standard deviation of the portfolio's returns, and both R and σ_R are in absolute dollar terms.

To highlight all of the sources of RAROC's bias, it is best to rearrange equation (2). As discussed earlier, if the RAPM system is to provide an unbiased evaluation of risk-adjusted performance even in efficient markets, the expected RAROC for any transaction or portfolio should be a constant and independent of its risk – in short, every transaction in an efficient market should be fairly and fully compensated for its risk. Using this logic, taking expectations of equation (2) and rearranging, we get equation (3):

$$\begin{aligned} E(R) &= E(RAROC) \times \alpha \times \sigma_R \\ &= k \times \sigma_R \end{aligned} \quad (3)$$

where $E(\ )$ is the expectations operator and k is a positive constant equal to the expected RAROC multiplied by the confidence interval.

Equation (3) looks very similar to many one-factor pricing models like the capital market line in Sharpe–Treynor's capital asset pricing model, or Ross's arbitrage pricing theory: k can be interpreted as a risk premium, the position's capital at risk as the relevant risk that is measured and compensated by the market, and the confidence interval as a "market risk-aversion" parameter. In these terms, it is clear that RAROC is based on an implicit assumption about how the market compensates risk with returns. The direct effect is that if RAROC is an unbiased risk adjustment method, equation (3) should be a good approximation to the way the market measures and compensates risks in equilibrium. If it is not a good approximation, RAROC will be biased and cannot be used to evaluate performance. And equation (3) is a very special risk/return pricing function – and one that is obviously false:

- *RAROC implicitly compensates only risk, whereas the market compensates both risk and capital.* To see this in the context of equation (3) notice that, as the portfolio's risk goes to zero, so does its expected return. But, in equilibrium, as risk goes to zero, the invested capital (if any) is compensated by the risk-free rate of return. By allocating only risk capital, RAROC implicitly assumes that risk capital alone is compensated by the market.
- *RAROC's implicit risk premium is arbitrary, while the market's is not.* The risk premium in equation (3) is a function of the confidence interval, which is set arbitrarily. As we will see, if the confidence interval is set too high, profitable businesses (on a risk-adjusted basis) will appear to be unprofitable; if it is set too low, businesses that destroy value will appear to generate excess returns.
- *RAROC's risk measure can be valid only for portfolios, never for individual transactions.* This is because capital at risk (or variance) is a total risk measure that includes both systematic and unsystematic risks, whereas the market compensates only the position's marginal risk contribution. To see the consequences of this bias, consider a long and a short position in the same asset. By equation (3), since both positions are risky from the bank's perspective, both are required to yield positive expected returns. But by combining both long and short positions, the bank can create a zero-risk, zero-return portfolio, implying that one of the expected returns must be negative. This contradicts equation (3), implying that RAROC cannot be used to evaluate individual transactions.

If we are to "fix" RAROC, we will have to make sure that it compensates invested capital as well as risk; that we choose the correct confidence interval so the risk premium reflects actual market prices; and that the risk measure is defined appropriately for both portfolios and transactions.

RAROC's capital bias arises because it ignores the economic capital invested in a portfolio. To demonstrate the necessary correction, suppose we were to start with an arbitrary reference portfolio with instantaneous expected returns (in per cent) equal to R' and instantaneous standard deviation of returns (in per cent) equal to σ'_R. Suppose further that the risk manager had γ economic capital to invest between this reference portfolio and a risk-free asset. If $\gamma = 0$, this is a self-financing portfolio, where if $\gamma > 0$, there is positive economic value invested in the portfolio.

Based on these definitions, it is possible to derive the set of possible risk/return combinations that can be achieved for different levels of relative investment in the risk-free and arbitrary risk portfolios. Defining R_p as the portfolio's absolute return and σ_p as the portfolio's standard deviation of absolute returns, we can represent these different combinations as a line in $R_p - \sigma_p$ space, with the exact formula for the line[4]

$$E(R_p) = \gamma \times R_f + \frac{(R' - R_f)}{\sigma_R} \times \sigma_p \quad \textbf{(4)}$$

Just as equation (3) was derived from the traditional RAROC calculation, equation (4) can be derived from a modified RAROC calculation. Rearranging equation (4) into a modified RAROC formula[5] (with capital in the denominator), we get

$$RAROC = \frac{R_p}{\gamma + \alpha' \times \sigma_p} \quad \textbf{(5)}$$

where

$$\alpha' = \frac{(R' - R_f)}{\sigma_R \times R_f}$$

If we ignore for the moment the implications for the choice of confidence interval, comparing equation (2) with equation (5) reveals how the traditional RAROC calculation needs to be changed to reflect both economic capital, γ, and risk capital, $(\alpha' \times \sigma_p)$: we simply need to add γ to the denominator. Therefore, the only additional information needed to implement this modified RAROC calculation rule is the economic value of the portfolio.

This analysis is not complete, however; the reference portfolio was arbitrarily chosen, implying an arbitrary implicit risk premium in equation (4) and, therefore, an arbitrary RAROC confidence interval in equation (5). The problem is that the market risk premium is anything but arbitrary, implying that RAROC's confidence interval must also not be arbitrary: if the two factors are not coordinated, RAROC will be biased.

To see this in concrete terms, consider again equation (5), which specifies that RAROC's confidence interval is equal to the risk premium on the arbitrary reference portfolio dividend by the risk-free rate of return. If the confidence interval is set too high, it will imply a risk premium which is unattainable by any portfolio in the market. Such a portfolio is represented as portfolio Z in the upper panel of Figure 4, where the shaded region represents risk/return combinations that are attainable in the market. Since such a high risk premium can never be achieved given current market

Figure 4 Adjusting for RAROC's pricing bias

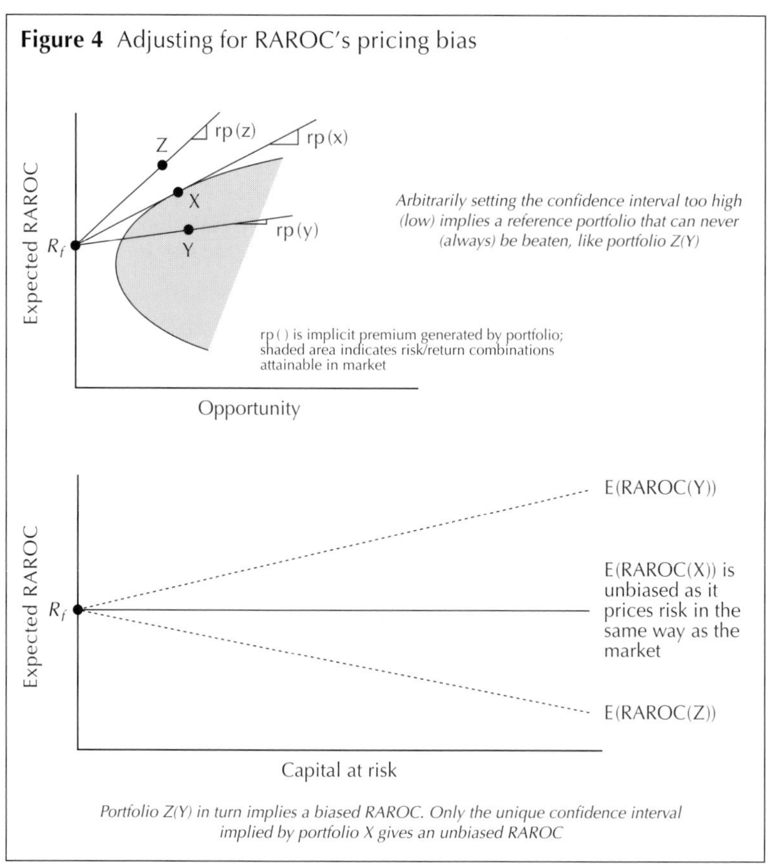

Portfolio Z(Y) in turn implies a biased RAROC. Only the unique confidence interval implied by portfolio X gives an unbiased RAROC

opportunities, the higher the risk accepted by the risk manager, the lower will be the expected RAROC. This implies that if the confidence interval is set too high, expected RAROC will be downward sloping and, therefore, biased. This is demonstrated in the lower panel of Figure 4.

Similarly, if the confidence interval is set too low, it will imply a reference portfolio (like portfolio Y in the upper panel) whose risk premium can always be beaten by portfolios that offer higher expected returns for the same level of risk. Since such a low-risk premium can always be beaten, the higher the risk accepted by the risk manager, the higher the expected RAROC. This implies that, if the confidence interval is set too low, expected RAROC will be upward sloping and therefore biased. This is also demonstrated in the lower panel of Figure 4.

The solution is to choose a reference portfolio that gives the highest achievable risk premium and therefore the highest achievable confidence interval. This portfolio is designated as portfolio X in Figure 4 and is found through a two-step process.

First, the set of portfolios that offers the highest possible expected return for a given level of risk is identified. This set is designated by the solid curve in Figure 4 and is often known as the "efficient frontier". Second, the portfolio which can be leveraged to the greatest advantage (portfolio X in the figure) is identified. Once this portfolio has been identified, the implicit risk premium can be determined and RAROC's confidence interval can be uniquely set. The result is a modified RAROC that reflects all of the portfolio's capital (both economic and risk) as well as the currently available market risk/return trade-offs:

$$RAROC = \frac{R_p}{\gamma + \alpha^* \times \sigma_p} \quad \textbf{(6)}$$

where

$$\alpha^* = \frac{(R^* - R_f)}{R_f \times \sigma_{R^*}}$$

It is easy to verify that if the risk manager chooses only mean variance-efficient portfolios, the expected RAROC will be constant and equal to the risk-free rate of return. Thus, the natural hurdle or benchmark rate for the modified RAROC calculation is the risk-free rate. This is an intuitive result since, by its very construction, the modified RAROC formula fully adjusts for all risks, making risk positions directly comparable with one another and against the risk-free rate of return.

Note that there is no natural, market-driven hurdle rate for the traditional RAROC calculation since the traditional formula ignores invested capital and sets the confidence interval in an arbitrary fashion. It is interesting to note that the above results depend only on the distributional assumptions and are not dependent on equilibrium. In fact, determining the optimal reference portfolio is a purely statistical exercise.

In terms of implementation, two points should be considered. First, the relevant risk premium is portfolio-specific (at least theoretically) since each risk manager faces a different set of instruments and market opportunities. Second, there are three methods of calculating the appropriate risk premium. Arranged in order of increasing accuracy – and increasing cost of implementation – these are: a constant risk premium for all businesses based on aggregate historical data; differentiated risk premiums by business unit based on historical data; and differentiated risk premiums by business unit based on current market conditions.

The problem with capital at risk (or standard deviation of returns) as a risk measure is that it cannot be applied to individual transactions – it is a total risk measure – whereas to evaluate individual transactions we require a measure of marginal risk contribution. Fortunately, there is a measure that is suitable for a mean variance framework: the position's covariance with the reference portfolio. The result is the risk/return pricing relationship given by

$$E(R_i) = R_f + \frac{(R^* - R_f)}{\sigma_{R^*}} \times \frac{\sigma_{i,\,R^*}}{\sigma_{R^*}} \tag{7}$$

where $E(R_i)$ is the transaction's expected return and σ_{i,R^*} is the covariance of transaction i with respect to the optimal reference portfolio. This implies a RAROC calculation rule for individual transactions that is slightly different from the rule used for portfolios:

$$RAROC = \frac{R_i}{R_f + \alpha^* \times \dfrac{\sigma_{i,\,R^*}}{\sigma_{R^*}}} \tag{8}$$

The only difference between equations (6) and (8) is that the risk measure has been changed from σ_p, a total risk measure, to $\sigma_{i,R^*}/\sigma_{R^*}$, a marginal risk measure. Note again that the results are driven purely by the assumed statistical properties of the model and do not rely on equilibrium.

1 I demonstrate later that RAROC calculations based on capital-at-risk allocations tend to generate profiles such as scenario A. Calculation rules that use regulatory standards to allocate capital tend to generate profiles such as scenario B, since regulatory capital allocations are not sufficiently differentiated in terms of the riskiness of underlying positions.

2 The precise assumption is that the price paths of all assets are governed by the following multidimensional stochastic differential equation:

$$dP_t = \mu(P_t, t)dt + \sigma(P_t, t)dB_t$$

where P_t is an N-dimensional vector of current asset prices, μ and σ both satisfy the Lipschitz and growth conditions, and B_t is an N-dimensional standard Brownian motion process.

3 This assumption can be replaced by the assumption that either the institution is only concerned with the first two moments of the return distribution or that returns themselves are normally distributed. Although these alternative assumptions make it possible to define a non-trivial orderly liquidation period, they are more difficult to defend on either theoretical or practical grounds, especially for derivative businesses.

4 Defining μ as the level of relative investment in the risky portfolio and R_f as the risk-free rate, the return on an arbitrary leveraged portfolio, R_p, and its standard deviation, σ_p, are given by the equations

$$E(R_p) = \mu \times R' + (\gamma - \mu) \times R_f \qquad \text{and} \qquad \sigma_p = \mu \times \sigma_R$$

Substituting out μ and rearranging gives equation (4).

5 The same correction can be accomplished by adjusting the numerator of the RAROC equation as opposed to the denominator. Rearranging equation (4) differently, we see that the appropriate adjustment to the numerator is to subtract the risk-free rate of return times the amount of value in the portfolio (eg, $r_f \times \gamma$). From an economic perspective, the returns are adjusted so that they mimic the returns of the same portfolio as if any net investment was self-funded at the risk-free rate. If this adjustment is made, no further adjustment is required in the denominator.

Many Happy Returns

Sanjeev Punjabi

Banks are increasingly using risk-adjusted performance measures (or RAPMs) for decision-making across different business lines. These measures take into account the risks embedded in the returns as well as the returns themselves and provide a common, aggregated framework to assess the contributions of various transactions and business units to the firm's value. So they can help business managers make informed, economic decisions and long-term strategic plans at various levels, including risk quantification and management, transaction evaluation, profitability enhancement, business performance measurement, capital allocation and risk-linked reward systems. They also provide tools to price new transactions effectively and enable higher value-added investments.

To carry out superior RAP analysis, comprehensive risk-exposure data and measurement systems and sophisticated portfolio methodologies, underpinned by extensively researched parameters, are extremely valuable.

RAPMs are invaluable in quantifying each transaction's and business area's regulatory and economic capital consumption, so making it easier for banks to calculate the level of regulatory and economic capital reserves. Regulatory capital adequacy procedures mandated by the Bank for International Settlements do not differentiate capital requirements based on the important risk determinants of varying counterparty credit quality and different diversifying or concentrating effects of transactions. Economic capital requirements are estimated as a function of the various economic risks inherent in the range of business activities.

DIFFERENT RAPM SPECIFICATIONS

Four common RAPM variants are ROC (return on regulatory capital), RORAC (return on risk-adjusted capital), RAROC (risk-adjusted return on regulatory capital) and RARORAC (risk-adjusted return on risk-adjusted capital). In each of these performance ratios, a measure of unadjusted or risk-adjusted return is divided by the required regulatory or risk-adjusted capital requirement. While performance is generally measured in similar ways, these RAPMs are distinct techniques for comparing return on capital and incorporating differing forms of risk adjustment. A common definition of the RAROC method of performance measurement for a transaction is:[1]

$$\textit{Adjusted income/Economic capital}$$

where

$$\textit{Adjusted income} =$$

$$\textit{Revenues} - \textit{Administrative expenses} - \textit{Expected loss} \pm (\textit{Transfer prices})$$

However, this measure is actually RORAC, not RAROC, because the adjusted income in the numerator does not include an adjustment for risk or unexpected losses, a measure of transaction risk. Hence, the numerator is simply risky return and not risk-adjusted return (RAR). Rather, the estimate of economic capital in the denominator captures transaction risks, for which economic or risk-adjusted capital is required.

RARORAC is a RAPM in which risk-adjusted return is divided by risk-adjusted capital. The risk-adjusted return component of RARORAC is valuable for performance measurement independent of the capital requirement. As a result, RARORAC enables, in a single measure, evaluation of the after-risk performance, risk contribution and capital requirements of a transaction or business. This article shows how the combination of risk adjustment in the numerators of the RAROC and RARORAC formulations makes these two measurement procedures superior to both ROC and RORAC.

Transaction or business risk is typically measured as the estimated volatility of the return distribution. The portion of this risk that contributes to the overall volatility of the bank's portfolio is undiversifiable and should be appropriately compensated. The specification and methodological derivation of the resulting suitable risk adjustment to adjusted income is presented below. This deduction to adjusted income results in a portfolio-based risk-adjusted return measure that incorporates different concentration and diversification effects and lends itself to straightforward implementation for a variety of financial instruments. It enables comparability of returns from instruments of various risk profiles relative to any portfolio. As a result, for example, in a portfolio containing both interest rate and equity products, returns due to a long position in long-maturity, high-grade corporate bonds can be quantified in comparison with returns accruing from a short position in short-dated Treasury options.

DERIVATION FROM CAPITAL ASSET PRICING THEORY

The risk-adjusted return is derived using the capital asset pricing model (CAPM). This specifies the relationship between expected asset risk premiums, the asset's undiversifiable risk (measured by its beta), and the riskless interest rate and expected market risk premium. For a commercial banking credit transaction (such as a term loan, revolver or standby letter of credit), revenues can accrue from up-front, agent, commitment or facility fees, and be spread over the funding cost for the drawn portion of the credit limit. The interest rate paid by the bank for funding the exposure can be proxied by the riskless rate of interest. Excess revenues from a typical credit transaction can be represented by $R' - R_f$, where R' are the revenues earned in the transaction and R_f is the cost of funding the borrowing. If R represents the adjusted return calculated after adjustments to R', the excess adjusted return (EAR) of the transaction is calculated as $R - R_f$. Since the receipt of transaction revenues is conditional upon there being no default

Figure 1 Comparison of return and risk of three assets relative to portfolio with the CEER/RAR measure

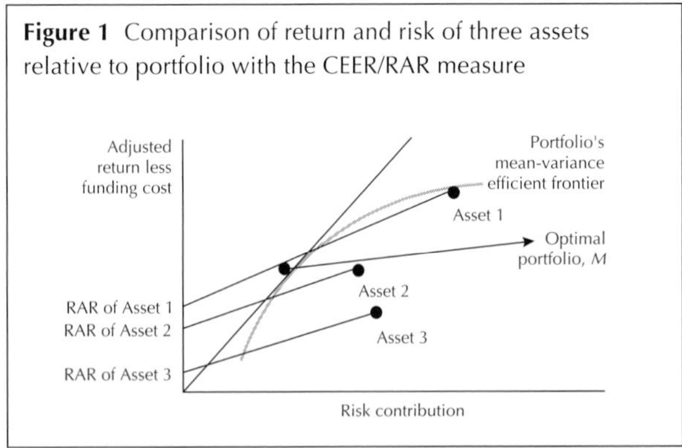

by the counterparty, the adjusted income is risky. The expected EAR for a transaction is therefore represented as $E(\tilde{R} - R_f)$. The one-factor Sharpe–Lintner CAPM states that

$$E\left(\tilde{R}-R_f\right) = \beta E\left(\tilde{R}_m - R_f\right) \tag{1}$$

where $\tilde{R}_m$ is the return on a mean-variance-efficient market portfolio and β is the beta of the transaction relative to the market portfolio. The optimised lending portfolio of a bank is considered to be a suitable proxy for the market portfolio as it comprises all investment opportunities available to the bank in the market-place. In this optimal portfolio, indicated by M in Figure 1, the portfolio return/risk is maximal. The ratio of the optimal portfolio return, minus the riskless return, to its standard deviation is the optimal (or maximum) Sharpe ratio.

Decomposing the beta of the transaction relative to the optimal bank portfolio into its components – the covariance of the asset's return with the optimal bank portfolio return and variance of the optimal bank portfolio return – equation (1) can be restated as:

$$E\left(\tilde{R}-R_f\right) = \frac{\text{cov}\left(\tilde{R}, \tilde{R}_m\right)}{\text{VAR}\left(\tilde{R}_m\right)} E\left(\tilde{R}_m - R_f\right)$$

This equation is identical to

$$E\left(\tilde{R}-R_f\right) - \textit{Maximum Sharpe ratio} \times \textit{Asset risk contribution to optimal portfolio} = 0 \tag{2}$$

where

$$\textit{Maximum Sharpe ratio} = \frac{E\left(\tilde{R}_m - R_f\right)}{\sigma\left(\tilde{R}_m\right)}$$

and

$$\textit{Asset risk contribution to optimal portfolio} = \frac{\text{cov}\left(\tilde{R}, \tilde{R}_{\text{m}}\right)}{\sigma\left(\tilde{R}_{\text{m}}\right)}$$

For any asset on the line tangent to the optimal portfolio *M* indicated in Figure 1, equality (2) holds. In other words, the risk-adjusted return specified by equation (3) is zero:

$$\begin{aligned} \text{RAR} = E\left(\tilde{R} - R_{\text{f}}\right) &- \textit{Maximum Sharpe ratio} \\ &\times \textit{Asset risk contribution to optimal portfolio} \end{aligned} \quad \textbf{(3)}$$

In Figure 1, we plot the expected EAR relative to the risk contribution of three different assets, which reside in a large, well-diversified portfolio. The mean-variance-efficient frontier for this portfolio, along with the optimal portfolio *M*, considered as the "market portfolio" in capital asset pricing theory, are also shown in this figure. The tangent line to this frontier represents the capital market line for the bank's portfolio, which signifies the set of opportunities that provide the highest return for any level of risk. The optimal portfolio has the highest Sharpe ratio.

After deducting the portfolio-based risk adjustment specified by equation (3) from the asset's expected EAR, the resulting RAR (also known as "certainty-equivalent" excess return) of the three assets enables these assets' return–risk levels to be compared with a single measure. The asset with the highest RAR is the most attractive because it provides the highest return relative to its risk contribution to the portfolio.

SHARPE RATIO AND RISK CONTRIBUTION

In the absence of the requirement to hold economic capital, RAR is a suitable RAPM to determine the relative attractiveness of assets. Modern portfolio theory indicates that the Sharpe ratio of the optimised portfolio is the relevant benchmark target and measures the reward-to-risk ratio offered by the market-place. However, the optimal Sharpe ratio indicated by theory is not achievable in reality.

A study by Asarnow (1996) suggests that measured Sharpe ratios can not only vary across different types of fixed-income instruments but can also be different by risk category of loans for the corporate loan market. Efficiency and integration of markets would suggest similar Sharpe ratios for varied asset and risk classes. Measurements of Sharpe ratios can be influenced by occurrences of higher than normal or lower than average losses on volatile sub-investment grade loans. The Sharpe ratios measured in Asarnow's and other studies are different for various asset classes – Treasuries, equities, corporate bonds, high-yield bonds, investment-grade loans and high-yield loans. This is due to several factors, the most significant being the segmentation of markets and investment strategies for various asset classes and their investors, and differing investor risk aversions for various levels of diversifiable and non-diversifiable risk. So the following need to be considered when setting a benchmark Sharpe ratio:

- the reward-to-risk ratio of the opportunity set presented by a wide range and the particular class of financial instruments in the market-place;
- the institution's desired hurdle rate, as determined from its target return on equity; and
- the portfolio management system's measurement of the Sharpe ratio.

It is advisable to link the Sharpe ratio to the credit portfolio management framework in use because of key variations in the methodologies and measurements used to mark-to-market the credit ratings and exposures of market-based credit instruments. Additionally, there may be variations in the portfolio parameters (default correlations and volatilities) of credit instruments.

Additionally, for a working implementation of RAR, it is better to use the risk contribution to the *actual* portfolio as the *optimal* portfolio is not a realistic objective for credit transactions – particularly for commercial lending products – for a number of reasons. Three of these are:

- *The competitive realities of the market-place* To achieve an optimal portfolio, a company would have to forgo many market-making opportunities and business relationships and concentrate on transactions that are hugely profitable relative to their risk contribution to the portfolio. However, the number of these opportunities is finite, and the spreads on them are driven down in an efficient market.
- *The credit paradox* Concentrations of credit build-up due to the "credit paradox".[2] An asset's risk contribution to the optimal portfolio does not adequately capture its risk contribution to the current portfolio if there are concentrations of the same or highly correlated assets. Using the current portfolio instead of the optimal one imposes a suitable penalty on large transactions that exacerbates concentrations and assigns a higher marginal risk contribution to transactions of counterparties to which the current portfolio has high credit exposure.
- *The difficulty in trading commercial lending products* As a result of the relatively high illiquidity of loans, asset weights in a portfolio of commercial lending credit products are significantly less amenable to alteration than a portfolio of traded instruments. While active trading of loans in the cash and credit derivative markets has been on the upswing, this market is, by and large, small and limited to certain types of loans.

APPLYING AND CALCULATING RAR, RAROC AND RARORAC

The risk adjustment in RAR enables relative-value analysis of assets with different expected excess returns and risk contributions to the portfolio. The risk contribution incorporates the asset's stand-alone risk, its correlation with that of the portfolio, and the portfolio's total risk. The risk adjustment is the market-based price of portfolio-linked risk; it is proportional to the asset's risk contribution and the Sharpe ratio of the portfolio. The objective of a portfolio manager, trader or account officer should be to undertake transactions with positive risk-adjusted return. In other words, a transaction's revenues should exceed its expected losses, risk adjustment, administrative expenses, funding cost and transfer prices.

However, a trading or lending portfolio may contain transactions with negative RAR. This can happen, for example, if unprofitable transactions are undertaken for liquidity or relationship reasons, if the pricing of the transaction inadequately compensates for the higher incremental marginal risk contribution due to asset concentration, or if an incorrectly conceptualised RAPM is used to evaluate the transaction.

The average RAR of all transactions in the portfolio is expected to be positive, which reflects the shareholder value that is added by the portfolio. We will set out an example involving two assets to illustrate the value of RAR for performance measurement and transaction evaluation (see Table 1). In this example, Asset 1 has a lower return and lower stand-alone risk than Asset 2. When the RAR measure is applied, we find that the asset with lower returns (Asset 1) is more attractive to a portfolio. Asset 1 has a lower stand-alone risk and lower correlation with the portfolio than Asset 2. So its estimated RAR is superior, despite its lower expected adjusted return. However, in another portfolio in which Asset 1 has a

Table 1 Use of RAR to evaluate two assets

	Asset 1		Asset 2
Expected annualised adjusted return less funding cost	4%		10%
Stand-alone credit, market and operational risk	6%		15%
Correlation of asset returns with current portfolio returns	0.1		0.5
Benchmark Sharpe ratio of portfolio		1.0	
Total risk of current portfolio		20%	
Calculation of RAR	4 – 1 × 0.1 × 6 × 20 ÷ 20		10 – 1 × 0.5 × 15 × 20 ÷ 20
Risk-adjusted/certainty equivalent excess return	3.4%		2.5%

higher correlation (than Asset 2) with the portfolio, transacting in Asset 2 might have greater appeal and value-added.

RAR, RAROC and RARORAC can be applied to a range of market-based credit instruments – interest rate and currency swaps, fixed-income options, forwards and equity and commodity derivatives. As suggested in Shimko (1997), both risk-adjusted profit and loss and value-at-risk (or economic capital) are important inputs to the calculation of RAPMs. Once suitable measures of the risk adjustments are calculated, the RAPM calculation is fairly straightforward. The risk measures for the credit exposure need to be calculated in the context of the correlation effects with the rest of the portfolio.

The panel on page 301, "Swap steps", illustrates an implementation of these RAPM calculations in four steps for the simple example of a leveraged, seven-year interest rate swap.

SELECTING A SUITABLE RAPM

The four RAPMs – ROC, RORAC, RAROC and RARORAC – distinctively measure return on capital and incorporate differing forms of risk adjustment. Using the correct RAPM will result in the correct view of performance and capital allocation at the business, customer and transaction levels of analysis. Pricing guidelines, institutional strategies and, ultimately, shareholder value are affected.

Figure 2 shows the expected change in various RAPMs for different risk ratings, which serve as a proxy for transaction risk contributions. Assume that a CCC rating represents high financial distress. The portrayed patterns of change in RAPM with risk ratings are illustrative and can vary with different assumptions of parameters. For instance, the desired "capital comfort" influences the steepness of the RORAC and RARORAC curves. The analysis assumes market efficiency, meaning transaction pricing reflects the counterparty's risk rating and implied default risk. This is demonstrated in Figure 2(*a*), in which expected revenues from a transaction or business increase systematically the lower the counterparty's rating. An analysis of spreads for a range of credit instruments would confirm this type of relationship. When the return for a transaction is divided by the required risk-adjusted capital, the resulting measure is RORAC. Higher-rated assets need relatively low capital reserves as they contribute less risk to the portfolio. Consequently, the RORAC for them tends to be high. Hence, we observe that RORAC increases for higher-rated assets and is negative for severely distressed assets.

With a changing transaction risk contribution, we would expect RAR to be flat (see Figure 2(*c*)). Capital asset pricing theory indicates that, after deducting the cost of systematic risk and non-risk costs, the expected risk-adjusted return across the entire market is, in fact, zero. A performing credit or trading portfolio will, however, have positive average RAR.

Figure 2 Variation of RAPMs with changes in risk ratings

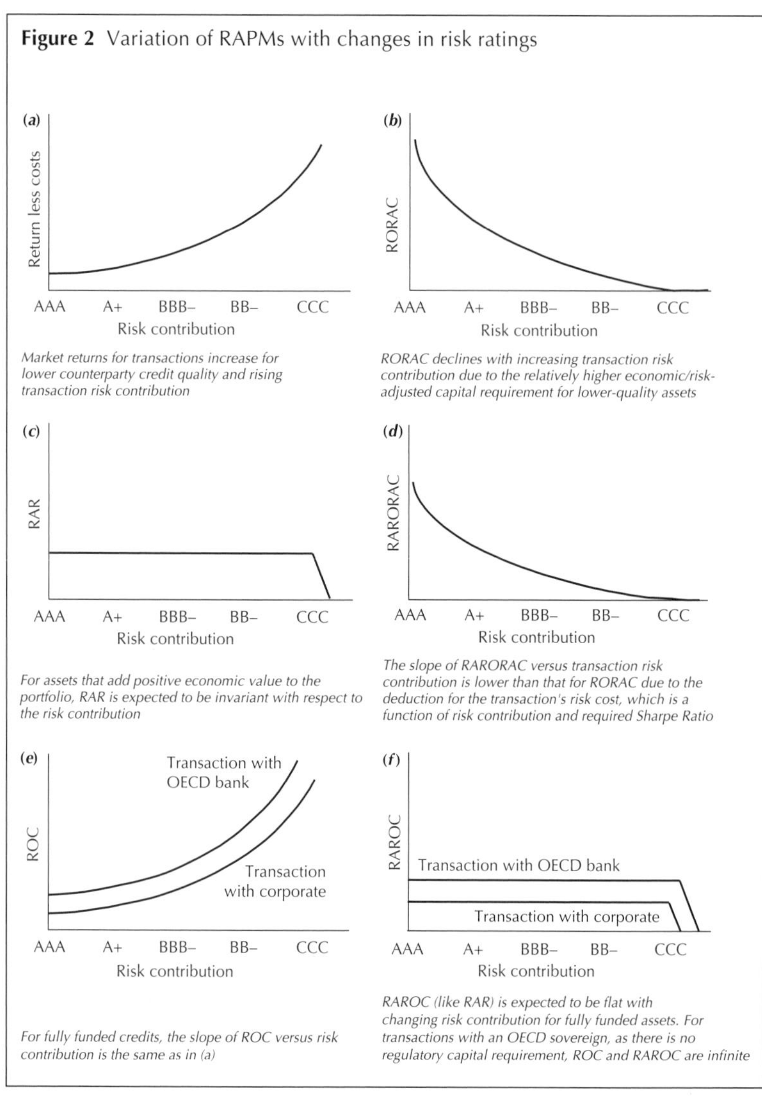

In Figure 2(*d*), the average anticipated RARORAC will increase for assets with lower risk contribution because of the significantly higher risk-based capital required for lower-rated assets. The deduction of risk costs in the numerator of RARORAC and absence of risk costs in the numerator of RORAC causes the pattern of increasing RARORAC for better-rated assets to be less steep than for RORAC.

If the capital requirement is measured by regulatory capital, ROC and RAROC are the counterparts of RORAC and RARORAC, respectively. With varying risk ratings, however, ROC and RAROC are remarkably

SWAP STEPS

Consider a leveraged seven-year interest rate swap with an OECD bank counterparty for a $100 million notional amount, with a mark-to-market of 6% of notional. Suppose further that the annualised expected loss and unexpected loss for this credit product are, respectively, 50 basis points of mark-to-market and 50 basis points of notional.

Step I The regulatory capital requirement for this swap is potentially:

(0.5% *of notional + mark-to-market*) × *counterparty risk-weighting*

Since there is a 20% regulatory risk-weighting for an OECD bank counterparty, the BIS tier 2 (8%) regulatory capital is $1.3 million × 0.08 = $104,000.

Step II Assuming that we want this credit exposure to have economic coverage for 10 times the contributed risk and the default correlation of this exposure with the rest of the portfolio is 1%, a simplified calculation of portfolio-based risk-adjusted capital is:

$$\sqrt{\text{default correlation}} \times \text{capital multiplier} \times \text{unexpected loss} \times \text{notional}$$

This amount is $500,000.

Step III Risk-adjusted return is calculated as:

economic profit – expected loss – risk cost to the portfolio

The risk contribution is $\sqrt{\text{default correlation}} \times \text{unexpected loss}$, which is $50,000. Assuming an economic profit of $250,000 and a required Sharpe ratio of 1, and calculating the expected loss and risk contribution to be $30,000 and $50,000, respectively, the RAR is $170,000.

Step IV Using RAR and the estimates of regulatory and economic capital, RAROC and RARORAC are determined to be 163% and 34%, respectively. The levered, long-term nature of the swap and high degree of required economic capital, despite the low default correlation with the portfolio, results in a lower RARORAC relative to RAROC.

Table 2 Risk-adjusted performance measures compared

Definition	ROC **Return on capital**	RORAC **Return on risk-adjusted capital**	RAROC **Risk-adjusted return on capital**	RARORAC **Risk-adjusted return on risk-adjusted capital**
Typical measurement	Excess adjusted return/ regulatory capital	Excess adjusted return/ risk-adjusted capital	Excess risk-adjusted return/regulatory capital	Excess risk-adjusted return/ risk-adjusted capital
Nature of measure	Measure of profitability relative to regulatory capital	Reflects profitability relative to desired economic (risk) capital	Incorporates market-based risk cost as well as regulatory capital requirements	Pure economic measure; based on bank's desired cushion and market risk adjustments
Hurdle rate	Difficult to calculate; the same hurdle rate may be used for all businesses not because it is correct but because it is easier to implement and communicate		Natural hurdle rate of zero resulting from deduction of risk and other costs; linked to changing business/portfolio composition and available market opportunities	
Advantage	Straightforward to implement and institutionalise	Links capital need to asset as well as to non-asset risks	Combines risk and regulatory costs in one measure	Produces risk-based decisions that appropriately differentiate assets
Limitation	Does not capture different transaction risks	Biased towards acceptance of low-risk assets[1]	Affected by lack of risk differentiation in regulatory capital	Ignores regulatory cost of doing business
Asset 1 (lower-risk) of table 1	$4/(8 \times 100\%) = 50\%$	$4/(\sqrt{0.1} \times 6 \times 10) = 21.1\%$	$3.4/(8 \times 100\%) = 42.5\%$	$3.4/(\sqrt{0.1} \times 6 \times 10) = 17.9\%$
Asset 2 (higher-risk) of table 1	$10/(8 \times 100\%) = 125\%$	$10/(\sqrt{0.5} \times 15 \times 10) = 9.4\%$	$2.5/(8 \times 100\%) = 31.25\%$	$2.5/(\sqrt{0.5} \times 15 \times 10) = 2.4\%$

Note: the simplified risk-adjusted capital calculation assumes a desired coverage of risk up to a capital confidence multiplier of 10. The 100% risk-weighting used to calculate ROC and RAROC assumes that both transactions are with a corporate counterparty. A capital multiplier of 8 is used for the calculation of regulatory capital requirements.

[1]Since banks with high desired ratings and low risk tolerance have an economic capital requirement that increases significantly with rising transaction risks, low-risk assets appear especially attractive despite contributing relatively low earnings. The RARORAC measure also results in a preference for transactions with less risk. A RAPM with risk capital in the denominator has this property because the market does not compensate for "capital comfort" but prices risk across investors of varying risk tolerance. Required "capital comfort" is greatest for commercial banks with a high credit rating, is less for investment banks, insurance companies and mutual funds (because of higher liquidity and more diversity of their asset portfolio), and is lower for hedge funds (whose risk appetite is arguably greater). For a RAPM to be unbiased (like RAR and RAROC), it is necessary that the average value of the measure with varying risk contribution be unchanged. This condition is not satisfied for RORAC and RARORAC.

dissimilar from RORAC and RARORAC. First, the former two should be higher for funded than for unfunded credits because the benefit of increased revenues from funded credits would overshadow the impact of higher regulatory capital requirements. In Figure 2(*e*) and (*f*) it is shown that ROC and RAROC should be higher for OECD bank counterparties than for corporate counterparties for the same risk rating. Owing to the absence of a risk adjustment in ROC in Figure 2(*e*) and a disregard for counterparty risk rating in regulatory capital requirements, the shape of ROC is the same as that of return less costs in Figure 2(*a*). Similarly, the shape of RAROC with changing transaction risk contribution in Figure 2(*f*) is the same as that of RAR in Figure 2(*c*).

Table 2 compares and contrasts the four RAPMs. The degree of complexity of these measures increases from ROC to RARORAC. Clearly, these RAPMs have varying benefits for any institution. The selection of an appropriate RAPM not only hinges upon the desirable properties of the measure, but also depends on the availability of systems and processes and the diversity of businesses in an organisation. We can summarise the characteristics of the four RAPMs as follows:

- The absence of the risk adjustment in ROC encourages risk-taking to earn the associated higher revenues. In the long run this is likely to lead to higher credit losses and lower shareholder value. Insufficient pricing would be demanded for riskier assets and high-credit quality assets would be shunned due to their relatively low returns.
- While the use of risk capital in RORAC is an improvement over ROC, low-risk and likely-to-be-lower-revenue transactions that earn high RORACs are pursued to a greater extent. For institutions whose desired capital "buffers" are relatively high, the outcome may be a proclivity toward less attractive transactions. As a result, the portfolio will be of high credit quality but earn lower revenues.
- The incorporation of risk and regulatory considerations in RAROC leads to the pursuit of assets that provide market-based compensation for risk and aim to optimise the use of available regulatory capital. This measure is very effective and practical since it attempts to maximise risk-adjusted profitability subject to market and regulatory constraints.
- The risk-based theoretical and economic underpinnings of the RARORAC technique make it invaluable in maximising risk-adjusted profitability while minimising risk capital. The practice of this decision-making procedure, in combination with other objectives such as revenues and earnings targets, is recommended. Due to the incorporation of risks in both the numerator and denominator of RARORAC, the accurate determination of risks assumes greater importance. A firm-wide use of this measure requires sophisticated methodologies and systems for measuring and tracking a variety of risks.

CONCLUSION

An overall objective of any firm is to make the best use of available capital by allocating it efficiently to different businesses. Banking institutions are required to hold regulatory capital in the spirit of the 1988 Basle Accord. The uniformity and generally straightforward nature of these standards and absence of economic risk considerations captured in counterparty risk ratings have prevented an accurate measurement of economic capital that reflects the underlying risk characteristics. In fact, the regulatory capital standards have led to incentives that are mostly inconsistent with the trade-off between risk and return. Risk-based capital allocation is preferable. Some common risk or economic capital measures are linked to coverage of unexpected transaction/portfolio losses up to a desired confidence level, earnings-at-risk and asset volatility.

Zaik *et al* (1996) provide a useful discussion of how Bank of America utilises RAROC methodologies and systems in determining capital allocations. This scheme incorporates the covariation of a business unit's portfolio with the rest of the bank's portfolio of assets and considers the risk contribution of each business unit to the overall volatility of the bank's market value.

Based on the capital consumed by a business unit relative to the allocated capital, a transfer pricing mechanism aims to "level the playing field". While diversification is a desirable goal, average correlation measures of risk contribution should also be considered for transaction evaluation and performance measurement purposes. Not only may market pricing for an asset not reflect the impact of likely concentrations of similar assets and poor correlations of this asset with other assets in particular portfolios but, also, business managers have no control over the composition of the rest of the bank's portfolio.

The RAROC and RARORAC procedures are valuable for both capital allocation and performance evaluation.[3] These measures evaluate risk-adjusted performance relative to regulatory and economic capital utilisation, respectively. RAROC enables performance measurement in light of the expected loss and risk costs of the transaction or business unit and allocates capital based on regulatory standards. RARORAC provides a mechanism for capital allocation tied to the aggregate risk profile; it takes into account the varying capital requirement across counterparty risk rating. The successful implementation of this procedure requires rigorous risk methodologies and measurements. The institution's assessment of its desired rating is significant in setting the target rate for RARORAC. For an institution with heavy regulatory capital consumption, closer adherence to a hurdle RAROC being achieved by new transactions becomes significant. In the reverse situation where an institution has substantial economic capital requirements, RARORAC has great value.

1 Smithson *et al* (1997) propose a similar measure. In their measure the transaction's adjusted income is computed by deducting expected loss, due to the possibility and severity of default, from the net income

2 The credit paradox refers to the specialisation and lending relationships established by commercial lending originators, resulting in concentrations of transactions (industry, geography, maturity, market sector) in the bank's portfolio

3 A detailed exposition of the firm-wide implementation of RAPM systems in concert with different capital allocation procedures can be found in Matten (1996)

References

Asarnow, E., 1996, "Corporate Loans as an Asset Class", *Journal of Portfolio Management* summer, pp. 92–103.

Lintner, J., 1965, "The Valuation of Risk Assets and the Selection of Risky Investment in Stock Portfolios and Capital Budgets", *Review of Economics and Statistics* 47, pp. 13–37.

Matten, C., 1996, *Managing Bank Capital: Capital Allocation and Performance Measurement,* John Wiley & Sons.

Sharpe, W., 1964, "Capital Asset Prices: A Theory of Market Equilibrium under Conditions of Risk", *Journal of Finance* 19, pp. 425–42.

Shimko, D., 1997, "See Sharpe or Be Flat", *Risk* June, p. 33.

Smithson, C., T. Po and J. Rozario, 1997, "Capital budgeting", *Risk* June, pp. 40–1

Zaik, E., J. Walter, G. Kelling and C. James, 1996, "Raroc at Bank of America: from theory to practice", *Journal of Applied Corporate Finance,* summer, pp. 83–93.

Reconcilable Differences

H. Ugur Koyluoglu and Andrew Hickman

In the past few years, major advances in credit risk analytics have led to the proliferation of a new breed of sophisticated credit portfolio risk models. Several models have been developed, including proprietary applications developed for internal use by leading-edge financial institutions and third-party applications intended for sale or distribution as software. Several have received a great deal of public attention, including JP Morgan's CreditMetrics/CreditManager, Crédit Suisse Financial Products' CreditRisk+, McKinsey & Company's CreditPortfolioView and KMV's PortfolioManager. These new models allow the user to measure and quantify credit risk comprehensively at both the portfolio and contributory level. As such, they have the potential to cause profound changes to the lending business, accelerating the shift to active credit portfolio management[1] and, eventually, leading to an "internal models" reform of regulatory credit risk capital guidelines.[2]

But before these models can deliver on their promise, they must earn the acceptance of credit portfolio managers and regulators. To these practitioners, this seemingly disparate collection of new approaches may be confusing or may appear as a warning sign of an early developmental stage in the technology. While these misgivings are understandable, this paper will demonstrate that these new models in fact represent a remarkable consensus in the underlying framework, differing primarily in calculation procedures and parameters rather than financial intuition.

This paper explores both the similarities and the differences among the new credit risk portfolio models, focusing on three representative models:

- ❑ "Merton-based", eg, CreditMetrics and PortfolioManager;[3]
- ❑ "econometric", eg, CreditPortfolioView; and
- ❑ "actuarial", eg, CreditRisk+.

Note that this paper examines only the default component of portfolio credit risk. Some models incorporate credit spread (or ratings migration) risk, while others advocate a separate model. In this aspect of credit risk there is less consensus in modelling techniques, and the differences need to be explored and resolved in future research. The reader should strictly interpret "credit risk" to mean "default risk" throughout.

Additionally, for comparability, the models have been restricted to a single-period horizon, a fixed recovery rate and fixed exposures.

UNDERLYING FRAMEWORK

At first, the models appear to be quite dissimilar – CreditMetrics is based on a microeconomic causal model of default; CreditPortfolioView is a

Figure 1 Conditional default rate transformation

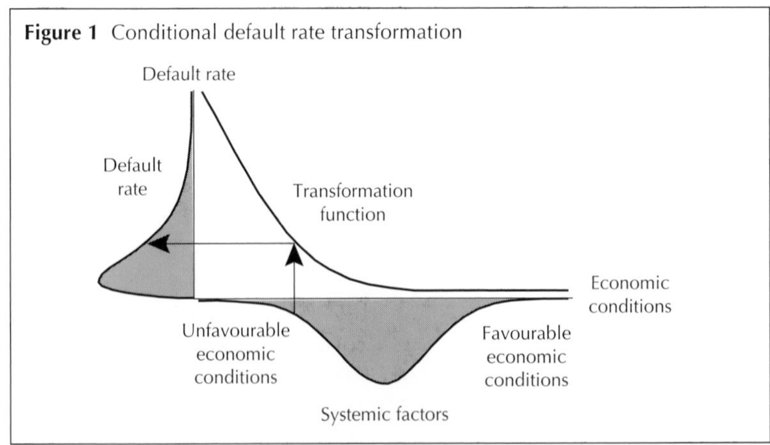

macroeconomic causal model; and CreditRisk+ is a top-down model, making no assumptions about causality. Despite these apparent differences, the models fit within a single generalised underlying framework, which consists of three components:

- *Joint default behaviour* Default rates vary over time – intuitively, as a result of varying economic conditions. Each borrower's default rate is conditioned on the "state of the world" for the relevant economic conditions. The degree of "correlation" in the portfolio is reflected by borrowers' conditional default rates varying together in different states.
- *Conditional distribution of portfolio default rate* For each state, the conditional distribution of a homogeneous sub-portfolio's default rate can be calculated as if borrowers are independent because the joint default behaviour is accounted for in generating conditional default rates.
- *Convolution/aggregation* The unconditional distribution of portfolio defaults is obtained by combining homogeneous sub-portfolios' conditional default rate distributions in each state and then simply averaging across states.

This generalised framework allows a structured comparison of the models, as follows.

Conditional default rates and probability distribution of default rate

All three models explicitly or implicitly relate default rates to variables describing the relevant economic conditions ("systemic factors"). This relationship can be expressed as a "conditional default rate" transformation function (see Figure 1). The systemic factors are random and are usually assumed to be normally distributed. Since the conditional default rate is a function of these random systemic factors, the default rate will also be random.

The Merton-based model relies on Merton's model of a firm's capital structure:[4] a firm defaults when its asset value falls below its liabilities. Default probability then depends on the amount by which assets exceed liabilities and the volatility of those assets. If standardised changes in asset value, ΔA_i, are normally distributed, the default probability can be expressed as the probability of a standard normal variable falling below some critical value, c. Joint default events among borrowers in the portfolio are related to the extent that the borrowers' changes in asset value are correlated.

Since the Merton model neither assigns the transformation function nor assumes a probability distribution for default rates explicitly, these relationships must be derived. The change in asset value can be decomposed into a set of normally distributed orthogonal systemic factors, x_k, and a normally distributed idiosyncratic component, ε_i:

$$\Delta A_i = b_{i,1}x_1 + b_{i,2}x_2 + \cdots + \sqrt{1 - \sum_k b_{i,k}^2}\,\varepsilon_i$$

where $b_{i,k}$ are the factor loadings and x_k, $\varepsilon_i \sim iid\ N[0,1]$.

Given the values of the systemic factors, the change in asset value will be normally distributed with a mean given by the factor loadings and factor values and a standard deviation given by the weight of the idiosyncratic factor. The default rate, conditioned on the systemic factors' values, can then be expressed as[5]

$$p_i \big| X = \Phi\left[\frac{c - \sum_k b_{i,k}x_k}{\sqrt{1 - \sum_k b_{i,k}^2}}\right]$$

For the single borrower or homogeneous portfolio case, the systemic factors can be summarised by a single variable, m, reducing the transformation function to

$$p\big|_m = \Phi\left[\frac{c - \sqrt{\rho}\,m}{\sqrt{1-\rho}}\right]$$

where $m \sim N[0,1]$ and

$$\rho = \sum_k b_k^2$$

is the asset correlation.

Since the cumulative normal function is bounded $[0,1]$ and concave in the relevant region, the resulting default rate distribution is bounded $[0,1]$ and skewed right, as in Figure 1.

The probability density function for the default rate, $f(p)$, can be derived explicitly, as follows:

$$f(p)=\varphi(m(p))\left|\frac{dm}{dp}\right| = \frac{\sqrt{1-\rho}\,\varphi\left(\frac{c-\sqrt{1-\rho}\,\Phi^{-1}(p)}{\sqrt{\rho}}\right)}{\sqrt{\rho}\,\varphi\left(\Phi^{-1}(p)\right)}$$

where $\varphi(z)$ is the standardised normal density function.

The econometric model[6] drives the default rate, $p_{i,t}$, according to an "index", $y_{i,t}$, of macroeconomic factors. The index is expressed as a weighted sum of macroeconomic variables, $x_{k,t}$, each of which is normally distributed and has lagged dependency:

$$x_{k,t} = a_{k,0} + a_{k,1}x_{k,t-1} + a_{k,2}x_{k,t-2} + \cdots + \varepsilon_{k,t}$$

and

$$y_{i,t} = b_{i,0} + b_{i,1}x_{1,t} + b_{i,2}x_{2,t} + \cdots + \upsilon_{i,t}$$

where $\varepsilon_{k,t}$ and $\upsilon_{i,t}$ are normally distributed random innovations.

The index is transformed to a default probability by the Logit function:

$$p_{i,t} = \frac{1}{1+e^{y_{i,t}}}$$

The index and macroeconomic variables can be combined in a single equation:

$$y_{i,t} = \left[b_{i,0} + \sum_k b_{i,k}\left(a_{k,0} + \sum_j a_{k,j}x_{k,t-j}\right)\right] + \sum_k b_{i,k}\varepsilon_{k,t} + \upsilon_{i,t}$$

consisting of a constant term and random terms representing systemic and index-specific innovations. For the single borrower or homogeneous portfolio case, these random terms can be summarised by a single normally distributed variable, m, so that the conditional default rate can then be expressed as

$$p\big|_m = \frac{1}{1+e^{U+Vm}}$$

where $m \sim N[0,1]$, and U and V represent the summarised constant term and coefficient to the random term, respectively.

Since the Logit function is bounded $[0,1]$ and concave, the resulting distribution is bounded $[0,1]$ and skewed, as in Figure 1.

The implied probability density function for the default rate, $f(p)$, is

$$f(p)=\varphi(m(p))\left|\frac{\mathrm{d}m}{\mathrm{d}p}\right|=\frac{1}{Vp(1-p)}\varphi\left[\frac{1}{V}\ln\left(\frac{1-p}{p}\right)-\frac{U}{V}\right]$$

The actuarial model[7] assumes explicitly that the default rate distribution follows the gamma distribution. Joint default behaviour is incorporated by treating the default rate as a random variable common to multiple borrowers. Borrowers are allocated to "sectors", each of which has a gamma-distributed default rate with specified mean and volatility. A borrower's conditional default rate is a scaled weighted average of sector default rates:

$$p|_X=\bar{p}\sum_k \omega_k \frac{x_k}{\mu_k}$$

where $\bar{p}$ is the borrower's unconditional default rate, ω_k represents the weight in sector k:

$$\sum_k \omega_k = 1$$

and

$$x_k \sim \Gamma[\alpha_k, \beta_k] \qquad \text{with } \alpha_k = \frac{\mu_k^2}{\sigma_k^2} \text{ and } \beta_k = \frac{\sigma_k^2}{\mu_k}$$

The gamma distribution is skewed right, as in Figure 1, but has unbounded positive support.

It is possible to derive the actuarial model's implied transformation function such that when applied to a normally distributed systemic factor, m, it results in a gamma-distributed default rate. The transformation function consists of all points (χ, ξ) that satisfy

$$\int_0^{\xi}\Gamma(p;\alpha,\beta)\mathrm{d}p=\int_{\chi}^{\infty}\varphi(m)\mathrm{d}m$$

Hence, the transformation function is given by

$$p|_m=\Psi^{-1}(1-\Phi(m);\alpha,\beta)$$

where

$$\alpha=\frac{\bar{p}^2}{\sigma^2},\qquad \beta=\frac{\sigma^2}{\bar{p}}$$

$m \sim N[0,1]$ and $\Psi(z;\alpha,\beta)$ is the cumulative density function of the gamma distribution.

Conditional distribution of portfolio default rate

Given fixed or conditional default rates, a homogeneous sub-portfolio's distribution of defaults follows the binomial distribution $B(k;n,p)$, which provides the probability that k defaults will occur in a portfolio of n borrowers if each has default probability p. CreditMetrics implicitly uses the binomial distribution by calculating the change in asset value for each borrower and testing for default – exactly equivalent to the binomial case of two states with a given probability. CreditPortfolioView explicitly uses the binomial distribution by iteratively convoluting the individual obligor distributions, each of which is binomial.

CreditRisk+ uses the Poisson distribution $P(k;pN)$, which provides the probability that k defaults will occur in a portfolio of n borrowers given a rate of intensity per unit time p. The binomial and Poisson distributions are quite similar; indeed, the Poisson distribution is the limiting distribution for the binomial distribution.[8]

Aggregation

The unconditional probability distribution of portfolio defaults is obtained by combining the conditional distributions of homogeneous sub-portfolio defaults across all "states of the world". Mathematically, this is expressed as a convolution integral.

The Merton-based and econometric models are conditioned on normally distributed systemic factors, and the independent loans' defaults are binomially distributed. Hence, the convolution integral for a homogeneous sub-portfolio with a single systemic factor is expressed as

$$\int_{-\infty}^{\infty} B\left(k;n,p\middle|_{m}\right)\varphi(m)\,\mathrm{d}m$$

The actuarial model's homogeneous sub-portfolio convolution integral, with gamma-distributed default rate and Poisson-distributed conditional defaults, is

$$\int_{0}^{\infty} P(k;np)\,\Gamma(p;\alpha,\beta)\,\mathrm{d}p$$

These integrals are easily evaluated; in particular, the convolution of the Poisson distribution and gamma distribution yields a closed-form distribution, the negative binomial distribution. It is the differences between sub-portfolios – differing exposure size or default probabilities, or multiple systemic factors, complex correlation structure, etc – that create difficulty in aggregation. In practice, then, the convolutions are evaluated by Monte Carlo simulation in CreditMetrics and CreditPortfolioView, while CreditRisk+ uses a numeric algorithm based on "banding" exposures. In all three cases the procedures are exact in the limit.

Figure 2 The models in relation to the generalised framework

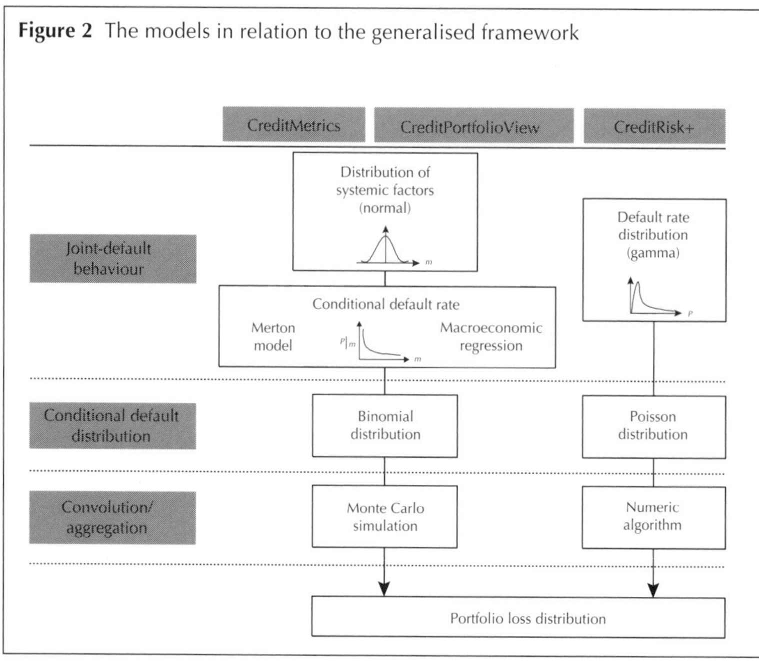

Figure 2 depicts the models as they are redefined in relation to the generalised framework.

HARMONISATION OF PARAMETERS

The preceding discussion shows that all three models depend critically on the unconditional default probability and joint default behaviour. While unconditional default probability is relatively straightforward, joint default behaviour appears in a different form in each model. The Merton-based model uses pairwise asset correlations; the actuarial model uses sector weightings and default rate volatilities; and the econometric model uses coefficients to common macroeconomic factors. Although these parameters are very different in nature, they contain equivalent information to characterise joint default behaviour.

Coefficients and correlations

The Merton-based model represents joint default behaviour with a set of asset factor loadings or, equivalently, a pairwise asset correlation matrix:

$$\Delta A_i = b_{i,1}x_1 + b_{i,2}x_2 + \cdots + \sqrt{1 - \sum_k b_{i,k}^2}\,\varepsilon_i$$

The systemic factors are defined to be orthonormal, so that

$$\text{correlation}\left[\Delta A_i, \Delta A_j\right] =$$

$$\frac{E\left[\Delta A_i \Delta A_j\right] - E\left[\Delta A_i\right]E\left[\Delta A_j\right]}{\sqrt{\left(E\left[\Delta A_i^2\right]-E\left[\Delta A_i\right]^2\right)\left(E\left[\Delta A_j^2\right]-E\left[\Delta A_j\right]^2\right)}}$$

$$= b_{i,1}b_{j,1} + b_{i,2}b_{j,2} + \cdots$$

The econometric model's "index" regression coefficients closely resemble the asset factor loadings of the Merton-based model. An "index correlation" is easily defined in a similar fashion to an asset correlation, and will be treated as equivalent, though they may provide slightly different results to the extent of differences in their respective conditional default rate functions.

Unconditional default rate and default rate volatility

The unconditional default rate and default rate volatility are specified directly in the actuarial model. For the Merton-based and econometric models, they are calculated by

$$\bar{p} = \int_{-\infty}^{\infty} p\,|_m\, \varphi(m)\, \mathrm{d}m$$

and

$$\sigma^2 = \int_{-\infty}^{\infty} \left(p\,|_m - \bar{p}\right)^2 \varphi(m)\, \mathrm{d}m$$

The parameters for the Merton-based (c and ρ) and econometric models (U and V) can then be solved to yield a specified unconditional default rate and default rate volatility. This defines the relationship between default rate volatility and asset correlation (see Figure 3).

Default correlation

Some models take a Markowitz variance–covariance view of credit risk portfolio modelling. Each borrower has a variance of default given by the variance for a Bernoulli variable:

$$\text{var}\left(\text{default}_i\right) = \bar{p}_i\left(1-\bar{p}_i\right)$$

For a large homogeneous portfolio, the portfolio variance approaches

Figure 3 Default rate volatility and asset correlation

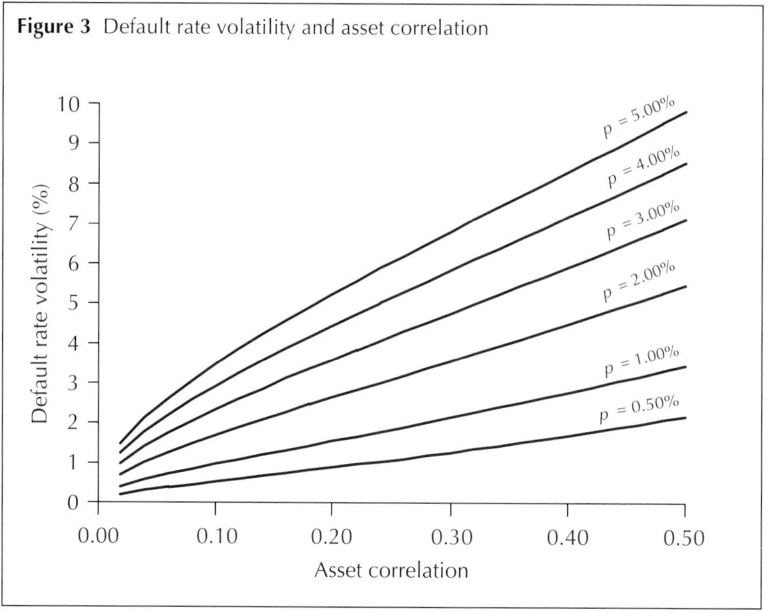

$$\sigma^2 = \bar{p}\left(1-\bar{p}\right)\rho_{\text{default}}$$

This provides the relationships between default correlation and default rate volatility and, therefore, asset correlation.

Mappings such as these allow parameter estimates to be "triangulated" by multiple methods, to the extent that model differences are not significant. For example, default rate volatilities can be used to estimate implied asset correlations in the absence of asset value data.

DIFFERENCES IN DEFAULT RATE DISTRIBUTION

The discussion above ("Underlying framework") demonstrates that substantial model differences could arise only from the differing treatment of joint default behaviour – the conditional default distributions are effectively the same and the aggregation techniques are all exact in the limit. The section "Harmonisation of parameters" provides the means to compare the joint default behaviour on an apples-to-apples basis.

This comparison will be illustrated for a homogeneous portfolio with an unconditional default rate, $\bar{p}$, of 116 basis points and a standard deviation of default rate, σ, equal to 90 bp.[9] Since each model produces a two-parameter default rate distribution, the mean and standard deviation are sufficient statistics to define the relevant parameters for any of the models, as above. To yield $\bar{p}$ = 116 bp and σ = 90 bp, the parameters for each model are as follows:

Figure 4 Default rate distributions compared

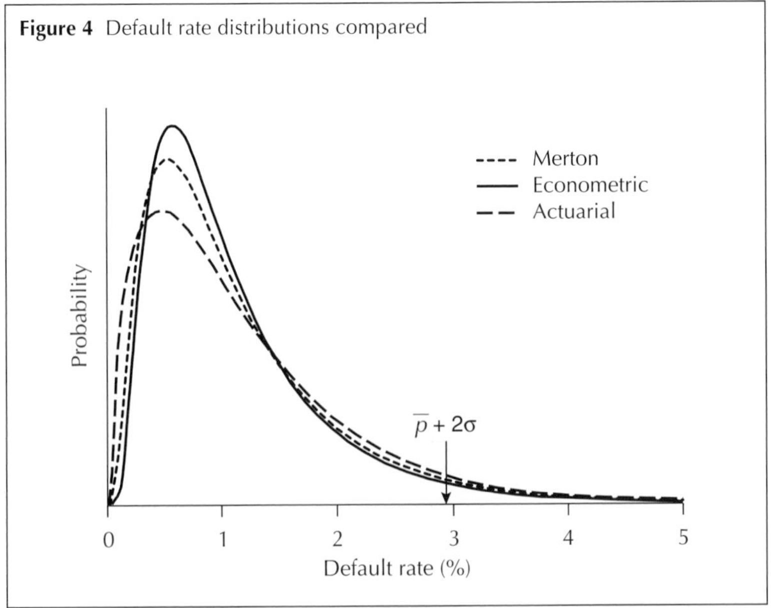

- Merton-based: $c = -2.27$, $\rho = 0.073$
- econometric: $U = 4.684$, $V = 0.699$
- actuarial: $\alpha = 1.661$, $\beta = 0.0070$.

In this example, the models' conditional default rate functions are virtually indistinguishable when the systemic factor is greater than negative two standard deviations. For extremely unfavourable economic conditions, the econometric model predicts a somewhat higher default rate and the actuarial model predicts a somewhat lower default rate. The default rate distributions (see Figure 4) are also very similar, with only minor discrepancies in the tails.

The degree of agreement in the tails of these distributions can be assessed with the following statistic:

$$\Xi_z(f, g) = 1 - \frac{\int_z^{\infty} \left| \mathrm{f}(x) - \mathrm{g}(x) \right| \mathrm{d}x}{\int_z^{\infty} \mathrm{f}(x)\mathrm{d}x + \int_z^{\infty} \mathrm{g}(x)\mathrm{d}x}$$

where $\mathrm{f}(x)$ and $\mathrm{g}(x)$ are probability density functions and z defines the lower bounds of the "tail", which will be defined arbitrarily as the area more than two standard deviations above the mean, ie, $z = \overline{p} + 2\sigma$. This statistic measures the amount of the probability distributions' mass that

Table 1 Tail-agreement statistics for the example distributions

Merton versus econometric	94.90%
Merton versus actuarial	93.38%
Econometric versus actuarial	88.65%

overlaps in the tail, normalised to the total probability mass of the two distributions in the tail. The statistic will be bounded $[0, 1]$, where zero indicates distributions with no overlapping probability mass and one indicates exact agreement. Table 1 provides the tail-agreement statistics for the example distributions.

Without a credible alternative distribution, this tail-agreement statistic provides a relative rather than an absolute measure. However, it can be used to test the robustness of the similarity to the parameters (Table 2).

The results in Table 2 demonstrate that the similarity of the models holds for a reasonably wide range of parameters. The models begin to diverge at a very high ratio of default rate volatility to default probability, particularly for very low or very high default probabilities. Accordingly, in very high quality (AA or better) or very low quality (B or worse) portfolios, model selection can make a difference, though there are scant data on which to base such a selection. In a portfolio with only moderate weight in very high or very low quality sub-portfolios, these differences should not be significant in aggregation.

Impact of parameter inconsistency

This finding of similarity should be taken with caution, as it hinges on harmonising parameter values. In practice, the parameters vary with the estimation technique. The different estimation techniques appropriate to different joint default parameters may result in inconsistent default rate volatility. Even mean default probabilities may vary considerably depending on the estimation technique, sample, etc. Unsurprisingly, when the parameters do not imply a consistent mean and standard deviation of default rate distribution, the result is that the models are significantly different. This case is illustrated by an example of three parameter sets that are not consistent, though plausibly obtainable for the same portfolio (see Table 3). Within any one of these three parameter sets, a comparison of the models yields results similar to those illustrated in Figure 4 and Table 1 – tail-agreement statistics average 91% and range from 82% to 95%. Large differences arise when the models are compared across the inconsistent parameter sets (see Figure 5) – tail-agreement statistics average only 76% and range from 65% to 85%, even when comparing the same model applied to each of the inconsistent parameter sets. The differences in parameters – well within the typical range of estimation error – have much greater impact than model differences in this example.

Table 2 Tail-agreement statistics versus parameter values

$\bar{p}$	$\sigma/\bar{p}$ 0.50	1.00	2.00	3.00
0.05%	98.10% 93.53% 91.71%	95.94% 88.50% 84.70%	91.16% 81.17% 73.13%	89.12% 78.99% 69.04%
0.10%	97.92% 93.75% 91.73%	95.57% 88.94% 84.78%	91.15% 82.16% 73.95%	88.40% 80.40% 69.73%
0.25%	97.61% 94.11% 91.79%	94.93% 89.73% 84.97%	90.35% 83.87% 74.83%	87.86% 82.92% 71.60%
0.50%	97.33% 94.42% 91.88%	94.41% 90.56% 85.30%	89.91% 85.71% 76.15%	88.09% 85.61% 74.28%
1.00%	97.06% 94.93% 92.04%	93.97% 91.69% 85.93%	89.89% 88.29% 78.57%	88.97% 89.38% 78.72%
2.50%	96.62% 95.82% 92.62%	93.62% 93.94% 87.79%	90.77% 93.65% 84.77%	91.33% 94.68% 87.53%
5.00%	96.33% 97.02% 93.55%	93.85% 96.70% 90.87%	92.79% 95.24% 91.38%	94.59% 81.79% 79.96%
10.00%	96.21% 98.55% 95.45%	94.92% 95.57% 95.22%	95.79% 72.95% 72.41%	na na na

na = not applicable because it is an unreasonable combination of parameters – model results become unstable. Each cell contains tail-agreement statistics for Merton v. econometric, Merton v. actuarial and econometric v. actuarial.

Table 3 Hypothetical inconsistent parameter values

	$\bar{p}$	σ	c	ρ	α	β	U	V	Model for comparison*
1	**2.26%**	**1.70%**	−2.00	8.5%	1.767	0.0128	**4.00**	**0.70**	Econometric
2	**1.52%**	**1.71%**	−2.16	14.4%	**0.790**	**0.0192**	4.60	0.95	Actuarial
3	**1.54%**	**2.63%**	**−2.16**	**26.2%**	0.343	0.0449	4.95	1.30	Merton

*In the inconsistent parameter case, the parameter sets' "models for comparison" were selected arbitrarily. Bold figures indicate parameters appropriate to selected model.

Figure 5 Conditional default rates for different models compared

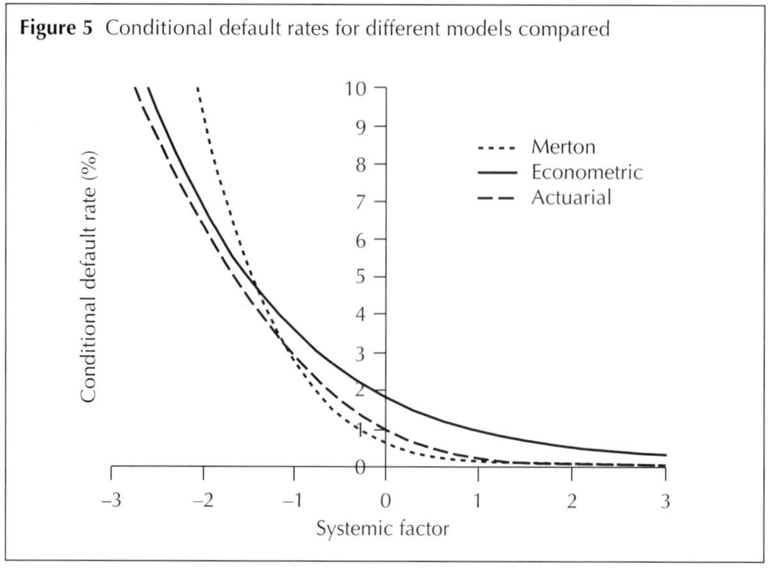

CONCLUSIONS

On the surface, the credit risk portfolio models studied here seem to be quite different. Deeper examination reveals that the models belong to a single general framework, which identifies three critical points of comparison – the default rate distribution, the conditional default distribution, and the convolution/aggregation technique. Differences were found to be immaterial in the last two of these, so that any significant differences between the models must arise from differences in modelling joint default behaviour which manifest in the default rate distribution. Further, when the joint default parameter values are harmonised to a consistent expression of default rate and default rate volatility, the default rate distributions are sufficiently similar to cause little meaningful difference across a broad range of reasonable parameter values. Any significant model differences can then be attributed to parameter value estimates that have inconsistent implications for the observable default rate behaviour.

Parameter inconsistency is not a trivial issue. A "naïve" comparison of the models, with parameters estimated from different data using different techniques, is quite likely to produce significantly different results for the same portfolio. The conclusions of empirical comparisons of the models will vary according to the degree of difference in parameters.[10] In such comparisons, it is important to understand the proportions of "parameter variance" and "model variance" if different results are produced for the same portfolio. The findings in this paper suggest that "parameter variance" is likely to dominate. Future studies should focus on the magnitude of parameter differences and the sensitivity of results to these differences.

Parameter inconsistency can arise from two sources: estimation error, which could arise from small sample size or other sampling issues; or model mis-specification. While default rate volatility may be immediately observable, even long periods of observation provide small sample size and risk non-stationarity. At the other extreme, asset correlations can be measured with reasonable sample size in much shorter periods, albeit with the risk of mis-specification in the return distributions and default causality assumptions in the translation to default rate volatility. Rather than conclude that parameter inconsistency potentially constitutes irreconcilable differences between the results of these models, this paper concludes that because the models are so closely related, the estimates are complementary and should provide improved accuracy in parameter estimation within the generalised framework as a whole.

A useful metaphor can be drawn from the success of the value-at-risk framework in modelling market risk. VAR has become the industry standard and the basis for regulatory capital requirements. But, in practice, VAR encompasses a variety of significantly different modelling and parameter estimation techniques – eg, historical simulation versus variance–covariance, delta–gamma versus exact Monte Carlo simulation, etc. The underlying coherence of the VAR concept – that risk is measured by combining the relationship between the value of trading positions to market variables with the distribution of those underlying market variables – ensures a consistency that is sufficient for widespread acceptance and regulatory change. Similarly, the underlying coherence of these new sophisticated credit risk portfolio models should allow them to overcome differences in calculation procedures and parameter estimation. Rather than dissimilar competing alternatives, these models represent an emerging industry standard for credit risk management and regulation.

The authors wish to thank Andrew Cross, Frank Diebold, Tom Garside, Mark Intrater, Andrew Kuritzkes, Hashem Pesaran, Til Schuermann, James Wiener and Tom Wilde for providing helpful comments and discussions. All errors are the responsibility of the authors alone. The opinions expressed herein are those of the authors and do not necessarily reflect those of Credit Suisse Financial Products, CSFP Capital Inc., or Oliver, Wyman & Company. This paper is an abridged version of "A Generalised Framework for Credit Portfolio Models", a working paper that may be obtained from the authors on request.

1 For example, see Kuritzkes (1998).
2 See International Swaps and Derivatives Association (1998).
3 The discussion that follows will focus on CreditMetrics as the example, but it also applies reasonably well to PortfolioManager.
4 See Merton (1974), Kealhoffer (1995) and Gupton, Finger and Bhatia (1997).
5 Vasicek (1987) develops this representation of the Merton model for a single factor.
6 See Wilson (1997).

7 See Crédit Suisse Financial Products (1997).

8 See Freund (1992).

9 These parameters were selected to match Moody's Investors Services "All Corporates" default experience for 1970–95, as reported in Carty and Lieberman (1996).

10 For example, Isda (1998) and Roberts and Wiener (1998) compare the results of several models on test portfolios. The former finds that model results are fairly consistent, while the latter finds that the models may produce quite different results for the same portfolio using parameters selected independently for each model.

References

Carty, L., and D. Lieberman, 1996, *Corporate Bond Defaults and Default Rates 1938–1995*, Moody's Investors Service Global Credit Research, January.

Crédit Suisse Financial Products, 1997, *CreditRisk+ – A Credit Risk Management Framework.*

Freund, J., 1992, *Mathematical Statistics*, fifth edition, Prentice Hall, New Jersey.

Gupton, G., C. Finger and M. Bhatia, 1997, *CreditMetrics Technical Document*, Morgan Guaranty Trust, 1997.

International Swaps and Derivatives Association, 1998, *Credit Risk and Regulatory Capital*, March.

Kealhoffer, S., 1995, "Managing Default Risk in Derivative Portfolios", in *Derivative Credit Risk: Advances in Measurement and Management*, Risk Books, London, 1995.

Kuritzkes, A., 1998, "Transforming Portfolio Management", *Banking Strategies*, July–August, pp. 57–62.

Merton R., 1974, "On the pricing of corporate debt: the risk structure of interest rates", *Journal of Finance* 29, pp. 449–70.

Roberts, J., and J. Wiener, 1998, "Handle With Care", Oliver, Wyman & Company, Working paper.

Vasicek, O., 1987, "Probability of Loss on Loan Portfolio", KMV Corporation, February 12.

Wilson, T., 1997, "Portfolio Credit Risk, Part I", *Risk*, September 1997, pp. 111–17.

Wilson, T., 1997, "Portfolio Credit Risk, Part II", *Risk*, October 1997, pp. 56–61.

Refining Ratings

Ross Miller

Difficulties in quantifying credit risk mean that it is measured with far less precision than market risk. Financial institutions that develop their own internal measures of credit risk usually use a "1 to 9" scale of creditworthiness for their exposures, taking their lead from the rating agencies' alphabetical scales, eg, from triple A to D. Even with the refinement of "notches", designated with a "+" or "–", the vast universe of credit risk is reduced to at most 30 levels. In reality, the broad range of pricing for corporate debt obligations in the marketplace indicates that there are far more than 30 categories of credit risk. In the high-yield debt market the illusion of "stability" provided by a broad categorisation scheme can easily be outweighed by its imprecision.

The better precision of market risk measurements is mainly due to the rich body of quantitative theory that has been developed for it. In particular, there are many cases where the arbitrage-based techniques of option valuation theory can be applied to market risk. Despite the numerous shortcomings of this theory (elaborated upon in *Risk* and other journals), its practical application leads to a fairly precise quantification of risk in a wide variety of settings.

Fortunately, these same option-theory roots can be applied to the quantification of credit risk in corporate settings. Indeed, the modern theory's developers – Fischer Black and Myron Scholes (1973) and Robert Merton (1973) – noted in their earliest works on options that the equity in any firm could itself be valued as an option. The value of the equity holder's implicit option is directly related to the likelihood of financial distress, at which point they will choose to limit any further liability from their stake in the firm by "putting" it at a price of zero to the debt holders. Generally, such financial distress will also result in a shortfall to the debt holders and the firm will default on its debt. Hence, the credit risk of the firm – ie, its propensity to default – is directly and quantitatively linked to the value of its equity. (It is usually even more difficult to find the default probability from debt prices because, historically, debt has been much less liquid than equity.) In those cases where the value of the equity is directly observable, such as when it takes the form of an actively traded security, one should be able, in principle, to "reverse engineer" the probability distribution of default from the market value of the equity, given the volatility and financial structure of the firm's assets. Without delving into the details here, the option-valuation approach to credit risk is far more difficult to make practical than its market risk counterpart.

This article develops and applies the statistical machinery needed to determine whether a particular quantitative method of measuring credit risk, using option valuation or other methods, represents a refinement over broader categorisation methods. Here the term "refinement" is used in a technical sense of partitioning the creditworthiness of firms in a way that yields more information than the original partition, in this case the alphabet-based ratings. This is a particularly challenging statistical problem because defaults are infrequent occurrences and the error structure of their estimates cannot be assumed to be normal or to follow any other regular distribution. The solution to this problem is to get the most out of the existing data and to apply non-parametric tests (which do not rely on distributional assumptions) to them.

We describe here a methodology for testing whether a quantitative credit rating system is a statistically significant refinement of a broader rating system. We developed it as part of an independent study commissioned by the Capital Markets Assurance Corporation (CapMAC), a financial guarantee company based in New York (which has since merged with another financial guarantee company, MBIA). CapMAC was specifically interested in KMV Corporation's Credit Monitor system – the first options-based credit rating system – and how it compared with Standard & Poor's (S&P's) notch-level ratings for US companies.[1]

S&P ratings are designed to provide intermediate to long-run indications of creditworthiness.[2] The ratings (in descending order of credit quality) are: AAA, AA+, AA, AA–, A+, A, A–, BBB+, BBB, BBB–, BB+, BB, BB–, B+, B, B– and so on. We did not use ratings below B– (CCC+, CCC, etc) in the study because of the sparseness of these data. We used S&P's senior unsecured debt ratings as reported by S&P's Compustat database service.

In contrast, KMV's ratings take the form of expected default frequencies (EDFs), which range from 0.02% (2 basis points) to 20% and are reported with basis-point precision, making for 1,999 different possible ratings. As the likelihood of default varies over the business cycle, there is no fixed mapping between KMV and S&P ratings. KMV provides EDFs for horizons ranging from one to five years – see Kealhofer, Kwok and Weng (1998) for more information about Credit Monitor and the relationship between EDFs and agency ratings. For this study, the one-year EDF, for which KMV provides the most information, is used. Although the EDF provides a cardinal measure of credit risk, the non-parametric methods used in this study will only examine its ordinal properties relative to S&P ratings.[3]

The test of KMV's predictive power relative to a S&P rating can be expressed as the following null hypothesis: given a S&P rating for a company, the KMV rating (EDF) provides no additional information about the likelihood that the firm will default over a specified period of time. Table 1 gives a grid of the EDFs for all companies rated by KMV Credit Monitor at the end of 1989 with a S&P rating of B–. The 87 EDFs are in ascending order (descending creditworthiness). The table also shows which of the 87 defaulted in the following three years. The null hypothesis states that the

Table 1 The pattern of defaults: 87 companies' "expected default frequencies" with actual defaults for 1990–92

0.02	0.04	0.13	0.15	0.16	0.16	0.26	0.26	0.28	0.28
0.30	0.30	0.43	0.48	0.51	0.51	0.56	0.63	0.65	0.68†
0.68	0.71	0.74	0.75	0.75	0.76	0.79	0.80	0.86	0.87
0.88	0.88	0.90	0.95	0.99	1.00	1.12	1.12	1.17	1.20
1.20	1.22	1.32	1.33†	1.35†	1.43	1.58	1.72	1.74	1.75
1.87	1.92	1.96	1.99†	2.06	2.07	2.16†	2.23*	2.54	2.64
2.65	2.71†	2.80	3.01	3.03	3.06	3.22	3.31	3.32‡	3.32
3.49	3.63	3.69	3.81	3.91	4.02*	4.12	4.13	4.97	5.75
6.95†	7.09*	7.76†	7.88	8.75	10.42	17.02*			

All companies were rated B– by S&P at the end of 1989.
*Defaulted in 1990; †defaulted in 1991; ‡defaulted in 1992. Remainder did not default during this period.

pattern of defaults should be random within that cohort; however, it is clear from the table that defaults came disproportionately from the companies with the highest EDFs. Of course, this is a single cohort at a single point in time. We will next show how to aggregate all cohorts at all points in time into a single non-parametric statistical test of the null hypothesis.

To do this, we again used companies with both S&P ratings and KMV Credit Monitor EDFs. This time we studied US companies at the end of each month from June 1986 to November 1996 – a total of more than 1,000. Defaults were taken from KMV's default database, including those reported by the rating agencies for rated issues as well as those for companies without rated debt.

The trick to aggregating the KMV data over both time and S&P rating categories is to convert each EDF into an ordinal ranking within its month and (notch) rating cohort. A natural ordinal measure is a percentile rank – with 100 being the best (lowest EDF) and 0 the worst (highest EDF). A means for calculating the percentile that both takes account of ties in ranking, which are quite rare for companies with higher EDFs, and is consistent across cohorts of different sizes is given by

$$\text{Percentile} = 100\left(\frac{\dfrac{\text{Worse}}{\text{Total}} + \dfrac{\text{Total} - \text{Better}}{\text{Total}}}{2}\right)$$

$$= 50\left(\frac{\text{Worse} + \text{Total} - \text{Better}}{\text{Total}}\right)$$

where *Total* is the size of the cohort, *Worse* is the number of firms in the cohort with worse credit ratings (EDFs) and *Better* is the number of firms with better ratings.

For example, in a cohort with 20 companies (the smallest allowed in the study), the company with the lowest EDF (assuming it is the only one) has

Figure 1 Distribution of KMV percentiles of defaulting firms six to 48 months prior to default

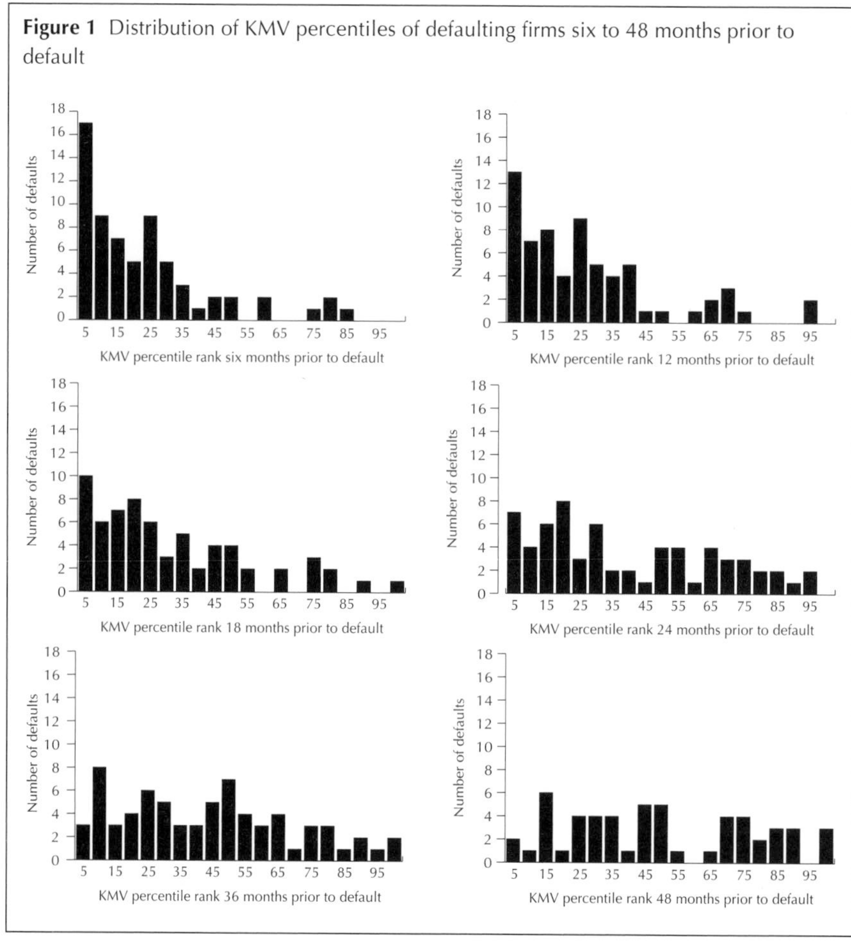

Better = 0 and *Worse* = 19, so, by substitution above, its *Percentile* = 97.5. If two companies are tied for third and fourth best EDFs, they would have *Better* = 2 and *Worse* = 16, giving *Percentile* = 85. The reason we set a minimum size for the cohort was to make the distribution of percentiles as continuous as possible, facilitating meaningful comparisons between cohorts. Also note that, by converting an EDF to a percentile, we are completely eliminating any bias that might result from EDFs as a whole being more or less optimistic about the overall rate of defaults than S&P ratings.

The null hypothesis we wish to test is that EDFs provide no more information than is contained in S&P ratings. Given the way the percentiles were constructed, the null hypothesis implies that the percentiles of the population of defaulting firms will have a flat (or uniform) distribution.[4] Furthermore, this distribution should be uniform any number of months prior to default.

The histograms in Figure 1 show that at six months prior to default this distribution is obviously far from uniform. As the default time nears the distribution becomes less uniform, which is what one would expect for any system with predictive power – ie, the nearer the event, the greater the predictive power. Nonetheless, just from looking at the graph of the distribution, it is apparent that there is still some predictive power 36 months prior to default.

APPLYING KOLMOGOROV–SMIRNOFF

The Kolmogorov–Smirnoff test is used to quantify the degree to which EDFs provide information not contained in S&P ratings. This test is a basic and well-understood tool of non-parametric statistics (see Siegel and Castellan, 1988, for details). In the one-sample version we can determine the significance with which a sample of data differs from a given baseline frequency distribution – in this case the uniform distribution.

The Kolmogorov–Smirnoff test works by calculating the maximum distance between the observed distribution of EDFs and the uniform distribution. This maximum distance is known as the *D*-statistic. By aggregating over all months and ratings we get at least 50 data points, for which both KMV and S&P ratings are known: 6, 12, 18, 24, 36 and 48 months prior to default, more than enough to perform a meaningful statistical test.

The results of this test are shown in Table 2. KMV Credit Monitor has very strong predictive value for up to 18 months prior to default. The predictive power remains statistically significant out to 36 months. At 48 months the significance level finally drops below 95%.[5]

An alternative non-parametric approach to showing the predictive power of EDFs relative to S&P ratings is to apply a binomial test to a division of the sample into two parts, with the fiftieth percentile as a natural cutoff point. The results of this test, which are not given here, as well as those for other natural percentile cutoffs (ninetieth, seventy-fifth, etc), confirm the results of the Kolmogorov–Smirnoff test. The advantage of the test is that it does not require the arbitrary choice of a percentile cutoff.

Table 2 Statistical significance of KMV default predictions

Months to default	Number of observations	Kolmogorov–Smirnoff *D*-statistic	Significance level (%)
6	66	0.5042	>99
12	66	0.4409	>99
18	66	0.3465	>99
24	66	0.2280	99
36	71	0.1775	95
48	54	0.1236	<80

DISCUSSION

This paper has demonstrated a statistical methodology for inferring that a quantitative credit rating system is a refinement of a traditional rating system – ie, it provides additional information. This demonstration was made with the use of a single, innocuous statistical assumption – that the number of firms in a cohort is large enough to make the distribution of percentiles nearly continuous. Generating results beyond those given here almost always comes at the cost of additional assumptions that could affect the validity of the analysis. For example, it is natural to try to turn the analysis around and ask whether, for a given EDF, a letter rating provides additional information. To do this analysis, the technique developed above cannot be applied without making further assumptions. The problem here is that whereas each letter rating-based cohort has associated with it a near-continuum of EDFs (see Table 1), virtually all cohorts based on a single EDF will contain few, if any, companies because the number of companies is small relative to the number of possible EDFs. The remedy of grouping EDFs together to get round this problem will not only require the use of arbitrary cutoffs but will also throw away information that may then be incorrectly attributed to the letter rating.

Additional assumptions are required to gauge the relative contribution of both the letter-based and quantitative rating systems simultaneously using regression analysis. In a regression, the two rating systems are used to generate two or more dependent variables. The independent variable is then either the default rate (for grouped data) or a dummy variable representing default (for individual data). Whichever way the analysis is set up, explicit assumptions as to the error distribution of the independent variables must be made to perform the regression. Given that neither rating is generated by a "natural" process that can be expected to have a predictable error term (eg, normally distributed), the results are likely to be quite sensitive to the distributional assumptions that underlie the regression.

On a more positive note, the analysis performed in this paper can be extended to compare two different quantitative credit rating systems with a common letter-based baseline.[6] Such a comparison can be directly implemented using the two-sample version of the Kolmogorov–Smirnoff test, a standard textbook extension of the single-sample version that we used.

1 All resources and data for this study were provided by CapMAC, who contacted KMV directly for the use of its historical data.

2 Additional credit information is available from S&P in the form of CreditWatch indications (positive, negative, stable and developing). However, S&P could not provide these data in a form suitable for a statistical study.

3 A rigorous test of the cardinal properties of KMV's Credit Monitor requires more data than were used in this study.

4 It is safe to ignore any small error that may be introduced because of the finite sample size and the possibility of ties in rankings.

5 Technically, the test only shows that the distribution of percentiles is not uniform. However, it is clear from Figure 1 that the difference is such that it confirms that EDFs provide predictive value directly.

6 Unfortunately, no other vendors of quantitative credit rating systems contacted by CapMAC would permit the general release of results from such a comparative test.

References

Black, F., and M. Scholes, 1973, "The Pricing of Options and Corporate Labilities", *Journal of Political Economy* 81, pp. 637–59.

Kealhofer, S., S. Kwok and W. Weng, 1998, "Uses and Abuses of Bond Default Rates", *CreditMetrics Monitor,* first quarter, pp. 37–55.

Merton, R., 1973, "Theory of Rational Option Pricing", *Bell Journal of Economics and Management Science* 4, pages 141–83.

Siegel, S., and N. Castellan, 1988, *Nonparametric statistics for the behavioral sciences,* McGraw-Hill, second edition.

A Credit Risk Toolbox*

Angelo Arvanitis and Jon Gregory

This paper presents new insights and techniques for the computation of credit loss distributions for capital allocation and active portfolio management. It focuses on portfolios whose exposures are marked-to-market and therefore vary randomly over time. The analysis is thus applicable to both loan and capital market derivative portfolios. We develop analytical expressions under restricted assumptions and a general simulation procedure. We demonstrate how default correlations, stochastic recovery rates, stochastic exposures and credit migration affect the capital computation. We present two Monte Carlo acceleration techniques that significantly reduce the simulation time. Finally, we discuss how portfolio optimisation can be developed within this framework.

The management of credit risk is becoming a standard responsibility of risk departments. There are several commercially available products for credit risk management (see References). In this paper, we present techniques for faster and more accurate calculation of credit loss distributions.

There are two general approaches to calculating credit loss distributions. The first is to make simplifying assumptions about the portfolio and derive analytical expressions. The accuracy of such an approach will vary with the characteristics of the portfolio and quite large errors can be introduced. Nevertheless, the method we describe here (which has not previously been applied in credit risk management) gives good results. The second approach is to use Monte Carlo simulation, which is flexible but slow. We describe two techniques that significantly speed up the simulation.

Another objective of this paper is to deal with the problems of modelling default correlations. No assumption needs to be made about the capital structure of the firm, nor are equity returns required to estimate the correlations. An important question that arises in this context is the simulation of correlated binary variables, corresponding to default events, given only marginal probabilities and pairwise correlations.

We introduce a new approach for modelling stochastic recovery rates that intuitively links the recovery amount to the severity of the default. This induces correlation between the recovery rates and also leads to a reduction in simulation time.

**This is an updated version of a paper originally published in* Risk *(December 1998), pp. 50–55. The authors are grateful to Jean-Michel Lasry for helpful comments and discussions. A longer version of the paper is available from the authors upon request.*

E mail: angelo_arvanitis@paribas.com; john_gregory@paribas.com

Figure 1 Error in estimating unexpected loss

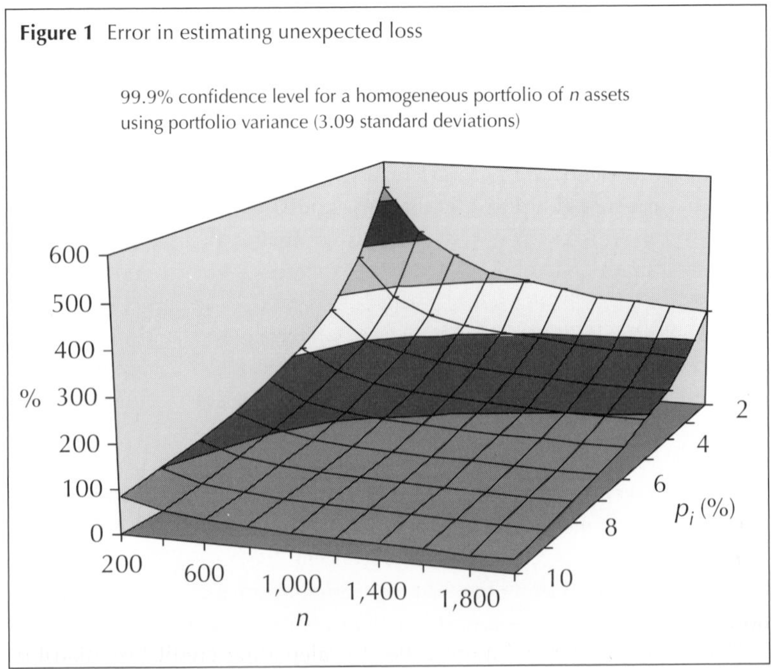

UNEXPECTED LOSS

A common measure in risk management is the unexpected loss. This is the worst loss incurred at a specified level of confidence and for a specified observation period; it is therefore used to measure economic capital. The period used in credit risk is generally in terms of years (rather than days as for market risk) since the underlying positions cannot be readily traded. The level of confidence is defined by the $(100 - x)$ percentile of the loss distribution, where x is determined according to the institution's credit rating.

For a normal distribution, the confidence level can be determined as a multiple of its standard deviation. But losses due to credit risk are highly skewed as adverse credit events are rare but give large losses. This means that a normal approximation is not valid, as illustrated in Figure 1. This shows the error, $(UL_{\text{stdev}} - UL_{\text{p}})/UL_{\text{stdev}}$, that would arise if one used the appropriate multiple of the portfolio's standard deviation, UL_{stdev}, rather than the true percentile, UL_{p}. For example, for a portfolio of 1,000 facilities each with default probability 2%, the unexpected loss is underestimated by 300%. To manage a portfolio of credit exposures one must estimate the whole loss distribution without relying on the normality assumption.

For a portfolio consisting of n assets or netted positions, the portfolio loss due to defaults up to a time T is given by

$$L(T)=\sum_{i=1}^{n}(1-\delta_i)X_i(T)d_i(T) \tag{1}$$

where $X_i(T)$ is a stochastic exposure given by the greater of the present value of the asset and zero, $\max(PV_i, 0)$, $d_i(T)$ is a binary default function with 1 indicating default and 0 otherwise, and δ_i is the recovery rate. The above expression cannot be calculated explicitly except when the number of assets is small.

SADDLE-POINT APPROXIMATION

When considering sums of independent random variables, it is convenient to consider the moment-generating functions (mgf). The mgf of a random variable V is

$$M_V(s)=E\left[e^{sV}\right]=\int_{-\infty}^{\infty}e^{st}p_V(t)\mathrm{d}t \tag{2}$$

This can be thought of as the Fourier transform of the pdf. When independent random variables are added, their distributions are convolved but their mgfs are multiplied. As multiplication is such a simple operation, a summation of independent random variables is best tackled by examining their mgfs. For the example we are considering – a weighted sum of binary variables with weights w_i and default probabilities p_i – the mgf is simply

$$M_L(s)=\prod_{i=1}^{n}\left(1-p_i+p_i e^{w_i s}\right) \tag{3}$$

One then has the problem of "undoing" the transform – ie, obtaining the pdf of L from the mgf M_L. This can be achieved by an inversion integral similar to equation (2). By suitably approximating the shape of the integrand, one obtains an analytical approximation to the pdf of L. This technique is known as the method of steepest descents or saddle-point method (Davison and Hinkley, 1988). The method also allows one to obtain analytical approximations to the tail probability without having to integrate the density function. The saddle-point method does not make any prior assumption about the shape of the loss distribution. The shape of the approximated pdf may have fat or thin tails, be symmetric or asymmetric, be unimodal or multimodal, and be bounded or unbounded. In the case of a loss distribution we know that it is bounded by 0 and the sum of all the exposures.

Figure 2 compares the saddle-point approximation with the true distribution in the $B(50, 0.10)$ and $B(50, 0.01)$ cases – ie, $n = 50$, p_i all equal. It is apparent that the saddle-point method gives better results than the

Figure 2 The saddle-point method

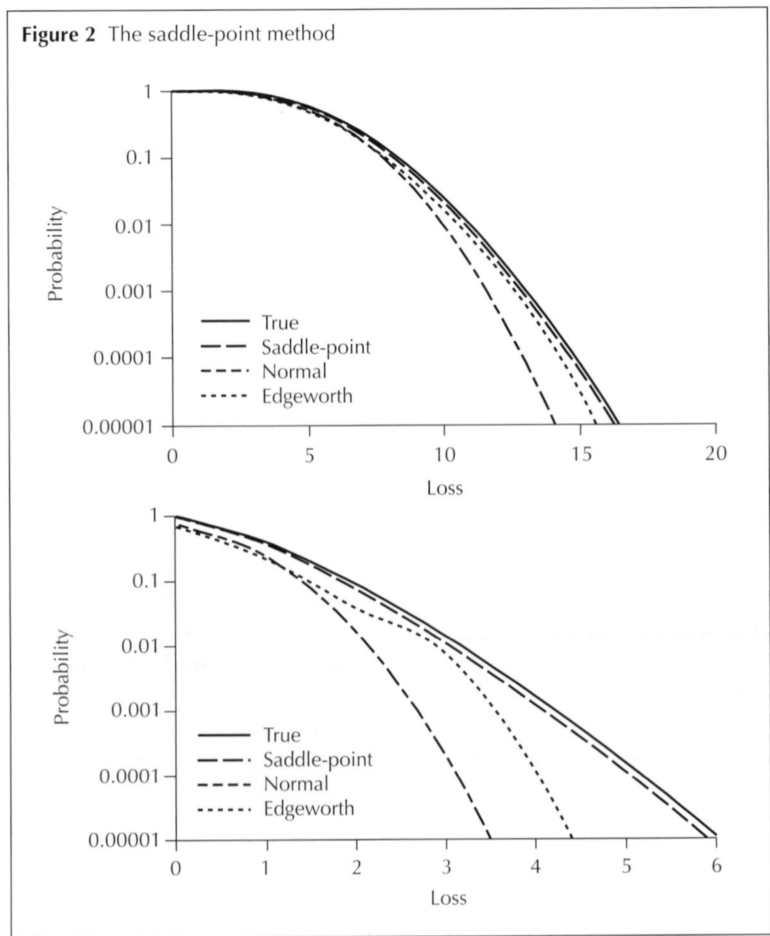

normal approximation, especially in the tails, and also outperforms the Edgeworth series (using two correction terms to the central limit theorem; see, for example, Johnston, Kotz and Balakrishnan, 1995). To quantify its performance, consider estimating the unexpected loss at the 99.9th percentile for the $B(50, 0.01)$ example. This corresponds to a tail probability of 0.001. The saddle-point method underestimates the economic capital by 3%, the Edgeworth correction by 17% and the normal approximation by 37%.

We have been able to use the saddle-point approximation to derive expressions for loss distributions that include variable exposures and default probabilities and we have also been able to incorporate correlation into the analysis. The calculations are at virtually no computational cost, and we believe the saddle-point approximation to be an excellent method for calculating tail probabilities of credit loss distributions.

SIMULATION METHODS

The analytical expressions presented in the last section are very powerful in calculating loss distributions and may be used for arbitrary (but deterministic) recovery rates, unequal exposures and unequal default probabilities. However, to include all the effects present in a real portfolio – such as stochastic exposures, stochastic recovery rates, correlations and credit migrations – we must use simulation. The method presented is not based on Merton's "firm value model" model (1974), though it has an interpretation in terms of the asset returns of the firm.

Default events are positively correlated, which increases the unexpected loss. The correlations are mostly influenced by macroeconomic factors that are reflected in the general state of the economy. The estimation of default probabilities and correlations can be done dynamically based on the credit spreads of bonds issued by the firm or the returns of the underlying equity. Alternatively, static estimates can be made using historical data. We estimate default correlations from historical data supplemented with information according to the industrial and geographical characteristics of each counterparty. We emphasise that our correlation model is not based on equity returns and allows any procedure for estimating the default correlations to be used.

A correlation structure for binary variables is not completely specified by its pairwise correlations. We must therefore define the higher-order correlations. To do this, we assume that the entire correlation structure can be determined from a multivariate normal distribution, for which the higher-order correlations are defined by the pairwise ones. It must be emphasised that this is by no means the only way to build the higher-order structure, although the approach has the intuitive interpretation that the multivariate normal distribution represents the standardised (zero mean and unit variance) asset returns of the counterparties.

The correlation framework is defined by mapping the binomial default probabilities, p_i, on to thresholds, $k_i = \Phi^{-1}(p_i)$, of a normal distribution. The probability that the two assets default is given by integrating the bivariate normal pdf – which is plotted in Figure 3, showing a correlation of 50%. The area bounded by the two normal variables, $k_i = \Phi^{-1}(p_i)$ and $k_j = \Phi^{-1}(p_j)$, defines the probability of joint default of assets i and j. As the correlation increases the density function is "squashed" along the diagonal, increasing the joint default probability.

We need to relate the correlations between the normal variables λ_{ij} to the correlations between binary variables ρ_{ij}. This can be achieved by equating the expectation of pairs of joint binary events to the joint probability of a correlated bivariate normal distribution:

$$E\left[d_i d_j\right] = \Phi\left(\lambda_{ij}, k_i, k_j\right) \tag{4}$$

Figure 3 The default process

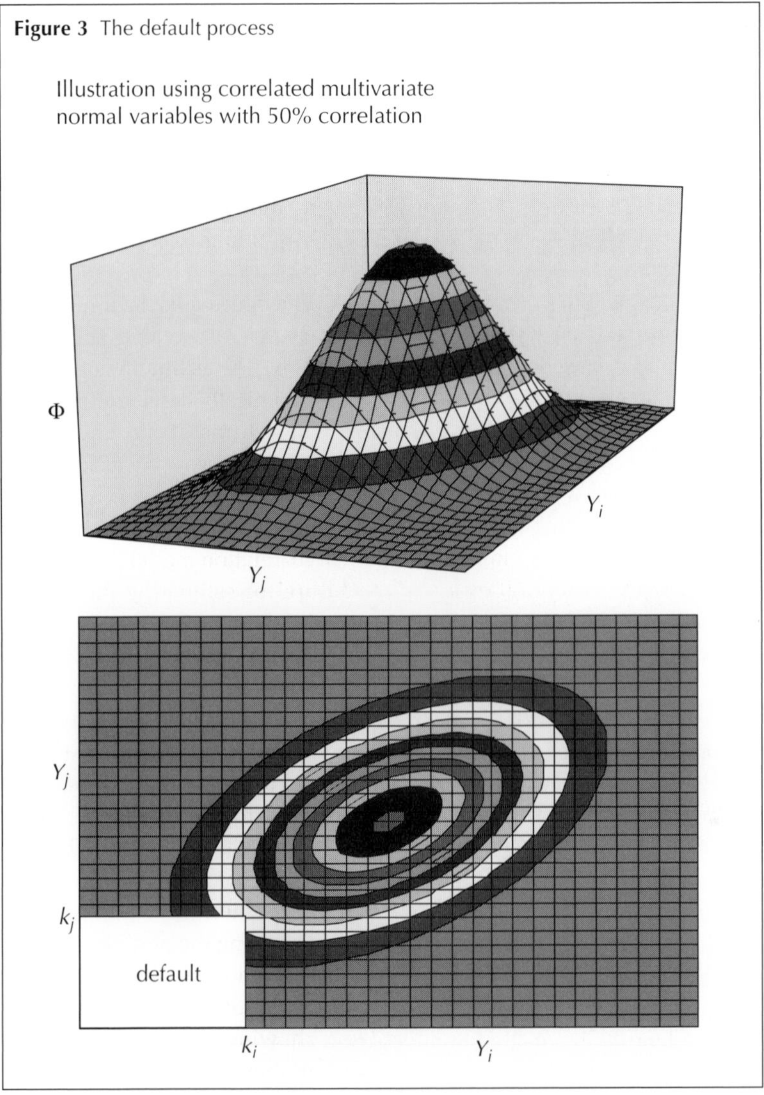

Using the standard definition of the correlation coefficient

$$\rho_{ij} = \frac{\Phi\left(\lambda_{ij}, k_i, k_j\right) - p_i p_j}{p_i(1-p_i)p_j(1-p_j)} \tag{5}$$

establishes a relationship between ρ_{ij} and λ_{ij} that can be solved numerically.

It is important to understand the full implication of the above formula. Without loss of generality, $p_i \le p_j$; so $\Phi(\lambda_{ij}, k_i, k_j) \le p_i \le p_j$ (as the probability

Figure 4 Maximum value for default correlation

As a function of the default probabilities of the two assets

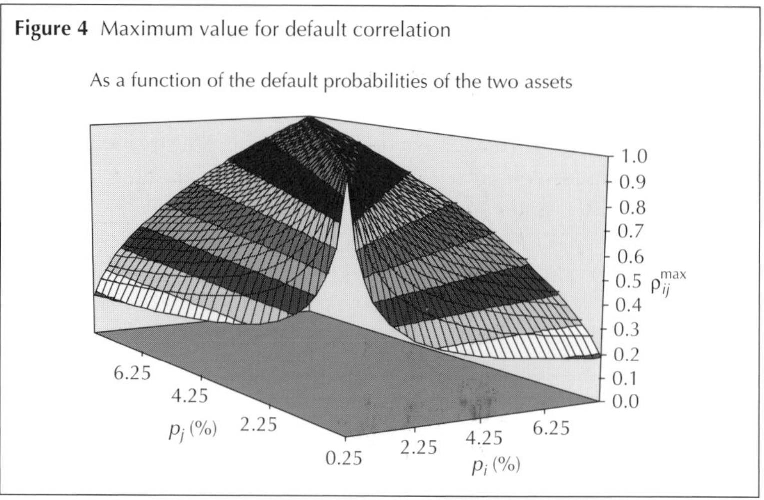

of a pair of events occurring is necessarily less than or equal to either of their individual probabilities), which gives

$$\rho_{ij} \leq \sqrt{\frac{p_i(1-p_j)}{p_j(1-p_i)}} \tag{6}$$

So the default correlation can reach unity if and only if the individual probabilities are equal. The maximum value that the pairwise default correlation may take with respect to the individual probabilities is shown in Figure 4.

Using this representation for the binary default events, it is possible to derive analytical formulae for the loss distribution. We do not discuss this approach further but instead proceed with Monte Carlo simulation for full flexibility. The same analysis can be performed by sampling from the α-stable instead of the normal distribution.

For a Monte Carlo simulation, we need a way of simulating correlated binary (default) events that involves drawing from the correlated multivariate normal distribution:

$$Y \sim N\left[\begin{pmatrix} 0 \\ 0 \end{pmatrix}, \begin{pmatrix} 1 & & \lambda_{ij} \\ & \ddots & \\ \lambda_{ij} & & 1 \end{pmatrix}\right] \tag{7}$$

The underlying correlation matrix represents the correlation between the multivariate normal variables and not the default events themselves.

We know that the covariance matrix can always be factorised as $C = AA^T$ for some matrix A (by Cholesky factorisation or diagonalisation on C). If u is a multivariate process with components independently drawn from the standard normal distribution, the vector Au has the required covariance matrix C.

Having determined the correlation between the normal random variables, the binary default variable d_i is given by the indicator function $I(Y_i < k_i)$, where Y_i is the ith element of the vector Au. The additional structure we have imposed ensures that the binary default variables match the default probabilities and correlations in the input data.

The simulation method we present includes stochastic exposures. It is important to compare this with the case in which the exposures are treated as constant, known as the "loan-equivalent approach". This approach makes three crucial assumptions. The first is that there is zero covariance between the exposures of the assets, which is unlikely. The second assumption is that the recovery rate is constant. We later present an analysis of a real portfolio in which this assumption leads to an underestimate of 25% of the unexpected loss. The last assumption is that the unexpected loss can be defined by the portfolio variance. The argument presented previously shows that this is not appropriate.

Our treatment of stochastic recovery rates follows from the default and migration model. In the event of default the recovery rate is defined by a series of further thresholds below the default threshold. Intuition suggests that a more extreme default leads to a lower recovery rate. This approach means that further random numbers need not be drawn and introduces correlation between the recovery rates. The form of the correlation is determined by the default correlation structure. The position of the recovery rate thresholds can be determined by matching the historical mean and variance, which depend on the seniority of the debt (eg, see CreditMetrics).

If default occurs at some time in the future, it is necessary to know the exposure distribution at the risk horizon. If the exposure is negative, default does not lead to a loss. A loss of up to the maximum exposure can be incurred when it is positive. The exposure distributions are estimated by simulating underlyings over many paths. Assets are then revalued, on a deal-by-deal basis, at a number of discrete time points on these paths. The exposure data are aggregated on a counterparty basis to account for the covariances between exposures, netting agreements and collateral.

We now apply the methodology above to a hypothetical example to illustrate the effect of the various factors on the loss distribution for a portfolio of swaps. Our initial analysis will consider only default events since they account for the majority of losses. We can estimate the distribution for the variable defined in equation (1) by averaging over many simulations.

Figure 5 shows the loss distributions for the swap portfolio obtained from four scenarios of varying complexity: a basic case (constant exposures and recovery rates and no default correlation), and then including default correlation, stochastic recovery rates and stochastic exposures. Table 1 summarises the findings. It shows the increase in the 99.9th percentile for

Figure 5 Tail of loss distributions

For swap portfolio under different assumptions

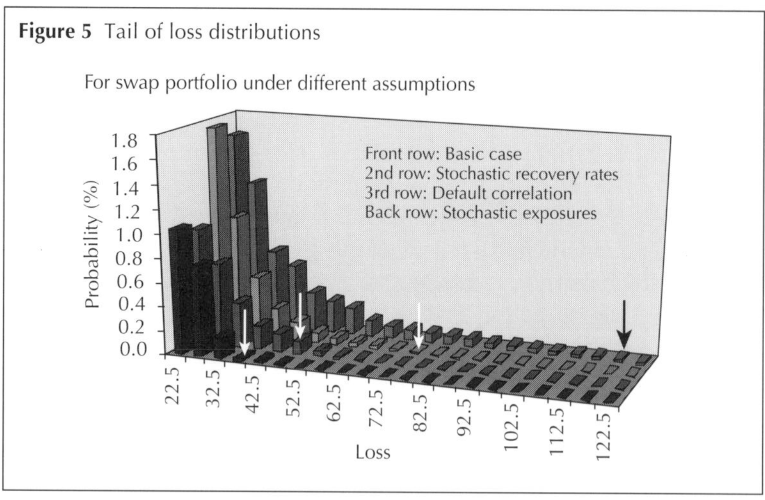

the effects studied and also shows the estimate for the loan-equivalent methodology.

The most dramatic effect in the estimation of capital comes from the introduction of stochastic exposures. This has important implications for loan-equivalent methodologies. Using constant exposures will almost always underestimate the true economic capital. The loan-equivalent measure accounts for only 69% of the true economic capital in this instance.

We have so far restricted our analysis only to losses from default events, but for a complete model we also need to consider credit downgrades and the volatility of the credit spreads even without credit migration. The migration process is defined as a simple extension to the default model whereby further thresholds are added for each migration probability (see CreditMetrics for a complete description of this procedure). Credit migration has two effects. First, credit downgrades lead to a loss in the market value of assets and facilities. Second, a downgraded counterparty is more likely to default.

Table 1 Economic capital estimates for swap portfolio under different assumptions

	Economic capital	**Relative increase (%)**
Basic case	36	–
Stochastic recovery rates	45	25
Correlated defaults	66	83
Stochastic exposures	124	244
All effects	177	392
Loan equivalent	122	229

Figure 6 Forward credit spread curves

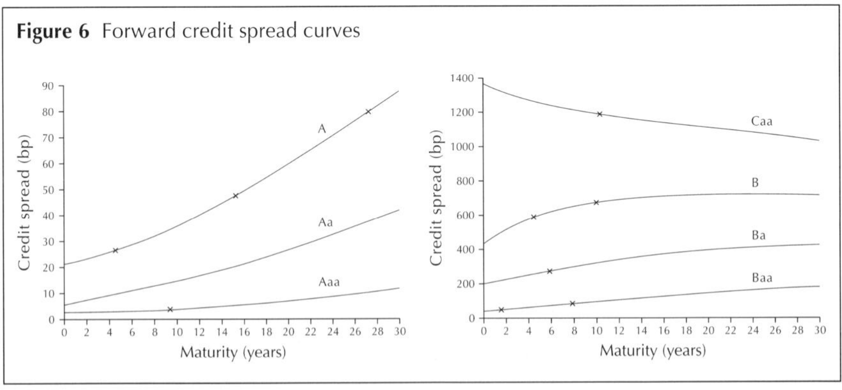

To calculate the loss due to credit migration, we have to be able to compute credit spread curves at future points in time for all credit classes. Jarrow, Lando and Turnbull (1997), and Arvanitis, Gregory and Laurent (1999) present a pricing model that is consistent with this framework. The latter model also accounts for the volatility of credit spreads within a rating class. This would be important for capital market portfolios, where losses are marked-to-market even if there is no downgrade. In Figure 6, we show the estimation of forward credit spread curves using the model presented in Arvanitis, Gregory and Laurent (1999), calibrated with US telecommunication bond prices on December 30, 1997.

The credit migration events have a significant effect on the mean of the loss distribution (a 16% increase for the swap portfolio considered in this example), but the tail is not affected as much (4% increase in unexpected loss). This is due to the fact that the tails of the distribution are defined by the most extreme losses from default events. The loss distribution for credit migration events only is much closer to normal but still has a fatter tail – an important observation for building models to assess the specific risk of bond portfolios.

Credit migration also causes a drift in default probabilities that must be taken into account when considering losses for multiple periods. For investment-grade portfolios, this will increase the probabilities of default over time since there is more chance of worsening credit quality.

Many simulations are required to get a good estimate of the loss distribution because the events that determine the tail of the distribution are rare. We describe two ways to speed up the convergence of the Monte Carlo simulation. The first technique is importance sampling, where the aim is to concentrate the simulations in the regions of most interest. Figure 7 shows the effect on convergence. The second method uses the analytical formulas discussed earlier to control the variation of a Monte Carlo estimator (see Figure 8). This approach represents a combination of the analytical and simulation methods, which is particularly powerful

Figure 7 Importance sampling

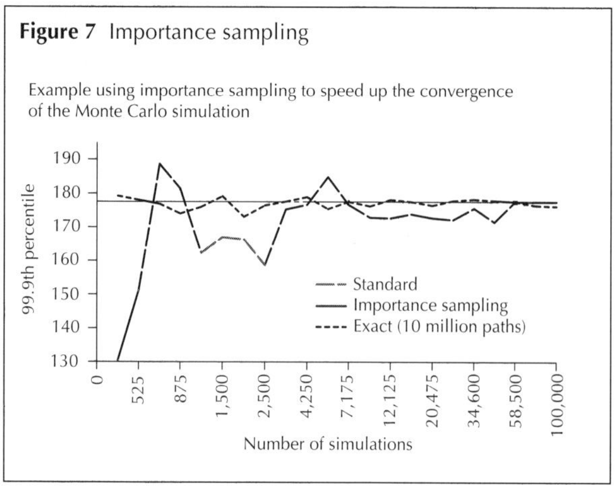

Figure 8 Control variate

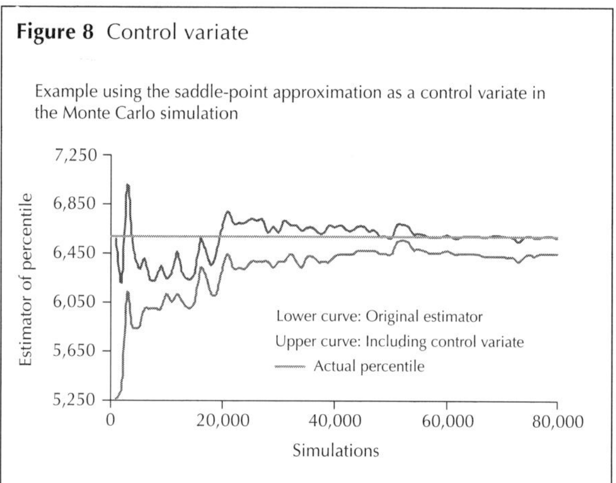

when the analytical approximation is close to the true distribution. Note that it is also possible to combine the importance sampling and control variate methods.

DEFAULT DATA

To estimate expected loss and capital for risk management, we need to use "real" default probabilities. A straightforward way of estimating these numbers is from historical data, since they reflect actual default experience. It is important to point out that as the default process is non-stationary (more defaults during recession than expansion of the economy), particular attention should be paid to the choice of the estimation interval.

From the prices of traded instruments we can only derive risk-neutral default probabilities, which reflect a combination of the real default probabilities and the risk premia. They are therefore inappropriate for risk

Figure 9 Portfolio optimisation

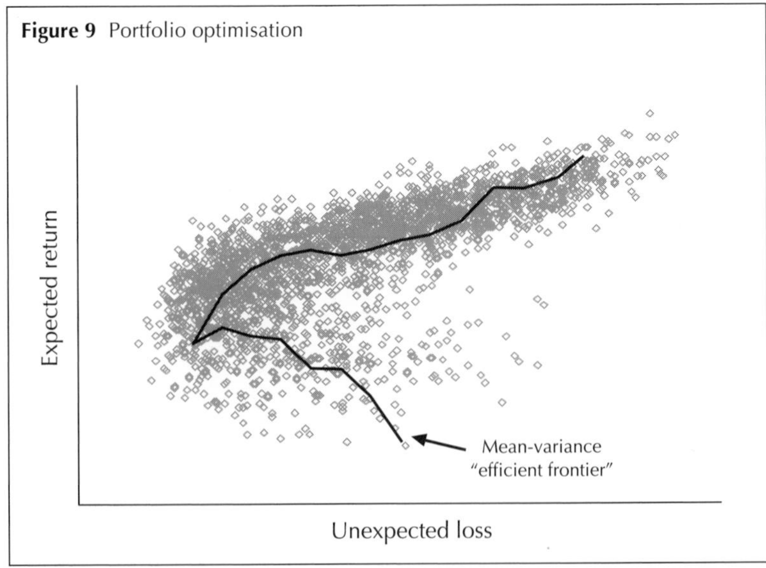

management. Risk-neutral default probabilities are substantially more volatile than the real ones, resulting in high volatility for the computed capital – which is not acceptable for most applications. On the other hand, for arbitrage-free pricing and hedging we should use risk-neutral default probabilities. They could be derived from the prices of standard default swaps, since these are the natural instruments for hedging counterparty risk in loan and derivative portfolios. If default swaps are not traded for a specific name, bonds would be the best alternative.

Similarly, default correlations can be estimated from either historical defaults or historical credit spreads, or ideally, they can be implied from the prices of securities that are sensitive to correlation, such as spread options or first-to-default swaps. Unfortunately, the latter instruments tend to be very illiquid.

CREDIT PORTFOLIO OPTIMISATION

As the loss distributions are skewed, the usual mean–variance optimisation can lead to inefficient portfolios, as shown in Figure 9. Credit portfolio optimisation aims to increase the ratio of expected return to capital (unexpected loss) by either increasing the former or reducing the latter. The lack of exact analytical results forces us to use simulation to compute the efficient frontier.

References

Arvanitis, A., J. K. Gregory and J.-P. Laurent, 1999, "Building Models for Credit Spreads", *Journal of Derivatives* Spring, pp. 27–43.

Credit Suisse Financial Products, 1997, *CreditRisk+*.

Davison, A., and D. Hinkley, 1988, "Saddlepoint Approximations in Resampling Methods", *Biometrika* 75(3), pp. 417–31.

Jarrow, R.A., D. Lando and S. Turnbull, 1997, "A Markov Model for the Term Structure of Credit Risk Spreads", *Review of Financial Studies* 10(2), pp. 481–523.

Johnston, N., S. Kotz and N. Balakrishnan, 1995, *Continuous Univariate Distributions* volumes I and II, John Wiley.

JP Morgan, April 1997, *CreditMetrics*.

KMV Corporation, *Portfolio Manager, Description, Usage and Specification, Version 4.0*.

Merton, R., 1974, "On the Pricing of Corporate Debt: the Risk Structure of Interest Rates", *Journal of Finance* 29, pp. 449–70.

Wilson, T., 1997, "Portfolio Credit Risk", *Risk* September, pp. 111–17; October, pp. 56–61.

Glossary

adjusted exposure the portion of the totality of all exposures that a bank would not be able to recover in the event of default

Amendment to the Basle Capital Accord (1996) the amendment of the 1988 Basle Accord to incorporate capital adequacy due to market risk

asset and liability management practice of matching the term structure and cashflows of an organisation's asset and liability portfolios to maximise returns and minimise interest rate risk

asset correlation correlation of returns from two risky assets

asset securitisation process whereby loans, receivables and other *illiquid assets* with similar characteristics in the balance sheet are packaged into interest-bearing securities that offer attractive investment opportunities

asset value of a firm the present value of all the expected future cashflows attributable to all the firm's lines of business. Under generally accepted accounting principles (GAAP), an asset is defined as the probable future economic benefits obtained or controlled by the firm as a result of past transactions or events

back-testing the validation of a model by feeding it historical data and comparing the model's results with the historical reality

banking book *see* **trading book**

bankruptcy the liquidation of a firm's assets when it is unable to meet its financial obligations; distinct from *default*

beta distribution a family of parametric probability distributions with two degrees of freedom defined on the interval [0,1]. One of the *Weibull* class of distributions

bond a debt security which bears interest and promises repayments of principal

Brownian motion a type of *Markov process* that is used to specify the stochastic process of asset prices – also known as the *Wiener process*

calibration (of a model) *see* **parameterisation**

call option contract giving purchaser the right to buy an underlying at a certain price on or before a certain date (*see also* **put option**)

capital allocation/attribution the allocation of capital to the business lines in a financial institution

capital charge the required regulatory capital imposed on banks by the supervisory bodies

capital market the market for the sale and purchase of medium- and long-term financial instruments

capital multiplier the *economic capital* necessary to protect a bank against the risk of unexpected credit default losses is a multiple of the *portfolio unexpected loss*. This multiple is the capital multiplier

capital ratio *see* **solvency ratio**

charge-off a debit to the reserve for possible credit losses. It is also called a bad debt

collateralisation the backing of a security by an asset

commitment normally means a loan and is composed of two portions: drawn and undrawn. A commitment is an amount the bank has agreed to lend, at a borrower's request, up to the full amount of the commitment

Comptroller of the Currency an officer of the US Treasury Department responsible for chartering national banks and with primary supervisory authority over them. All national banks are required to be members of the Federal Reserve System and are insured by the Federal Deposit Insurance Corporation

concentration risk *see* **credit risk concentration**

contingent option option where the premium is higher than usual but is only payable if the value of the underlying reaches a specified level. Also known as a contingent premium option

correlation of credit quality the correlation of the *credit ratings* or rating changes of entities in a portfolio

correlation of default *see* **default correlation**

counterparty risk weighting *see* **risk weighting**

country risk the risk that borrowers within a country will not be able to repay their obligations to foreign creditors because of negative political or general economic factors. Also known as sovereign risk

coupon interest rate payment on a bond

covenant a term or provision in a loan agreement; can be options the bank reserves to itself or options granted to an obligor

credit concentration *see* **credit risk concentration**; *see also* **credit paradox**

credit derivative a specific class of financial instruments whose value is derived from an underlying market instrument driven primarily by the *credit risk* of private or government entities. The underlying instruments of credit derivatives are generally in the form of corporate debt and securities issued by sovereign entities

credit enhancement any method or technique that reduces the credit exposure of a transaction with a counterparty

CreditMetrics the framework used by JP Morgan for quantifying credit risk in portfolios of credit products, fixed-income instruments and financial instruments subject to counterparty default

credit migration short of a default, the extent to which the *credit quality* of an obligor or counterparty improves or deteriorates

credit paradox the dramatic rise in the loan spreads required as exposure to the same obligor increases. The phenomenon forces many banks to take on larger amounts of credit exposure in search of larger spreads, thereby exposing themselves to an even larger probability of suffering from default. *See also* **credit risk concentration**

credit quality the credit quality of a firm at a specific point in time is measured by the probability that it will be able to pay off its contractual obligations. The first instance of failure to do so is defined as *default*

credit repo credit repurchase agreement

credit (or default) risk the risk that a loss will be incurred if a counterparty to a transaction does not fulfil its financial obligations in a timely manner

credit risk concentration (concentration risk) if a loan portfolio is highly concentrated in terms of exposure to a specific industry or country, it is highly susceptible to correlated *default* and *credit migration* events. The opposite of *diversification*

credit risk models models that attempt to quantify credit risk – eg, value of the firm models; recovery of promised payoff models; instantaneous risk of default models

credit swaps agreement between two counterparties to exchange disparate cashflows, at least one of which must be tied to the performance of a credit-sensitive asset or to a portfolio or index of such assets. The other cashflow is usually tied to a floating-rate index (such as Libor) or a fixed rate, or is linked to another credit-sensitive asset

default failure of a firm to make a payment on a *coupon* or reimburse its debt

default correlation the degree to which the default of one obligor is related to the default of another. The quantity that ties the *risk contribution* of a risky asset to the portfolio

default point critical *threshold* for defaulting posited by KMV Corporation on the basis of the observation that a firm is more likely to default when its asset value reaches a certain critical level somewhere between the value of total liabilities and the value of short-term debt. Defined by KMV as the "book value" of the firm's liabilities – roughly approximated by the sum of the short-term debt and one-half of the long-term debt

default probability *see* **expected default frequency**

default process in most cases of default there are transitions between credit ratings (*credit migration*) before the default state is reached; this is known as a multi-state default process. A two-state default process consists of the two possible events "no default" and "default" at the analysis horizon

density function (of a distribution) the area under the density curve across an interval represents the probability over that interval

distance to default an index defined by KMV Corporation as the distance between the expected *asset value of a firm* at the analysis horizon and the *default point*, normalised by the standard deviation of the future asset returns

diversification putting your eggs in more than one basket as a way of reducing risk

draw-down referring to a loan facility, the amount of the *commitment* drawn by the obligor. *See also* **usage given default**

drift mathematically, the deterministic component of a Brownian motion indicating the general slope and direction of the random motion

economic capital capital necessary for the bank to remain solvent in the event of *extreme loss*. Economic capital is the number of standard deviations away from the *expected loss* that is necessary to protect the bank from insolvency in the event of extreme losses in the bank's portfolio due to default risk. Also known as "risk capital". *See also* **value-at-risk**

EDF *see* **expected default frequency**

EL *see* **expected loss**

event risk a risk defined as a change in value of an asset or position due to occurrences such as a merger or acquisition, changes in market conditions, political upheavals or other unforeseen circumstances

expected default frequency (EDF) the probability that an obligor will default before the maturity of the contracted obligation to pay. Such probabilities can be estimated from historical data or analytically using options theory. Same as probability of default

expected exposure the amount the bank can expect to lose, on average, over the period of time in which it extends credits

expected loss (EL) the average loss the bank can expect to incur on an asset over the period up to a specified horizon. *See also* **unexpected loss**

exposure vulnerability to loss from unanticipated events

extreme loss loss arising from defaults of catastrophic magnitude, which tend to occur more frequently when market conditions deteriorate beyond a certain point

extreme value theory an actuarial science that focuses on extreme events and their associated tail probabilities; it looks explicitly at extreme outcomes and provides a series of natural models for them. The tail of an empirically observed loss distribution, however incomplete, can be fitted to some analytical "extreme distribution", facilitating the analysis of tail or extreme events

Federal Reserve Board the governing body of the central bank of the US. Composed of a seven-member Board of Governors, 12 regional reserve banks and depository institutions that are subject to reserve requirements

first-passage time mathematically, the first instantaneous occurrence of an event, such as default

forward (transaction) agreement to exchange a predetermined amount of currency, commodity or other financial instrument at a specified future date and at a predetermined rate

Fréchet distribution an extreme value distribution with unbounded support to the right. Includes the log-gamma, Cauchy and Student's *t* distributions. *See also* **generalised Pareto distribution**

game theory a theory of individual rational decisions taken under conditions of less than full information concerning the outcomes of those decisions

generalised Pareto distribution a class of theoretical distributions of extreme values with three degrees of freedom parameterised as scale, location and shape. Includes the *Gumbel* (double exponential), *Fréchet* and *Weibull* distributions. *See* **extreme value theory**

Group of Ten (G10) countries Belgium, Canada, France, Germany, Italy, Japan, Netherlands, Sweden, the United Kingdom and the United States

Gumbel (double exponential) distribution an extreme value distribution. Includes the normal, exponential, gamma and lognormal distributions. *See also* **generalised Pareto distribution**

hedge a strategy to reduce exposure by effecting a transaction that offsets an existing position

hedge fund private investment partnerships that seek above-average returns through aggressive portfolio management. Due to their private nature, hedge funds are allowed to use leverage, short sales and other non-traditional techniques to enhance returns

hold-to-maturity bank assets that are not classified for immediate sale

hurdle rate rate of return required in a business enterprise

illiquid asset essentially, a lack of liquidity in an asset or in a portfolio of assets held by a transactor. The condition is always relative, since almost all assets vary in degree of liquidity. A corporate loan is less liquid than, say, a US Treasury security

indenture legal contract specifying the relationship between the issuer and the holder of a security

industry index refers to the officially designated S&P index classification by industries

interest rate risk the risk to borrowing or investment posed by interest rate changes

internal (credit) risk rating a bank's own assessment of the risk associated with an entity as opposed to the ratings issued by credit rating agencies. Essentially, the bank's primary indicator of risk for individual credit exposures and used to provide guidance for setting *loan loss reserves,* profitability analysis and loan pricing analysis

ISDA International Swaps and Derivatives Association

joint distribution a multivariate distribution that depends on two or more variables

joint probability of default the probability that one obligor will default if another defaults

Jumbo CD normally refers to certificates of deposit (in the US) with at least $100,000

leptokurtosis phenomenon when the probability distribution has a larger mass on the tail and a sharper hump than is consistent with the assumption of a normal distribution

leverage (1) the opportunity for large gains or losses from a small initial investment as widely associated with derivatives or (2) the relationship between a firm's equity and its debt

leverage ratio the ratio between a firm's equity and debt

LGD *see* **loss given default**

liquidity risk a risk that the market might dry up and make it impossible to sell out of a position without incurring large losses

loan an agreement whereby one party provides monies to another party for a set period in return for regular payment of interest and principal

loan loss reserve (or provision) the amount of reserve capital a bank needs to set aside to cover *expected losses*

loan pool an aggregate of several bank loans

loan portfolio a collection of *illiquid assets,* eg loans, held by an institution in its banking book

loan pricing calculator means of determining the *required spread* the bank needs to charge as compensation for taking on additional credits in an existing portfolio given a desired level of risk-adjusted return

loss given default (LGD) the fraction of the exposure amount that will be lost on default or, more appropriately, the fraction of the debt the bank is not likely to recover from the obligor once it has defaulted

loss probability distribution the probability distribution of loss in portfolio value

loss severity degree of loss in the event of default. *See* **loss given default**

macroeconomics the study of the behaviour of the economy as a whole

market risk "risk of losses in on- and off-balance sheet positions arising from movements in market prices" (BIS)

Markov process an ordered set of discrete random variables, each of which has at any time a given state or value dependent only on the state of the variable immediately before it. It assumes that only the current value of a stochastic (random) variable is important in predicting future values of that variable

Markov property (condition/process) of a system, that its evolution in time depends only on the state that preceded it

mark-to-market valuation valuing securities on the basis of the current market values of a counterparty's obligations

martingale property posits that the conditional expectation of a future value of that random variable is the current one

mean excess function graphical method of determining the *threshold* in an extreme value distribution; an empirical estimate of the expected overshoot of a threshold when exceedance occurs. *See also* **extreme value theory**

model risk the risk arising from the misuse of financial models, including mis-calibration and incorrect specification

Monte Carlo simulation technique used to determine the likely value of a derivative or other contract by simulating the evolution of the underlying variables many times over. The discounted average outcome of the simulation gives an approximation of the derivative's value. Monte Carlo simulation can be used to estimate the *value-at-risk* (VAR) of a portfolio. Here, it generates a simulation of many correlated market movements for the markets to which the portfolio is exposed, and the positions in the portfolio are revalued repeatedly in accordance with the simulated scenarios. This results in a probability distribution of portfolio gains and losses from which the VAR can be determined

netting refers to the offsetting of transactions between two parties with settlement of the net difference

notional amount the quantity of an underlier (the primary instrument or variable) to which a derivative contract applies

obligor-specific risk risk associated with a particular client; tends to increase with diminishing company asset size

off-balance sheet item (OBSI) an item not on a financial institution's balance sheet; includes swaps, futures, options, foreign exchange and interest rate risk

offsettings transaction a procedure for terminating an option's position

operational risk risk of loss arising from inadequate systems and control, human error or management failure

outstandings generic term referring to the portion of the bank's asset that has already been extended to a borrower (in the case of loans and bonds) and also to other receivables in the form of contractual payments which are due from its customers. If on default a borrower is unable to fulfil its contractual obligations or the receivables fail to come in, the bank is exposed to the entire amount of the outstandings. Examples of outstandings are *term loans*, credit cards, *bonds* and receivables

pairwise correlation of default the correlation between the defaults of two assets. *See* **joint probability of default**

parameterisation the subjective choice of parameters used as inputs to a risk model; also known as "calibration"

parametric distribution a probability distribution whose shape and form are specified by certain parameters

par bond a bond selling at par

Pareto distribution *see* **generalised Pareto distribution**

pay-down the amount by which the par value of securities maturing is in excess of those sold

payoff the return from an instrument or position

portfolio expected loss the simple sum of individual *expected losses* from all the risky assets in a portfolio.

portfolio unexpected loss unexpected loss at portfolio level. Unlike *portfolio expected loss*, this loss is *not* equal to the linear sum of the individual unexpected losses of the risky assets making up the aggregate portfolio. Because of diversification effects, the portfolio unexpected loss is very much smaller than the sum of the individual unexpected losses

portfolio variance the square of the standard deviation of the portfolio's return from the mean

prompt corrective action (FDICIA 1991) imposes increasingly strict limits and punitive actions on a bank as its *capital ratio* declines

put option an option contract that gives the holder the right to sell the underlying security at a specified price for a fixed period of time

RAPM *see* **risk-adjusted performance measurement**

RAROC *see* **risk-adjusted return on capital**

rating the evaluation of an issuer's investment quality by a rating agency

recovery rate the extent to which the face value of an obligation can be recovered once the obligor has defaulted

regulatory capital sufficient capital imposed by regulators on banks that must be maintained to provide a cushion to absorb losses which would otherwise cause a bank to fail

required spread the *spread* the bank needs to charge given a particular level of return

risk-adjusted performance measurement (RAPM) calculation of performance using a risk adjustment (ie, risk-weighted) process. *See also* **risk-adjusted return on capital**

risk-adjusted return on capital (RAROC) the expected *spread* over economic capital, calculated for individual assets or portfolios

risk adjustment the process whereby returns from dissimilar business lines are measured on a comparable basis according to their riskiness

risk-based capital standard/adequacy generally referred to as the BIS capital rules

risk capital *see* **economic capital**
risk contribution the incremental risk that the exposure of a single asset contributes to the portfolio's total risk
risk-free rate a theoretical interest rate at which an investment may earn interest without incurring any risk
risk-neutral a theoretical condition whereby investors require no compensation for taking risk
risk-weighted assets (RWA) assets weighted in accordance with their relative credit riskiness
risk weighting when calculating the amount of capital which the Bank for International Settlements (BIS) advises should be set aside to cover the credit risk generated by derivative transactions, banks first calculate a "credit equivalent amount" and then multiply this figure by the appropriate counterparty risk weighting (eg, 20% for OECD incorporated banks). The product of this calculation is the final risk-weighted amount

securitisation *see* **asset securitisation**
shape parameter controls the shape of a probability distribution
short squeeze (or bear squeeze) rising prices due to a lack of supply; a short squeeze causing losses for those who have a short position
solvency ratio the formula for setting down the size of the balance sheet credit run by a financial institution based on the riskiness and size of the capital; also known as a capital ratio
sovereign debt when the obligor is a state or government
specific risk risk of changes in the value of an individual security due to factors related to the individual issuer of the security (eg, credit quality and liquidity) that are outside of broad market movements
spot rate rate paid for commodities when they are offered for immediate payment and physical delivery
spread difference between the yield on a risky debt and the *risk-free rate*
stress-testing analysis that gives the value of a portfolio under a range of worst-case scenarios
strike price the price level of the underlying asset at which an option may be exercised
structured note/vehicle structured notes are OTC products that bundle several disparate elements to create a single product, generally by embedding options in a debt instrument such as a medium-term note
subordinated debt a debt that is ranked lower than another security in the priority of its claim on the issuer's assets
synthetic option replicating the payment of an option using cash or, more often, futures
systemic risk a risk that threatens the whole financial system due to the failure of one participant or an event

term loan a loan with a payment of interest where the principal is usually paid out some years later

term structure of interest rates relationship between interest rates on the same securities with different maturities

threshold the point in a distribution marking onset of extreme tail events

threshold level level of a firm's asset value that determines its credit rating

total return swap swap agreement in which the total return of bank loans or credit-sensitive securities is exchanged for some other cashflow, usually tied to Libor, or other loans or credit-sensitive securities. It allows participants effectively to go long or short the credit risk of the underlying asset

trading book bank portfolio containing securities that are actively bought and sold for the purpose of making short-term profit, in contrast to the banking book, which generally consists of loans.

transition matrix an array of transition or migration probabilities from one credit rating to another

transition probability the probability that the *credit quality* of a firm will improve or deteriorate; quantifies *credit migration*; *see* **transition matrix**

Treasury bill a non-interest bearing security issued by governments to finance national debt

Treasury bond a long-term government security

UGD *see* **usage given default**

UL *see* **unexpected loss**

undiversifiable risk the amount of credit risk that cannot be diversified away by placing or removing an asset in a portfolio; also called systematic risk

unexpected default rate the distribution of future default rates is often characterised in terms of an expected default rate (eg, 0.05%) and a worst-case default rate (eg, 1.05%). The difference between the worst-case default rate and the expected default rate is often termed the "unexpected default rate" (ie, 1% = 1.05 – 0.05%)

unexpected loss (UL) uncertainty in the amount of loss in portfolio value caused by market conditions. This uncertainty, or more appropriately the *volatility* of loss, is the so-called *unexpected loss*. Unexpected losses are triggered by the occurrence of *default* and unexpected *credit migrations*

usage given default (UGD) fraction of a loan *commitment* that has been drawn at the time of an obligor's default. *See also* **draw-down**

value-at-risk (VAR) formally, the probabilistic bound of market losses over a given period of time (the holding period) expressed in terms of a specified degree of certainty (the confidence interval). Put more simply, the VAR is the worst-case loss expected over the holding period within the probability set out by the confidence interval. Larger losses are possible but with a low probability. For instance, a portfolio whose VAR is $20 million over a one-day holding period, with a 95% confidence interval, would have only a 5% chance of suffering an overnight loss greater than $20 million

value of the firm models propose that the underlying process driving a firm's default (or credit rating change) is the firm's asset value (after Merton, 1974). *See also* **credit risk models**

volatility measure of the variability (but not the direction) of prices or interest rates

Weibull distribution an extreme value distribution with unbounded support to the left. Includes the beta and normal distributions. *See also* **generalised Pareto distribution**

Wiener process *see* **Brownian motion**

workout special payment arrangements formulated for the potential or actual default of a loan

worst-case default rate the highest rates of default that are likely to occur at a given moment or period in the future, with a given level of confidence

worst-case (credit risk) exposure estimate of the highest positive market value a derivative contract or portfolio is likely to attain at a given moment or period in the future, with a given level of confidence

worst-case (credit risk) loss estimate of the largest amount a derivatives counterparty is likely to lose, with a given level of probability, as a result of default from a derivatives contract or portfolio

zero-coupon bond a bond that makes no interest payments

***Z* threshold** the mathematical positioning of joint probability of default into distinct bands or zones

Select bibliography

CAPITAL AND RISK-ADJUSTED PERFORMANCE MEASUREMENT

Allen, R. (1996), "Together They Stand", *Firmwide Risk Management, Risk* Supplement July, pp. 21–31.

Berger, A. N., R. J. Herring and G. P. Szegö (1995), "The Role of Capital in Financial Institutions", Working paper, University of Pennsylvania – Wharton, January.

Froot, K. A., and J. C. Stein (1998), "Risk Management, Capital Budgeting, and Capital Structure Policy for Financial Institutions: An Integrated Approach", *Journal of Financial Economics* 47, pp. 55–82.

Greenspan, A. (1998), *BIS Review*, January–March.

James, C. (1996), "RAROC-Based Capital Budgeting and Performance Evaluation: A Case Study of Bank Capital Allocation", Working paper, University of Florida.

Matten, C. (1996), *Managing Bank Capital* (Chichester: John Wiley and Sons).

Merton, R. C., and A. F. Perold (1993), "Theory of Risk Capital in Financial Firms", *Journal of Applied Corporate Finance* 5, pp. 16–32.

Modigliani, F., and M. H. Miller (1958), "The Cost of Capital, Corporation Finance, and the Theory of Investment", *American Economic Review*, June, pp. 261–97.

Office of the Comptroller of the Currency (1997), *Handbook for Asset Securitization*.

Punjabi, S. (1998), "Many Happy Returns", *Risk*, June, pp. 71–6. Reprinted in the Appendix to the present volume, pp. 295–307.

Stewart III, G. B. (1991), *The Quest for Value* (New York: HarperCollins).

de Swaan, T. (1998), *BIS Review*, January–March.

Wilson, T., 1992, "RAROC remodelled", *Risk*, September, pp. 112–9. Reprinted in the Appendix to the present volume, pp. 283–92.

Wong, M., and S. Song (1997), "A Loan in Isolation", *AsiaRisk*, June, pp. 21–3.

Zaik, E., J. Walter, G. Kelling and C. James (1996), "RAROC at Bank of America: From Theory to Practice", *Journal of Corporate Finance* 9, pp. 83–93.

CREDIT RISK

Credit Risk Supplement (1998), Special Report, Risk Publications, March.

Crouhy, M., and R. Mark (1998), "A Comparative Analysis of Current Credit Risk Models", Working paper, Canadian Imperial Bank of Commerce, October.

Das, S., ed. (1998), *Credit Derivatives: Trading and Management of Credit and Default Risk* (Singapore: John Wiley).

Gupton, G. M., C. C. Finger and M. Bhatia (1997), *CreditMetrics – Technical Document* (New York: JP Morgan).

Koyluoglu, H. U., and A. Hickman, A. (1998), "Reconcilable Differences", *Risk,* October, pp. 56–62. Reprinted in the Appendix to the present volume, pp. 308–22.

Li, D. (1998), "Constructing a Credit Curve", Credit Risk Supplement, *Risk,* November, pp. 40–4.

Manuels, E. J. (1997), "Modern Loan Portfolio Management and the Role of Loan Portfolio Models", Unpublished manuscript, Erasmus University Rotterdam, Faculty of Economics, August.

CREDIT RISK RATINGS

Anon. (1998), "Winning the Ratings War", Credit Risk Supplement, *Risk,* November, pp. 28–9.

English, W. B., and W. R. Nelson (1998), "Bank Risk Rating of Business Loans", *Finance and Economics Discussion Series,* Federal Reserve Board.

Miller, R. (1998), "Refining Ratings", *Risk,* August, pp. 87–99. Reprinted in the Appendix to the present volume, pp. 323–29.

Treacy, W. F., and M. S. Carey (1998), "Credit Risk Rating at Large U.S. Banks", *Federal Reserve Bulletin,* Federal Reserve Board, November.

Udell, G. F. (1987), "Designing the Optimal Loan Review Policy: An Analysis of Loan Review in Midwestern Banks", *Prochnow Reports,* Madison, Wisconsin, p. 18.

DEFAULT PROBABILITIES AND DEFAULT CORRELATION

Keenan, S. C., and L. V. Carty (1998), "Commercial Paper Defaults and Rating Transitions: 1972–1998", *CreditMetrics Monitor,* Third Quarter.

Lucas, D. J. (1995), "Default Correlation and Credit Analysis", *Journal of Fixed Income,* March, pp. 76–87.

Moody's Investor Services (1997), *Rating Migration and Credit Quality Correlation, 1920–1996,* Global Credit Research, July.

Standard and Poor's (1996), *CreditWeek,* April 15, pp. 44–52.

Standard and Poor's (1997), *Ratings Performance 1996: Stability and Transition*, Special Report, February.

Zhou, C. (1997), "Default Correlation: An Analytical Result", Working paper, Federal Reserve Board, May.

EXTREME VALUE THEORY

Embrechts, P., C. Kluppelberg and T. Mikosch (1997), *Modelling Extremal Events for Insurance and Finance* (Berlin: Springer-Verlag).

Embrechts, P., S. Resnick and G. Samorodnitsky (1998), "Living on the Edge", *Risk*, January, pp. 96–100.

McNeil, A. J. (1998), "Estimating the Tails of Loss Severity Distributions Using Extreme Value Theory", *ASTIN Bulletin* 27, pp. 117–37.

McNeil, A. J. (1998), "History Repeating", *Risk* 11(1), p. 99.

McNeil, A. J., and T. Saladin (1997), "The Peaks over Thresholds Method for Estimating High Quantiles of Loss Distribution", Working paper, ETH Zurich.

Reiss, R. D., and M. Thomas (1997), *Statistical Analysis of Extreme Values* (Basel: Birkhauser Verlag).

Zangari, P., (1997), "Catering for an Event", *Risk*, July, pp. 34–36.

HISTORY

Anon. (1989), "An Interview with FDIC Director C. C. Hope", *Journal of Commercial Lending*, January.

Hicks, J. D. (1960), *Republican Ascendancy: 1921–1933* (New York: Harper & Row), p. 110.

McElvaine, R. S. (1981), *The Great Depression: America 1929–1941* (New York: Times Books), p. 38.

Williams, E. J. (1995), "Risk Management Comes of Age", *Journal of Commercial Lending*, January.

LOSS EXPERIENCE: RECOVERY RATES, LOSS AND USAGE GIVEN DEFAULT

Altman, E. I. (1989), "Measuring Corporate Bond Mortality and Performance", *Journal of Finance* 44, pp. 909–22.

Altman, E. I., and V. Kishore (1996), "Default Rates and Returns in the High Yield Debt Market: 1991–1997", Working paper, New York University Salomon Center.

Altman, E. I., and A. Saunders (1997), "Credit Risk Measurement: Developments Over the Last 20 Years", *Journal of Banking and Finance* 21, pp. 1721–42.

Altman, E. I., and H. J. Suggitt (1997), "Default Rates in the Syndicated Bank Loan Market: A Mortality Analysis", Working paper, New York University Salomon Center, December.

Asarnow, E., and D. Edwards (1995), "Measuring Loss on Defaulted Bank Loans: A 24-Year Study", *Journal of Commercial Lending* 77, pp. 11–23.

Asarnow, E., and J. Marker (1995), "Historical Performance of the U.S. Corporate Loan Market: 1988–1993", *Journal of Commercial Lending*, Spring, pp. 13–32.

Carey, M. (1998), "Credit Risk in Private Debt Portfolios", *Journal of Finance*, August, pp. 1363–87.

Carty, L. V. (1996), "An Empirical Investigation of Default Risk Dynamics", PhD dissertation, Columbia University.

Carty, L. V., and D. Lieberman (1996), Moody's Investor Services, *Corporate Bond Defaults and Default Rates: 1938–1995*, Special Report, January.

Carty, L. V., and D. Lieberman (1996), Moody's Investor Services, *Defaulted Bank Loan Recoveries*, Global Credit Research, Special Report, November.

McDonald, C. G., and L. M. Van de Gucht (1996), "The Default Risk of High Yield Bonds", Working paper, Louisiana State University.

Society of Actuaries (1996), *1986–1992 Credit Risk Loss Experience Study: Private Placement Bonds* (Schaumburg, IL).

Standard and Poor's (1995), "Corporate Default Level Off in 1994", *Creditweek* (New York), May.

MATHEMATICS

Abramowitz, M., and I. A. Stegun, eds (1964), *Handbook of Mathematical Functions*, National Bureau of Standards.

Arvanitis, A., and J. Gregory (1999), "A Credit Risk Toolbox", *Risk*, December, pp. 50–5. Reprinted in the Appendix to the present volume, pp. 330–42.

Fishman, G. S. (1996), *Monte Carlo – Concepts, Algorithms, and Applications* (New York: Springer-Verlag).

Gordy, M. B. (1998), "A Generalization of Generalized Beta Distributions", *Finance and Economics Discussion Series*, Federal Reserve Board, April.

Harrison, J. M. (1990), *Brownian Motion and Stochastic Flow Systems* (Melbourne, Florida: Krieger).

MathSoft, Inc., *Mathcad 7*, Cambridge, MA.

REGULATORY ISSUES AND INTERNAL MODELS

Bank for International Settlements (1988), *Reserves and International Liquidity*, Monetary and Economic Department, June.

Basle Committee on Banking Supervision (1988), *International Convergence of Capital Measurement and Capital Standards*, July.

Basle Committee on Banking Supervision, Bank for International Settlements (1996), *Amendment to the Capital Accord to Incorporate Market Risks*, January.

Federal Reserve System Task Force on Internal Credit Risk Models (1998), *Credit Risk Models at Major U.S. Banking Institutions: Current State of the Art and Implications for Assessments of Capital Adequacy*, May.

Gilibert, P. L. (1995), "Bank Capital Regulations and Guarantees on Bank Loans", *The Financier* 2, May, pp. 50–8.

International Swaps and Derivatives Association (1998), *Credit Risk and Regulatory Capital*, March.

Jones, D., and J. Mingo (1998), "Industry Practices in Credit Risk Modeling and Internal Capital Allocations", Working paper, Federal Reserve Board.

Wall, L. D., and P. P. Peterson (1996), "Banks' Responses to Binding Regulatory Capital Requirements, Federal Reserve Bank of Atlanta", *Economic Review*, March/April, pp. 1–17.

RISKY DEBT

Black, F., and J. Cox (1976), "Valuing Corporate Securities: Some Effects of Bond Indenture Provisions", *Journal of Finance* 31, pp. 351–67.

Blauer, I., and P. Wilmott (1998), "Risk of Default in Latin American Brady Bonds", *Net Exposure*, March/April.

Hull, J., and A. White (1995), "The Impact of Default Risk on Options and Other Derivative Securities", *Journal of Banking and Finance* 19 (December), pp. 299–322.

Jarrow, R. A., D. Lando and S. Turnbull (1997), "A Markov Model for the Term Structure of Credit Risk Spreads", *Review of Financial Studies*, Summer, pp. 481–523.

Jarrow, R. A., and S. Turnbull (1995), "Pricing Derivatives on Financial Securities Subject to Credit Risk", *Journal of Finance*, March, pp. 53–85.

Litterman, R., and T. Iben (1991), "Corporate Bond Valuation and the Term Structure of Credit Spreads", *Financial Analysts Journal*, Spring, pp. 52–64.

Longstaff, F., and E. Schwartz (1992), "Valuing Risky Debt: A New Approach", Working paper, University of California – Los Angeles.

Mark, R. M. (1995), "Integrated Credit Risk Measurement", Chapter 8 in *Derivative Credit Risk – Advances in Measurement and Risk Management* (London: Risk Publications), pp. 109–39.

Merton, R. C. (1974), "On the Pricing of Corporate Debt: The Risk Structure of Interest Rates", *Journal of Finance* 29, pp. 449–70.

Nielsen, L. T., J. Saá-Requejo and P. Santa-Clara (1993), "Default Risk and Interest Rate Risk: The Term Structure of Default Spreads", Working paper, INSEAD, France.

Schönbucher, P. J. (1996), "The Term Structure of Defaultable Bond Prices", Working paper, University of Bonn.

Shimko, D., N. Tejima and D. van Deventer (1993), "The Pricing of Risky Debt when Interest Rates are Stochastic", *Journal of Fixed Income,* September, pp. 58–66.

Index